Sex after Fascism

Sex after Fascism

MEMORY AND MORALITY IN
TWENTIETH-CENTURY GERMANY

Dagmar Herzog

PRINCETON UNIVERSITY PRESS
PRINCETON AND OXFORD

Copyright © 2005 by Princeton University Press
Published by Princeton University Press, 41 William Street,
Princeton, New Jersey 08540
In the United Kingdom: Princeton University Press,
3 Market Place, Woodstock, Oxfordshire OX20 1SY

Library of Congress Cataloging-in-Publication Data

Herzog, Dagmar, 1961–
Sex after fascism : memory and morality in twentieth-century Germany /
Dagmar Herzog.
p.   cm.
Includes bibliographical references and index.
ISBN 0-691-11702-0 (cl : alk. paper)
1. Sex—Germany—History—20th century. 2. Germany—Moral conditions. I. Title.
HQ18.G3H47   2005
306.7′0943′0904—dc22   2004040126

British Library Cataloging-in-Publication Data is available

This book has been composed in Sabon

Printed on acid-free paper. ∞

pup.princeton.edu

Printed in the United States of America

10   9   8   7   6   5   4   3   2   1

Contents

Introduction

WHAT IS THE RELATIONSHIP between sexual morality and mass murder and its aftermath? In view of Nazism's horrific crimes, sexuality might be seen as a frivolous or inappropriate subject for scholarly study of twentieth-century Germany. Yet precisely the opposite is the case.

Careful attention to the history of sexuality prompts us to reconsider how we periodize twentieth-century German history; it changes our interpretation of ruptures and continuities across the conventional divides of 1918, 1933, 1945, 1968, and 1989. Consideration of the history of sexuality and insistence on integrating the history of sexuality with more traditional topics of historiography can also challenge our assumptions about key social and political transformations and provide new insights into a broad array of crucial phenomena. To neglect the history of sexuality, for example, is also to fail to care about the content or force of antisemitism both during the Weimar Republic and in the early years of the Third Reich. Similarly, if we set sex aside as irrelevant, we lose opportunities to comprehend the extraordinary appeal of Nazism both to those Germans who sought the restoration of conservative family values and to those who benefited from Nazism's loosening of conventional mores. Nor can processes of popular secularization or religious renewal be understood without attention to the history of sexuality. Likewise, to disregard conflicts over sexuality is to risk misunderstanding the extensive emotional repercussions of Germans' military and ideological defeat in World War II, and its consequences especially for German manhood. Perhaps most significantly, to treat sexual issues as marginal is also to miss how the postwar Federal Republic of Germany, in striving to be incorporated into the Cold War West, was able to manipulate the memory of Nazism and to redirect moral debate away from the problem of complicity in mass murder and toward a narrowed conception of morality as solely concerned with sex.

Sexual politics functioned as a main locus for recurrent reconstructions of the memory and meanings of Nazism. Because the reworking of sexual mores had been such an important feature of the Third Reich, attempts to come to terms with the legacies of fascism in Germany could not help but address sexual matters. No less pertinent a factor, however, was the unexpected revival of Christian authority in the political realm in the western zones and then subsequently the Federal Republic of Germany. As it turns out, to delineate the ways in which sexuality, memory, and morality repeatedly intersected in postfascist Germany is also to shed light on Germans' efforts to grapple with the possible relationships between pleasure and evil.

This book was originally conceived as a study of the generation of 1968 in West Germany. Seeking to understand how Nazism and its legacies were interpreted in the 1960s, especially by the New Left student movement, I was struck by the preponderance of arguments that the Third Reich was a distinctly sexually repressive era and that to liberate sexuality was an antifascist imperative. Numerous New Leftists argued directly that sexuality and politics were causally linked; convinced that sexual repression produced racism and fascism, they proposed that sexual emancipation would further social and political justice.

Members of the West German New Left student movement, along with many of their liberal elders, defended activism on behalf of sexual emancipation on the grounds that sexual repression was not merely a characteristic of fascism but its very cause. As one author put it, "it would be wrong to hold the view that all of what happened in Auschwitz was typically German. It was typical for a society that suppresses sexuality."[1] Another argued that "brutality and the lust for destruction become substitutes for bodily pleasure. . . . This is how the seemingly incredible contradiction that the butchers of Auschwitz were—and would become again—respectable, harmless citizens, is resolved."[2] Or as yet another phrased it even more succinctly: "In the fascist rebellion, the energies of inhibited sexuality formed into genocide."[3] In the 1960s these views were widely held, and they provided moral justification for dismantling the postwar culture of sexual conservatism. To liberate sexuality, it was believed, would help cleanse Germany of the lingering aftereffects of Nazism.

For many commentators in present-day reunified Germany, more than fifteen years after the collapse of communism, it has become standard to denigrate the rebellions of the later 1960s for their utopian romanticism and fierce anticapitalism. But in their historical moment, those rebellions—and not least the sexual element in them—were signally important. They fundamentally reconfigured familial, sexual, and gender relations and all codes of social interaction. They undermined the authority of political and religious conservatives who had dominated West German political life for nearly two decades, and they succeeded in reorienting society-wide moral discussion and debate toward global concerns like social injustice, economic exploitation, and warfare.

As my research unfolded, I found that the New Left's interpretation of the Third Reich's sexual politics as profoundly repressive had been almost uniformly adopted in recent scholarship on Nazism as well. I also found, however, in researching the more immediate post–World War II period, that numerous commentators in that period had a completely different interpretation of the Third Reich. They argued that the Nazis had encouraged sexual licentiousness or even suggested that their sexual immorality was inextricable from their genocidal barbarism. Indeed, for many of these more immediate postwar observers, the containment of sexuality and the restoration of marriage and family were among the highest priorities for a society trying to overcome Nazism. It increasingly appeared as though the postwar culture of sexual conservatism was not (as the New Left believed) a watered-down continuation of a sexually repressive fascism but rather had itself been developed at least in partial reaction *against* Nazism.

The puzzles presented by the contradictory postwar interpretations of Nazism—and the utterly conflicting lessons drawn from them—led me to broaden the scope of my study. If I was going to explain the New Left's viscerally intense but also highly mediated relationship to the Nazi past, I had to expand my focus considerably. This entailed reconstructing debates over sexual mores under Nazism, as well as the evolution of postwar interpretations of Nazism. It also required an examination of the sexual culture of the first two postwar decades, first in the western zones under military occupation and then in the Federal Republic of Germany, in order to clarify in what climate the generation of 1968 had come of age and against which it would subsequently rebel. But it also became important to explore the comparative context of developments in the Soviet zone of occupation and then in the German Democratic Republic, in order to see how the development of postfascist sexual moralities differed in East Germany, especially due to the dramatically reduced presence there of those two main social forces—consumer capitalism and the Christian churches—which each in its own way kept sexual matters so integral to politics and culture in the West. In addition, I wanted not only to understand how the convictions about Nazism held by members of the generation of 1968 informed its efforts to remake German society from the 1960s to the 1980s but also to see how those efforts—and indeed the meaning of 1968 itself—had been reinterpreted yet again in the wake of German reunification in 1990.

In short, I began to consider questions of continuities and discontinuities (and complex mixtures thereof) in twentieth-century German history through the lens of conflicts over sexual morality. It seemed that the history of sexuality in Germany and other aspects of German history articulated constantly with one another—though always again in different ways—and thus could not be told separately. It also became clear that the generation of 1968 was not the first to believe that sexual and other kinds of politics were intrinsically connected. Sex was a crucial theme for politics even before the Third Reich began. It was closely linked with antisemitism.

After Germany's defeat in World War I, in the politically and economically unstable experiment with democracy called the Weimar Republic, Jews were—for the rising National Socialist movement as well as for many across the political spectrum—powerfully identified with sexual liberality. Not coincidentally, the sexual demonizing of the Jewish man became a major element in early National Socialist campaigns, and during the Third Reich the equation of Jews with sexual immorality helped facilitate first their exclusion from German society and subsequently their murder. Issues of sexual morality were central as well to the Christian churches' initial defense of National Socialism after Adolf Hitler's ascension to power in 1933—and thereby of the moral legitimation of the regime—even while differences of opinion over sexual mores subsequently emerged as a source of tension between the churches and the Nazis. Attending to this conflict over sex between the churches and the Nazis during the Third Reich in turn brings us much closer to an understanding of why the postfascist period in West Germany, under the leadership of the Christian Democratic Party (CDU), would be so strongly marked by a preoccupation with sexual propriety.

It is not least because scholarship on the Christian churches and scholarship on sexuality under Nazism have generally proceeded separately (all the more remarkable since sexual matters are often central to an erosion of faith) that so many scholars continue to presume that the Third Reich's sexual politics can best be characterized as prudish and conservative. For this turns out to be an only partially accurate reading. Without a doubt there were massively repressive elements in Nazi sexual politics: from the torture and murder of homosexual men to the incarceration of prostitutes to the forced sterilization of proletarian women whose purported promiscuity was taken as a sign of mental deficiency, from the prosecution of Jewish-Gentile sex in the so-called race defilement trials to the grotesque reproductive experiments and sexual sadism practiced on Jewish and other prisoners in the concentration and death camps. But none of this evidence justifies the conclusion that the Third Reich was repressive for everyone. What has routinely been downplayed since the 1960s is that Nazi policy and practice, for those broad sectors of the populace that were not persecuted, was anything but sexually repressive. Indeed, and this was especially apparent in the regime's vigorous attacks on the Christian churches, Nazism advanced an often ribald and unapologetic celebration of sexual activity; it avidly promoted both pre- and extramarital heterosexual sex.

There were also for the duration of the Third Reich regime-encouraged tendencies toward the maintenance of conventional sexual morality. Sexually conservative values were preserved in the bourgeois middle class and among church-affiliated individuals and groups of all social strata.

Nazi spokespeople did on many occasions appropriate and actively disseminate these values; for instance, examples of Nazi sex advice materials advocating premarital chastity and marital fidelity—especially for women—abound. But these traditional mores were also intensively combated by the regime.

Ultimately, and despite the contrary impulses, Nazism perpetuated and intensified certain aspects of the sexually liberalizing tendencies underway since the early twentieth century, even as it sought to harness those liberalizations—and the growing popular preoccupation with sex—to a savagely racist, elitist, and homophobic agenda. This was the distinctive innovation of Nazi sexual politics. The goal was not so much to suppress sexuality. Rather the aim was to reinvent it as the privilege of nondisabled, heterosexual "Aryans" (all the while *claiming* to be "cleaning up" sexual morality in Germany and overcoming the "Jewish" legacy). What needs to be confronted, in short (and what the 68ers could not accept), is that this advocacy of sexual expression coexisted with virulent racism and mass murder.

Indicatively, moreover, no one in the immediate post–World War II era recalled the Third Reich as a sexually conservative time. On the contrary, observers remembered a steady liberalization of heterosexual mores over the course of the first half of the twentieth century. One question this book thus pursues has to do with how the close imaginative linkage created by Nazism between sexual libertinism and genocide was coped with and misremembered in the post-1945 period.

At its heart, then, this book is concerned with how, in the postwar era, for complicated and overdetermined—if never fully conscious or rationalized—reasons, conflicts over sexual mores could become such an important site for managing the memory of Nazism and Holocaust and coming to terms with their inheritance. Thus I investigate the history of sexuality: laws, values, beliefs, and practices; such matters as contraceptive techniques, the treatment of sexual minorities, or the prevalence of pornography; how people talked about anxieties and about pleasures. But the book also charts *what else* was getting worked through when Germans fought with each other over sex and traces the continual reinterpretations of Nazism that occurred within postwar debates over sex. As such, the book can be read in at least two ways. It is a history of conflicts over sexual morality in Germany from the Third Reich to the present. But the book also advances a conceptual argument that has to do with memory. My aim in presenting a revised assessment of the sexual politics of the Third Reich, as chapter 1 will do, is not just for its own sake (though that too), but also in order to lay the groundwork for the remainder of this study. For a central question pursued in this study concerns how the memory of the connections between Nazi sexual enticements and Nazi racism came to be so energetically forgotten, only to be replaced by the new (and now more familiar, if also unevenly applied) "memory" of Nazism as sexually constrictive and uptight. With this question in mind, each chapter offers a different perspective on the relationships between sexual and other kinds of politics. Throughout, the book is concerned with the mechanisms of, and reasons for, the repeated reimaginings of the national past.

Chapter 1 offers a reinterpretation of Nazism's sexual politics against the background of developments in the Weimar Republic. I emphasize how under Nazism both sexually conservative and sexually liberalizing claims were advanced through antisemitic argumentation and how Nazis "remembered" and represented Weimar in sexualized terms. I suggest the often disconcertingly protopostmodern elements of Nazi thinking about sexual orientation and desire, explore the ways young people in particular were encouraged to depart from their parents' mores as well as the depth of the conflicts between Christians (especially Catholics) and Nazis over the status of premarital chastity and of marriage, and conclude with a discussion of the impact of total war on sexual mores. Chapter 2 then turns to the liminal moment between the end of World War II and the early years of the Federal Republic of Germany (founded in 1949). On the one hand, this was an era of considerable sexual liberality; on the other hand, it was also a time when the meanings of Nazism were actively renegotiated via impassioned discussions of sex. In these years of transition from fascism to Western democracy, diverse constituencies distanced themselves from select aspects of Nazism while they pursued fresh rationales for the continuation of other—and some of the more disturbing—elements of Nazi ideology.

Chapter 3 analyzes the claustrophobic and conformist climate of the mid-1950s to early 1960s in West Germany. Beginning with the early 1950s debate over censorship of sexually suggestive images and texts, and the need to promote sexual decency and protect young people from smut, I argue that the official sexual conservatism of this era can be understood not only as an inevitable by-product of the dominance of the Christian Democratic Party during these years but also as a powerful strategy for mastering German guilt and shame over the Holocaust. This chapter also charts the evolution of sexualized interpretations of Nazism. While in the early 1950s, commentators still emphasized Nazism's antibourgeois component and explicitly linked Nazi encouragements to nonmarital sexuality with Nazism's crimes, the Auschwitz trial of 1963–65 in Frankfurt am Main marked the emergence of the theory of the petty bourgeois and sexually repressed Holocaust perpetrator that was to become so important to the New Left student movement.

Chapter 4 turns to the sexual revolution that swept West German society after the mid-1960s. In this chapter, I examine the very real effects of

New Leftists' beliefs about Nazism, manifest in their critiques of the family and experimentation with communal living, antiauthoritarian child-rearing, and nonmonogamy—but outline as well the immense appeal of New Left perspectives also far beyond New Left circles. At the same time, I am concerned to foreground New Leftists' acute discomfort with the mainstream sexual revolution unfolding all around them, and the vehemence of their efforts to forge links between liberated sexuality and struggles for social and political revolution. I argue that the New Left can best be understood not just as it presented itself (i.e., as an antifascist movement) but even more as an anti*post*fascist movement, one whose activism around all aspects of sex and gender relations was formulated in reaction against the postfascist settlement of the 1950s—even as Nazism and the Holocaust were continually invoked as negative moral reference points.

Chapter 5 returns to the immediate postwar moment in the Soviet zone of occupation and then analyzes sexual mores under East German communism from 1949, when the German Democratic Republic was founded, until 1989, when it disintegrated. The evolution of East German sexual mores illuminates a different possible postfascist trajectory. In contrast to the West, where discussion of sex was such a key means for mastering the Nazi past, in East Germany discussion of sex constantly circled around hopes for the future. Far from being insignificant in comparison with such issues as political dissent or the perpetual shortage of consumer goods, sex became a crucial focus for the regime in its efforts to encourage citizens to endorse more fully the socialist project. This chapter concludes with an examination of the ways the unique sexual culture of East Germany became a major object of former easterners' nostalgia in the wake of German reunification in 1990.

Finally, chapter 6 explores what happened to the anticapitalist impulse within the West after the perceived failure of the student revolts of the late 1960s. The chapter spans the three decades from the aftermath of 1968 to the turn from the twentieth to the twenty-first century, and charts the impact of the collapse of East Germany and of German reunification on the ways 1968 and its meaning and import would be interpreted. If chapters 3 and 4 examine the logics whereby New Leftists' beliefs about Nazism as "sex-hostile" were created (and document the ardor and fervor of New Leftists' faith that sexual liberation would be both a cause and a key component of the achievement of political and social justice), and chapter 5 provides a contrasting perspective on how the connections between sexual and other kinds of politics could be conceived, then chapter 6 chronicles the dashing of New Leftists' faith that sexual freedom had anything whatsoever to do with social justice in the first place. Against the background of both spreading sexual liberalization and recurrent announcements that sexual desire and intensity were in steep decline, chapter 6 also traces the rise of—and vehement backlash against—feminism that occurred in the 1970s and 1980s and the effects of the ensuing gender conflict on how the Third Reich was understood, and the lessons drawn from that understanding. It concludes with a look at the current status of German debates over sexuality and memory after Nazism.

In aiming to illuminate how we might think about the ever-altering connections between sexual and other kinds of politics, the book shows how sex can be the site for talking about very many other things besides sex and working through a multitude of other social and political conflicts. At the same time, specifically the contrast of developments under three regimes—fascist, democratic capitalist, and state socialist—offers an opportunity to ground historically investigations into the relationships between social structures, ideologies, bodies, and minds and to consider how, in the twentieth century, sex could become such an extraordinarily significant locus for politics, one of the major engines of economic development, and such a central element in strategies of rule. "Sex is not a natural act," the psychologist Leonore Tiefer once wrote; the seemingly most intimate parts of our lives are strongly shaped by social forces, even as the dynamics of the interrelationships between the social and the individual are elusive and constantly changing.[4] The challenge is to take such matters as sexual practices, or subjective accounts of the dissociation or connection between physiological sensations, fantasies, and emotions, as legitimate objects for historical inquiry.

Throughout, a crucial point—and each chapter reveals another dimension of this phenomenon—is that memories were not preserved and passed on in some pure, uncontaminated fashion. Rather, "memories" of the Third Reich were continually constructed and reconstructed after the fact, so much so that these subsequent memories were even *more* influential—in political and social conflicts, and in individual psyches—than the actual complicated original reality. Each memory was always also an interpretation, mixing kernels of truth about the past with powerful emotional investments that had much to do with an evolving present. The ways that Nazis constructed Weimar, or the ways former citizens of East Germany, after reunification, constructed their experiences under communism, or the ways former New Leftists in the early twenty-first century have reimagined the significance of 1968, offer further expositions of this theme. Moreover, and while the literature on postfascist memory in Germany is large, what attention to the workings of memory in conflicts over sex in particular offers us is an extraordinary insight into how memories get "layered"—that is, the ways each cohort and constituency approached both the immediate and the more distant past only through and against the interpretations of its historical predecessors.[5] What becomes apparent, in short, is the intricate mutual imbrication of different eras in German history. In seeking to make sense of this imbrication in a particular location, I hope to offer perspectives that are relevant for scholars studying memory cultures also in other national contexts. The aim is to explore the processes by which certain central cultural understandings—with enormous and quite concrete consequences for how lives are lived—are achieved. Precisely, then, by historicizing how German constructions of the Nazi past evolved, and the remarkable impact those constructions have had (and continue to have), the book considers the lasting power not just of real but also of fictive memories.

CHAPTER ONE

Sex and the Third Reich

Remembering Nazism

Sex was no marginal matter for the National Socialists. Rather, sexuality in all its aspects was a major preoccupation for the regime and its supporters for the duration of the Third Reich. While racism of any kind has necessarily always been also about sex, this was especially true for National Socialism.

The Third Reich was an immense venture in reproductive engineering. But no less important than the dual project of prohibiting (through sterilization, abortion, and murder) the reproduction of those deemed "undesirable" and of encouraging and enforcing (through restrictions on contraception and abortion, financial incentives, and propagandistic enticements) the reproduction of those prized as healthy heterosexual "Aryans" were at least three further dimensions of sexuality. First, there was a manifest effort to manipulate the range of often conflicting psychological and physiological reactions that sexuality can evoke: arousal and inhibition, anxiety and satisfaction, attachment and repulsion, ennui and envy, ecstasy and longing. This stimulation of affect and sensation was used both to bind people to the regime and to mobilize antisemitic and other forms of racist and eugenic sentiment. Second, there was the special usefulness of sexual politics as a device for reworking moral languages. Not only did Nazis both attack Christian values *and* appropriate them for their own purposes, speaking constantly of the "sanctity" of racial purity, the "salvation" of Germany, and "guilt" and "sin" against the race or the *Volk*. They also drew on profound (and strongly church-fostered) associations between sex and evil—and between sex and Jews—in order to make the disenfranchisement and murder of Jews appear morally legitimate.

Third, and not least, there was a powerful desire to penetrate the mysteries of the human organism, a ferocious "will to know" about the functioning of psyches and bodies that, over and over, crossed the border into violence.[1] Some of the patients in their regular practices and the inmates of prisons, concentration camps, and death camps provided gynecologists, urologists, endocrinologists, and other physicians with human "material" for an array of invasive investigations into sexual variability, desire and response, drive and dysfunction. What is difficult to grasp is the double truth of, on the one hand, the hideous hubris and scientific uselessness of so many of the so-called reproductive experiments conducted under Nazism (with due attention to those physicians who utilized the concentration and death camps to transfer their research focus from chicken, rabbits, and mice to humans) and, on the other, the often conspicuously protopostmodern "successes" achieved by German physicians in such areas as artificial vagina construction, the use of (recently discovered) hormones to treat erectile dysfunction, as well as such decidedly more ambiguous ventures as the treatment of nonnormative orientations or the attempt to establish the efficacy of female orgasm for the likelihood of conception (by determining how far sperm had traveled past the cervix three minutes after coitus).[2]

What is clear, however, is that all the manifestly brutal aspects of Nazi sexual politics were not embedded in a broader antisexual attitude but, rather, coexisted with injunctions and encouragements to the majority of Germans to seek and experience sexual pleasure. Yet this assessment is not the prevailing view. Scholars continue to presume that the Third Reich was marked by pervasive sexual repression.

In addition to the standard scholarly consensus that the Third Reich was sexually repressive and conservative, there are other recurrently surfacing readings of Nazism—in literature, film, journalism, and popular culture—that in some way emphasize Nazism's purported sexual perversity. These popular interpretations have multiple variants that coexist—and at times overlap—uneasily both with each other and with scholars' assumptions about Nazism's sexual repressiveness. These interpretive approaches can be loosely distinguished into five strands: fascism as decadent; fascism as intrinsically homoerotic; fascism as femininity gone awry; Adolf Hitler's own gender-bending as the key to his ability to seduce a nation; and fascism (or even the Holocaust itself) as the titillating backdrop for hard-core pornographic fantasies. These approaches do not constitute the opposite of the "repressive hypothesis" but neither can they be completely subsumed under it. Instead they serve that hypothesis variously as extensions, supports, or counterpoints.

A first popular strand emphasizes morbid decadence and sadomasochism as the hallmarks of both Italian and German fascism. The tendency here has been to universalize the potential for pleasure in evil—for example, to treat everyone as a potential collaborator with fascism—and thereby to evacuate all historical specificity in analysis; a related effect is to provide a theory of human cruelty that roots cruelty in sexual deviance and/or boredom while simultaneously often glamorizing or eroticizing the perpetrators. The classic instances are to be found in Italian art films of the 1960s and 1970s, but there were comparable tendencies in French and German cinema as well. As the Italian Liliana Cavani, director of *The Night Porter* (1974)—which depicts the doomed sadomasochistic love affair between a concentration camp inmate and a guard—put it at once vacuously and grandiosely: "I think there is a certain portion of sadism and masochism, and thereby also a certain portion of National Socialism, in each of us."[3]

A second strand, developed already in the 1930s and amplified considerably in the decades since, stresses what it deems to be the (usually male) homosexual subtext in Nazism, even as adherents of this school remain quite inconsistent, even incoherent, about whether this homosexuality was actual/manifest or repressed/latent.[4] This approach extrapolates from the fact that Ernst Röhm, head of the brown-shirted Nazi stormtroopers (*Sturmabteilung*, or SA) and a close associate of Hitler's, was well known to be homosexual. (Hitler had Röhm murdered in the "Night of the Long Knives" in June 1934—along with other members of the SA and sundry political rivals—when Röhm's overweening ambitions conflicted with Hitler's need to curry the army leadership's favor; Röhm's homosexuality, which had not bothered Hitler before, became a convenient justification for the killings.)[5] Dozens of articulate and careful scholars have shown that, although the Röhm case does teach us that for a while homosexuality at the highest echelons of the Nazi Party was tolerated or simply found to be politically irrelevant (even as Communists and Social Democrats in Germany and in exile and anti-Nazi Anglo-American observers alike tried to get political mileage out of the Röhm affair), to extrapolate from Röhm to all of Nazism is not only historically inaccurate but serves above all two aims: tarring homosexuality in general with the brush of fascism and genocide and diverting attention from the escalated homophobic persecution and the tormenting and murder of male homosexuals, which indeed became a hallmark of Nazism.[6]

Yet popular assumptions of Nazism as a homosexual movement have remained remarkably durable. Presumptions of an inherent link between Nazism and homosexuality are, however paradoxically, nourished by the incontrovertible sense that Nazism—in historian Geoffrey Giles's apt formulation—"institutionaliz[ed] . . . homosexual panic."[7] In other words, elite institutions like the SS (*Schutzschaffel*)—initially a subset of the SA, which functioned as Hitler's bodyguard but which developed into an empire all its own under the leadership of Heinrich Himmler, providing guard duty in concentration camps and staffing numerous other aspects of the policing and killing processes—depended precisely on heightened masculinism and male bonding, even as the homoerotic elements of that bonding could not be permitted to turn into homosexual activity.[8] In a late twentieth- and early twenty-first-century climate characterized both by historical ignorance and persistently lingering homophobia, it has been an arduous and delicate matter for scholars to develop analytic frameworks that can encompass not only the lethal homophobia that came to characterize Nazism but also the attraction that the Nazi movement could initially have exercised also for some homosexual men and to bring into view not only the terrors that defined homosexual lives during the Third Reich but also the unevenness of policy and government control.[9] Differentiated and nuanced scholarship is now well underway, on the experiences of both male homosexuals and lesbians.[10] (Although lesbianism was not criminalized in Nazi Germany—it did remain criminalized in Austria throughout the Nazi period and afterward—lesbians nonetheless suffered intensified surveillance and were occasionally imprisoned in concentration camps under the rubric of other purported offenses, such as "asocial" behavior.) Yet, simultaneously, there are still commentators who are drawn to a form of simplistic Freudianism that equates the pleasure in brutality so widely evident in the Third Reich and the territories it conquered with "regression" to what is (unhelpfully) called the "anal-sadistic" stage. In this way linking up with notions of Nazism as decadent, the theories of fascism as a form of arrested development almost inevitably reinforce rather than challenge homophobic reflexes that have nothing to do with historical analysis.[11]

A third recurrent and highly speculative strand of argumentation feminizes fascism. It does so either by highlighting what are thought to be Nazism's peculiar attractions for women or, alternatively, by representing Nazism's evil as especially incarnated in such legendarily beautiful and malicious female perpetrators as Irma Grese, a guard at Auschwitz and Belsen, or Ilse Koch, the wife of Buchenwald commandant Karl Koch.[12] The impulse to investigate many German women's apparently powerful attraction to Nazism has been legitimately motivated not least by the intellectual puzzle of why a movement that explicitly announced its antifeminism and called for "emancipation from emancipation" would nonetheless find resonance among women. In pursuing this line of inquiry, scholars have among other things discovered that although Nazism claimed it would return women to the home and to the tasks of childbearing and child-rearing, in fact the Third Reich saw numerous tendencies toward female emancipation in work, in family relations, and in sexuality.[13] Yet the challenge remains to find the right balance between refusing assumptions that German women were somehow more irrationally enthralled by Hitler than were German men (a staple of misogynist commentary that it has taken decades of feminist writing to dislodge) and acknowledging that there is still something worth pondering and analyzing in such phenomena as the crates full of love letters women from all over Germany wrote to Hitler or the fact that crowds of women—*and* of men—cheered ecstatically at the sight of Hitler and testified to his magnetic appeal.[14]

Still other commentators focus on the sexually aberrant qualities of Adolf Hitler himself. This tendency, at times complexly entangled with one or more of the others, insists on the singular libidinous attraction Hitler supposedly held either for German women specifically or for the German masses as a whole. Foreign or exiled contemporaries, seeking to make sense of Hitler's astonishing success with the public despite his overt banality, often sought the explanation in sexual irregularity, locating it variously—and with blithe inconsistency—either in Hitler's own apparently dysfunctional and bizarre romantic relationships with a number of women, or in his rumored perverse sexual predilections, or in his comfort with homosexual comrades-in-arms, or in his own purportedly "feminized" quality—exhibited by his failure to fit securely into a stereotypical masculine identity. Ignoring the fact that Hitler's own anomalous personality could hardly explain the monstrousness of the Third Reich as a whole, journalists then and since have pandered to and fostered a leering public fascination with both perversity and evil that continually collapses one into the other.[15]

Finally, for complex reasons, the Third Reich also often serves as the locus for hard-core pornographic films. Whether this phenomenon appeals to the same public fascination with both perversity and evil that makes Hitler's eccentricities such a frequent focus of public attention, or simply banks on the shock value of bringing eroticism and cruelty into the same frame of reference, or—as sociologist Lynn Rapaport has proposed—amplifies violent porn's more general function of allowing viewers to master in fantasy matters that would otherwise be deeply unsettling and threatening, there is no question that pornography based in Nazi contexts sells well and has a mass audience.[16] The recurrent pornographization of Nazism and the Holocaust in the postwar era (and, vice versa, the use of Nazi insignia and props or Holocaust locales and plots in pornographic materials) in high and popular culture alike has a double effect.[17] On the one hand, the persistent linkage of pornography and Nazism in literature and film and in the popular imagination actually captures some truths about the Third Reich that are too frequently suppressed in scholarly writing about the era; it is as though these cultural phantasms serve as the repository of intuitive insights that apparently could not be integrated into academic scholarship.[18] On the other hand, and simultaneously, the pornographization of Nazism indisputably also functions to trivialize Nazism's horrors and thereby to ward off serious confrontation with those horrors and their implications.

Despite these several popular strands, the standard scholarly assumption, so widely held that it is seldom documented in detail, is that Nazism was at its core antisex. The conventional periodization suggests that the Third Reich's sexual politics can best be understood as a reactionary backlash against the freedom and openness of the Weimar Republic. Throughout the 1980s and 1990s, for example, and also in the early twenty-first century, the Third Reich has been routinely described, in an assertive sort of shorthand, as "sex-hostile," "pleasureless," characterized by "rigid-bodily sexual norms of behavior" or "official German prudery."[19] The visceral intensity of Nazi antisemitism was said to have had its source in an external projection of "unconscious guilt produced by repressed sexual desires" in "innumerable" Germans.[20] Under Nazism, "sexual abstinence until an early marriage was the highest command."[21] Furthermore, "whatever Weimar had thought and partially practiced as progress, was radically denied or terminated," and Germans' willingness to be "distracted away from eroticism and sexuality" was indicative of a deeper and more lasting "political German masochism, a joyful subordination and . . . willingness to deny one's own feelings."[22] "National Socialists' fear of sexuality" is deemed to be incontrovertible.[23] So too is the notion that in the Third Reich, "sexuality and its representation were now thoroughly tabooized."[24] Indeed, as Jeffrey Herf summarized the problem in 1999, "historians of German society and culture under the Nazis" have proceeded as though "the connection between Nazism and sexual repression" were simply "intuitively obvious."[25]

In this regard, George Mosse's pathbreaking studies are paradigmatic for inquiries into sexuality and Nazism. In such works as *Nationalism and Sexuality* (1985) and *The Image of Man* (1996), Mosse largely took at face value the National Socialists' claims to be restoring clean and orderly family life. Although he made numerous perceptive points about the tensions between camaraderie and homoeroticism inherent in the Nazi ideal of male bonding and about the conflicting injunctions to fidelity to the community of males (the *Männerbund*) and to heterosexual family life with which Nazism confronted its male followers, Mosse was committed to an overall interpretation of Nazism as "a movement that made every effort at middle-class respectability."[26] Seeing Nazis primarily as inheritors of a culture of bourgeois constraint rather than that culture's critics, he argued at length that the ubiquitous nudes of the Third Reich were in actuality devoid of eroticism, and he described Nazism as far more preoccupied with sexual propriety than sexual liberation.[27]

Challenging and recasting the terms of debate about sexuality under Nazism, this chapter argues that the sexually inciting elements of Nazism have been neglected. There can be no doubt that in its thorough racialization of sex and in its heightened homophobia, the Third Reich's sexual politics represented a definitive and violent backlash against the progressivism and tolerance possible in Weimar. Yet for much of the populace

Nazism brought with it not only a redefinition but also a perpetuation, expansion, and intensification of preexisting liberalizing trends. In part, the liberalization would be the result of the massive disruptions caused by war, labor mobilization, and population transfers and the general climate of moral anarchy as mass murder escalated. But the liberalization of heterosexual mores was also, already before World War II, actively advanced as part of NSDAP policy. For the regime ultimately offered, to those broad sectors of the populace that it did not persecute, many inducements to pre- and extramarital heterosexuality—not only for the sake of reproduction but also for the sake of pleasure—and numerous celebrations of marital bliss. Indeed, one could potentially think of Nazi affirmations of sexual pleasure both within and outside of marriage also in the context of the broader modernization of consumer culture under Nazism, from the marketing of Coca-Cola to the new travel opportunities afforded by the Strength through Joy (*Kraft durch Freude*) program.[28]

It is frequently emphasized that the extraordinary disruptions of World War I—with couples separated, women having acquired greater independence, thousands of men maimed and millions killed, Germany humiliated and defeated and forced by the victorious Allies to accept democracy under socialist rule—ushered in the more sexually liberated Weimar era, and then that the general Weimar atmosphere of experimentation and the pursuit of pleasure, especially evident in such large metropoles as Berlin and Hamburg, was abruptly cut short by the Nazi rise to power in 1933. But this periodization overlooks two important points. First, the liberalization typically associated with Weimar began before World War I. It is indicative, for instance, that authors writing in the 1930s and 1940s place the onset of sexual liberalization at the very start of the twentieth century.[29] Moreover, physicians' reports routinely reveal that premarital heterosexual intercourse among all classes of women as well as men and an increasing use of contraceptive strategies (both before and during marriage) were becoming standard practice before 1914.[30] Just as significant is the second point: even as the liberalized mores continued to spread ever further in the populace, there were also, already during the years of Weimar, the beginnings of a conservative (and explicitly Christian-led) countermobilization against that liberalization.[31] In short, Nazism came to power at a time of already competing tendencies toward liberalization and renewed restraint.

Yet another lacuna in the historiography of the Third Reich concerns the interconnections between sex and religion. Almost invariably, these subjects are treated separately. In particular, the relationship of sexual matters to Nazism's impact on processes of secularization has hardly been acknowledged. Yet Nazism's sexual politics only come into focus if one considers them in the context of the history of religion. To make sense of

Nazism's sexual politics requires recognition not only of the fierce rivalry that raged in the Third Reich between the Nazi Party and the Christian churches but also of the overlaps in personnel and commonalities in values between them. Much has been written about the churches under Nazism.[32] But while the Nazi campaign to charge Catholic priests with homosexuality is sometimes mentioned, little is said in this scholarship about other sexual issues. This is surprising not least because the competition and cooperation between Nazis and Christians over sexual mores provided the single most important context for the regime's elaboration of its own particular sexual vision.

Without question, Nazis were conflicted among themselves over sexual mores and some certainly did seek a return to more conservative values and behaviors. Nazi-affiliated sexual conservatives did not hesitate to challenge the regime directly when they felt that traditional norms were being undermined.[33] And throughout the Third Reich, a wealth of regime-endorsed writings advanced the argument that racial purity and national recovery depended on premarital chastity, monogamous and prolifically procreative marriage, and wholesome family life. These commentators counseled young people: "Do not succumb to your urges."[34] They asserted that sexual abstinence before marriage was "fundamentally appropriate to our type and race [*Art und Rasse*]" and praised the regime for "liberating" youth from "premature sexualization" through sports; repeatedly they quoted the well-known slogan by the popular writer Walter Flex: "Staying pure and becoming mature—that is the most beautiful and most difficult life-art."[35] They railed against the "Bolshevik contamination of our sexual morality" and called for greater "joy in reproductivity" (*Fortpflanzungsfreudigkeit*).[36] They complained about the culture of "free love" and insisted that "the sole inner *purpose of family and of marriage*" was "*to give the Volk healthy children and to raise them to be healthy, decent German women and men.*"[37] Advice literature directed at youth and writings by self-styled experts in the fields of "racial research" and "political biology" frequently advanced the ideals of sexual restraint and self-control.[38] Conservative constituencies could always find texts that reflected their concerns.

Many other Nazi-identified spokespersons and publications, however, worked to detach emancipatory impulses from their association with "Marxism" and "Jewishness" and to redefine sexual liberation as a "Germanic," "Aryan" prerogative. Among the challenges confronting us is therefore the need to make sense of the inseparability of antisemitism and other forms of racism from both anti- *and* pro-sexual Nazi efforts. While there was no master plan for sexuality under Nazism and no coherent policy (but rather a cacophony of often competing injunctions), it is clear that over time a decisive trend against traditional mores emerged.

Although Nazism has been misremembered and misrepresented as sexually repressive for everyone, what Nazism actually did was to redefine who could have sex with whom. The persecution and torture of homosexuals, for example, provided a crucial context for the constant injunctions to heterosexual activity. And the abuse and murder of those deemed unworthy of reproduction and life because of their purported "hereditary" or "racial" characteristics constituted the background against which those classed as superior were enjoined to enjoy their entitlements.[39] The legitimation of terror and the invitation to pleasure operated in tandem.

Studying how sex was experienced, represented, and discussed in the Third Reich thus provides singularly important insights into the workings of Nazi ideology. What a reading of a broad array of Nazi writings on sex suggests is that no prior regime in history had ever so systematically set itself the task of stimulating and validating especially young people's sexual desires—all the while denying precisely that this was what it was doing. This chapter, then, is concerned with analyzing the ways Nazi propagandists embedded inciting solicitations of desire and emphatic celebrations of heterosexual activity in a variety of disavowing mechanisms. It examines as well the double move by which Nazis both assaulted Christian standards of sexual behavior *and* borrowed from Christian language and converted it to their own purposes. While the chapter is attentive to the gaps as well as the congruence between regime rhetoric and individual practices, it also begins from the premise that one of the notable features of sexuality as a realm of existence is that it foregrounds the inextricability of representation and experience.

For historians of sexuality it has become increasingly standard to turn away from the work of Sigmund Freud to that of Michel Foucault, even as it is likely that we need both of them in order to understand and convey the distinctive qualities of life and death in a viciously savage but wildly popular dictatorship obsessed with issues of both reproduction and enjoyment. Yet the peculiar interpretive difficulties raised by the topic of sexuality under Nazism make it even more valuable to revisit the work of such an intermittently neglected theorist of sex and power as Herbert Marcuse. Few terms capture as well as Marcuse's famous "repressive desublimation" the regulatory components also of emancipatory injunctions.[40] In addition, Marcuse was one of the first to specify how Nazism's hubristic racism was inseparable from its attempts to reorganize sexual life, how central the politicization of the previously more private realm of sexuality was to the Nazis' political agenda, and how it was that sexual excitation could become a mechanism for social manipulation.

Scholars of *Alltagsgeschichte* (daily life history) have long pointed out that developments within the so-called private sphere change according to rhythms that diverge substantially from those of high politics. The shapes of such daily life activities (like shopping or socializing with co-workers or childrearing) transform in response to events and pressures that may not always be clearly linked to what political regime happens to be in power. In some ways, sex fits the *Alltagsgeschichte* model, but in other ways—especially because Nazis ascribed tremendous importance to sex and strove to reshape sexual mores—it does not. Ultimately, the majority of the population experienced the Third Reich not as a sexually conservative time but rather as one in which the general processes of liberalization of heterosexual mores that had been ongoing since the beginning of the twentieth century were perceived both as simply progressing further and as escalating under the combined effect of official Nazi encouragement and eventually the disruptive impact of total war. Under Nazism, this growing liberality was handled in a double way: it was *both* decried as Jewish *and* celebrated as an Aryan privilege.

SEX AND ANTISEMITISM

Sexual demonization of Jews was a pervasive feature of antisemitism already during the Weimar years. Building on older associations of Jews with carnality and Christians with spirituality, the twentieth-century version emphasized the threat posed by a rapacious, bestial Jewish male to innocent German femininity. Typical was an early right-wing election campaign poster from 1920 which showed an unattractive Jewish man paired with a beautiful non-Jewish woman beside a coffin labeled "Deutschland."[41] Also typical from this time was a cartoon of the Jewish male as a repulsive large octopus raping Germania, the female representative of Germany.[42] The racist novelist Artur Dinter, author of the best-selling *Die Sünde wider das Blut* (The Sin against the Blood, 1921)—it was said to have been read by 1.5 million Germans—not only reinforced the antisemitic cliché of the Jewish pimp who violated young girls under his control, but also argued that one drop of Jewish sperm permanently contaminated a German woman. Even if she later partnered with a German man, the children they had together were nonetheless polluted by her earlier encounter with a Jew.[43] Hitler made Dinter's notion of "the sin against the blood" his own, and *Mein Kampf* (My Struggle, 1925) famously included a passage in which Hitler fantasized how "for hours the black-haired Jew-boy, diabolic joy in his face, waits in ambush for the unsuspecting girl whom he defiles with his blood and thus robs from her people."[44] The antisemitic Nazi newspaper *Der Stürmer* (The Stormtrooper), founded in 1923 and edited by Julius Streicher, elaborated on these themes in dozens of variations, ranting repetitively about male Jews' supposed compulsion toward sexual criminality (including rape, pedophilia, and systematic seduction of German girls into prostitution). It printed hundreds of images of the Jewish man as a vulgar, animalistic, or diabolical figure driving German womanhood into disaster.

Yet there was a countervailing association between sexuality and Jewishness in Weimar: the representation of Jewish Germans as leaders in various campaigns for sexual liberalization. This association contained more than a small amount of truth. Jewish medical doctors and political activists were indeed often at the forefront of campaigns to abolish Paragraph 218 (which criminalized abortion) and Paragraph 175 (which criminalized male homosexuality) as well as the broader efforts to make contraceptive information and products more widely available and to assist couples (through sex enlightenment films and sex and marriage counseling centers) not only with family planning but also with achieving greater sexual satisfaction. The prominent physician Max Marcuse, for instance, made the (at the time radical) claim that "*The purpose of sexual activity is the achievement of pleasure.* Nothing more and nothing less." His major work, *Der Präventivverkehr* (Preventive Intercourse, 1931), not only explained in detail how condoms might be properly stored for repeated use (since most working-class couples could scarcely afford them) but also offered the advice that oral and anal sex were excellent strategies for preventing conception.[45] Another prominent activist, Magnus Hirschfeld, was the leader of the movement for homosexual rights in Weimar Germany (which had hundreds of thousands of supporters); he had also established the Institute for Sexual Science in Berlin in 1919, which included a sex counseling center as well as the major library in Germany for sexological research (subsequently burned by the Nazis). He stood not only for homosexual rights but—like Marcuse—for an accepting attitude toward premarital heterosexuality and to contraceptive use both before and during marriage.[46] Max Hodann, another well-known physician, provided some of the earliest sex advice writings for proletarian youth.[47] And the abortion rights activist Friedrich Wolf was a leader in the fight against Paragraph 218 (which in the final years of Weimar had developed into a huge mass movement) and was the author of the widely seen play (and then movie) *Cyankali*, which dramatized poor women's desperation over unwanted pregnancies.[48]

However, and despite these and numerous other examples of Jewish sex rights activism, the idea of Jews as the main advocates of sexual liberalization was also a racist, right-wing construct. Taking shape already in the later years of Weimar, this construct became even more important after the Nazis came to power in 1933 and, in fact, became central to the Nazis' retrospective representation of the Weimar Republic as a whole (fig. 1.1). Weimar was reduced to sex. All the complexities and contrary political and social impulses of German life between 1919 and 1933 were

Figure 1.1. *Der Stürmer*, April 1929, p. 1. The naked and bound blonde woman represents "Truth," and the signs pasted over a copy of *Der Stürmer* say "confiscation," "court," "prohibition," and "temporary injunction." She is being tied up by the state prosecutor and the police and the caption below her reads "Down with the truth!" On the right side, a stereotypically Jewish upper-class man seems to be clasping hands with the same prosecutor and policeman as he stands before a sign calling for passersby to "leave the church" and engage in "free love," "fight against Paragraph 175 (criminalization of homosexuality)," and "kill the fruit in the mother's body." The caption below him reads: "Thank you, gentlemen!"

obscured and displaced by an image of Weimar as a hothouse of decadence and promiscuity, a time of the "most vulgar stimulation of steamy, debauched eroticism."[49] Weimar was described as a "Jews' republic" (*Judenrepublik*) in which, among other things, magazines for homosexual men and women "burst out of the ground like mushrooms after the rain" and abortion rights were defended by Jews in order to "secure their dominion over the Aryan peoples."[50] In addition, since the Weimar Republic had been governed by socialists, since many of the sex counseling centers in Weimar had been set up as services provided by the Socialist and Communist parties for their predominantly working-class members, and since many of the Jewish physicians active in various sexual-rights campaigns were also leftists, it was simple for Christian conservatives and Nazis alike to assimilate the phenomenon of sexual rights activism to the larger phantasmagorical menace of "Judeo-Bolshevism."

Even the founder of psychoanalysis, the Austrian Sigmund Freud, decidedly not a leftist, was portrayed as part of the same pernicious conspiracy. Freud's purported proclivity for seeing sex everywhere and at the root of all individual and social phenomena (an interpretation of his work that Freud categorically rejected) became a constant motif for Nazi authors. Freud was accused not only of having a "dirty fantasy" that projected sexuality onto children but also of inventing the idea of an id—or "unconscious force"—solely to keep the consciences of "Nordic" people from bothering them when they engaged in masturbation or extramarital relations. Freud's teachings, it was claimed, robbed people of all ethical orientation as they struggled to master their own drives. Individuals were cast into the Jews' "Asiatic world view: 'Enjoy, because tomorrow you'll be dead.' "[51]

As one pediatrician complained, for the Freudian the human being "existed only as a sex organ, around which the body vegetates."[52] Psychoanalysts and doctors—"mostly of Jewish extraction"—who defended homosexual rights were labeled "pimps under the cover of scholarship" (*Zuhälter unter wissenschaftlichem Deckmantel*).[53] Sex education experts influenced by psychoanalysis were declared to be "Jewish sex criminals."[54] When massive public book burnings organized by Nazi student organizations took place in 1933, a demonstrator recited (as Freud's work went into the blaze): "Against soul-corroding overestimation of the drive-life [*Triebleben*], for the nobility of the human soul! I give to the flames the writings of Sigmund Freud."[55] As late as 1942, theologian Heinz Hunger (who in postwar West Germany would become a highly regarded specialist on youth sexuality) simultaneously insisted that there was "nothing original" about psychoanalysis—for to claim otherwise would be "to give too much honor to the unproductivity of the Jewish race"—and declared that "the whole of psychoanalysis is nothing other than the Jewish nation's rape of Western culture." Psychoanalysis was "*Volk*-damaging" in its overemphasis on that which lay "below the navel."[56] Throughout the Third Reich, Freud remained a favorite object for Nazi attack, even as Nazi psychotherapists and physicians appropriated his ideas (while denying they were his); borrowing from Freud while simultaneously denigrating him was a common Nazi-era strategy.[57]

Similarly, Magnus Hirschfeld and Max Marcuse became major targets for Nazi venom. As one Nazi-identified doctor put it, "the psychoanalysts are not yet the worst. Far more offensive is that which gathers around Magnus Hirschfeld, the director of the Institute for Sexual Science, and around Mr. Marcuse & Co. Here, one can be sure, there is a quite conscious effort to destroy the German soul."[58] Hirschfeld's contention that sexual orientation was biologically determined and his widely reported success organizing Germans in favor of the abolition of Paragraph 175 were both labeled appalling. But Hirschfeld distressed conservatives also because he promoted an ethics of consent. Challenging the standard Christian view that premarital intercourse was by definition a sin, Hirschfeld emphasized that the key moral issue was that there be no coercion in sexual encounters. Marcuse too argued that also nonmarital love relationships, if based on mutual respect and affection, were ethically legitimate. Nazi commentators voiced their outrage at what they considered an insidious attempt to "obscure the simple concepts of right and wrong and relocate the boundaries between them" and (rejecting what they deemed a Jewish celebration of sexuality as a central force in human life) announced that they had rid Germany of this "abominable specter of the idol worship of sex appeal."[59]

Nazis eager to advance a sexually conservative agenda drew on the ambivalent association of Jews with both sexual evil and sexual rights. Attempting to mobilize antisemitism for sexually conservative ends, they argued that Jews undervalued spirituality and love and overvalued sensuality and physical contact.[60] Far from advocating a natural sexuality, Jews exhibited a "disgusting lechery."[61] Or: "The Jew just has a different sexuality from that of the German."[62] Jews were working "*to strike the Nordic race at its most vulnerable point: sexual life.*"[63] Jewish doctors' willingness to provide abortion services was portrayed as above all a calculated attempt to destroy the racially superior German *Volk*.[64] In the course of 1933, the marriage and sex counseling centers associated with the Left were ransacked and destroyed (in a center in Düsseldorf, Nazi stormtroopers took the contraceptives for themselves); Jewish doctors and counselors lost their jobs, fled into exile, or were imprisoned or deported and later killed. Meanwhile, marriage counseling centers emphasizing strictly "racial" and "hereditary" matters flourished under Nazism.[65]

What was being denied in the constructions of Jews as the primary proponents of contraceptive use and as the main celebrants of sexual pleasure and of diversity and perversity in desire was that what these activists had offered was what also millions of non-Jewish Germans had fervently wanted. Indicative of such longings was that the birthrate in Germany had been declining in all classes since at least the start of the twentieth century.[66] Significantly, moreover, and despite the monetary and other incentives proffered by the Nazis—including higher taxes on singles and childless couples, marriage loans (amortized through the birth of each child), and Mother's Cross awards for prolific childbearing—nearly a third of all couples married in 1933 were still childless five years later, and a further quarter of them had only one child.[67] And while the birthrate did rise in the first five or six years of the Third Reich, this was due not to a rise in the number of children per couple but rather to a rise in the number of marriages. "All the efforts of the authorities to break the mold of the two-child couple failed."[68] Even churchgoing Christians reportedly considered the use of contraception commonsensical.[69]

Some contemporaries say that they never saw a condom during the Third Reich.[70] But condom use was openly advocated in the leading Nazi sex advice manual.[71] And other contemporaries assert that in the Third Reich condoms were available in "abundance," in "vending machines on metro and railway platforms, in public toilets," and that the machines in public toilets also carried "tubes of Vaseline."[72] (It would not be until the 1950s that many of these "rickety old automats" were dismantled.)[73] Until the advertisement and sale of mechanical and chemical contraceptives were outlawed by Heinrich Himmler in 1941 (although condoms were exempted from this ruling), diaphragms, cervical caps, and spermicidal tablets and gels were available in pharmacies, beauty salons, and directly from the companies producing them; even after 1941 mail-order companies found ways to circumvent the law.[74] Moreover, information about the rhythm method, just developed in the early 1930s, continued to be available during the Third Reich.[75] And despite the much harsher penalties for abortions instituted by the Nazis, abortions were still avidly sought, and "for all the public pressure, the birthrate in the Third Reich did not ever equal the rates from the last years of the 'decadent' 1920s."[76]

It is crucial to register as well how significant a topic and goal sexual pleasure—for women as well as for men—had become in Germany in the early decades of the twentieth century. While assertions of the breadth and depth of sexual misery were prevalent, there was clearly also considerable hopefulness that this misery could be alleviated.[77] Many women experienced anxiety about pregnancy as not only orgasm-inhibiting but also libido-suppressing. Coitus interruptus could be unnerving and stressful for both partners; disinfectant-soaked sponges placed in front of the cervix before coitus or postcoital douches often irritated and inflamed the vaginal area and made sex painful rather than pleasurable; bacterial contamination of diaphragms and cervical caps could lead to infection. And illegal abortions performed inexpertly and under less than aseptic conditions could also cause infections and uterine damage. Lack of privacy in overcrowded proletarian housing could make relaxation difficult. Heavy alcohol use especially among men often made marital sexual encounters little more than violations for the women. But without question, the possibility of greater sexual satisfaction was also becoming an increasingly important ideal for broad sectors of the population, both women and men; many articulated a profound yearning for something better in their lives. Against this background, it was no wonder that the sex counseling clinics established by the Socialist and Communist parties had been unable to keep up with mass demand.

As the Third Reich unfolded, the most striking aspect of sexual conservatives' writings was their dismay in the face of non-Jewish Germans' apparent disinterest in conforming to more constrictive mores. As one author observed critically in 1933, after the Nazis' ascension to power, "a large proportion of our *Volk* comrades, male and female, insists nowadays on the standpoint of complete 'free love,' love without any inhibition, that is, love that is not love, but rather a purely animalistic activation of the sex drive."[78] While references to Jews continued to function as a negative counterpoint to underscore the value of a sexually conservative perspective, precisely some of the most conservative texts also included important evidence of just how unpopular sexual conservatism was.

In a book published in 1938, for example, the Nazi-identified physician Ferdinand Hoffmann fumed that "approximately 72 million condoms are used in Germany each year" and that "in the surroundings of big cities, evening after evening, the roads into the woods are covered with automobiles in which, after the American pattern, so-called love is made." Premarital heterosexual intercourse was near-ubiquitous in Nazi Germany, Hoffmann said. "A young man who does not have a girlfriend is a priori a dummy; a girl without a boyfriend is a 'homely Gretchen type.' " This was not just a matter of boys sowing their wild oats; girls too played the field. The idea that anyone should stay chaste until marriage "possesses absolutely no more validity." Perhaps 5 percent of brides were still virgins; many had already had numerous boyfriends. Even after marriage Germans did not often remain faithful to their spouses. Hoffmann imagined a map on which "all the crisscross relationships of broken fidelities and adulteries are drawn; a filigreed network of lines would bind cities and towns and villages."[79]

Eager to persuade Germans of the value of more conservative mores— a single standard of premarital abstinence and marital fidelity for both women and men, and an end to the use of contraceptives—Hoffmann declared that "the demand for the full living-out of sexuality is a typical Jewish-liberalistic one, and the news should gradually have gotten around, that everything which on the Jewish side has become a battle cry, solely serves disintegrative and not constructive aims. The Jew has never talked us into something that could help us." Singling out Max Marcuse for special censure, Hoffmann raged against Jewish doctors who, during the years of the Weimar Republic, had had the audacity not only to provide birth control information and equipment but also to advance a sexual morality centered on pleasure. The trouble was that, although the populace had largely embraced Nazism in political terms, and Germans were appropriately antisemitic in most parts of their lives, they were evidently loath to let go of their emancipated sexual habits. Trying to pin on Jews what he simultaneously admitted was a pandemic phenomenon, Hoffmann sought to reconcile his own contradictions by surmising that, due to the machinations of Jewish doctors, pop-song writers, and filmmakers, individualism and materialism had come to "saturate the personality of the individual not only through to his economic interests, but through to his erotic deep structure [*erotische Tiefenschicht*]." As a result, numerous people believed that one could be a "good citizen of the Third Reich, if one is simply a good political soldier, and for the rest one can organize one's love-life . . . in accordance with the previous liberalistic perspectives." Few things could be further from the truth, Hoffmann cautioned his readers. "There are not two sides to the Jewish question, and it is not admissible to damn the Jew in his political, economic, and human manifestations while secretly, for personal convenience, to maintain the customs he has suggested in the realm of love- and sex-life." There was little doubt that sex remained the site, Hoffmann complained, at which it was "evidently the most difficult to be a good National Socialist."[80]

This was only the most elaborate exposition of the theory that "Jewishness" was deeply rooted also within non-Jewish Germans.[81] Population policy expert Paul Danzer, for example, writing in 1936 in the journal *Völkischer Wille* (Racial Will), argued that whether Jews

> exploited our economy, whether they confused our legal life or encouraged social divisions, all that pales before the very most serious damage they have done to our *Volk*, the *poisoning of marital and sexual morality*. . . . Just remember the semitically saturated entertainment- and theater-literature, the film making of the past decades, and the persistent effort that was made from that side in the ripping asunder of all moral barriers, the glorification of adultery and sexual uninhibitedness!

And yet Danzer, too, like Hoffmann, worried openly that the German masses could not care less about cleaning up their sexual act. Despite the Nazis' political victory, men continued to see it as an "indispensable proof of their masculinity, to run after every skirt and in so doing notch up as many successes as possible. . . . And one cannot say that the female sex is much more narrowminded."[82] Similarly, another leading "race expert" complained that "the notions about sex life, marriage, and family" promoted in Weimar had "eaten . . . more deeply" (*tiefer . . . einfressen*) into the German *Volk* than any "purely political teachings" from that era.[83]

Likewise, an NSDAP-affiliated physician vociferously lamented in 1937 how "we have experienced a revolution in ways of understanding the world and a *völkisch* awakening like never before. And yet we thoughtlessly repeat the Jewish or Jewish-influenced vulgarities concerning the relations of the two sexes. . . . It is astonishing how little our great National Socialist revolution has moved forward in this area!"[84] Another Nazi medical doctor a few years later marveled in outraged alarm that, contrary to expectation, the Nazi revolution had not been able to reverse the German public's love affair with the rubber industry. Although the marketing of contraceptives, in his view, was nothing but "the means for racial suicide," and "one had thought this was a symptom of the Jewish-Marxist *Volk* destruction. . . . on the whole, unfortunately, nothing has changed."[85] Yet another variation on these themes appeared in the work of a Berlin urologist who condemned what he saw as an unfortunate pressure on men to please women sexually. In racially coded terms, he blamed this pressure on Jewish doctors and psychoanalysts who put into women's heads the idea that women too were capable of orgasm. He recommended that men return to "'automatic-egotistical' sexual intercourse," warning that solicitous concern for women only led to erectile dysfunction and prostate problems.[86] However paradoxically, this was not a form of antisemitism in which Jews were abjected. Sexually conservative Nazis—whether intentionally or not—reinforced the idea that what Jews supposedly represented also had undeniable appeal for vast numbers of non-Jewish Germans. In addition, and even more significantly, the arguments made by sexual conservatives indicate that they believed that the Nazis' ascension to power was not exactly experienced as sexually repressive by the majority of non-Jewish Germans.

Meanwhile, the need for greater conservatism was not the sole message about sex promoted by Nazism. For there was also another strand of Nazi argumentation about sex, one that was far more deliberately inciting and one explicitly aimed at encouraging playful, pleasurable heterosexuality among those ideologically and "racially" approved by the regime. Importantly, however, this second strand of argumentation too was thoroughly saturated with antisemitism. For these pro-sex advocates, references to the supposed shamelessness and impropriety of "Jewish" versions of sexuality functioned preeminently as a technique of disavowal—a strategy to distract attention away from Nazism's own inducements to premarital and extramarital sexual activity.

INCITEMENT AND DISAVOWAL

Nazis were acutely aware that the regime was already in the mid-1930s developing a reputation for urging teenagers to engage in premarital intercourse, and they strove to manage the ensuing controversy—domestically and internationally—both by denying that they were doing any such thing *and* by avidly defending their own policy and practice. While in 1934 leaders in the Bund Deutscher Mädel (Federation of German Girls) still received a directive to encourage their young charges to have premarital love affairs under the rubric "top secret," by 1935 at the latest there was nothing particularly secret anymore about what went on in some (though surely not all) of the local BDM chapters.[87] In Dresden, for instance, Victor Klemperer noted the following in his diary in 1935: "Annemarie Köhler tells us in despair that the hospitals are overcrowded with fifteen-year-old girls, some pregnant, some with gonorrhea. The BDM. Her brother has vehemently refused to allow his daughter to join."[88] As of 1937, the Social Democratic Party (SPD) in exile reported the news that in the Hitler Youth "promiscuity is the concretely accepted situation."[89] And in 1938 the American sociologist Clifford Kirkpatrick was at pains to present his major study on *Nazi Germany: Its Women and Family Life* as offering a more complex and rounded portrait than the (by then already cliché) image of regime encouragement to "the conceiving of illegitimate children" and "polygamy."[90]

In the early 1940s Herbert Marcuse, at that point working for the U.S. Office of Strategic Services, strove to articulate how the effectiveness of Nazi culture had rested not least on its "abolition" of taboos and its "emancipation of sexual life." Although Marcuse suggested that the trends he was identifying could not be found in official regime pronouncements or documents but rather needed to be gleaned from an assessment of social and cultural dynamics, he noticed that "inducement" to the pursuit of sexual pleasure was pervasive. As Marcuse put it, "the destruction of the family, the attack on patriarchalic and monogamic standards and all the similar widely heralded undertakings play about the latent 'discontent' in civilization, the protest against its restraint and frustration. They appeal to the right of 'nature,' to the healthy and defamed drives of man. . . . They claim to reestablish the 'natural.' " At the same time, however, "the new individual liberties are by their very nature exclusive liberties, the privilege of the healthy and approved." Marcuse certainly pointed out that under Nazism "personal satisfaction has become a controlled political function" and that while "the abolition of these taboos" was "one of the most daring enterprises of National Socialism . . . the liberty or license implied in this abolition serves to intensify the 'Gleichschaltung' [coordination] of individuals into the National Socialist system." Yet he was quite clear about the inciting effects of Nazism and its encouragement particularly of "extra-marital relations between the sexes." In particular, Marcuse pointed "to the deliberate herding of boys and girls in the training camps, to the license granted to the racial elite, to the facilitation of marriage and divorce, to the sanctioning of illegitimate children." Marcuse observed that "all this is, of course, in line with the population policy of the Reich." But he was quick to note as well that "the policy has still another aspect, which is far more hidden and touches the roots of National Socialist society." The aim, Marcuse surmised, was to tie individuals to the NSDAP by urging them to pursue pleasure: "The abolition of sexual taboos tends to make this realm of satisfaction an official political domain. . . . The individual recognizes his private satisfaction as a patriotic service to the regime, and he receives his reward for performing it."[91]

Yet despite Herbert Marcuse's claim that Nazis did not put their comfort with and advocacy of pre- and extramarital sex into writing, this is not the case. Not only sexual conservatives like Ferdinand Hoffmann or Paul Danzer but also more sexually liberal Nazi-identified authors published freely. The mid-1930s—a few years into the Third Reich as the regime strove to consolidate its hold on the populace—saw a particular efflorescence of discussion of the acceptability of premarital and extramarital coitus; Nazi-endorsed authors openly espoused both.

That premarital intercourse was the standard popular practice was considered quite uncontroversial by a number of Nazi authors. In one widely discussed 1936 essay, for instance, the physician Walter Gmelin reported on his work evaluating couples' "racial" and "hereditary" suitability for marriage and also commented on the extant high incidence in Germany of premarital intercourse. Although Gmelin found that less than 5 percent of the women and men he interviewed were virgins—indeed, most had begun to have intercourse in their late teens and early twenties, approximately seven years before they married—Gmelin did not find this trend alarming. And although he pondered why the majority had more than one premarital partner (and some had several dozen), he nonetheless insisted that premarital sexual experience was a good thing, a phenomenon to be read above all as "a healthy reaction against the social inhibitions and against morality preachers," a sign that "also today—in spite of everything—people at the age of sexual maturity satisfy the drive given them by nature!" In fact, Gmelin interjected, those few who denied having had premarital experience "certainly did not display above-average hereditary resources [Erbgut]."[92]

As Gmelin's aside about "morality preachers" suggests, Nazi-affiliated authors espoused their pro-sex vision especially in attacks on the Christian churches. Also in 1936, for example, the jurist Rudolf Bechert energetically defended extramarital affairs. In the context of explaining a proposed new law that would give illegitimate children the father's name and equal rights with legitimate children to financial support, Bechert ventured this:

Nonmarital bonds are superior to marriages in many ways. It is not just life experience that proves that nonmarital connections rooted in sexual love are an unchangeable fact; rather all of human culture teaches that they can represent

the highest moral and aesthetic value. Without sexual love no poetry, no painting, indeed, no music! In all cultured nations concubinage is *not criminalized*,
with churchy Italy ahead of all the rest. . . . Never can nonmarital sexual intercourse be prevented.

Indeed, Bechert concluded effusively: "Love is the only true religious experience in the world."[93]

Such an emphatic rejection of Christian moralizing—coupled with a
glorification of sex—was even more evident in a 1937 book by the physician Carl Csallner. Csallner advocated a double standard. Premarital experience for men was fine, even useful (and extramarital experience constituted an often understandable lapse), but female chastity before and
during marriage was imperative; Csallner thought it unacceptable that a
wife might have a comparative basis by which to judge her husband's
lovemaking skills. But he certainly thought sexual intercourse deserved to
be energetically defended against traditional religious scruples. Csallner
opined that only "unnatural sanctimoniousness" and "clerical cant" had
turned the sexual drive, which was "wanted by nature and spontaneously
presses toward activity," into something "base and mean . . . a deadly
sin." The sexual drive, in Csallner's view, was "great" and "holy." For
Csallner, the human being's "greatest individual experience of bliss lies in
the accomplishment of the sex act"; raising the sex act "out of the sphere
of naive psychophysiological sensation" and to "the level of eternal values" in order to "anchor it in the transcendental" actually made for hap-
pier and better sex and allowed the individual to partake of even greater
joy.[94] The Nazi pedagogue Alfred Zeplin put the matter yet more succinctly (as he unveiled his five-point plan for encouraging premarital heterosexual sex while discouraging masturbation and homosexuality).
"*Sexual activity*," Zeplin announced, "*is not sinful, it is sacred.*"[95]

As these remarks imply, sexual matters were central to processes of
secularization. In the early twentieth century, in the context of conflicting
impulses toward secularization and searching for existential purpose-
fulness, the yearning for romantic love—both its more immediate and its
enduring joys—was already, and was becoming even more, invested with
truly existential import. Hans von Hattingberg, an acclaimed psychotherapist and medical doctor, put the point eloquently in a book published in
1936: "After so much of faith has been destroyed, faith in love is for
a growing number of people the only faith to which they still cling."[96]
Secularization, in short, involved not just increasing numbers of people
disaffiliating themselves from churches or rejecting church teachings; it
was also very much about a reworking of languages and attitudes, a sort
of compromise formation in which this-worldly matters were described
as having divine significance.

In this context Nazi-identified writers not only defended pre- and extra-marital sex but also avidly celebrated marital passion. Many Germans would remain uncomfortable with the most radical Nazi challenges to the institution of marriage, especially the open calls for infidelity and illegitimacy. But most would have been hard pressed to challenge the Nazi rhetoric of romance. After all, also according to contemporaries, this was an era in which "the erotic bases of marriage" were "pushed so much to the fore."[97] The deliberate sacralization of human love thus became a crucial aspect of National Socialism's reconfiguration of notions of morality and furthering of ongoing processes of secularization. Without question, Nazism was concerned to advocate "racially" desirable matches and the production of numerous "healthy" children. But to read Nazis' paeans to the delights of love as simply tactical embellishment of what was actually a narrowly reproduction-oriented agenda would be to miss the ways Nazi advice givers inserted themselves into the most elemental desires for personal happiness—how much, in short, Nazism's appeal lay (in a Foucaultian sense) in the positive rather than negative workings of power—even as the glorification of heterosexual romance would provide the context for (and distracting counterpoint to) defenses of some of the most grotesque and violent aspects of Nazi politics.

The tendency to treat passion and romance as divine was certainly a key component of Nazi sex advice writings that sought to enhance marital mutuality and shared pleasure. So, for instance, the medical doctor and psychotherapist Johannes H. Schultz, a prolific writer of essays on psychotherapeutic theory and practice and author of the widely circulated regime-endorsed advice manual *Geschlecht-Liebe-Ehe* (Sex-Love-Marriage, 1940) described intercourse as a "sacred" act and a lastingly loving marriage as "holy land."[98] Schultz is, to this day, most famous for being the inventor in 1920 of "autogenic training," a system of self-hypnosis, relaxation, and breathing techniques to enhance overall well-being that has been exceedingly popular in Germany and eventually found adherents the world over. Liberal antiguilt arguments were the hallmark of his texts, and he was especially noteworthy for his strong defenses of affectionate parenting and of child and adolescent masturbation and for his particular attention to women's pleasure. For example, although scholars often assume that Nazi childrearing advice advocated emotional coldness and lack of physical affection, Schultz on the contrary extolled mothers who lavished kisses on and cuddled their infants, insisting on the importance of this attention for later sexual health and self-esteem.[99] Moreover, Schultz not only defended masturbation as "a necessary transitional phase of youthful life-searching" with no negative physical consequences whatsoever and raged against the "crippling in their love lives of quite numerous valuable people" by "punishment-threatening, coldhearted," antimasturbation "tyrants." He also lamented the inadequate attention given to female sex education in all social strata and the apparently ongoing problem of female frigidity. Declaring himself pleased that the worst suffering was over ("with profound gratitude every older physician will celebrate the fact that a ghost of his youth, the 'daughter of the upper bourgeoisie' with corset, hypocrisy, and lasciviousness, belongs to the past"), Schultz nonetheless worried that not enough women had overcome the damage of a repressive education and found their way through to the "vibrant humanness" they so richly deserved. And he stressed to his readers that sexual desire and pleasure in women were absolutely normal and desirable: to encourage fear of sex in girls or to treat sex as something indecent was to have "sinned" against female youth. "A mature woman with a normal body, healthy organ function, and proper development is without question always fully love-capable."[100]

In his advice manual, Schultz repeatedly emphasized the importance of orgasm for both women and men. He called his readers' attention to the sensitivity of the clitoris, encouraged gentle breast fondling, and recommended stimulating the front wall of the vagina during intercourse. He also celebrated the "most fiery physical passion" as well as the "shared diving-into the blisses of pure bodiliness, and finally the self-finding in the mystery of highest union." In addition, Schultz spelled out the diversity of possible experiences for men, distinguishing between quick and superficial orgasms and those, usually growing out of a longer lovemaking episode, which could lead to a "very intensive resolution," "extraordinarily profound destabilizations and shakings of the entire organism."[101]

Schultz was hardly unique in his concern with enhancing sexual relations within marriage.[102] Although doctors in the Third Reich frequently remarked that technique alone could not produce satisfying sex (as they insisted that spiritual and emotional connection between partners was equally if not more important), they also repeatedly emphasized the importance of educating themselves and their patients about the best strategies for enjoyable lovemaking. As one physician remarked in a public lecture to his colleagues, "it is not necessary for a doctor to study the Kama Sutra of Vasyayana, the Indian arts of loving, or to promote them in detail. But it is necessary to become clear about the fact that in many people's habits of life and love a thriving marital communion is being sinfully thwarted and that the doctor, through enlightenment, can foster good in this area." This physician advised his fellows to keep up with the latest research on herbal and hormonal remedies for enhancing libido and not to shy away from recommending new positions for intercourse.[103]

As human love, or the longing for it, was felt by many to be the only spiritual content left in people's lives, what evolved was a kind of proto–New Age sentimentality that intersected with both deistic nature-loving

Nazi racism and with what people genuinely experienced as involving their deepest longings and most supreme experiences of happiness. When jurist Bechert declared that "love is the only truly religious experience in the world" or psychotherapist Schultz opined that "love is . . . the greatest gift that this life can give!" or the official SS journal *Das Schwarze Korps* (The Black Corps) announced that romantic love was "the highest this-worldliness of life fulfillment," critics would have had difficulty explaining what could possibly be wrong with these ideas.[104]

Indeed, *Das Schwarze Korps*, launched in 1935, quickly became a main venue for the promotion of Nazi ideas about the reprehensibleness and unnaturalness of prudery and the potentially transcendental qualities of human sexual expression. One of the most popular weeklies of the Third Reich—printed in hundreds of thousands of copies—and one enthusiastically endorsed by the regime, this paper was read far beyond SS circles (its circulation would be second only to the serious news weekly *Das Reich*, launched five years later).[105] In an entertaining and acerbic style, *Das Schwarze Korps* advanced its recipe for national happiness and health. The paper continually appealed to its readers' earthy common sense *and* feeling of superiority over others. Cartoons, feature pieces, photographs of attractive adults and children, and serial short stories alternated with accessibly editorialized reports on political happenings at home and abroad. The overall tone was conversational and informative and—especially in the prewar years, and continuing into the early war years while the military campaign still went well for Germany—also decidedly cheerful. Even in the more desperate later years of the war, as the paper championed the ever more crass and histrionic clamor of the regime for each and every individual's total self-sacrifice on behalf of the nation, it never lost its distinctively ironic tenor. This tongue-in-cheek and sardonic tone did not disguise the paper's many ruthless attacks on Jews, the handicapped, homosexuals, "asocial" criminals, and political critics of the regime—including, for example, unabashed calls for murder of the disabled—but certainly it contributed mightily to the paper's morally disorienting effect.

Christian efforts to draw the population away from Nazism, especially by documenting Nazi encouragement of naked self-display and of pre- and extramarital heterosexuality, provided a recurring joke for the journal from its inception. The paper often reprinted excerpts from Christian complaints about Nazi policies and injunctions, only then to repudiate these complaints in the most forceful terms, even as, simultaneously, the elaborating remarks actually confirmed aspects of the Christians' criticisms (although they reversed the Christians' assessments). At the same time, the paper delighted in detailing craven Christian accommodation to Nazism and shared acceptance of Nazi values.[106]

Das Schwarze Korps obsessively mocked Christian efforts to defend the sanctity of marriage and aligned itself with young people's impatience with traditional bourgeois mores. "Eager clerical 'moralists'" had "pathetic complexes"; "*original sin*" was a "foreign" and "oriental" idea; medieval Christianity's dogmatism was designed to bring down the "vibrant" and "life-affirming" Germanic and Nordic peoples.[107] When a female author remonstrated in another Nazi journal about how men treated women as objects and argued that Germanic tradition demanded that men be more respectful of an unmarried woman's chastity, *Das Schwarze Korps* rebuked her and rebutted her version of history. The paper declared that what she took to be Germanic tradition was nothing but another example of "the pathological tendency to Catholic virginalism."[108] In no uncertain terms, *Das Schwarze Korps* attacked "the denominational morality . . . that sees in the body something to be despised and wants to interpret what are natural processes as *sinful drives.*" Children should be taught by their parents that sex "is not unnatural sin, is not repulsive vice, but rather the God- and nature-willed, highest fulfillment of human existence." The paper explicitly blamed Christians for redirecting "healthy drive-forces" into "unnatural" paths, and it brashly defended sex with "frivolous, immoral" girls as much less dangerous than "youthful aberrations toward one's own sex."[109] Thus, the rejection of homosexuality in *Das Schwarze Korps* was not combined with a more general sexually conservative attitude but rather with an intensified encouragement of premarital heterosexual activity.

Many Nazi "experts" advanced a social constructionist view of sexuality that insisted that sexual identity was variable and vulnerable. The key idea, as one author summarized it, was that "with respect to homosexuality there is no stark either-or, no incurable fateful naturalness, but rather many transitional stages and in-between forms."[110] (This view was presented not least as a vigorous refutation of Magnus Hirschfeld's belief that homosexuality was constitutionally determined. As another writer put it—as he derogated Hirschfeld's belief in a (physiological, chemical or hormonal) congenital etiology of homosexuality—homosexuality was without a doubt an expression of a "neurosis, in which the bisexuality inherent in every person has been foregrounded in an abnormal way.")[111] In this context, social constructionist approaches did not ameliorate antihomosexual sentiment but rather exacerbated it. Nazi Party member Hans Bürger-Prinz, director of the psychiatric and neurological clinic at the University of Hamburg, for example, advanced his career under Nazism by promoting theories of homosexuality as a deficit of heterosexual vitality.[112] The punitive intensification of homophobic persecution in the Third Reich—escalating especially from 1937 on and promoted vigorously by *Das Schwarze Korps*—was fueled precisely by the idea that homosexuality was very much a possibility lurking within the majority of men and that, for many men, it was a phase they literally went through in their youth.

Specifically the notion that sexual orientation was fluid, for example, also informed the work of psychotherapist Johannes Schultz as he evaluated individuals being prosecuted for homosexuality. Through his deep-breathing techniques and reassuring, affirmative sex advice (both of which bore some disconcerting similarities to techniques and advice advanced by the anti-Nazi left-wing sex radical Wilhelm Reich), Schultz could fairly portray himself as a man committed to enhancing heterosexuals' sex lives. Yet this same man was also an advocate of murder who behind closed doors choreographed torture. During the Third Reich, Schultz openly endorsed the "extermination" (*Vernichtung*) of the handicapped, expressing the hope "that the institutions for idiots will soon in this sense be emptied."[113] He was also personally involved in making concrete decisions about which of those men accused of homosexuality would be set free and which would be sent to a concentration camp (and hence often also to death). Schultz theorized that there were two kinds of homosexuals. Some he considered "hereditarily ill" and therefore unredeemable; others he designated as "dear little brother" (*liebes Brüderchen*) types whom he thought could benefit from help. In Schultz's own words, "a thoughtful psychotherapist" like himself could transform such a man into a heterosexual. At the Göring Institute in Berlin, Schultz and a commission of co-workers instructed accused homosexuals to perform coitus with a female prostitute while the commission watched. Whoever performed heterosexually to their satisfaction under these conditions was set free; whoever did not, and hence had revealed his incurability, was sent to a concentration camp.[114]

Notions of fluidity in sexual orientation informed the stance of *Das Schwarze Korps* as well. The paper did attack homosexuals as dangers to the *Volk* and traitors to the state. But it also blamed "bourgeois moralists" for being so busy presenting the "natural aim" (i.e., sex with a woman) as a "shameful sin" that they permitted a youth's still completely "*unspecific*" "sexual yearning . . . to be given a false aim—same-sex love." It is worth paying close attention to how *Das Schwarze Korps* went out of its way to acknowledge the ubiquitous potential of homosexual feeling in men. Guessing what readers might be guiltily thinking, while also cleverly offering readers the out that their feelings might have been "unconscious," the paper made a point of saying that "above all we know that every person in his development unconsciously goes through a phase, in which he is to a certain extent receptive to the poison [of same-sex desire]." For "the drive-life awakens in a stage of life, in which the other sex cannot yet appear as the conscious ideal."[115] In earlier essays, *Das Schwarze Korps* had already self-consciously thematized the way Nazi single-sex organizations provided a worryingly conducive environment for homosexual relations.[116]

In *Das Schwarze Korps'* view, 98 percent of accused homosexuals were fully capable of heterosexuality; they were simply "seduced" "fellow travelers" whom the state could help therapeutically to become "healthy." But the remaining 2 percent (by the paper's count, forty thousand men) would be turned into "a crystallization point of repulsion"; *Das Schwarze Korps* uncomplicatedly endorsed "brutality" against these men and voiced nostalgic appreciation for the ancient Germanic and Friesian customs of castrating homosexuals or drowning them in swamps.[117]

Meanwhile, just as sexually conservative mores were expressed through antisemitism, so too were Nazis' particular versions of sexually emancipatory ideas. Yet *Das Schwarze Korps* handled the purported "Jewishness" of sex differently than sexual conservatives did; as with homophobia so also with antisemitism, *Das Schwarze Korps'* techniques were deliberately self-reflexive. Even as *Das Schwarze Korps* castigated Christianity for its hostility to sex, the journal continually worked to distance Nazism from any possible association with Weimar-era liberality; it did so by deliberately calling attention to the comparison between Weimar and Nazism. Thus, for instance, the journal contrasted the kind of "propaganda for nudism" purportedly evident during the Weimar era (or, as *Das Schwarze Korps* put it, during "the years of Jewish domination," when "the Semitic manipulators" were busy working to undermine "every natural order, such as marriage and family") with the aims of National Socialism, which were to resist "that prudery . . . which has contributed to destroying the instinct for bodily nobility and its beauty in our *Volk*," and "to represent the noble body in its natural shape" (for "the pure and the beautiful were for the uncorrupted German never a sin").[118]

Over and over, the paper denied that it advocated "free love" (this it associated with "Marxism"), and it insisted that Nazism supported and sought to restore marriage (in opposition to what it described as "Jewish" attacks on this institution).[119] It repeatedly described Nazism as a movement that above all demanded "*cleanliness*" in "*matters of love*" and the realm of "*sex*" (*Sexus*).[120] But simultaneously, frequently in the same articles, the paper defended both illegitimacy and nonreproductive premarital and extramarital heterosexual intercourse. It also printed numerous pictures of nudes—paintings, statues, and photographs—and defended nudity as pure, natural, and life-enhancing.[121]

The preference of Nazi leaders for nude figures (of both genders in sculpture but above all nude women in paintings) was indeed a subject of considerable popular amusement and heated debate. Paintings of female nudes constituted one in ten of all paintings presented at the Third Reich's annual national art exhibitions.[122] Nudes were displayed not only in museums but also in state ministries and municipal buildings; the style was almost always decisively nonabstract and often hyperrealist. The nudes of painters like Adolf Ziegler (president of the Nazi Reich Chamber of Art), Ivo Saliger, Sepp Hilz, Johann Schult, Julius Engelhard, and Paul Mathias Padua were particularly prized by the Nazi regime. Ziegler's and Padua's distinctly graphic nude paintings were much admired by Adolf Hitler but also readily available for public viewing at the national art exhibitions. Popular humor pungently expressed the point: Ziegler was given the title "the master of German pubic hair" (*Meister des deutschen Schamhaares*), and Hilz and Padua were jestingly ranked as "officers of the underbelly [*Unterleibl*]."[123]

It was precisely in awareness of both conservative objections and smirking popular skepticism of Nazi intentions with regard to nudity that *Das Schwarze Korps* assertively defended its value. Along these lines, for example, in 1938, in two full-page photo spreads, *Das Schwarze Korps* showcased the "beautiful and pure" nudity advocated by Nazism (exemplified by pulchritudinous naked women luxuriating in sun, sand, and sea) and juxtaposed this with the "shameless moneymaking" of the previous "cultural epoch" (illustrated by photos of half-clothed and excessively made-up women from what look like Weimar dance halls) (fig. 1.2). Once more, as it had so often done in its attacks on Christian sexual conservatives, *Das Schwarze Korps* chastised those who "campaign against the supposed immorality of National Socialism." The paper accused regime critics of playing into the hands of Nazism's enemies, deeming them "vermin" whose invocation of "the cultural will of the state" for their own prudish agenda was an "insolence" and against whom only "the police" could bring relief.[124]

Not only the continual self-labeling as "pure" and "clean," then, but also the fiercely hyperbolic attacks on Jews, Marxists, and Weimar-era cultural arbiters for *their* purported advocacy of extramarital sex, pornography, and nakedness, served to deflect from Nazi advocacy of those very things. *Das Schwarze Korps*, in short, expressly disavowed exactly the activities in which it was engaged. It did just that which it said it was not doing. Incitement and disavowal were inseparable.

Considering the strategies employed by *Das Schwarze Korps* in this way also offers a fresh perspective on that other most popular and rabidly antisemitic Nazi journal, *Der Stürmer*. *Der Stürmer* could simply be interpreted as an example of Nazism's sexually repressive, conservative side. Indeed, in view of its relentless obsession with "documenting" Jewish sex criminality and the prevalence in Germany of "race defilement" (i.e., consensual sex between Jews and non-Jews), reading it one could easily get the impression that non-Jews seldom if ever had sex with one another. Yet at the same time, it is readily apparent that in its narrative pacing, its luxuriantly detailed descriptions of sex crimes, and its many pictures of

Figure 1.2. *Das Schwarze Korps*, 20 October 1938, pp. 10, 12. The left side is entitled "Beautiful and Pure," The right side (opposite page) is entitled "Shameless Business." The quotation from Hitler's *Mein Kampf* declares that "Public life must be freed from the suffocating perfume of our modern eroticism, just as from every unmanly prudish dishonesty. In all these things the goal and the path must be determined by concern for the preservation of the health of our *Volk* in body and soul."

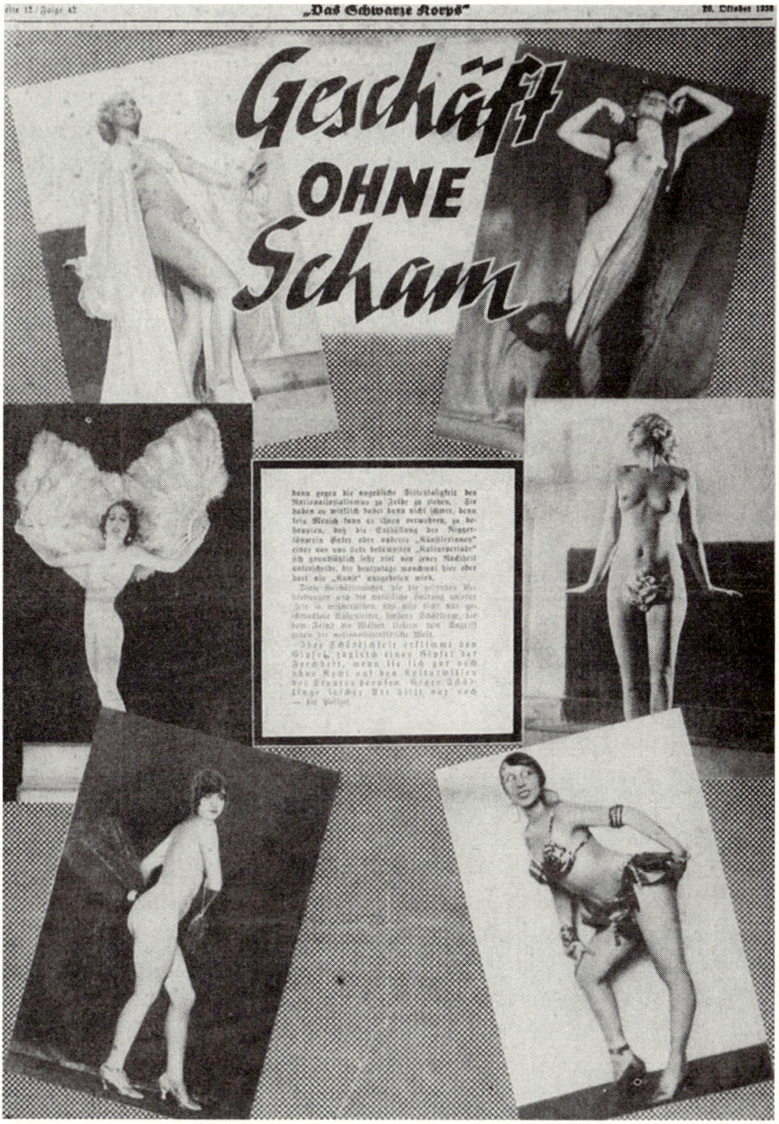

eite 12 / Folge 43 „Das Schwarze Korps" 26. Oktober 1938

Geschäft ohne Scham

dann gegen die angebliche Sittenlosigkeit des Nationalsozialismus zu Felde zu ziehen. Sie haben es wirklich dabei dann nicht schwer, denn kein Mensch kann es ihnen verwehren, zu behaupten, daß die Entblößung der Negertänzerin Baker oder anderer „Künstlerinnen" einer von uns stets bekämpften „Kulturperiode" sich grundsätzlich sehr viel von jener Nacktheit unterscheide, die heutzutage manchmal hier oder dort als „Kunst" angeboten wird.

Diese Geschäftemacher, die die gesunden Bestrebungen und die natürliche Haltung unserer Zeit so mißbrauchen, sind also nicht nur geschmacklose [illegible], sondern Schädlinge, die dem Feind die Waffen liefern zum Angriff gegen die nationalsozialistische Welt.

Ihre Schädlichkeit erklimmt den Gipfel, zugleich einen Gipfel der Frechheit, wenn sie sich gar noch ohne Recht auf den Kulturwillen des Staates berufen. Gegen Schädlinge solcher Art hilft nur noch — die Polizei.

naked blondes defiled by big-nosed Jews, *Der Stürmer* served as pornography (fig. 1.3). While it is impossible to know with which characters in *Der Stürmer*'s scenarios readers identified (was it the sexually successful Jewish man, the violated or seduced non-Jewish woman, the outraged non-Jewish male or female voyeur?), the multiplicity of possibilities for libidinal identification may have been precisely the point and could help to explain the paper's immense appeal, especially for teenage boys. What is clear is that *Der Stürmer*'s recurrent detailed descriptions of sexual outrages gave readers crucial moral permission to hate without guilt (since Jews were continually described as aggressing on Germans) *even as* the ubiquitous declaration that Nazism was battling filth provided a ready excuse to display naked women and keep people's attention fixed on sex.

This manipulation of the discourses of sexual morality was particularly evident at those moments when the regime managed to have things both ways at once: to present itself as the guardian of good taste and pristine morals *and* to titillate and pander to the pleasures of looking. A classic instance of this deliberate duality can be found in the women's journal *Frauenwarte* (Women's Watchtower), which in 1940 offered its own two-page photo spread contrasting, on the one hand, images of women in bikinis and skimpy cabaret costumes with, on the other, more demurely clothed healthily athletic women as well as women wearing the traditional German dirndl (fig. 1.4). But unlike the photo spread in *Das Schwarze Korps* two years earlier, which among its cabaret scenes had included a picture of African American dancer Josephine Baker so as to clarify that these images belonged to "the previous cultural epoch" (i.e., Weimar), the *Frauenwarte* declared that all the images on its scantily clad side had been taken from pictures "that appeared in German illustrated periodicals in the last few weeks." Indeed, the journal pointed out that these images were being presented to the German *Volk* in "millions of copies." At the same time, and remarkably, the *Frauenwarte* labeled these images, as well as ones it claimed to have found in recent German film and theater productions, as "Jewish—all too Jewish." Striking a remonstrating pedagogical pose toward other Nazis, the *Frauenwarte* elaborated that

> The National Socialist idea is profoundly life-affirming. Nothing could lie further from it than prudery. . . . A beautiful girl is certainly not created to be a nun but—and that is the difference between yesterday and today—also not to be a coquette! The shallow and frivolous degradation of the woman into an object of pleasure, the repulsive warping of a healthy, natural feeling for the body in the manner of a crass and undisguised sexual greed, this whole distorted, unhealthy atmosphere belongs exclusively to the chapter of Jewish disintegrative propaganda [*jüdische Zersetzungspropaganda*]! We will maintain a watchful eye so that such tendencies do not, under some falsified excuse, spread again among us.

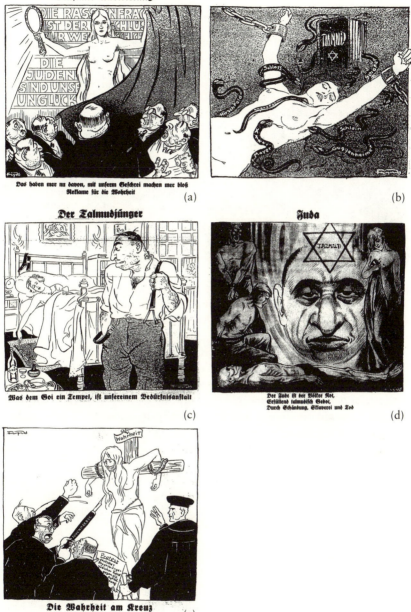

Figure 1.3. Cover images from *Der Stürmer* (*beginning upper left and reading left to right*): January 1935, January 1929, November 1932, August 1935, and February 1930.

Figure 1.4. *Frauenwarte*, February 1940. The captions on the left say: "They think: Chic and cheerful. We think: Trashy and trying too hard." The captions on the right say: "They think boring? We think: Healthy and beautiful."

On this somewhat surprising note—the idea that, seven years into the Third Reich, some (other) Nazis were behaving like Jews—the *Frauenwarte* concluded that the only explanation could be "how deeply the Jewish contamination has worked specifically in this area."[125] Once again, then, incitement and disavowal were inextricable. The purposely incoherent good-cop, bad-cop routine was evidently far more effective than any unified message could have been. In this way, multiple constituencies might be addressed at once. Sexual conservatives were never directly censored but rather were both published *and* mocked. Overtly sexual images and pro-sex messages were both lauded *and* rhetorically chastised.

THE CHRISTIAN RESPONSE

Numerous Catholic and Protestant church leaders and laypeople championed the Nazi ascension to power. And in the first months of the Third Reich, Christian support for the regime only grew. Protestant pastors praised Hitler as a "marvelous gift from God" and a "through and through decent, clean character," and celebrated the Nazis' rise to power as a "miracle"; "the immense power of international Jewry" was deemed a "frightening" threat, while Hitler was providential: "It is absolutely certain that God sent us this man and through him protected us from a great danger."[126] Catholics, who had often been skeptical about Nazism during Weimar, were now thrilled to find a government that shared their hostility to both communism and liberalism. With the exception of a handful of courageous clergymen, the majority of church representatives expressed no particular concern about Nazi antisemitism, except insofar as they cautioned that racial loyalties should not outweigh fidelity to God. As Guenter Lewy has written of German Catholicism, "from the time Hitler came to power all the German bishops began declaring their appreciation of the important natural values of race and racial purity."[127] And, as Susannah Heschel has noted of German Protestantism, while "Christian support for National Socialism was an unrequited affection," there is no question that most theologians and clergymen rushed to meld Nazism and Christianity.[128] Leading Protestants endorsed Nazi efforts to "push back 'Jewish influence' in public life" and argued that—because since the crucifixion of Christ, Jews "stood under God's curse"—Jews should be given only the "status of guests" (not citizens) in Germany and should "relinquish any decisive involvement" in the life of the German *Volk* and state.[129] Many Christians, both Protestant and Catholic, shared the view that Jews were responsible for the sexual immorality that purportedly pervaded Weimar culture.

Initially, Christians thought Nazism could help them recover the ground lost to widespread popular secularization. Defensive in the face of many aspects of modernity, they believed Nazism would protect—as Hitler himself had phrased it—"positive Christianity."[130] Christians also thought Nazism would help to restore conservative sexual mores.

Indeed, distress over what they identified as Weimar's debauched sexual climate was a major reason for some Christians' early endorsement of the Nazi regime. Conservative Christian clergymen and lay activists believed they had finally found the ally they needed to combat Germany's sexual dissolution. As a Catholic scholar put it in 1933, not only was National Socialism "by its nature an opponent of Bolshevism, liberalism, relativism," but in addition "National Socialism is an outspoken opponent of public indecency" and of the "liberalistic permissiveness" that was "dominating" modern civilization:

> We Catholics have protested tirelessly in countless press campaigns, pamphlets, sermons, conference resolutions, and parliamentary proposals against trash and smut [*Schund und Schmutz*]. But this effort remained mainly in the theoretical realm, because we were not the state. But now, National Socialism has the power to be effective, and in its attacks against the cesspool of the big city we already see the result.[131]

In that same year, Protestant activist Adolf Sellmann of the Western German Moral Purity Association was no less enthusiastic, and for the same reasons. "Overnight things got different in Germany. All smut and trash disappeared from public view. The streets of our cities became clean again," Sellmann said. He saw his organization's fifty-year battle for "the morality and strength of the *Volk*" as finally achieving its aims.[132] The churches and conservative religious associations were especially pleased with the Nazis' March 1933 "battle against public immorality" (*Bekämpfung der öffentlichen Unsittlichkeit*), and welcomed early Nazi actions to close brothels and gay and lesbian bars, to clean city kiosks of pornography, and to curtail the activities of nudist organizations.[133] A Catholic journal effused about these "sharp measures against the different forms of public immorality" and declared "we stand behind the efforts of the government 100 percent."[134] Another Catholic journal raved about "the new government's level-headed yet firm approach toward filth wherever it is visible . . . therefore *Siegheil!*"[135]

Christian observers also interpreted Nazism as a force for improving the status of marriage. In this spirit, for instance, a Protestant pastor in 1934 touted "the great national shift" and "different perspective" in sexual values brought by the Nazi ascension to power and adumbrated in Hitler's *Mein Kampf*. Whereas during Weimar advice writings had emphasized specific sexual techniques such as those promoted by the Dutch advice writer Theodor van de Velde, Hitler was now showing the way to "a completely different understanding of wedlock than in the era of individualism." Christians rejected egoism in marital sex and instead celebrated the "millionfold bliss" of loving mutual sexual reciprocity; they were also firmly committed to "lifelong and monogamous marriage." Nazi racialism did not conflict with Christian values but rather was consonant with them. "Naturally," this pastor wrote, "in the *völkisch* state racial hygiene will be the highest principle for the formation of marriage and the ethos of marriage in the *völkisch* state will in essence receive its content from the *Volk* and from the race."[136]

Along related lines, the Catholic eugenicist Hermann Muckermann authoritatively argued in 1933 that for the sake of the preservation of the "'untouched, elemental nature of the German people' he wanted to 'push back racially foreign, particularly Jewish influence in the shaping of our culture.'"[137] And in 1935 Muckermann again complained about "certain Jewish writers" who had, in his view, "devastated precisely that realm that has to do with the sexual purity of our *Volk*." At the same time, Muckermann also opposed Jewish-Christian marriage even if the Jewish partner was baptized: "I therefore emphatically insist that marriages between native-race Germans [*heimrassigen Deutschen*] with those of foreign race [*Fremdrassigen*], which could deform the native race, should be avoided. One should not invoke the baptism that makes a Christian out of a Jew. Baptism makes a person into a child of God, but it never changes his hereditary composition [*sein Erbgefüge*]. Thus foreign-race people should marry their own kind, and the native-race people should stay among themselves. That is full of blessings for both."[138]

Within just two to three years, however, Christian spokespeople also found reasons to feel disillusionment over the Third Reich's sexual politics. Increasingly, they noticed that developments in the Third Reich were not proceeding in a sexually conservative direction. Among other things, Christians began to complain that under Nazism marriage was being reduced to a breeding institution, while its spiritual elements were being denied. The archconservative Protestant organization Weisses Kreuz (White Cross), for example, initially supportive of the Nazis, worried in 1935 that the "new German morality" advanced by the Nazis was actually contrary to Christian teachings.[139] That same year, the archbishop of Freiburg warned the faithful that Nazis who treated marriage as "nothing but a sexual connection for the service of the *Volk* and state" were "false prophets" who placed human beings in the same category with animals.[140] And in 1936 a Catholic jurist also contrasted Christian notions of marriage with what he deemed "animalistic" attitudes: he was appalled that young people were being encouraged to choose mates based on a "good figure," "athletic ability," and "sex appeal."[141] Another Catholic author cautiously implied that the Nazi attacks on Christian marriage were in continuity with liberal critiques of the institution in prior decades.[142] Christians complained as well—as, for example, a Protestant commentator on sex education did—that daily newspapers in the Third Reich so frequently printed stories about "sexual aberrations."[143]

Christians also angrily assailed Nazis' defenses of disrobement and apparent intention to reintroduce the very "culture of nakedness" (*Nacktkultur*) they had claimed they would abolish. Along these lines, for instance, in 1936, the Protestant pastor Stephan Vollert, in a letter to the editor of the main Nazi Party newspaper, the *Völkischer Beobachter* (Racial Observer), chastised the journal for printing "obscene pictures" and demanded to know whether images of nude women were really proper objects for "German art." For his part, he said, he had "been ashamed, as I held the paper in my hands, and immediately I cut out two pictures and shredded them. After all, you should consider that this paper gets into the hands of the simple folk and children."[144] Similarly, when the Nazi Party's Office for Racial Policy (Rassenpolitisches Amt) published a calendar with nude images, Catholic priests in Westphalia organized a campaign against its sale, arguing that the pictures were "piggish" (*schweinig*) and "indecent" (*unanständig*).[145]

Christians began to note ever more openly that the Third Reich was a disappointment when it came to sexual mores, and they above all started to sound the alarm about Nazi promotion of sexual activity outside of marriage. An evangelical Protestant missionary and journal editor from Württemberg in 1935 explicitly lamented that, although "at first we believed that morality would improve in the Third Reich, today *this hope reveals itself more and more as false.*" He further charged that "*fleshly lust*" and a "*spirit of uncleanness*" were at work in the Third Reich. (Interestingly, however, he also went out of his way to validate the Third Reich's "message about *race, blood, and soil*" as "at least in part valuable and true.")[146]

In March 1935 the major exhibit *Das Wunder des Lebens* (The Miracle of Life) opened in Berlin, introducing viewers, through photographs, artworks, and accompanying texts, to Nazi racial theory. The exhibit included a slogan that endorsed nonmarital sex—as long as the child born of such union was both racially and eugenically "healthy": "Immaculate and holy is the conception out of worthy love—immaculate and holy is the birth of life of a healthy type" (*Unbefleckt und heilig is die Empfängnis aus würdiger Liebe—unbefleckt und heilig ist die Geburt wohlgearteten Lebens*). At once a mockery, an imitation, and a radical redefinition of the Catholic praise song for the Virgin Mary, this slogan exemplified the Nazi strategy of appropriating while rejecting Christianity. Yet even though the exhibit also included a series of photographs of visibly handicapped individuals as part of the Nazi campaign to legitimize its sterilization program, these eugenic elements were not what one Catholic journal found most objectionable. Instead, and while the journal deemed the exhibit as a whole to be "impressive" and expressly affirmed the importance of the exhibit's injunctions to individual and collective mental and physical health, it explained that the exhibit's "decisive weakness" was the absence of references to God as the originary source of "the miracle of life." And it singled out the slogan about "worthy love" as especially "dangerous" above all because "many an unhappy girl, who has today become an illegitimate mother" might interpret the slogan too "willfully" and feel a sense of "entitlement" rather than shame.[147] Along related lines, a Protestant commentator praised the Nazi innovation of "racial hygiene" but also warned that, while "physically unsuitable people can through the law be prevented by the state from marrying," "moral weakness and evil" were harder "to eliminate among the young." Violations of the sixth commandment really were the worst and most consequential of all sins. "Nothing is so likely to precipitate the downfall of a *Volk* than the failure of the individual in the sexual realm."[148]

At times, Christian commentators appeared to treat the Nazi cult of the body and encouragement to sexual licentiousness as more troubling than antisemitism. Even when the regime introduced the Nuremberg Laws in September 1935, which forbade marriages and also sex between Jews and non-Jews, the churches on the whole cooperated with the laws (the only exceptions involved Jewish converts to Christianity). Indeed, one Catholic journal praised the legislation for providing important "'safeguards' for the general character of the German people," while the Protestant theologian Martin Rade, editor of the journal *Christliche Welt* (Christian World), affirmed that the Nuremberg Laws "guarantee the maintenance of the purity of the race for those peoples whose Aryan character is unchallenged."[149] And "aside from a small minority of Protestants gathered in the anti-Nazi 'Confessing Church' [*Bekennende Kirche*]," most Protestants—in the words of one contemporary—"*never* made any criticism of the regime's anti-Jewish policies."[150]

Christians also continued to share with Nazi antisemites assumptions of an intrinsic link between Jewishness and sexual liberality, even as they started to suggest that Nazism was turning out to be no better when it came to sex. For example, when the Nazis in 1935 escalated their rhetorical attacks on the Catholic Church—in part by describing Catholic casuistries in sexual mores as themselves "directly pornographic" and marked by "spiritual degeneracy and lechery"—a Catholic theologian noted caustically that the recent media reports on the lurid details of Catholic teachings on sex were achieving a popular notoriety far exceeding even that of "*Magnus Hirschfeld* at the height of his sexual propaganda!"[151]

A year later, the Catholic priest Matthias Laros, author of the advice book, *Die Beziehungen der Geschlechter* (The Relations of the Sexes, 1936), praised the Nazis for their dedication to race and *Volk* but also held Nazism responsible for exacerbating further the dissolution of sexual mores. "The era has succumbed to a horrifying barbarism and overstimulation of the sexual drive, especially since all inhibiting barriers of tradition have been trampled," Laros observed. The "false prophets" of a relaxed sexual morality were carrying their pernicious teachings also "into church-affiliated circles" and "everywhere, into the smallest village." The "entirety of public and private life has today been gripped" by an "insane *overvaluation of the sensual-sexual*." Laros singled out as especially abhorrent the new Nazi encouragement of coed sports at the workplace. As male and female co-workers did their morning exercises together in a half-clothed state, women and girls were obliged to "reveal their female secrets to a great extent": "All talk of naturalness and the beauty of the body cannot do away with the consequence, that on the male side an intensified sex drive results, and on the female side, if she has retained her true femininity, the most delicate bodily shame has been damaged and moral feeling deadened." Laros challenged readers to resist such "methods of the culture of nudism." And distancing himself from *both* Nazis and Jews (even as he reinforced the association of Jews with un-Christian sexual values), Laros declared that "the church, unconcerned by all semitic or antisemitic fashions of the day, holds fast to the . . . Christian structure of marriage."[152]

There were Protestants as well who shared the Nazis' antisemitism but publicly dissented from the regime's evolving sexual politics. The well-known Protestant publicist Wilhelm Stapel was notable in this regard. Stapel protested in 1935 that the new Nazi forms of deism and paganism involved a "tendency toward nudism" (and was promptly attacked in *Das Schwarze Korps* as a result).[153] Yet in 1933, in his contribution to a major anthology of antisemitic texts, Stapel had seen fit to complain about how Jews were constantly criticizing Germans and denigrating "*our* moral concepts: reputation, modesty, bravery, patriotism, fidelity to the Führer, loyalty to the *Volk*, and so forth. . . . Continually they are objecting to our natural morality [*Sittlichkeit*]. . . . Jewish domination is the most insufferable form of rule. There would be no antisemitism if only Jews could keep their mouths shut."[154] (And in 1937 Stapel would once again seek to ingratiate himself with the regime when he published a book that analyzed "the literary dominance of Jews in Germany, 1918–1933.")[155]

In general, Protestants evinced more perplexity about how to respond to Nazism than Catholics did. Protestant theologians, pastors, and activist laity repeatedly articulated confusion about how best to respond to the pseudospirituality of Nazism, with its "romantic, idealistic" search for God in "the language of flowers and sounds or the wealth of our spiritual inwardness," and they scrambled to counter the Nazi charge that Christianity was a downbeat and depressing religion incompatible with the life-affirming message of Nazism.[156] They also encouraged one another to take seriously and to engage in earnest dialogue with Nazis. Thus, for instance, in the pages of the Protestant journal *Seelsorge* (Counseling), the theologian Adolf Allwohn summarized what he saw as the important contribution of his colleague Alfred Dedo Müller toward understanding the National Socialist phenomenon of "natural theology." Müller, Allwohn advised, could help pastors understand "the natural searching for God of the contemporary human being": "For our pastoral stance toward those who have become alienated, it is decisive that we do not 'simply dogmatically condemn to death' the natural theology of our time, for example, the religious conception of *Volk* and race, but rather come into 'a genuine conversation and true meeting' with it."[157]

Catholics were on the whole clearer about the decisive differences between Christianity and what they saw as the "neopagan" tendencies of Nazism. When the self-defined pagan journal *Flammenzeichen* (Mark of Fire) advocated in 1935 that "sex education of youth in the Third Reich" be released from the claims of "positive Christianity" with its "Jewish-

Pauline" tendencies and its "inappropriate feelings of shame," it also—as *Das Schwarze Korps* would so frequently do as well—announced that its own unabashed advocacy of coed nudity had nothing in common with the "dirty pedagogical work of the Marxist era." On the contrary, *Flammenzeichen* opined, a healthy sex education, a "racial ideal of beauty," and the exclusion of "bad hereditary resources" from the "hereditary stream" (*Erbstrom*) of the *Volk*, would all be best served by leaving behind Christian anxieties about "original sin" and encouraging adolescents regularly to view the opposite sex unclothed. Far from feeling intimidated, the *Katholisches Kirchenblatt* (Catholic Church Paper) forcefully criticized these opinions and complained vociferously about what it saw as a massive and "nowadays over and over again" repeated misrepresentation of Christianity as inevitably hostile to sex or to nature more generally.[158]

Yet Catholics and Protestants alike were acutely aware that Nazis used the realm of sexuality in particular to make Christianity look backward and foolish, and they struggled over how best to react effectively to the endlessly repeated popular and regime announcements that Christian prudery profoundly damaged the *Volk*.[159] While in the years leading up to the war Christian commentators on sex were increasingly placed on the defensive, by the time the war broke out their protestations had become largely irrelevant. At the same time, Christian self-criticism about sexuality evolved into a genre all its own under Nazism.

Conceding that the Christian churches had often promoted a sex-hostile attitude, for example, the prolific Protestant advice writer Theodor Haug in 1939 not only celebrated "the gift that God has given us in the powers of sex" but also castigated his fellow Christians for their sex-negative attitude and their fixation on sexual sins to the exclusion of all others. "According to the judgment of Jesus," Haug declared, "we should see and treat sins of sex more mildly [than other sins]. Jesus spoke much more serious words against the rich than against whores. The isolating of sexual problems has brought much harm and rigidness into Christianity." Notably, Haug reported as well that Christians in his day were not exactly resistant to engaging in premarital sex and that, indeed, the ready availability of contraception was what made premarital sex so appealing. Announcing that "today birth control of some sort is nearly universal, also among Christians," Haug elaborated further: "Since with the use of protective means pregnancy does not have to be feared as it used to be, ['friendship' including bodily love] is widespread also in circles that before now hardly knew of it. It becomes a question also for those who live in a Christian environment. Why should sexual need in the long waiting period before marriage not be resolved in this way?"[160]

Catholic writers too sought to prove that Christianity had its pro-sex elements. The Austrian Catholic Church official Theodor Bliewies referred to "the God-given sex drive" and declared that "in itself the sexual is good, holy, and something beautiful." While continuing to insist that sex be reserved for matrimony—even as he noted that "the majority of girls lose their innocence around the age of sixteen"—he chided Christians for how "our prudery and dishonest shamefulness are co-responsible for the way year after year thousands of young girls run into disaster."[161] Another Catholic commentator, also distressed at the growing acceptance of premarital sex as inevitable, complained that Christianity was assumed to be antisexual and "life-hostile." Attempting to reserve sexuality for marriage, he emphasized that "holiness is very well compatible with a healthy marital life appropriate to nature" and that "Christian moral teaching sees in the natural drives, also in the sexual drive, not something bad, something that must be expurgated root and branch, but rather something wanted by God, something that God, the Creator of Nature, has put in the human being."[162] And a Catholic professor complained that sermons too often "stigmatize infractions against the sixth commandment as the gravest sins, indeed even as *the* sin"; in his view this habit led to "unnecessary conflicts of conscience" and "to the conviction that the demands of sexual morality cannot be fulfilled at all"; after all, he argued, most young people were ultimately supposed to be preparing themselves not for celibacy but for marriage.[163] In short, the success of both popular and regime pressures for liberalized sexual attitudes was measurable not least in the extent to which Christians too absorbed this message, even as they struggled to integrate a more sex-positive attitude with their own distinctive hope that sexuality be confined to marriage.

One German Jesuit author in 1939 tried both to grant the Nazi point that Christian prudery was a problem and to turn the Nazi obsessions with race and military triumph into a means to influence Nazi sexual politics in a more conservative direction. Lamenting that Christian morality was subjected to constant attack and ridicule, he nonetheless agreed that prudery was "unhealthy" and simply "masks an inner unfreedom vis-à-vis the sexual." Yet he also made the case that in "a hostile world," the atmosphere of sexual license prevailing in the Third Reich could only lead to "cultural decline" and "the death of the *Volk*." He further deplored how "the free intercourse of the two sexes has become so *unbridled* that really no normal human being still sees noble naturalness in it." While the younger generation in Nazi Germany celebrated its own "freedom" and " 'unembarrassed naturalness' " (*unbefangene Natürlichkeit*), the Jesuit took the view that "this much-vaunted 'unembarrassedness' is nothing but *shamelessness* in the deepest sense of the word." And like the priest Matthias Laros before him, he argued that the trends of the era were deleterious especially to women: "Above all the moral dignity of women is dirtied and desacralized [*beschmutzt und entweiht*]." Yet his efforts to put his case in terms the regime would hear reinforced racist and nationalist Nazi values more than challenged them. "There is no question," he argued, "that sexual morality is in bad shape in all strata of our *Volk* and that thereby the physical health and the strength of the *Volk* is threatened. Indeed, moral degeneration has progressed so far that it must necessarily lead to the death of the nation, if a moral renewal of our *Volk* does not take place."[164] The regime, however, remained quite undeterred by such warnings, just as it failed to be impressed with Christian efforts to reframe Christianity as a sex-validating religion.

Adolf Hitler and Heinrich Himmler were both dismissive of church teachings on sexuality. Himmler, who had become the second most powerful man in the Reich (as he consolidated the police forces, including the Gestapo, and an ever-growing SS, under his own jurisdiction), bluntly deemed monogamous marriage to be "the Catholic Church's satanic achievement" and labeled the church's rules on marriage "immoral."[165] Himmler believed that not only divorce or premarital sex but also extramarital affairs ought to be formally encouraged. Two months after the invasion of Poland, at the end of October 1939, Himmler promulgated an order (officially endorsed by Hitler) to the entire SS and police:

> Beyond the boundaries of perhaps otherwise still necessary bourgeois laws and customs it will also outside of marriage be an important responsibility for German women and girls of good blood, not lightly, but rather in profound moral seriousness, to become the mothers of children of soldiers who are going to the front and of whom fate alone knows whether they will return or fall in battle for Germany.[166]

Hitler too appears to have been fully supportive of Himmler's fantasies that one day bigamy would be instituted for the male racial elite.[167] Domestically and internationally, both during and immediately after the war, the commonsense consensus on Hitler's views was that sexual activity— whether inside or outside marriage—strengthened a soldier's resolve to fight for the Reich. In his pronouncements to a small circle of intimates, Hitler deemed church hostility to sex "only laughable," and opined that "one cannot come at a soldier with the religious doctrine of abstinence in the realm of love if one wants him to stay steeled for battle." He also declared that "If the German man as a soldier should be prepared to die unconditionally, then he must also have the freedom to love unconditionally."[168] Already during the war, an American magazine quoted Hitler to the effect that "providing sexual gratification must be one of the main devices of our propaganda. . . . I shall not spoil the fun for any of my lads. If I demand the supreme effort from them, I must also give them the right to carouse as they please, not as it suits a lot of church-going old women."[169]

The war years brought a reduced presence of Christian publications; much of the church press was simply shut down.[170] But the war brought no change in Nazi disdain for Christian mores. As race theorist Hans Endres told an audience of high-ranking Nazis and their guests in 1941: "We have been raised in criminal bigotry, because the Oriental Christian mentality has suppressed our healthy Germanic instincts in sexual matters. Our younger generations . . . must become proud of their bodies and enjoy the natural pleasures of sex without being ashamed."[171] The war years also saw a further deployment of the antisemitic strategy of disavowal: blaming Jews for non-Jewish Germans' sexual licentiousness even as in the same breath that licentiousness was defended as normal and natural. Military doctor Joachim Rost, for instance, in 1944 took direct jabs at Sigmund Freud and a certain "Viennese school" for their efforts to find the roots of all drive-life in the sex drive. And he declared that in the aftermath of the First World War, "the demand for free love, nurtured by the parasites on our *Volk* . . . went hand in hand with a denigration of higher ethical feelings." But simultaneously, Rost defended the sex drive as a powerful and important force, wondered aloud whether "*one can ever demand of a grown human being the mastery of the strongest of all drives, the sex drive?*" and also announced that "male natures with strong drives" are "frequent among the good soldiers," and they "naturally find a limitation of sexual activity oppressive." Moreover, in an extended analysis of the ways military men spoke among themselves about the legitimacy of adultery, Rost noted that quite a few contended that sexual activity outside of marriage was acceptable so long as there was no emotional involvement with the sex partner.[172]

Over time, the regime simply became far bolder in its challenges to traditional mores. In 1938, for example, the regime instituted new divorce legislation that made divorce and remarriage easier. Emotional noncompatibility could now be seen as grounds for divorce, especially if a couple could prove that it had already lived separate lives for at least three years (an innovation that had long been resisted by the Christian churches). Other grounds for divorce could be found in failure to engage in sexual intercourse and thereby fulfill one's "marital duties," in the use of contraception, and in childlessness.[173] While early on in the Third Reich the Nazi mouthpiece *Völkischer Beobachter* had announced explicitly that Nazism *opposed* divorce (while invoking the popular phrase "marriages are made in heaven"), by 1939 the same paper was publishing articles that not only sought to help women accept the new divorce regulations but glorified divorce and remarriage as an appropriate means of following "the inner law of one's life and nature."[174]

By 1942 at the latest the regime directly encouraged marital infidelity also outside of the military and SS elite and even idealized those wives who were sympathetic to their husbands' affairs. An official Nazi journal explained the state of the law for civil servants: a man's adulterous affair was no longer perceived as injurious to his wife. The law looked with special favor on husbands whose wives had "given permission for" the affair with another woman. The legal focus was on questions of racial appropriateness between partners and the likelihood of racially appropriate reproduction in *both* the marriage and the affair. The concern, however, was not solely with reproduction. As long as the wife approved, the law explicitly permitted a husband's extramarital dalliance whether or not it involved coitus. Fooling around became a man's legal right. (The only matter that worried lawmakers was the possibility that "the other woman" might seek ambitiously and aggressively to bind the husband— a civil servant and therefore of prestigious status—to her for a longer time and thereby cause financial difficulties for the wife.) Here too, however, incitement and disavowal worked together. For the essay's lead sentence on the state of the law asserted a traditionalist and conservative stance: "Adultery and antimarital [*ehewidriges*] behavior regularly constitute a transgression of duty." Only then did the essay go on to contradict this opening stance with numerous qualifications that clarified the instances when adultery was permissible.[175]

While some German Protestant and Catholic clergymen were already imprisoned in concentration camps for their outspoken resistance to Nazism, the reconfigured leadership of the Protestant Church and the bulk of the Catholic leadership endorsed the war effort with great fervor and called on their faithful to do so as well. In 1939 Nazi propaganda minister Joseph Goebbels subsided in his assaults on the churches, wanting them to help mobilize the German people for war. They complied. The Protestant Church leadership announced at the occasion of the German invasion of Poland in September 1939 that "the German Protestant Church has always stood loyally bound to the fate of the German people. . . . So also in this hour we unite with our *Volk* in prayer on behalf of the Führer and the Reich." After the successful blitzkrieg on Poland, Protestant leaders offered this message from the pulpits: "And with thanks to God we combine thanks to all those who in only a few weeks have made possible such a tremendous turn of events: the Führer and his generals, our brave soldiers on land, in the water and the air." And Catholic bishops intensified their support for Hitler once war began. A prayer book developed by the Catholic bishop for the Wehrmacht said that the military was "the school of bravery, the birthplace of great heroes, a showplace of honor and fame" and told soldiers to fight "with God for Führer, *Volk*, and fatherland!"[176] Although Poland was a Catholic country, and German army atrocities against Polish clergy were known, the German cardinals and bishops enjoined German Catholics to pray for the Wehrmacht's success and rang church bells to celebrate Germany's victory. Similar celebrations ensued in the course of 1940 as the German army occupied Denmark, Norway, the Netherlands, Belgium, and France. And upon hearing the news of the 1941 invasion of the Soviet Union, Protestant leaders assured Hitler "once again, in these overwhelmingly intense hours, of the unchangeable loyalty and willingness to serve of the entire Protestant Christendom of the Reich." Hitler was praised for "having put a stop to the Bolshevik danger in our own land" and for "calling now for our people and the peoples of Europe to the decisive battle against the sworn enemy of all order and all Western Christian culture."[177]

Yet even as the war in the Soviet Union became, at one and the same time, immeasurably more difficult for the German army and also inseparable from the process of genocide, one of the most influential Protestant bishops, August Marahrens, continued in 1943 to demand that his pastors convince their congregants that "we are in a war that demands our entire commitment and this war must be pursued with unflinching devotion, free of all sentimentality."[178] The Catholic leadership behaved no better. As Michael Burleigh grimly summarized the relationship between Nazism and the Catholic Church:

> Catholic clergy also helped the regime camouflage a war of racial-ideological murder in Russia by presenting it as a "crusade" against atheistic Bolshevism, a formula which barely covered murdering Jews in Catholic Poland. Nor did the Church protest the confinement of multifarious victims in concentration camps, beyond half-hearted attempts to bring spiritual solace to Catholics detained within them. And with the exception of a few brave men such as Provost Bernhard Lichtenberg of Berlin, who died in Dachau because he insisted on praying each day for deported Jews, protests regarding antisemitic measures were largely confined to the fate of "non-Aryan" Christians rather than Jews *qua* Jews. Even when in late 1941 the Catholic bishops protested proposals compulsorily to divorce partners in mixed marriages, Cardinal Bertram felt moved to insist that his words were not motivated by "lack of love for the German nation . . . or of underestimation of the harmful Jewish influences upon German culture and national interests."[179]

This cooperation between the churches and Nazism in matters of militarism and antisemitism provides important context for subsequent self-presentations by the churches as both resisters to and victims of the Nazi regime.

Certainly not all Christians shared the church leaderships', by turns, obsequious deference to and fanatic support for the regime. Many of the most earnest Christians, those who were horrified by the overall trajectory of the Third Reich and its hideous and callous disrespect for human rights—whether of Jews, of the handicapped, or of political dissenters—

were also sickened by what they saw as the Third Reich's hubris in the realm of sex. Indeed they saw the massive inhumanity and the *Herrenmensch* feeling of entitlement to rule breaking as somehow connected. As a "prayer for peace" formulated by members of the breakaway anti-Nazi Protestant "Confessing Church" put it in 1938 (during the diplomatic crisis over the Sudetenland), at once allusively and pointedly:

> We poor sinners confess before Thee the sin of our church, its leadership, its congregations and its shepherds. . . . We have tolerated a false gospel all too much. . . . We confess before Thee the sin of our people. Thy Name has been taken in vain by it, Thy Word fought against, Thy Truth suppressed. Publicly and secretly much injustice has occurred. . . . Life is being wounded and destroyed, marriage is being broken, property stolen, and the dignity of the neighbor is being damaged. Lord our God, we lament before Thee these our sins and the sins of our *Volk*. Forgive us and spare us from Your punishments. Amen.

Several days later, four state bishops were called upon by the government to censure the prayer; they did so, deeming it inappropriate "for patriotic and religious reasons."[180] Strikingly, however, and although the comment about marriage is certainly not the prayer's main emphasis, it is worth noting that even before total war engulfed much of Europe, precisely that minority of Christians who had a critical perspective on Nazism saw Nazism's constitutive savagery and its boundary pushing with respect to sexual mores as linked. This tentative intuitive insight would become for a brief time more widely advanced in the immediate aftermath of the war, only in subsequent decades to be forgotten as new versions of the Third Reich came to hold sway.

TOTAL WAR

There are several ways to interpret the Second World War's impact on sexuality in the Third Reich and the territories it conquered. The first emphasizes non-Jewish Germans' suffering. It calls attention, on the one hand, to the enormity—for a nation and for a continent—of tens of millions of couples and families ripped apart, sometimes for years, sometimes forever, and it stresses, on the other hand, the particularity and intensity of individual fear and pain in the face of loss of loved ones, as well as the difficulty of repairing relationships after long and arduous separations (in those fortunate cases when people were able to return to one another).

A second approach emphasizes the ordinariness and unexceptionality of most sexual experiences in wartime and the persistence of conventional patterns of behavior despite the war. "Sex in the Third Reich," as one woman who lived in Nazi Germany said many decades later, "was totally normal."[181] In this rendering, older people mostly stayed faithful to their partners despite the long bouts of separation. Young people variously flirted, had infatuations, strove to remain virgins, had conflicts with parents over their romantic choices, had surreptitious sex, and so forth. Perhaps they used the occasion of a stint in the Reich Labor Service or in an auxiliary service role for the military to experiment with individuals or with practices that they might not have considered in the more closely monitored settings of their own communities. But there were no dramatic departures from inherited norms. Still, this account of sexuality under Nazism does acknowledge the brothels instituted for soldiers in the armed forces but, again, these are labeled unexceptional. As one man (a teenager during the Third Reich) remarked with casual dismissiveness: "All armies in the world have brothels."[182]

A third interpretive framework contends that there was little that could be normal anywhere in a society in which the majority of the populace enthusiastically supported a violently racist government. This view focuses on the suffering that those not persecuted by the Nazi regime imposed on those who were persecuted—even as it also acknowledges that both the conditions of terror and the complexities of human nature make judgments in many cases complicated, and it emphasizes how complicity and victimization can coexist in the same individuals. (For example, a woman victimized because of her gender may yet have exercised the power to torment her community's Jews.) This perspective is also grounded in the knowledge that the genocide of European Jewry was no secret in Nazi Germany. While ordinary citizens may not have known about Auschwitz and other death camps, the majority of the German populace knew about the mass shootings of Jews in Poland and the Soviet Union, which constituted a significant portion of the Holocaust.[183] The majority was also aware of the programs for sterilization and murder of the disabled, as well as innumerable other violent aspects of Nazi rule. Scholars who view Nazism in this framework, moreover, frequently emphasize that matters of romance, sex, and reproduction were especially significant sites of suffering in a continent subjected to Nazi domination.

Scholarship written from this perspective details the countless intimate invasions in the Nazi strategy of rule, and it sees the cruelties committed in wartime as at least in part an extension and elaboration of processes underway since the beginning of the Third Reich. This approach insists that crucial aspects of the history of sexuality under Nazism include the anguish and humiliation of women and men forced against their will to be sterilized under the auspices of the "Law for the Preservation of Hereditarily Healthy Offspring," and the excruciating impact of the Nuremberg Laws "for the Preservation of German Blood and Honor" on tens of thousands of Jewish-Gentile couples and their families. It also emphasizes the ripple effect of these and other laws, as many couples hesitated even to seek a marriage license for fear that medical or juridical investigation would disclose (real or concocted) evidence of mental illness in the family or inappropriate racial lineage. This interpretation foregrounds the strong class dimension of Nazi racism and the ways social factors were interpreted in biologistic terms; it is also sensitized to the differential impact on men and women of Nazi gender ideology and regulations about reproduction, and it exposes the especially punitive treatment of proletarian women designated variously as "prostitutes," "asocials," or "mentally deficient." It emphasizes the perniciousness of both the pronatalist and the antinatalist dimensions of Nazi reproductive policy, and it examines the intensified criminalization of abortion as well as the abortions performed on women against their will (not just those deemed "mentally deficient" but also Jews, Sinti and Roma, and foreign laborers). This approach further stresses the Nazis' radical expansion of the prosecution and punishment of homosexual acts between men, the cruel treatments to which men accused of homosexuality were subjected, and the tens of thousands who were imprisoned and the thousands who were murdered for their homosexuality. It sees the wartime prohibitions on sex between Germans and foreign forced laborers and prisoners of war on the home front and the prohibitions on sex between German soldiers and female citizens in (some but not all of) the occupied territories and nations, as well as the draconian penalties for incursions against these laws, as an extension of the longer-standing Nazi obsession with controlling both reproduction and intimate contacts.[184]

Yet a fourth way of telling the story highlights the dynamic of total war itself. Total war is war that places every technical, material, and human resource in the service of the production of death. Total war involves and mobilizes to the fullest extent both numerous battlefronts and the home front; the home front not only becomes a battlefront of its own but is essential to the war effort through its production of ammunition and other war-related objects and its reproduction of future soldiers.[185] And as Magnus Hirschfeld and his colleagues pointed out in their analysis of the sexual mores both destroyed and spawned by the First World War, war is not only (or not even so much) the result of human sadistic impulses but rather the opposite: sadism is produced by war. The conduct of war depends on, creates the conditions for, and encourages the expression of sadism—often on a mass scale. War alters human nature. It reconfigures the relationships between sex, pleasure, and violence, and it does so in multiple ways. Drawing on Freud's insights, Hirschfeld and his colleagues saw war as a force that caused human beings to regress and return to an earlier stage of civilization. "War," Freud had written, "strips us of later cultural layers and lets the primitive person within us become visible again." Or, as Hirschfeld and his associates put it, already in the First World War group actions and interactions and individual personalities underwent a process of barbarization that ultimately left none untouched. And they quoted a military officer who explained the aim of this process: "Primitivization [*Verrohung*] at the front achieves a more brutal conduct of war, and primitivization of the homeland awakens and maintains the feelings of hate against the enemy that are actually foreign to any civilized people."[186]

This dynamic of the First World War became exponentially more apparent in the Second World War. While World War I had already been experienced as cataclysmic by all the combatant nations, the conduct of World War II, especially the Wehrmacht's actions on the eastern front and its involvement in the operations of the mobile killing units of the SS and SD (*Sicherheitsdienst*), broke every previous rule of warfare. Thus, it was not only that the war made the Holocaust possible in the first place. Rather, war and genocide became inseparable processes.[187] Meanwhile, it would be willfully blind to deny the sexual elements of either war or genocide, from the decisive separation of sex from sentiment in the hastily assembled and coercively staffed military brothels to the "practically necrophiliac" practice of consorting with women in an enemy village one night only to murder the villagers the following morning, from the deliberate rape of women in the killing fields to advance dehumanization and to make killing easier for the perpetrators to the hallucinatorily inventive sadisms practiced in the ghettos and concentration and death camps.[188]

To grasp fully both the experience of the Second World War and how life in the later years of the Third Reich would subsequently be interpreted in the postwar era, it is essential that all four of these registers of reality be acknowledged. Trauma and banality, life as usual and unimaginably perverse cruelty, coexisted. Indeed, they often collapsed into each other. Certainly, this was true for perpetrators. "You can trust your Daddy. He thinks about you all the time and is not shooting immoderately," one fond father wrote to his family about his role in the roundups and mass executions of Jews in the Soviet Union, signing the letter with "Lots of kisses and greetings for the children, For their dear mummy a long deep kiss."[189] "Highly esteemed, dear Reichsführer! . . . I thank you from the bottom of my heart for the presents and the pleasure which you have given us all. My husband is very fond of chocolate and took some with him to the concentration camp. . . . My husband is very pleased at the interest that you have shown in his experiments. At Easter he conducted the experiments for which Dr. Romberg would have shown too much restraint and compassion," the wife of a doctor engaged in murderous research on prisoners of war in Dachau wrote to the leader of the SS.[190] In completely different ways, it could be true for victims. Describing the intensity of sexual connection experienced in a stalled streetcar in the midst of bombing raids, Gad Beck, a homosexual and member of the Jewish underground resistance in Berlin, remembered that it was "very romantic . . . because in such a drastic time one tends toward romanticism. When bombs are going over your head, and one even hits close by, then you simply seek the nearness of the other person beside you."[191] It could also be true for bystanders. One woman described how after a bombing raid—in the sheer relief of still being alive after emerging from the bomb shelter—she went around the corner with a random man to have quick but satisfying intercourse.[192] For others, the spousal separations caused by war allowed wives and husbands to seek out new and more emotionally meaningful relationships, which sometimes, but not always, led to new marriages.[193] And court records from the war years and doctors' case studies from the postwar years testify amply to how the mass mobility forced by the war shaped individuals' romantic histories.

On the one hand, the Nazi leadership had trouble persuading the German populace of the value of its more radical sexual plans. For instance, popular misgiving about the *Lebensborn* homes founded by Himmler was widespread. These were maternity homes for wives of SS men and "racially fit" unwed mothers. But ordinary citizens nervously spread rumors that the homes were in actuality also for selective breeding—with especially attractive (and racially endorsed) women matched with particularly handsome SS men they barely knew. (The serious scholarship on this concludes that such encounters never occurred, even as it acknowledges that Nazi activists planned that they someday would; there is, however, evidence that, although there may not have been deliberate couplings, there were nonetheless incidents of artificial insemination undertaken by Nazi doctors with a view to "nordifying" (*aufnorden*) the German gene pool.)[194]

Moreover, on a far more quotidian level, by no means were all Germans eager to endorse the regime's emphasis on sexual incitement. Many parents felt keen distress at the idea that their underage daughters should become illegitimate mothers, and many young women and men were repelled by the idea that they ought to become breeders for the Führer or have any sex outside of a long-term commitment.[195] For many girls especially the concept of virginity until marriage remained a sincere and idealistic goal.[196] Nor were many wives and girlfriends pleased with the Nazi encouragement of sexual infidelity among men as long as those men selected "racially appropriate" partners. And many soldiers at the front were rent with anxiety by the thought that their wives or sweethearts were cheating on them.[197] The concerns of these constituencies may thus provide an important explanation for the regime's tendency to permit sexually conservative voices to coexist alongside more radical pronouncements. Indeed, the historian Gudrun Schwarz has expressed consternation at the contrast between the ease with which Nazis were able to make their anti-Jewish policies palatable to the populace and the difficulty they appear to have had convincing most Germans that marriage and marital fidelity were antiquated ideals.[198]

On the other hand, the combination of Nazi policies and the dynamics of total war did indisputably contribute to a loosening of sexual mores. On the western front, there were long stretches of time when occupation forces were not engaged in battle and thus had more opportunity for leisure; in addition, there were fewer prohibitions, or in some countries like Norway or Denmark (supposedly of kindred racial type) no formal prohibitions at all, on consorting intimately with the local population. Recent estimates suggest that one in ten Danish and one in five Norwegian women under the age of thirty were at some point during the war romantically and sexually involved with German men; approximately one in ten of these relationships, in turn, resulted in illegitimate offspring—perhaps ten thousand all told for both nations. An official estimate for the number of illegitimate children of French women and German men is even higher.[199] On the eastern front, by contrast, battles were brutal and constant, battalions were continually on the move and the tide turned repeatedly both for and against Germany. Here there were severe penalties for sex with supposedly racially inferior peoples. Yet the very same racism that lay at the root of those regulations also facilitated the military's unofficial permission to rape local women as a strategy of warfare. Clearly soldiers also ignored or circumvented the regulations and sought out consensual sex—even at the risk of direct confrontation with their commanders over the matter.[200]

It was standard for military leaders to encourage their troops to engage in sexual activity. Condoms were distributed to soldiers (twelve per month) with the expectation that they be used for nonmarital sex; men boasted of their sexual prowess by wearing the packages visibly through their breast pockets.[201] Soldiers also availed themselves of local as well as Wehrmacht-sponsored brothels (fig. 1.5). As one soldier wrote after the war to his former fellows: "Dear war comrades, have you forgotten so soon how in Smolensk, Odessa, and Simferopol you went into the Russian houses? That in the retreat in the final years in the East Russian women had to come along with your battalion. . . . Do you still remember how you stood in the long queues in the brothels of Paris and Le Havre, Lille and Besançon, Norway and Italy, in the Baltics and in Greece . . . ?"[202] Another former soldier, an earnest Christian, remembered his acute discomfort as a teenager in the Wehrmacht at the pressure articulated by fellow soldiers that every young man must be sexually active: " 'Every little Hans must have a little Sabine' [*Jedem Hänschen sein Sabinchen*], that was the motto. It was disgusting. The Nazis constantly insisted that

Figure 1.5. Brothel pass for Wehrmacht soldiers stationed in the Netherlands. From Andreas Gaspar, *Sittengeschichte des zweiten Weltkrieges*. The instructions say (under A): "Intercourse only with a condom! After intercourse immediate sanitation! Pick up your identification number!" B names the brothel and the "partner" (Lilly). C is a certificate showing that the soldier has undergone post-intercourse "sanitation."

sex before marriage or outside of marriage was morally acceptable, even necessary."[203] But others experienced the official encouragement as marvelous. One man, a young officer at the time, recorded in his memoirs the delight he and his comrades felt in the last months of the war when, stationed in a western occupied nation, an auxiliary service contingent of twenty-one girls and young women arrived. The lieutenant major made a speech before his assembled young charges. Gesturing toward the overwhelming sense of impending catastrophe (summarized in the then oft-repeated catchphrase "Enjoy the war—the peace will be awful"), he instructed that there should be neither petty fights nor jealousies and insisted that precautions be taken against accidental pregnancy. Otherwise, he said: "Nothing may be noticed by the outside world. On the other hand, one may not forbid fucking. . . . Further: no sex in the normal sleep barracks (so that the goody-two-shoes will not be disturbed). But so that you can bang away, we have prepared an extra barrack with ten straw sacks, that is, for ten couples!" As the memoir recorded, "These encouraging words let everyone hit the high point of exuberant euphoria."[204]

Women and girls in the Reich Labor Service had ample opportunity for sexual encounters. One woman remembered the Reich Labor Service as having a "very sexual climate . . . a thoroughly sexual climate." Females in the Reich Labor Service were deliberately brought together with young military men for coed "social evenings"; the expectation was clearly that romantic pairings would occur. If there was no one who appealed to a particular girl, it was "difficult to get out of there." Even after Germany's defeat at Stalingrad in 1943, the mood in the Third Reich was still one of "dancing and partying." The overall message young people received was that Nazis were in favor of premarital sex. It was not just that reproduction was desired; "in general, the Nazis were in favor of fun" (*sie waren doch auch sonst für Spass*).[205]

Meanwhile, women on the home front often had romantic and sexual relationships not only with German men to whom they were not married but also with "foreigners" (the close to four million forced laborers and almost two million prisoners of war brought into the Reich to work in agriculture and military industries to compensate for German men at war). The Nazi Office of Racial Policy was aghast at how "unmindful of their duty to the *Volk*" so many German women and girls proved to be: "Many German women and girls . . . are not ashamed to strike up a friendship or even intimate relations with these men of an alien *Volk*. They allow themselves to be plied with drinks quite openly in the pubs and then disappear with these men, who don't even speak German, into parks, adjacent woodlands, and meadows." The SD reported with further annoyance that "Not all are women of loose morals, though this may well be true for the majority. The accused women include innocent farm girls of good reputation and family background, and also soldier's wives, some happily married for many years." How German men behaved in the occupied territories was not unknown on the home front, and some German women sought to express their own version of gender egalitarianism. For example, after a woman in one German town was paraded through the streets with her head shorn and a sign reading "I sullied the honor of German womanhood" (for having had an affair with a prisoner of war), some of her female townspeople "let it be known that they disapproved of this action. A few women also ventured to ask whether the same would be done to a man who had an affair with a French woman while in France."[206]

What bears emphasis is that these developments of the war years were not solely due to the pressures of war. Nazi prewar policies were just as significant. Yet Nazi encouragement of pre- and extramarital heterosexuality not only for the purpose of procreation but also for the pursuit of pleasure was precisely the aspect of Nazi policies that would be assiduously forgotten in the postwar era. That the regime that had been sexually inciting was also responsible for continent-wide carnage and the systematic torture and murder of its own citizens and millions of citizens of other nations made it especially desirable to erase the memory of popular receptivity to Nazism's pleasure-enjoining aspects. Specifically the fact that the taboo breaking with regard to sexual mores had been accompanied by such massive rupture of the taboo against killing those powerless to resist made it both psychologically and politically congenial to excise certain elements from the retrospective portrait of Nazism while highlighting others.[207]

In the late 1940s and early 1950s, the antibourgeois and sexually transgressive aspects of Nazism were still remembered and recorded by commentators across the ideological spectrum. By the late 1950s and early 1960s, however, these memories had receded. In their place, new interpretations of Nazism took hold, nudged along not least by reformed ex-Nazis and former Nazi sympathizers who now, as both bona fide democrats and (simultaneously) authoritative witnesses to the Third Reich, promoted an array of half-truths and outright falsifications. Assertions were made, for example, that Nazism had been so intent on raising reproductive rates that contraceptive products and information had been completely unavailable.[208] Alternatively, it was stressed that the Nazi movement was strongly motivated by homosexual impulses (even as the Nazi persecution and murder of homosexuals were completely suppressed).[209] Young people born during or shortly after the war and who grew up in the 1950s were offered only the most selective (not to say distorted) stories about sexuality under Nazism. "All I ever remember hearing about was the sexually 'clean' Nazi, the very proper Nazi," one woman raised in northern Germany said. And a man who grew up in the 1950s Rhineland noted that "all I ever heard about was the queer Nazi."[210]

Only a very few of those who had lived through the Third Reich still publicized a dissenting view of Nazism's sexual politics. The successful (non-Nazi) Nazi-era film director Arthur Maria Rabenalt wrote in 1958, for instance, that Nazism had not been nearly as sexually strict or reproduction-oriented as it was (by then) standard to claim. In his memoirs, Rabenalt wrote: "The National Socialist will to eroticism, the self-evident avowal of sex expressed itself far beyond these functionalist necessities, in a very frank, generous and unbourgeois way." He added that under Nazism, "marriage was promoted and propagated as the fundamental cell of state formation, yet it was anything but sacrosanct." Rabenalt observed that under Nazism "the erotic—as long as it stayed within the framework of the racial laws and conformed to the so-called healthy sensibility of the *Volk*—faced no limit," and that promiscuity among youth was freely tolerated. In sum, and repeatedly contrasting Nazi sexual attitudes to (in his view) far more prudish and "sterile" Stalinist values, Rabenalt characterized Nazis as stalwart champions of the "all-powerful sexual drive."[211] It would take quite a long time before these perspectives on sex in the Third Reich would again be seriously countenanced.

CHAPTER TWO

The Fragility of Heterosexuality

TOPIC NO. 1

The postwar months and years were not a time of silence about Nazism. Indeed, in the immediate aftermath of the Second World War, sexuality became a central focus of efforts to master Nazism—and its defeat. Especially in the western zones of occupation, postwar discussions of sex proved a singularly important site for efforts to come to terms with the recent past. From church-affiliated Christians on the one side to the defenders of "healthy" pro-sex sensualism on the other, from medical professionals to mainstream journalists and middlebrow advicegivers, postwar commentators, far from suppressing references to Nazism, invoked it with frequency. Public debate about sexual practices, attitudes, and mores became a key means to negotiate the transition from fascism to Western democracy. That sexuality emerged as a main topic through which this transition from Nazism to democracy was managed had everything to do with the dramatic turmoil in sexual relations that accompanied the end of the Third Reich, a turmoil that some experienced as deeply disturbing while others found it exhilarating. Sex had become, as the slang term went, "Topic No. 1" (*Thema 1*).[1]

In this heightened public attention paid to sexual matters, numerous contemporaries lamented what they variously termed "the marital crisis," "the sexual crisis," or "the sexual misery of our time."[2] "Marriage is in danger" was a frequent refrain.[3] One author titled his 1947 book "The Tragedy of the Bedroom," while another writer in 1949 opined that "marriage is sick through and through"[4] (fig. 2.1). And a year later, yet another author continued to lament the "the statistically unmeasurable extent" of "the sexual misery."[5] Complaints were widespread that there was no longer any erotic energy, tension, or attraction between men and women. It was not, however, that people had stopped having sex—on the contrary.

Medical doctors diagnosed a hectic sexual activity that was nonetheless experienced as emotionally meaningless for the participants. As one physician noted in 1950, a tendency toward self-absorption had grown since the war, and within relationships there now existed a "disinclination to invest more emotional capital than necessary." Prospects, in his view, were dismal. Eroticism had disappeared: "What remains is only the performance

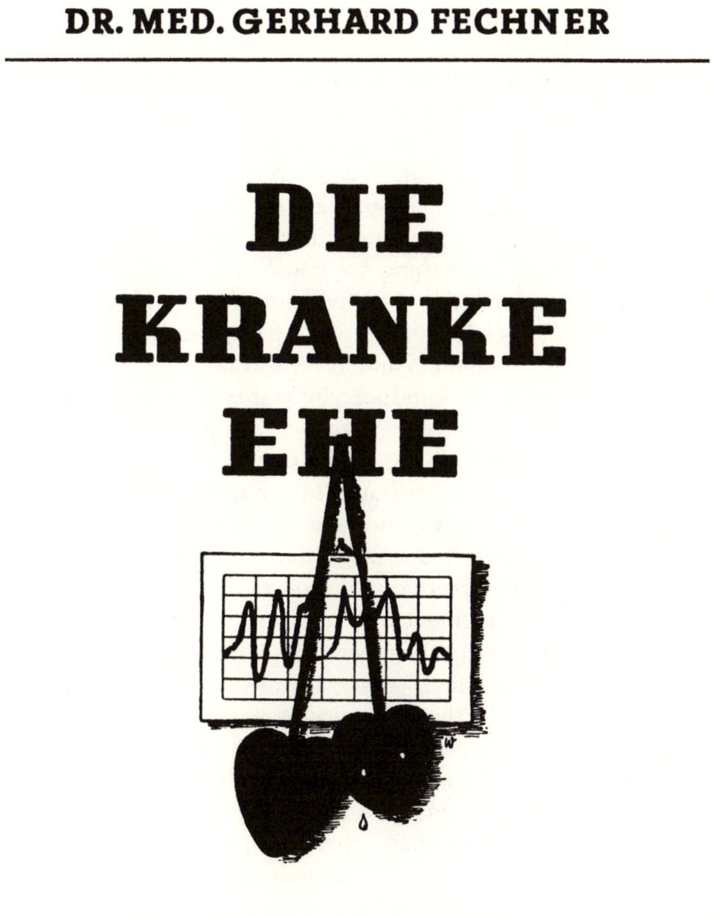

DR. MED. GERHARD FECHNER

DIE KRANKE EHE

Figure 2.1. “Sick Marrriage.” Title page for Dr. Gerhard Fechner’s book *Die kranke Ehe* (Hamburg: Grupe, 1949).

of the sex act as such." Men in particular, he averred, had trouble caring about their female partners. Men tended "toward more infantile behaviors" and were often unable to let go of a "certain last autistic remnant." While men continued to have sex with women, they were really just having sex with themselves.[6] In 1951 another doctor contended that precisely the cataclysmic intensity of the war years had damaged nearly all Germans' capacity for romantic connection. In "the most recent past," he wrote, the mobilization of countless "young-blooded" bodies of both sexes, "the concentration of all forces into violence and highest achievement," and "finally the pressure of an uncertain personal and universal fate hanging over everything" led even the "previously satisfied or morally strict" to become uninhibited. "Everything we call 'love,'" he said, "came away badly." Sex itself was reduced to a "primitive act," and whatever lack of quality the participants felt they simply "attempted to compensate for by the quantity of such encounters and adventures."[7]

The chaotic circumstances induced by war were in many ways exacerbated further in the wake of war. Massive unemployment, hunger, inadequate and overcrowded housing, and the uprooting and dislocation of millions of refugees each contributed to the general state of emergency. As a memoir about the postwar moment succinctly stated, this was a time of "anarchy in Germany."[8] Yet far from distracting people's attention away from sex, "the complete dissolution of all order" seemed to bring with it an even greater incidence of "indiscriminate sexual intercourse." As one physician observed, "While in other countries the end of the war proceeded in quiet orderliness," this was not so "in Central Europe, especially in Germany. . . . In these conditions it was often people who had barely met, who would never again in life see one another . . . who engaged in unrestrained sexual intercourse."[9] As venereal diseases, especially syphilis and gonorrhea, spread rapidly, placards that rhetorically asked "Do you even know each other?" (*Kennt Ihr Euch überhaupt?*) were posted in numerous places.[10] The main difficulty, however, according to many observers, was not material but metaphysical. Human beings' basic capacity for relationality had been impaired.

Nor did marriage provide any safe haven from the chaos. An extraordinary amount of marital discord succeeded the often multiyear separations between spouses caused both by the war and by the imprisonment of hundreds of thousands of German men (and some women) in Allied prisoner-of-war (POW) camps. The initial joy at reunion was often followed by delayed-reaction conflicts. "Marital crises are multiplying ever more," one author noted five years after war's end.[11] News articles, feuilleton stories, popular advice columns, and professional literature alike repeatedly emphasized both the pressing need to help individuals leave unhappy partnerships through divorce *and* the possibility that with great effort, sensitivity, and mutual forgiveness damaged relationships might be repaired.[12] The problem, moreover, as one newspaper put it in 1947, was not just that requests for divorce were "on a steeply rising curve." The very concept of marriage was under siege; what was urgently needed was "an unmistakable, positive affirmation of the nature and value of marriage."[13] One out of six marriages in Germany ended in divorce, ten times as many divorces as in the pre–World War I era.[14] And although the divorce rates reached a peak in the late 1940s and the situation stabilized in the early 1950s, marital conflict remained a topic of considerable public concern. Some couples were so young and had married in such a hurry while hardly having developed a relationship that after the war they faced each other practically as strangers. For somewhat older couples, it was not just the time of separation per se that felt insurmountable; the strongly divergent experiences spouses had were often nearly impossible either to communicate or to overcome.

Husbands (brutalized by what they had seen or done in battle and/ or devastated by defeat and imprisonment) and wives (strained beyond exhaustion by the burden of managing families alone under wartime conditions) frequently had trouble reconnecting at all. As one commentator noted, many men came home from POW camps "feelingless and cold, reserved . . . either hardened and wooden or irritable and nervous." And if upon his return a man rejected his wife no matter "how lovingly she received him and strove to give herself to him . . . after years of yearning for affection and goodness, contact and safety"—perhaps not least because she too had aged and toughened and no longer matched the "fantasy image" of her he had carried inside himself in his "homesick dreams"—then her "profound disappointment" could easily make her as well become "indifferent" and contribute her part to the growing alienation within the marriage.[15] Or, as another commentator pointed out, the independence so many women had acquired during the war often made it feel absolutely "insufferable" to now be expected "once again to subordinate themselves to the man."[16] However, far greater than the resulting number of divorces, one Protestant pastor noted, were the "undivorced but shattered marriages" that continued on despite "spiritual emptiness, alienation, embitterment, and desolation."[17]

At the same time, rather than persisting in unhappy marriages, millions of women were not able to marry (or remarry) in the first place. This was due to the painful arithmetic of (what was consistently referred to as) a several-million-strong "surplus of women" (Frauenüberschuss) after the overwhelming number of male war deaths. Some commentators, especially Christians, sought to validate single women's sense of pain but urged them to find fulfilling lives through service to society. And a number of energetic female authors declared that living with a man was not as exciting or gratifying as it was made out to be and that no one need condescend to the single woman. Yet most commentary added insult to injury as it eschewed earnestness and indulged in either acerbic or merely glib wit. As the best-selling women's magazine *Constanze* wryly put it in 1948, with 1,250 women to every 1,000 men, "which woman, in view of such an oppressive statistical surplus of female marriage partners can still ask, What is the man like? rather than simply, Where, where is the man?"[18] A few daring writers recommended that two women might share the same man (although the main tendency was to make coy references to the possibility of such threesomes while claiming to be opposed to them). Others titillatingly but patronizingly speculated that the dearth of men was leading to higher incidences of both female masturbation and lesbianism.[19] The overarching tendency in the press, however—and this had tremendous consequences—was both to pity the involuntarily single woman and to aggravate every already married woman's sense of anxiety that she was about to lose her man. A contributor to the newly founded scholarly *Zeitschrift für Sexualforschung* (Journal for Sex Research), for example, only exacerbated the atmosphere of competition between women when he referred to the "threat to healthy normal marriage created by the current large surplus of women . . . for the excess of female sexuality cannot simply in every case be forced into professional-spiritual sublimation!"[20]

Meanwhile, adding to the sense that the inherited sexual order was dissolving nearly overnight was the widespread fraternization between German women and soldiers of the occupying Allied armies. American soldiers were especially popular. Initial prohibitions on fraternization quickly gave way when they proved unenforceable. In any given week, U.S. military authorities discovered in consternation, more than a quarter of all their troops were having sex with German women.[21] Distinctions between prostitution and dating blurred completely, to the great distress also of more conservative Germans.[22] While certainly "the great majority of women and girls in Germany did not have relationships with American soldiers," either because they remained faithful to German husbands and sweethearts, disdained the former enemy, or were just not interested, there was no question that the Americans were the most attractive among the new arrivals.[23] The feeling was mutual. As the American *Reader's Digest* reported in 1946 under the caption asking "Why So Many GIs Like the Germans Best," the answer was simple: so many of the women were remarkably amenable. Whereas in France the only sexually accessible women were professional prostitutes, the moment the GI crossed the border into Germany "women in general were at his disposal" and "he was submerged in a sea of willing Fräuleins." The *Reader's Digest* also offered an explanation of sorts (which however questionable it might be in hindsight also highlights just how commonsensical, in the mid-1940s, the sexually inciting elements of the Third Reich were felt to be). It was not only that these women had "been deprived of their men for so long." Another reason for their ready sexual availability was "the breakdown of morality which resulted from Nazi preachings. The women of Germany had been taught that it was their duty to the state to refuse nothing to German soldiers on leave, even strangers. They decided to refuse nothing to Americans either."[24] Or as a quip circulating among GIs at the time put it, German women appeared to be the loosest "this side of Tahiti."[25]

Indeed, and as these reports already suggest, far from accepting the assessment that they were miserable, numerous Germans—women not least among them—were finding in the postwar moment an agreeable era of "erotic liberality" (*erotische Freizügigkeit*).[26] Evidence of postwar Germans agonizing about a state of crisis was matched by evidence of Germans unreservedly and emphatically celebrating sexual pleasure and sexual freedom. In a way that would come to seem unimaginable for those who remember the much more conservative mid- to late 1950s, in the late 1940s and early 1950s the idea that "unsatisfied urges" made people "neurotic" was widely held.[27] Sexual "harmoniousness" was considered essential for a durable marriage.[28] And, above all, nonmarital heterosexual activity was taken to be not merely prevalent but thoroughly reasonable. In a survey carried out in 1949 by *Constanze* together with the Institute for Statistical Market and Opinion Research, for example, six out of ten West Germans questioned declared that sex between unmarried adults was not immoral, and less than three out of ten insisted that it was.[29] Among West German men under the age of thirty, 97.8 percent believed premarital coitus to be either simply permissible or truly necessary.[30] Yet this did not reflect a sense of male prerogative only. As one jurist observed, "very many young people nowadays say with complete bluntness that one 'should not buy a cat in a sack [i.e., marry someone with whom one has not yet had sex].' " But he also added: "Just as openly, only in less drastic terms, young girls declare that they would experience it as disrespectful and insulting if a man wanted to marry them without beforehand giving them the opportunity to acquire clarity about whether they are also physiologically compatible."[31] Furthermore, women and girls were not impressed by efforts to curtail their premarital sexual exploration. As one satirical poem reminded those German men who were distressed at German women's easygoing relationships with the new occupiers, former German soldiers would simply have to wait for a full ten years, because "for that long we must still kiss / men from the U.S." After all: "How did you do it when you were away? / Did you not have girls and women by night and by day? / So shut up and be quite still / every girl can do what she will."[32]

Not only did German women more confidently seek premarital experiences, but—apart from general expressions of moral outrage or irritation over competition with the occupiers—growing numbers of German men were also increasingly comfortable with this trend. As numerous commentators noted, men just no longer valued female virginity as much as they once had. The medical doctor Heinz Graupner asserted in 1949 that the old double standard had fallen away: "In the eyes of men female virginity has lost meaning also with respect to the future wife. . . . Nowadays it is no longer made into a problem for a girl if her first experience did not lead to marriage. We have to accept this state of affairs, even if we don't like it: it is the general condition of our present."[33] And in 1950 the sexologist Hans Giese remarked on "the ever increasing disappearance in the past two or three decades of the significance of female virginity in the erotic imagination of male consciousness."[34] That same year, one fortyish German man describing his search for a suitable wife confirmed this point, albeit with some ambivalence: "Nowadays one can go far, really far, before one finds a decent girl 25 years or older who has until now only had honorable relationships. (I am not asking for her to be a virgin!)"[35]

In addition, and notably—especially in view of the more conservative attitudes that would characterize the later 1950s and early 1960s—in this postwar moment the reality of female desire and capacity for sexual satisfaction were considered well-established facts. Although reports were widespread that close to or upward of 50 percent of women had trouble achieving orgasm during coitus (undoubtedly not least because of anxiety about pregnancy), the idea that female orgasm was both possible and important was pervasively held.[36] In a second (and more elaborate) 1949 survey, this one undertaken by the weekly paper *Wochenend* (Weekend) and the Institute for Demoscopy in Allensbach, not only did 71 percent of those questioned approve of premarital sex and a mere 16 percent disapprove; more than half described premarital experience also for women as *beneficial*, while more than a quarter went so far as to assert that it would be detrimental for a woman, sexually speaking, to be a virgin on her wedding day. Gender was not a key differentiating variable. Not only did men and women tend to present similar views, but those between the ages of twenty and fifty were also largely in agreement with one another. Only those older than fifty, especially those socialized before 1900, inclined toward greater strictness.

Meanwhile, 89 percent of the men and 69 percent of the women among the more than one thousand people interviewed admitted to having had premarital sex. The sole significant variable found by the study had to do with church attendance: the quarter of the population that attended church regularly tended more strongly to disapprove of premarital relations. Yet even in this constituency, fully 44 percent declared that premarital sex was just fine.[37] The numbers endorsing—and admitting having engaged in—premarital sex in West Germany at this time, especially among the women, were considerably higher than the comparable figures from England or the United States.[38]

Expounding on the sense that heterosexual mores had relaxed considerably was also a favorite activity across disciplinary and ideological divides. One commentator in a religious periodical complained in 1949 that "in broad circles a new sexual-moral attitude has emerged and spread that trivializes sexual intercourse and puts it on the same level as eating or drinking."[39] Other Christian activists in the postwar years repeatedly protested what they saw as a climate of "erotic overstimulation and damned sexualism," "an overheated atmosphere," and the "progressive sexualization of the entirety of life."[40] The prominent University of Freiburg jurist Karl Siegfried Bader, addressing the founding meeting of the German Society for Sex Research in 1950, asserted as uncontroversial that in the course of the first half of the twentieth century the countryside had become just as sexually liberal as the big cities, and that "the morals code of the bourgeois era is now strongly defended by an ever smaller residual group . . . the old strict order has acquired the taint of the obsolete, the ridiculous." He also announced that "the transformations of the sexual order were primarily caused by the raising and—at least partial—recognition of the woman's entitlement to the acknowledgment of *her* needs. What distinguishes today's sexual order from that of the beginning of the century is the greater assertion of female sexual rights."[41] Indicative as well is the reaction in Germany to the publication of the first Kinsey report in the United States in 1948. Reviewers in the German press in the late 1940s could only marvel and scoff at the pathetic backwardness of American attitudes. Reviewers declared themselves aghast at what they saw as the puritanical American notion that sexual desire was the preserve of men and pitied the American woman who disliked sex and the American man who employed inadequate sexual skill. All this stood in sharp contrast to the "sexual freedom" and "true eroticism" of the Europeans.[42]

Finally, then, as both the complaints about sexual crisis and the strutting self-confidence about sexual skills imply, the outpouring of writings about sex in the first postwar years provide crucial insights into periodization. For far from seeing the proliferation of pre- and extramarital sexual activity and relationships—as scholars have subsequently tended to do—primarily as an effect of the initial postwar economic hardship and military occupation, or as a dramatic departure from past behaviors, contemporaries (regardless of their other differences) emphasized, as Bader had, what they saw as a steady liberalization of heterosexual sexual mores in the first half of the twentieth century.[43] No one in the later 1940s or early 1950s, for example, argued that the Third Reich had been generally antisex. Many even articulated directly their view that the Nazis themselves had further spurred the liberalization.

The change in West Germany that thus requires explanation is the one that would take place in the mid-1950s. For so many of the sexually conservative attitudes now customarily associated with the 1950s, and particularly with the especially stuffy West German version of them—the obsession with the niceties of proper manners, the prescriptive consignment of sexuality only to marriage, the devaluation of sexuality and hostility to its open discussion and display in general, and the belief in particular that women were less sexual than men and that overt sexual desire and agency on women's part were unrespectable—consisted of convictions that only became consolidated gradually in the course of the early 1950s. Popular magazines in the first years of the 1960s expressed more conservative views on gender and sex than did those in the late 1940s.

While for quite a few years it was not at all self-evident what sort of sexual politics would emerge from the wreckage of 1945, by 1953 at the latest, the postwar window of sexual liberality had been shut down. In its place a reconstructed and redomesticated heterosexuality had emerged. Yet postwar discussions of sex were a locus not just for the normalization of perceived-to-be-destabilized gender relations but also for the normalization of Germanness more generally. What requires particular attention, then, are the meaning-making processes engaged in by postwar Germans and the ways Nazism was represented in postwar accounts. For it was precisely within postwar discussions about such seemingly mundane issues as sexual dysfunction or the yearning for private happiness that central aspects of the traumatic and shameful past were addressed. And, as it turns out, while many (though not all) constituencies sought to distance themselves at least from some aspects of Nazism, there would be a considerable amount of unapologetic continuity as well.

CHRISTIAN MORALITY

The prominence of the Christian churches in western Germany (in contrast to the demotion of the churches' role in the Soviet socialist zone of occupation) was a crucial factor in making sex a constant topic of public debate. In the western zones in the postwar period, the churches reacquired tremendous prestige and influence. This was due in part to the American occupiers' (largely mistaken) assumption that the churches had provided something of a bulwark against Nazism—and the occupiers' concomitant decision to allow the churches to run their own denazification procedures. And it was ultimately due in large part to the choice of the Christian Democrat Konrad Adenauer in 1949 as the first postwar chancellor of the Federal Republic. As chapter 3 explores more fully, under Adenauer—not least because of his appointment of the ultratraditionalist Catholic Franz Josef Wuermeling as minister for the family in 1953—a particularly conservative brand of Christian values in matters of sex, gender, and family policy would become firmly ensconced in the law of the land. This development was not universally welcomed. As one German who had experienced both the Third Reich and its aftermath remembered in the late 1990s, "people resented that so much, when the Catholic Church got power again."[44]

It is also important to keep in mind, however, as this last remark already indicates, that in the initial postwar period, Christians—Protestants and Catholics alike—still felt themselves to be very much on the defensive with respect to popular mores. Christians were also acutely aware that irritation at church teachings about sex fostered a broader trend toward secularization. The conservative Protestant theologian Paul Althaus worried openly in 1949 that Christianity had acquired a bad reputation especially for being antisex. Christian ethics, he confessed, had for centuries "not done justice to the meaning of sexual love," and "many of our contemporaries are full of mistrust against Christianity precisely in this area."[45] For Catholic commentators, sexual matters were precisely the site at which secularization took hold in people's souls. Thus, the Catholic scholar and doctor Otto Bernhard Roegele in 1948 named as an "open secret" the fact "that the sexual problematic moves human beings more than anything else, qualitatively and quantitatively," and that this matter, more than any other, was what "estranges them most frequently from religion."[46] Another Catholic commentator in the same year also observed that priests felt all too painfully that issues of sex and the control of reproduction were "the point from which the whole religious life of the family is paralyzed."[47]

Christian spokespersons often presented sexual propriety as the cure for the nation's larger moral crisis.[48] At times they suggested that sexual immorality under Nazism, as much as popular complicity in disenfranchisement and murder, was a main source of that crisis. Some commentators explicitly elaborated moral equivalencies between Nazi crimes and postwar hedonism. One Protestant synod, in its postwar call to its flock to turn away from the godlessness of Nazism, expressed equal if not greater concern about the "forgetting of respect and modesty between man and woman . . . the crumbling of chastity"—and the way these supposedly made Germany a "laughingstock among foreign nations"—than about "the violence and murder" that "arose in our land" or about what it euphemistically referred to as "the taking of property and bread" from "the politically disfavored and Jews."[49] Another Protestant statement in 1946 stressed that it was the church's responsibility to speak out not only against "the sin of yesterday" (here it referred obliquely to the "horrors and crimes" of the Nazis) but just as much against "the sin of today": "the licentiousness and lack of dignity with which women and girls today surrender themselves and men profane female honor."[50] The Catholic Church issued related statements, not only identifying Nazism with secularism and lamenting and criticizing the "secularization" of wartime and postwar marital arrangements, but also contrasting (elliptically but pointedly) "the dark memories of the past years" with the need for "Christian family life" in the present.[51] The Catholic bishop of Passau sounded much like the Protestant commentators when he declared that "I have described how during the war years disgrace was heaped on the name of Germany. I must now add that no less disgrace has been brought to the name of Germany through all those careless women and girls who, in frivolous disregard for God's sixth commandment, through their shameless attitude humiliate not themselves but the entirety of the *Volk*."[52]

Some commentators made the displacement of attention away from the immorality of killing to the need for postwar sexual morality quite explicit. The popular Catholic priest Johannes Leppich, for example, in his open-air sermons attracting tens of thousands of listeners, announced provocatively (as he chastised his listeners for both fraternization and intra-German promiscuity and blamed "hackneyed Goebbels-phrases" for popular denigration of female virginity):

> It is true: we have a terrible war behind us, a war that has left behind demolished churches and houses and a multitude of war dead. But destroyed churches and houses can be rebuilt, and every day enough human beings are born. No—that is not what is ruining Germany. And if one asks me, Is our *Volk* being ruined, or does it still have a future? then there is only one answer: we are dying once more at the hands of our women and girls, who every day throw what is most sacred in them into the dirt.[53]

There was also in the postwar years—and this is crucial to register—a progressive version of Christianity being articulated, one that drew different lessons from the Nazi past than Christian conservatives did. This strand of Christianity combined longing for a renewal of serious spirituality with openness to aspects of socialism and with a profound opposition to remilitarization.[54] These antifascist Christians expressed, just as conservative Christians did, the conviction that Nazism had been nothing less than a "rebellion against God," and that in the Third Reich people had behaved as though they "were like God."[55] They argued that "the collapse of the present is in its deepest origins a religious catastrophe."[56] And they struggled in anguish over the best means to remake Germans' souls in the wake of so many people's emotional entanglement with Nazism.[57] Yet these more progressive views were minority ones, and already by the early

1950s antifascist Christians conceded that their hopes had been dashed. Moreover, the left-leaning tendencies of antifascist Christians also typically did not extend to matters of sexuality and reproduction.

Perhaps the single most powerful basis for a postwar Christian consensus that sexual restraint should be reintroduced in Germany was precisely the deep perception that there had been a close connection between Nazi inducements to criminality and to sexual pleasure. Catholic physician Anton Hofmann, for example, in his sex advice book of 1951 analyzing the "sexual crisis" of his present, not only criticized the way "NS-schools and the like" had forced "premature sexual contact" on young people under the guise of "'natural-free experiencing' of the erotic event." He also directly linked Nazi encouragement of sexual activity with Nazism's other transgressions. Hofmann contended that the disrespect for the spiritual dimension of life evident among people overly obsessed with erotic pleasure was intimately associated with disrespect for the bodies of others and therefore facilitated brutality and mass murder. Or, as he put it, as he lumped together "overvaluation of the body" with "godlessness and cruelty," what needed to be understood was "the paradoxical matter that the same person who raises the body to dizzying heights, in an instant can sacrifice the bodies of a hundred thousand others."[58]

Yet both the emphasis on an interpretation of Nazism as, above all, an anti-Christian movement and the calls to restore conservative sexual mores also worked to obscure Christian accommodation to and support for Nazism. For every earnest effort to deal with the metaphysical crisis that the Third Reich had indisputably caused, there were many other Christian spokespersons who took the occasion to advance self-exculpatory narratives about the Christian churches' relationship to Nazism.[59] Also antifascist Christians' hesitation to defend reproductive rights, and visceral hostility to abortion in particular, cannot be separated out from this wider ambiguous context.

Catholics directly invoked Nazism as they mobilized opposition to abortion and also most forms of contraception. Thus, for example, the priest Hermann Heilweck, while defending the rhythm method of birth control, sharply attacked other methods. Anyone who implied that the method chosen did not matter, since the aim of contraception was in all cases the same, was "unconsciously acting in accordance with the principle common under Hitler—that the ends justify the means—a principle that was at fault for so many heinous crimes." Heilweck argued as well that "believing Jews" shared Christians' conviction that "all unnaturalness" (i.e., any mechanical or chemical means of birth control) was to be rejected.[60] Walter Dirks, who had been a prominent Catholic progressive in Weimar and was coeditor of the influential postwar Catholic intellectual journal *Frankfurter Hefte*, declared bluntly in 1946 that abortion was "the path of least resistance, the easy solution, the capitulation—the perfect solution, if one has managed to shut one's eyes before the single uncomfortable fact that the killing of human life is murder—all one has to do is walk in the footsteps of the SS doctors." Dirks also drew a direct parallel between the courage it took to bear an unplanned pregnancy to term and raise the child and the courage it took to resist Nazism.[61] It could be no coincidence that Dirks was expressly directing his remarks against socialists and communists who were trying in the postwar moment to revive Weimar-era arguments in favor of abortion rights for women as they launched what turned out to be a futile campaign for the abolition or liberalization of antiabortion law.

Along related lines, the Catholic physician Hermann Frühauf, also writing in the *Frankfurter Hefte*, acknowledged only in passing that the Nazi reproductive agenda had involved not just the enforcement of abortions for "eugenic" and "racial" reasons but also an active attempt to stem the abortion rate among those sorts of women the regime hoped would reproduce prolifically. What emerged was a distinctly one-sided reading of Nazism's abortion politics (in which, after all, the involuntary abortions performed on tens of thousands of supposedly "unworthy" German and foreign forced-laborer women was the other side of the coin of the intensified prosecution and punishment of voluntary abortion—including, from 1943 on, the death penalty for abortion providers). Frühauf's main message, like Dirks's, was that a comprehensive antiabortion stance was the only way to be truly anti-Nazi. According to Frühauf, whoever favored abortion rights, "whether he intends this or not, whether he understands this or not, serves those forces and powers that trespass against humanity; he finds himself at a particularly dangerous point on that precipitous slope, that in its last consequences leads to the gas chambers of some Auschwitz."[62] Similarly, the Catholic priest Romano Guardini, also writing in the same venue, compared abortion on the grounds of economic hardship for the mother-to-be with Nazism's willingness to kill on the grounds of ethnic origin.[63] Deeply held beliefs that abortion was no different from murder led antiabortion commentators to reach for the strongest language available to make their case; for them, their Christianity simply *was* their antifascism.

For conservative Catholic commentators, the focus on abortion served wider purposes as well. The image of abortion—due undoubtedly not least to abortion's quite concrete prevalence in the first few postwar years—apparently functioned to condense a whole cluster of negative feelings about Nazism and to fuse distress over its genocidal policies with revulsion at its encouragement of popular libertinism. Maria Probst, for instance, representative to the Bundestag of the conservative Bavarian Christian Social Union (CSU), an affiliate of the ruling Christian Democratic Party (CDU), declared that any modification of Paragraph 218, the law prohibiting abortion, would be disastrous:

> This is not about the woman's so-called democratic right of self-determination with respect to her own body. This is a matter of the existence or nonexistence of another life. . . . I can only indicate the moral consequences here. Naked materialism, uninhibited sexuality, dying eros, growing neglect of youth, declining respect for the woman are results that must be taken very seriously. . . . It is a fact that childlessness frequently reduces the impulse to hard work and to thriftiness. . . . Even to relax Paragraph 218 partially would mean the state was permitting murder. Here the course would be set whose final step must lead to a new Auschwitz.[64]

Also Probst's CSU colleague Franziska Gröber imaginatively merged abortion and Nazi crimes—even as, simultaneously, she unapologetically repeated Nazis' (rather Lamarckian and scientifically insupportable) ideas about genetics: "Women who manage to kill the life they carry under their heart will also manage to kill any life. Then in addition to that comes genetic inheritance [*die Erbfolge*]; about that no one has today yet spoken. . . . If . . . a mother has already herself murdered two children, do you think that has no consequences for genetic inheritance? Will you be surprised if we then once again have concentration camps here or if out of such families more murderers are born? You will not have to be surprised about this!"[65] That Probst unselfconsciously expressed punitive affect about "work-shy" tendencies, or that Gröber's arguments lacked even the semblance of logical coherence, did not seem to matter. What was most significant and consequential was the accumulation of intense emotion that linked sexual freedom with death.

While the resistance to decriminalizing abortion provided an important fulcrum for efforts to renegotiate sexual values in the postwar years, the project of renegotiating those values was a far larger one. In the postwar situation of existential and ethical disorientation, both Catholics and Protestants also emphasized what they diagnosed as an omnipresent condition of sexual anomie. Conservative Catholic activists at the beginning of the 1950s, for instance, found in the evidence that some eighty sex-aid companies in the Federal Republic attracted tens of thousands of customers each month "a powerless attempt to extricate oneself from the general apathy and despair."[66] The head of the Social Service Office of the Protestant Church in Westphalia called attention to what he saw as a pervasive phenomenon of "satiety" or "ennui" (*Überdruss*) "resulting from the overvaluation of the erotic."[67] A conservative Christian woman writing in *Die Welt der Frau* (The World of the Woman) argued that "the plebeian freedom of the drive destroys every more tender relationship between the sexes, all higher development of humanity."[68] And Christian commentator

Hans March argued along similar lines that "once upon a time people repressed sexuality, now they are repressing love." This, he believed, was the source of much "bewilderment" and "suffering." Sex, he said, was available to "everyone, at any time"; what people were having trouble with were intimate relationships.[69]

Another prevalent approach, however, adapted the public's evident preoccupation with sexual happiness to a Christian message. Catholics and Protestants alike made the case that—contrary to Nazi-fostered clichés—Christianity was actually pro-pleasure. One of the main strategies among postwar Christian writers was to argue that Christian marital sex was especially ecstatic and that it offered more pleasure than secular vice. The Switzerland-based Protestant physician Theodor Bovet, for example, who published frequently in Germany and was extraordinarily popular and influential there, liked to announce that "for the Christian there is no contradiction between eros and divine love."[70] Catholic theologian Franz Arnold, complaining about what he saw as the Nazi stereotype that Christianity encouraged a "negation of nature . . . a defamation of eros and sex" (and lamenting that this "widely held notion" had "survived the downfall of the Third Reich and its blood mythos"), also argued that marital sex was a great thing.[71] In the "fundamental biblical texts," Arnold contended, "sexual pleasure within marriage is considered to be the God-willed *creation-ecstasy* [*Schöpfungswonne*] of those who carry on the work of the Creator in accordance with His thoughts."[72] Catholic commentator Roegele felt encouraged in 1948 that finally, "in our days," the Catholic Church's "traditional *defamation of the bodily* is dissolving," but he still felt that too many priests used the Sunday sermon to emphasize "the forbidden . . . the sinful" and wondered whether this was not the main reason for the oft-lamented "ineffectuality of the usual Sunday sermon." Roegele thought it would be better to stress that also the "bodily act" was an "*essential*" aspect of marriage, indeed that it was an inseparable part of the sacramental quality of marriage.[73]

Hans Wirtz's best-selling sex advice book for Catholics, *Vom Eros zur Ehe* (From Eros to Marriage, 1946), put this case even more strongly. Already popular under Nazism, the book sold even more copies after the war. It managed to get the apostolic imprimatur but was also a paean to the joys of wedded sex. In Wirtz's view, sexual satisfaction for both partners was essential to a healthy marriage; Wirtz encouraged husbands to become ever more expert at bringing their wives to orgasm. Although always invoking various church authorities, Wirtz on page after page also referred to the "weakness of the flesh," "the incredible force of the drives," the strength of "the sexual motor," the "revolt of the blood against the spirit," and "the giving of a thousand joys," as well as to the idea that "*eros* and *sexus* are essential to marriage. They are its *center*, not a side realm. They are its main point."[74]

Despite other variations, the unifying theme in Christian writings was the sanctity of marriage, and this certainly provided a major contrast to Nazism. What remains striking is how urgently Christians apparently felt they had to advance innovative arguments about the great sexual experiences to be found in marriage in order to get a public hearing in this era. Church-affiliated authors were in truth anything but prudish when it came to describing all the delightful, God-willed sexual activity that could be enjoyed by any couple joined in Christian union. But they also did not hesitate to predict dire outcomes for anyone who defied such advice. Catholic advice giver Hofmann, for instance, himself a fervent defender of women's "equal right" to the "rapturous haze" of orgasm (in fact, his argument against coitus interruptus was not just that seeking to prevent pregnancy was against church law but also that it deprived the woman of climax) stated as well that if a man had premarital sex, he heightened his risk of suffering from erectile dysfunction later in life and would probably be ruining all hope of marital happiness as a consequence. In general, Hofmann warned, "the full blissful richness of sexual love can only remain preserved undiminished for that person who has not violated it with untamed greed."[75] The Protestant Bovet was even more blunt: "Happy love is only possible within marriage." In his sex advice book specifically for girls, Bovet declared that whoever "wants to experience the whole pleasure of love [*die ganze Lust der Liebe*] cannot even consider experiencing it before or outside of marriage. It is as impossible as harvesting grapes in the snows of March. Only those who do not have an inkling of or do not respect mature love-lust can allow themselves the attempt to preempt it prematurely." Bovet went so far as to assert that "the majority of girls who wish for or tolerate premarital intercourse are not somehow especially passionate but, on the contrary, are those who repress their feelings or are indeed frigid."[76] Evidently, these advice writers hoped that their readers would be too fearful to gamble that such authoritatively delivered claims might simply be wrong. But the other point worth underscoring is that fear alone would not have drawn in an audience at this time; in post-Nazi Germany, Christians were clearly convinced, they had to make their case for more conservative mores on the grounds of pleasure.

At the same time, and despite their careful self-distancing from Nazism, Christian writers on sex also often picked right up where Nazi sex commentators had left off. This was particularly true when it came to the theory of eugenics, which retained a special hold on numerous postwar Christian thinkers. They appeared not in the least troubled by the fact that eugenic thinking had extraordinarily pernicious consequences under Nazism but rather veiled their ongoing attachment to eugenics (if only minimally) by bundling it together with paeans to orgasms and marital sex. For instance, the influential Catholic Werner Schöllgen not only offered the factually false but pro-orgasmic (and under Nazism recurrently advanced) argument that "often the actual source of a woman's infertility lies in her frigidity. . . . The full love experience thus has an objective meaning with respect to the child." He also spoke of pregnancy prevention as "biological suicide" and contended expressly that "the eugenic idea" had not lost its value despite "the abuse in the Third Reich."[77] Christian physician Meta Holland in 1950 reprinted her popular *Vor dem Tore der Ehe* (Before the Gate of Marriage)—which had previously appeared in 1936—in slightly altered form. The 1950 edition simply removed from the 1936 edition the glowing references to Hitler and the "purity of mores" in the "new Germany" along with her impassioned defense of the National Socialist sterilization program from a purportedly Christian point of view. It retained not only references to the claims of "race" and "tribe," but detailed delineation of the "eugenic" situations that made reproduction inadvisable or even immoral.[78] Catholic commentator Ernst Karl Winter in 1951 both emphasized the sacramental quality of Christian marriage (remarking as well that although "it was not in itself already the rediscovered paradise, it nonetheless indisputably carries within itself the possibility for the rebirth of [that paradise]") and declared that couples were obligated to conceive *"the highest number of physically and psychologically valuable offspring"* that they possibly could under their particular circumstances.[79] The pro-pleasure Protestant Bovet, for his part, insisted on the need to "be concerned with the healthy inheritance of our *Volk*." Bovet bemoaned the fact that "the less valuable elements, especially the mentally deficient, reproduce themselves approximately twice as much as healthy families. It is therefore absolutely necessary, if we do not one day want to be completely flooded by those [elements], that everyone who feels himself to be healthy . . . give life to as many children as possible."[80]

Defending Sex

While there were continuities between Nazism and postwar Christian commentators on sexuality, Christians at least could point to their critique of pre- and extramarital sex as *the* decisive difference between Nazi ideology and their world view. Secular defenders of nonmarital sex in the postwar period had a much more difficult time. The overtly risqué sex advice journal *Liebe und Ehe* (Love and Marriage), launched in Regensburg in 1949, represented a classic example of these difficulties (fig. 2.2). The journal was available by subscription and at magazine kiosks across the country, and it was important enough to attract contributions from dozens of popular medical and other publicists. It was one of the very few postwar venues in which pre- and extramarital heterosexuality (and,

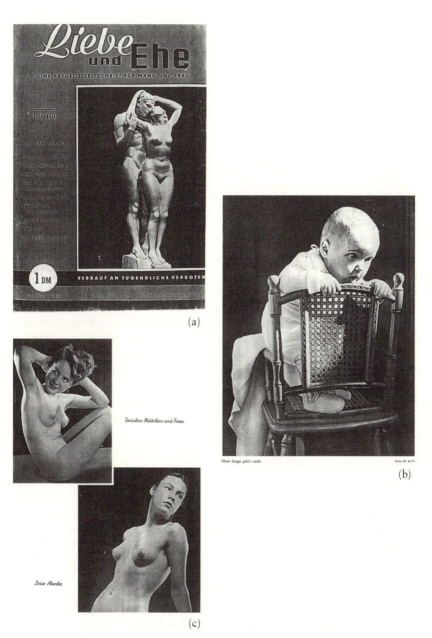

(a)

(b)

(c)

Figure 2.2. *Liebe und Ehe* 1, no. 1 (1949). Cover page (a); inside front cover (the caption for the picture of the baby reads: "can't do without that tongue!" and is clearly meant as a joke about cunnilingus) (b); and p. 21 (the captions say "between girl and woman" and "quiet resistance") (c).

although to a far lesser extent, also lesbianism and male homosexuality) were written about repeatedly and in detail. It is hence also no surprise that *Liebe und Ehe* would be sharply censured as "a dirty publication" by the federal government's Committee for Youth Welfare.[81] And it is striking how sensitive the (anonymous) editors were to antipornography sentiment. The photographs of female nudes, which had been so prevalent in the 1949 issues—replete with coy captions such as "between girl and woman" or "quiet resistance"—disappeared in the early months of 1950.[82] Contributors to *Liebe und Ehe* were clearly also sensitive to the strong association between Nazism and sexual incitement. As one contributor mockingly put it, it had been "reserved for National Socialism to wield a blow against German morality by establishing public processionals on the streets [to the brothels]."[83] Another noted as uncontroversial fact that the Nazi state was "morally degenerate" and had "specifically in the realm of family life championed principles that were utterly at variance with the custom and law of the centuries-old Western Christian culture."[84]

Numerous essays in *Liebe and Ehe*'s pages thus strove to find a new language in defense of the moral value of frank discussion of sex. The journal continually vacillated between assertions of the legitimacy of nonmarital sexual love and insistence on the importance of pleasurable sex to stable marriages. Contributors even drew on religious language. For example, as medical doctor Gerhard Ockel put it in 1951 in an essay endorsing cunnilingus as an "actually totally natural caress": "Wherever there is true love, is always sacred land, and all doing is pleasing to the Creator-power."[85] Or, as Dorothee Löhe put it in 1950, defending the nude sculptures of Georg Kolbe that had been so popular also during the Third Reich, it was obvious that "behind these naked human beings stands a chaste Creator." Kolbe, in her view, was motivated by a "deeply humble love of God and human beings."[86] In its search to make sex and sexual pleasure socially appropriate goals and topics, moreover, *Liebe und Ehe* continually moved back and forth between calling for greater sexual freedom and insisting that the public had already, as it were, voted with its bodies. Authors repeatedly expressed delight at the way, as one put it in 1950, "morality concepts have been in recent times extraordinarily transformed."[87] Or, as another author noted with pride, young girls in his day ("and by no means just the 'easy ones'") were turning away from their parents' mores and announcing "'I have a *right* to premarital love.'"[88]

Nonetheless, as with Christians, *Liebe und Ehe* too gave evidence of some unapologetic continuity with Nazi attitudes. And this was not just because of the strong resemblance between the sculptures of nudes favored by the journal and Nazi-approved artwork. Antisemitic and eugenic convictions were also expressed. One article asserted that "until the second world war the girls of the eastern states, especially also the eastern Jewesses, formed the main contingent of world prostitution."[89] And the author who had made fun of how the Nazis administered prostitution also wrote an essay in which he criticized the Nazi regime's and the Federal Republic's policy of giving "child money" to especially "child-rich" families—not, however, on the grounds that the Federal Republic's policies constituted an offensive continuation of Nazi attitudes toward the value of reproduction, but rather on grounds that under *both* regimes such policies only ended up benefiting the "irresponsible," alcoholic, and "unbridled." Indeed, the essay's main purpose was to defend eugenic sterilization of the "less talented" in the interests of the future health of the German *Volk*, now "pressed together into the most constricted space."[90]

Yet far more telling was the way Nazism functioned as a source of humor. It was above all the regime's racism, though also its homophobia, that commentators in *Liebe und Ehe* found amusing. Nowhere in its three years of existence did the journal articulate horror over these hateful elements of the Third Reich. Instead, the humor trivialized Nazism. A good example of humor about Nazi racism appeared in 1950 in an imaginative set of fake personal ads in cartoon form. Beginning with a sexy vestal virgin in 1500 B.C. and ending in a dystopian postatomic war future in 1958, the author, Hans von Hohenecken, offered a "little cultural history" of sexual mores. Von Hohenecken not only managed to make fun of post–World War II women's desperation to find a mate: the tattered woman in the nuclear wreckage of 1958 is looking for an "English-speaking Sibiro-Russian" and is willing to put up with being a man's "secondary wife" (*Nebenfrau*). He also treated as comedic (even as he underscored the reality of) both the persistence of racist attitudes into the post-Nazi period and the ineffectuality of denazification when he had the unattractive middle-aged former Nazi Party official in 1948 assure all potentially interested females that he had been cleared, that he had a home of his own and a secure pension, and that only young women "of the best race and attitude" need apply.[91]

A thoroughly incoherent multipart 1951 essay on "Sexual Problems in the SS" provided another prime example of *Liebe und Ehe*'s jesting side. The author, Martin Brustmann, a doctor of sports medicine, gave equal attention to what he saw as the SS's heterosexual, homosexual, and homophobic proclivities. Brustmann made fun both of the "exhaustion to the point of work-incapacity" induced in young SS men by the hordes of women willingly offering themselves to them, and of Himmler's disorientation in the face of spreading homosexual incidents within the SS. Among other things, Brustmann was especially entertained by the way Himmler's homophobia bore resemblance to the teachings of the Old Testament (i.e., the "Jewish" part of the Bible), a fact Himmler had been "embarrassed" to have pointed out to him. Unable, moreover, to decide whether the enforced policy of nude bathing encouraged the always well-built SS men in torrid fantasies of each other's "bronzed thighs," or whether homosexuality was the result of criminal elements "sneaking" their way into the SS, Brustmann reported both that the SS curriculum included analysis of differential male penis size and that Himmler had been "forced" to institute the death penalty for homosexuality because male prostitutes were stealing SS uniforms and making big money offering johns the chance to "desecrate the Führer's dress." Interspersed with these discussions, Brustmann offered details of Himmler deputy Reinhard Heydrich's supposedly persistent problems with premature ejaculation.[92]

Brustmann also shared the news that circumcision (because of infected foreskins) was "one of the most frequently performed operations within the SS":

> The lengthening of the duration of coitus due to circumcision, which made the problem of the frigid woman relatively infrequent among Jews and Mohammedans, now also benefited the SS, and it repeatedly brought on raucous hilarity when the SS men had to let themselves be told that they owed the advantages of this operation to that place in the Bible's Old Testament in which Jehovah sealed his covenant with Israel.

Distancing himself from Nazi racism by designating the circumcision story as a key example of "the paradox" and "the cunning of history," Brustmann at other points also repeated racist Nazi stereotypes (among other things, announcing himself amused at how many regime-serving Germans needed to be declared "honorary Aryans" because the much-fabled *Jud Süss* had managed to leave behind such "numerous traces" of his sexual activity across southern Germany).[93] In short, by repeatedly shifting his point of view, Brustmann made it possible for readers both to identify *with* the laughing Nazis and to laugh *at* them. This doubleness of identification and disidentification with Nazism was an important tactic in early efforts to manage the memory of the Third Reich.[94]

There were further tactics for managing the memory of Nazism in *Liebe und Ehe*. These tactics depended on the diffuse but powerful assumption that heterosexual relations in postwar Germany were not in a healthy state. Calls to restabilize the family and reorder gender relations provided important occasions for obscuring the contributory role played by both Nazism and total war in the production of the postwar sexual crisis.

For example, Gerhard Giehm, in his 1948 book on "the treatment of mental and nervous sexual disorders," excerpted in *Liebe und Ehe*'s first issue, distanced himself from the peculiar intensity of concern with sex in postwar Germany. Giehm declared that the postwar period's preoccupation with sex had something to do with the totality of Germany's defeat: "The 'sexual gospel' is the bible of the sick, the conquered, and abnormal. It was the faith of the defeated in the transvaluation of all values." And he defined the "sexual gospel" as "that dogma about the preeminence of the sexual in the spiritual life of human beings, which gained significance in the debacle of the postwar time, but which soon will be superseded once the atmosphere of decline has been overcome." Giehm instead yearned for "healthy relations of the sexes, which, strengthened through the tie of the child, pass on the inheritance of the present and past to the future, in order in this way to make the existence and rights-to-recognition of a *Volk* eternal." In this way, Giehm succeeded in displacing "that dogma about the preeminence of the sexual" away from Nazism and onto its defeat. At the same time, he effectively denied the manifest continuities between his vision and Nazism's. For Giehm also engaged in antisemitic allusions, denigrating those interested in "drive-drivenness" and "the mysterious regions of the unconscious" (clear references to Freudianism and Jewishness, which he associated with sexual "sickness") while calling in quasi-Christian terms for "the resurrection of a healthy humanity." And Giehm further invoked the time-honored but Nazi-reinforced distinction between the Jew and the Greek when he contended that the new age had "smashed the commandment tablets" of the previous moment and soon would be "celebrating the human of antiquity."[95]

Seemingly much more innocent tactics were evident in Dorothee Löhe's effort to revive traditional gender relations in her defense of the Kolbe statue (of a man protectively guarding the woman also striding forward beside him). Her praise of the spirituality of these nudes provided Löhe with the hook for fantasizing about the restoration of a kind of "coupledom" in which the man would once again be the stronger partner, and in which a new race of people, a new humanity (*ein neues Geschlecht*), would be regenerated by this reinvigorated couple. Her concluding hope was that these new human beings, "through their loving union," would "find their way back to the paradise we seem to have lost."[96] What was evident here, as in Giehm, was a kind of postfascist nostalgia, even as it was left decidedly unclear to what the nostalgia referred. Was the fascist era the lost paradise, or was the paradise some prefascist time? And what caused the paradise to be lost? Nazism? Or its collapse—or something else? Löhe's abstruseness about causes was not unique but rather part of a much more prevalent phenomenon in the late 1940s and early 1950s.[97] Meanwhile, the fervent hope for regeneration of heterosexual relationships that she also expressed showed just how signally important the restoration of conservative gender relations would become in the project of mastering both Nazism and its downfall.

RESTORING GERMAN MANHOOD

In the aftermath of Germany's defeat, as one man confessed to his psychiatrist, "I could not adjust to a world in which I would no longer be ruling over others." The end of the war was, in his view, unfortunately also the end of "the five-year rule of the minority over the majority." In his opinion, he had become "a victim of the era. . . . I had been betrayed, my faith in the destiny of Germans as lords of the earth had been broken."[98] It was not only privately that sentiments like these were expressed, and some commentators reflecting on the defeat of Nazism expressly analyzed its psychological and even physiological dimensions.[99]

German masculinity was thought to be in particular trouble. Physician Walter Frederking, when asked in 1947 to comment on the "crisis of marriage," put the problem like this: "The dominance of the man, which was so strongly emphasized in the Third Reich, has collapsed to a considerable degree. . . . In addition, the male gender is hit harder in its soul by the lost war than the female." Frederking noted that "all these confusions and shifts now reach deep into the drive-life and the events of the body. The doctor naturally hears much about this. Again and again he is told how frequently the male bodily functions are impaired, and those affected are also able to tell that they have heard similar things from many an acquaintance." At the same time, however, Frederking observed that "the female feeling- and drive-life is apparently not disturbed to such an extent." Frederking alluded to German guilt—though possibly he was also referring to ambivalence about denazification.[100] But his main aim was to solicit women's participation in restoring new life to "the fundamental relationship between man and woman." Sadly remarking that it was impossible at that point to know how gender relations would be configured in the future, Frederking took comfort in the knowledge that "the most important thing about the relations of the genders to each other will after all remain that they are different from each other."[101]

Along related lines, as one anonymous man informed the female readers of *Constanze* in 1948, men were not the superb types they once had been. Strategically asserting that "The men feel it, more or less, that something is rotten in the state of man. . . . We men are finished," he proposed that the man's decline "as husband, as politician, as 'head of the household,' as lover—as man pure and simple" had multiple sources, not least of which was that "We no longer have a gun in our arms and we can no longer tell you heroic stories." Meanwhile, however, the author also managed both to ridicule Nazis as the ultimate male losers—people who should have been "thoroughly spanked" because, "although even the stupidest must have known after Stalingrad that their looting expedition crisscrossing through the world would go wrong, they nonetheless for years went on sacrificing millions of human beings in order to rescue their own pathetic lives"—*and* to blame overly rigorous denazification and the lost war for the decline in high-quality manliness. The only solution was to restore heterosexual domesticity. Calling woman "the healthier sex," with "the stronger weapons," the author enumerated those weapons as "her whole great unshakeable nature, her instinct for the practical and immediate, her dexterity" in running the household, and the "singular magic" with which, in a time of pitifully low male salaries, the woman managed daily to get lunch on the table and keep the laundry clean.[102]

Yet another contribution to *Constanze* in 1948 came from the writer and psychologist Walther von Hollander, one of the most influential advice givers of the postwar period. In his three-part essay on "The Man in Crisis," von Hollander acknowledged that women were experiencing a "generalized disappointment" with the men in their lives. In the most recent war, women had found out for themselves that "the average man is no hero" and that apparently "also in this respect men were no longer worth unquestioning female surrender." This tragedy was experienced concretely in one marriage after another with the "return home of the conquered man." Yet even as he hinted at the reasons for the decline of a certain brand of masculinity, announcing that what was most corroding marriages was "the question of guilt . . . guilt for all this catastrophe and mess," and acknowledging that "the man with his politics, his greed for power . . . his worship of violence, his cockiness when successful, and his whininess in defeat" were core causes of both the most disastrous effects of Nazism and the disjointed state of postwar affairs, von Hollander was already working to set things right.[103]

Astutely pointing out, both in this essay and in response to a reader's letter, that women had not exactly been guiltless either under Nazism (while Germany was still undefeated, had women not "preferred the man of power, the victor?" and did women not themselves "worship power" and "love uniforms"?), von Hollander nonetheless, and simultaneously, elaborated normative notions of gender difference and trivialized—again by leaving deliberately fuzzy—what it was about Nazism that made it so catastrophic (the crimes or the defeat?).[104] It would thus be no surprise that in the later installments of the essay, von Hollander was able to suggest that "only one thing" could lead women and men out of the current "abyss," and that was love. Criticizing what he saw as the proliferation of "casual love" and insisting on women's "inextinguishable yearning for the superiority of the man," von Hollander lamented that most postwar women lacked "that pliancy and femininity, that atmosphere of the playful, the cheerful vibrancy, that the man simply needs from the woman." As von Hollander summarily observed, "That by becoming similar to the man, woman has become more empty of love as well, this seems to us to be proven. That love, the woman's true life-element, can only be re-created by the woman, seems to us clear."[105]

Women too made comparable arguments. Thus, for instance, in a *Constanze* essay by Else Feldbinder on "He and She 1948," Feldbinder, like many of her male contemporaries, also decried what she saw as the loss of "spiritual tension" between the sexes and therefore of "the magic of eros." Feldbinder regretted as well that "the maxim of equal rights has dissolved the maxim of chivalry." And significantly, while acknowledging long-term trends toward equality of the sexes existing since the French Revolution and simultaneously hoping that the transformation of gender relations was a temporary aberration due to the inevitable "brutalization" produced by total war, Feldbinder nonetheless singled out "the Nazi era" for ruining the "majority of men" with its "plebeian heroism" and for "trampling down every seed of a chivalrous feeling in a whole generation." As in the writings of von Hollander, so also for Feldbinder, the way to cure Germany of its ills was to bring back high-quality romance.[106]

The point that deserves to be emphasized is that the restoration of heterosexual domesticity as an ideal via an intensely normative rhetoric of romantic love was anything but an innocent apolitical enterprise. This is not just because it involved a cruel slap at those who remained involuntarily single, or because it cajoled those women "lucky" enough to be married into putting up with all manner of male deficiencies (from bossiness to boorishness to unwillingness to participate in housecleaning or childrearing). The rhetoric of romantic love, and the injunction to women to redevelop their "cheerful" femininity and to rebuild German men into more "chivalrous" exemplars of manhood, also had the effect of banalizing Nazism and downplaying many of its most hideous aspects. The argument *all you need is love* pretended that all that had to be overcome were dysfunctional relationships. Meanwhile, and quite concretely, the breezily upbeat suggestions for restoring vibrancy and constancy to heterosexual partnerships also played their part in diverting attention from the ongoing persecution of homosexuals in the postwar era.

PARAGRAPH 175

The gradual reconstruction of a domesticated heterosexuality coincided with a renewed commitment to the criminalization of homosexuality among men. Although initially there was a moment of openness and freedom with regard to homosexual activity among men in the postwar period, it did not last long. While antisemitism in the postwar period became largely confined to the private sphere and was replaced by a (however superficial) official philosemitism, homophobia reacquired respectability. Nazi-era assumptions about sexual orientation profoundly shaped postwar approaches to the subject.

Paragraph 175 criminalized "coitus-like" behavior between men, and was adopted from Prussia's legal code when Germany unified in 1871. Activists in the Weimar Republic, under the leadership of Magnus Hirschfeld, came close to getting it wiped off the books; had the NSDAP not taken over the reins of government in 1933, it was possible that it could have disappeared that year.[107] The National Socialists both expanded the scope of the law (in part through the addition of 175a) to all same-sex activity between men; this included mutual touching or even individual masturbation engaged in side by side and in some cases even "erotic glances." The Nazis also significantly sharpened and expanded the scope of punishments for violations of the paragraph to include longer prison and workhouse sentences, sentences to concentration camps, and castration. But the Nazi era also saw an efflorescence of theorizing about homosexuality.

As discussed in chapter 1, one of the distinctive features of Nazi conceptualizations of homosexuality was the contention that homosexuality was a potentiality in almost all men. Although Nazi-era publicists often assumed that homosexuality was an ineradicable identity for a distinct minority, the fact that they were perpetually preoccupied with sorting out what they thought was the very small number of "true" homosexuals from the larger group of "pseudohomosexuals" also suggested the familiarity many commentators had with the idea, as one doctor put it in 1937, that there were "fluid *transitions*" (*laufende* Übergänge) between hetero- and homosexuality.[108] Some specialists fantasized that hormonal treatments could turn even "true" homosexuals into "normal feeling and therefore, in every area, normal acting members of our *Volk* community."[109] Others emphasized psychotherapeutic approaches. Nazi-era writers recurrently thematized how difficult it could be for men to develop desire for women, and thus they competed to understand the kind of homosexual activity engaged in by youth "in puberty, when the sexual character is not yet sharply delineated," or to offer perspectives on men who "could not . . . find the way to the woman" because of "failure to breach the barrier of pubescent insecurity."[110] While at least some of these perspectives could have been used for antihomophobic purposes, they all in fact facilitated the expansion—and murderous radicalization—of criminal prosecutions for homosexuality.

The brutal impact of Paragraphs 175 and 175a during the Third Reich was public knowledge in postwar Germany, and in the initial postwar years courts across Germany came to quite different decisions on violations of Paragraph 175 or 175a. Sometimes they upheld harsh sentencing, often in conjunction with elaborate defenses of the law's ongoing necessity, while at other times they rejected jail and prison sentences entirely, either opting for court-ordered psychiatric treatment or, in a few cases, openly challenging the legitimacy of the law and letting defendants go free with just a small symbolic fine (or a remark that the time served was already adequate). Most cases did result in sentencing, but, again, there were courts that chose reduced prison terms—for example, fifteen months instead of the prescribed five or ten years. It was apparent to all parties involved that court behavior varied by region, and by individual judges, and that the administration of the paragraph was in a state of limbo.[111]

Whether their aim was to abolish or to defend Paragraph 175, both sides struggled to find persuasive arguments to advance their cause. In this indeterminate situation, defendants could have little way to guess what strategy might be effective in court. Some defendants (and their lawyers) used the same tactic developed under Nazism (and which had often been essential for any chance of survival then); they insisted that they were in truth heterosexual and were guilty only of a momentary lapse. As the liberal magazine *Der Spiegel* observed, to admit to homosexuality during the Third Reich meant the defendant's "path into the concentration camp (pink triangle on the breast) and, at some point, castration were certain."[112] Others risked the opposite strategy, now that the Third Reich had been defeated; they averred that they were in truth homosexual, that homosexuality was a powerful part of their lives, and that they really had no choice but to conflict with the law. In essence, they threw themselves on the mercy of the court. Sometimes, as in Frankfurt in 1950, during a massive police and court action which brought 700 investigations and 140 prosecutions (many of them based on denunciations proffered by one young male prostitute), defendants faced the same man as judge, Kurt Romini, who had also been their prosecutor during the Third Reich. Testifying to their "irresistible natural drive" toward homosexual activity could not convince the self-styled expert Romini, who remembered these men from a few years earlier. (The action ended in numerous prison sentences and at least six suicides [fig. 2.3].)[113]

Those in favor of abolishing the paragraph, or of rewriting and limiting it considerably (for instance, decriminalizing homosexual acts conducted in private between consenting adult men, while retaining as crimes homosexual prostitution or sex with a minor) were themselves in disagreement over how best to present their case. The best-known campaign, coordinated by the sexologist Hans Giese and his Institute for Sex Research in Frankfurt under the broader auspices of the German Society for Sex Research, made the case that the paragraph was incompatible with the Basic Law (West Germany's equivalent of a constitution) on two grounds:

Figure 2.3. *Freundschaft*, March 1951. Mourning the suicides in the wake of the 1950–51 Frankfurt am Main trials of men accused of homosexuality. *Freundschaft* (Friendship) was one of the few homophile magazines published in the 1950s.

that it conflicted with the Basic Law's guarantee of each individual's right to "free development of the personality" (guaranteed as long as this development did not contradict "moral law" [*das Sittengesetz*]), and that the paragraph conflicted with the Basic Law's guarantee of equality between men and women (since lesbian activity was not illegal and men were thus unfairly treated).[114]

Giese contended that thinking about sex in Germany had to change in more substantive ways as well. Sex needed to be taken seriously on its own terms, in its "own peculiarity," and one should stop making the mistake of "postulating sexuality as a means for the reproductive preservation [*Arterhaltung*] of humanity (or a group or even race)." Sexuality, Giese argued, was first and foremost "a drive that belongs to the sphere of interpersonal contact." But Giese also stressed the damages done by criminalizing sexual behavior: homosexuals were reduced to playacting, to seeming rather than being, for most of their lives. According to Giese, the constant performance by gay men of a straight self led "usually to neurosis, occasionally to criminality, in a few rare cases to the breakthrough of genius"; the need to suppress the drive due to the "unignorably intolerant stance of the public" led to derailing lapses; the vulnerability to blackmail was ever-present; self-destructiveness was almost inevitable.[115]

At the same time, Giese's strongest supporters advanced quite divergent arguments against Paragraph 175. Thus, for instance, one of the lawyers involved in the campaign, Horst Pommerening, made a point of emphasizing that every so-called perversion among heterosexuals was legally irrelevant and thus that the law's punitive treatment of homosexuals was incoherent on its own terms. He also stressed both how powerfully felt a homosexual disposition was—like an "*Ur*-drive" (*Urtrieb*)—and that homosexuals varied as much as heterosexuals, with both ranging from the libertine to the idealistic and nobly tender.[116] The law professor Karl Siegfried Bader, while also explicitly favoring decriminalization, actually disagreed with Giese that the paragraph was unconstitutional. Bader was convinced that the German populace was on the whole so hostile to homosexuality that—given the Basic Law's reference to the vague but potent category of "moral law"—there could be no hope of arguing that the paragraph was inconsistent with the Basic Law. While worried that moving too fast would lead to a homophobic popular backlash, Bader did believe that consenting homosexual acts between adults should not be a crime; what consensual adults did behind closed doors was their business, and the law had no place there.[117]

Those not directly involved with the campaign made yet other anti-175 arguments. A liberal-minded higher court in Hamburg in 1951 made a double point as it set aside the prison terms ordered by a lower court for two homosexual defendants. The higher court's ruling not only asked people to "consider what a role the sex drive plays in the life of human beings," and thus to what an extent the law's insistence that a homosexual suppress his drive made demands on the homosexual that "go far beyond the demands that the law otherwise directs . . . at a human being." The court also challenged those jurists who acted as if homosexual behaviors mattered in legal decision making by noting the variability of *heterosexual* behaviors; it pointed out succinctly, as Pommerening had, that just as promiscuity or perversity was legally irrelevant among heterosexuals, so also they ought to be legally irrelevant among homosexuals.[118]

The newsmagazine *Der Spiegel*, a forceful opponent of Paragraph 175, clearly saw those who continued to uphold the paragraph and supported renewed persecution of homosexuals as part of a broader politically conservative agenda. With withering sarcasm, the magazine speculated as to the various potential paranoid and repressive motives for the massive wave of arrests in Frankfurt. (These included: homosexuals could do nothing to replenish the badly depleted German population; homosexuals would infiltrate the civil service; homosexuality could not be tolerated because no sexual activity whatsoever before or outside of marriage was permissible.) *Der Spiegel* also cited the Kinsey report as advancing the sensible notion that there was no scientific basis to traditional classifications of "normal" and "abnormal"; at best, one could speak of "common" and "uncommon" behaviors. And the magazine wondered what exactly the difference was between someone who had once or twice been involved with a male prostitute and someone who had occasionally "fallen into a female hooker's trap."[119]

Supporters of Paragraph 175, however, took the view, as one jurist phrased it, that the purpose of the paragraph was to protect "the German *Volk* in its moral and healthful strength."[120] Numerous jurists also refuted the imputation of gender injustice by arguing that women's sexuality was dramatically different from men's. Women were more "shy" and "reticent" and in their love lives tended more toward "solid ties" than men. Lesbianism simply did not cause the same social problems that male homosexuality did; lesbianism did not constitute the same affront to the public.[121] Most frequently, supporters of the paragraph strongly emphasized the need to protect youth and repeatedly invoked the belief that male homosexuality was a contagious condition that would spread ineluctably unless forceful punitive action was taken. Over and over they stressed the vulnerability of youth to homosexual "seduction."[122]

Most Christian commentators opposed decriminalization. A book published by the archconservative Catholic moral purity organization, the Volkswartbund, actually pleaded for consistency and asked that lesbianism be criminalized as well. The book doubted whether there was any such thing as inborn or "true" homosexuality or, if so, argued that it must affect only a tiny percentage of people. Paragraph 175 was essential for the purpose of deterrence and because homosexuality simply was a "moral perversion and thereby a crime against nature"; because the Basic Law protected marriage, "consequently those who disdain marriage must be punished."[123] The journal *Christ und Welt* (The Christian and the World) expressed repugnance at the idea advanced by Giese's campaign that sexual self-determination could be seen as part of the guaranteed "free development of the personality." "Divine law" opposed this. "Sick" people might be innately homosexually disposed, but for someone to acquire a full-fledged homosexual identity, the disposition needed to be triggered. This is why homosexuality could not be legalized, even if psychiatric care might be better than prison terms. The rise in incidence of homosexuality, especially among youth, was "frighteningly high" and "unmistakably spreading." Clergymen needed to utilize the "depression" often presented by incarcerated homosexuals to help lead these people "back to the center of existence and to an inner renewal."[124]

The support given by the churches to antidecriminalization efforts had a decisive impact.[125] By 1954 a judge at the Federal Constitutional Court could summarily observe that "case law nearly unanimously takes the view that Paragraph 175 is compatible with the Basic Law."[126] Recurrent efforts to challenge Paragraph 175—either on grounds of unconstitutionality or on grounds that it represented an inheritance of Nazi *racial* law and hence should be considered invalid due to the occupiers' revocation of all laws related to Nazi racism—all failed.[127] The law was not modified until 1969. During the 1950s and 1960s, close to 100,000 men suspected of homosexual acts were registered in police files; every year brought between 2,500 and 3,500 convictions. As the historian of religion and anti-175 activist Hans Joachim Schoeps once remarked in retrospect, "for homosexuals, the Third Reich actually only ended in 1969."[128]

The persistence of homophobia into the postwar era has been well documented. What has been less frequently acknowledged is that, to a remarkable degree, the notion that men had a potentially bisexual disposition, and that young men in particular were vulnerable to conversion via seduction, was explicitly named as *the* reason for retaining Paragraph 175. This, and not, as is often assumed, any concern with homosexuals' failure to reproduce or refusal to live up to ideals of tough manliness, was the decisive conceptual legacy of Nazi homophobia for the postwar period. As one Protestant pastor surveying the state of postwar juridical decisions concluded in 1953, "what remains is the necessity . . . to protect developing youth during the time of their bisexual lability and homosexual receptiveness."[129] While an acute and deeply felt awareness of the fragility of heterosexuality might well have led to identification across the fluid and entirely permeable boundaries that distinguished one sexual orientation from another, that awareness instead became the very thing to bolster those boundaries.

It is quite likely that one key factor in making the notion that homosexuality could best be understood as a deficit of heterosexual attraction appear plausible to postwar Germans had to do with the actual experiences of men during the Second World War. However ironically, the war launched by a virulently homophobic Nazi regime put millions of men into homosocial environments. While some men stayed faithful to their girlfriends and wives on the home front and others turned to (consensual or coerced) sex with women in the territories militarily occupied by Germany, yet other men (or sometimes the same men) turned to each other. He had been the "whore of the company," a man said starkly after the war, in the context of having been caught once again in a homosexual act.[130] Three other men caught after the war argued that they had only turned to sex with men because of the racial prohibitions against sex with women in the occupied territories.[131] Another man described how he had avoided the greatest hardships in military service by serving as a "boy toy" (*Lustknabe*) for four military officers who, every two weeks, played cards and drank and then took turns penetrating him.[132] In the survey conducted in 1949 by the Institute for Demoscopy, 23 percent of the men questioned admitted having "contact with" homosexuality at some point in their lives.[133] Also indicative is that among the battery of herbal and hormonal remedies alleged to cure the ills of an unfulfilled and dysfunctional sex life that were marketed in the postwar years (with names like "Sexogen," "Sanursex," "Sexal," and "Libidin"), doctors especially praised the hormonal remedy "Bisexon." They found it effective in addressing the triple threats of premature ejaculation, impotence, and male homosexuality—an imaginative linkage that underscores once more how homo- and heterosexuality were understood to exist on a continuum.[134] Indeed, postwar doctors expressly assumed that any soldier who was "unable to find the way to the woman" (i.e., his wife) after his return home must have had either literal homosexual experiences or at least unconscious homosexual attractions during war and postwar imprisonments.[135] Not only, then, did postwar homophobia accompany a more general effort to return sexuality to the marital framework from which it had so demonstratively escaped during the Third Reich and the immediate postwar period. The revitalization of homophobia under democratic and Christian auspices appears also, at one and the same time, to have been fueled by individual memories of encounters with homosexuality in wartime and to have depended on the suppression of those memories.[136]

THE PEOPLE OF THE FUTURE

There are many ways to think about the ascendance of conservative norms in the course of the 1950s. One point that deserves emphasis is the extent of masochism expected from women. Another area that clearly deserves emphasis, and that manifested itself so peculiarly and disturbingly in post-Nazi Germany, has to do with the ever-symbiotic relationship between hetero- and homosexuality. These developments could be read simply as variants on the ways Cold War McCarthyite witchhunts destroyed American homosexuals' lives (even as homophobia during the 1950s in the United States was also used to police heterosexuals' behavior), just as the expectation of female self-sacrifice had its American counterpart as well.[137] But that would be missing a number of larger issues specific to German history.

The open and extensive discussion in the late 1940s and early 1950s of heterosexual dysfunction, and the flux and contest of competing interpretations of the state of sexual crisis, ought to be read not just as a prelude to the injunctions to and policing of conformist domesticity that came to characterize the later 1950s. This moment needs also to be taken seriously on its own terms as a time when a remarkable range of social actors acknowledged the complexities of sex—when rather than treating sex as an inevitably coherent and marvelous whole in which desire, mutuality and satisfaction, activity and feeling, were all in seamless continuity, the component aspects were picked apart. What felt out of kilter, and was thrown into question, were the very notions of desires and drives. And no less striking was the evident attention given to the interrelationships between social conditions, ideologies, bodies, and psyches—the shared conviction, no matter how different the analyses were otherwise, that sex was a social and political and not just a personal matter.

Yet the increasingly stultifying sexual conservatism evident in the 1950s would not be just the German version of an international trend in the West toward conservative gender roles and saccharine familialism. Instead, the insistence on sexual propriety that ultimately came to dominate West German culture in the mid- to late 1950s provided a displaced but nonetheless profoundly significant means for Germans to manage the legacy of guilt and shame over the Holocaust and so many other grotesque and brutal aspects of Nazism.[138]

Numerous scholars are beginning to call for a more differentiated portrait of what used to be described as the postwar era of "amnesia" or "silence" about the Nazi past, a silence supposedly only broken by the student rebellions of the late 1960s. As the writings on sex in the postwar period confirm, there was no particular silence. It was specifically through the talk, the incessant insistent chatter, not the silence, that memory was

managed and Nazism normalized. Among the divergent—mutually conflicting and overlapping—postwar constituencies of church-affiliated authors, sensualists, medical professionals, and mainstream advice givers,
there was not just a repudiation of Nazism but rather a variety of compromise formations that consisted of contradictory mixes of rupture and continuity, acknowledgment and disavowal, exaggeration and trivialization.
Nazi racism and militarism were considered outrages by some, but for
many they were jokes; eugenic ideas retained appeal among otherwise
opposed constituencies. Strong masculinity was in disrepute and heterosexuality was in crisis *both* because of Nazism *and* because of its defeat;
women were both emboldened and endangered by this state of affairs.
Homosexuals purportedly continued to pose a danger to youth precisely
because all people innately had bisexual capacities. Above all, straight
male egos needed boosting. Out of this incoherent jumble the sexual conservatism of the mid- to late 1950s and early 1960s emerged. Heteronormativity in the contemporary United States, it has been observed, "con-
sists less of norms that could be summarized as a body of doctrine than
of a sense of rightness produced in contradictory manifestations."[139] This
notion is useful for understanding some of the dynamics at work in post–
World War II West Germany as well. For there it was exactly the discor-
dant clamor of often mutually conflicting attempts to manage the postwar
"sexual crisis" and "marital crisis" that ultimately together contributed
to the normalization of the memory of Nazism—and to the ability to find
new justifications for the continuation of some Nazi-era policies.

The pressure to adopt conservative conformity would be so overwhelming to young people coming of age in the mid- to late 1950s that,
by the time they rebelled in the mid- to late 1960s, they had no idea that
the late 1940s had once been described as an era of "erotic liberality" or
even "erotic overstimulation," and that there had once been a moment
when numerous members of their parents' generation had openly debated among themselves whether promiscuity was happy-making or
not.[140] When the 1960s most famous sex reformer Oswalt Kolle announced in 1969 that the masses had "for centuries been kept from the
most simple basic information," no one challenged him on this point.[141]
Liebe und Ehe had ceased publication at the end of 1951. The main sexological book series, *Beiträge zur Sexualforschung* (Contributions to Sex
Research) became—with the exception of only a few volumes—increasingly conservative in the course of the 1950s. Among other things, contributors attacked Kinsey's methods, associated lesbianism with criminality, and concerned themselves with the elucidation of sexual pathologies
and the elaboration of norms of properly reproductive familialism.[142]
Meanwhile, *Constanze* became ever more of a fashion magazine; already
by the mid-1950s its pages were filled with advice on humoring one's

husband, home decorating, and correct behavior, and there was no hint of its former liberality in sexual matters. Gone were the days when a contributor to *Constanze* could nonchalantly write that a marriage entered into for financial maintenance was both an outdated and a "moldy arrangement," or when another could assert as self-evident the idea that "it is by no means a settled matter, whether one, if one must forgo marriage, must also forgo the experience with the man."[143] Christian literature came to dominate the sex advice market, and with Family Minister Wuermeling's direction and support—and despite the emergence of a few new liberal voices in the late 1950s—conservative politicians and publicists continued to set the terms of public debate about sex until well into the 1960s. By the late 1960s, the young rebels could rightly complain that there was no mention of pleasure in sex enlightenment literature; reproduction and venereal disease formed the main topics. Already by 1963, when the survey on sexual attitudes first conducted in 1949 was repeated, the percentages of interviewees endorsing and admitting to premarital sex had dropped by more than ten percentage points.[144]

Lost to subsequent memory was also what commentators in the later 1940s and early 1950s had known full well, and uncontroversially: that Nazism itself had encouraged pre- and extramarital heterosexuality. The resolution of the postwar "sexual crisis" in a conservative direction was accompanied by the erasure of the memory both of the postwar liberality and of the very fact of the existence of a considerable amount of pleasurable activity during the years of mass murder. Numerous statements made by members of the generation of 1968 attest to their belief that their parents' lives had been shaped by "prudery" and "taboos," and that "in the 1930s they had had communicated to them an unhappy, lifeless, pleasureless attitude."[145] New Leftists were convinced that "obscenity was not symbolized by a naked female body but rather the polished boots of a general"; they had not a clue, for example, that images of naked female bodies—often with quite graphic detail—had actually been pervasive in Nazi sculpture and painting.[146] The avant garde role played by the New Left student movement within the sexual revolution of the 1960s was nurtured by intensely held convictions that the Third Reich was sex-hostile and pro-family, and that the Holocaust was the perverted product of sexual repression. Yet, as the next chapter describes, the conservative sexual mores of the mid- to late 1950s and early 1960s were not a direct inheritance from Nazism, as the student movement believed, but rather a new postwar invention, developed also in complex reaction against Nazism.

At the same time, what cannot be emphasized enough is that while the fact that the Third Reich had been in many respects a quite libertine time for "racially fit" heterosexuals was expeditiously elided, many of the most cruel aspects of Nazism were uncomplicatedly endorsed. Indeed many medical experts continued to advance the same arguments they had made before 1945 and found themselves approvingly cited for doing so. Numerous commentators clearly felt there was not much to be embarrassed or ashamed about. Postwar legal commentators on homosexuality routinely invoked Nazi-era specialists as though they continued to be uncontroversial experts and noted with calm neutrality rather than horror the intensified persecution homosexuals had experienced under Nazism. Murderous homophobia, or experiments done on prisoners, were apparently nothing from which one needed to distance oneself.[147] Postwar physicians also cited the research done on female prisoners' menstrual cycles while they were awaiting execution as though there was no problem with the context in which the research had been done.[148]

Nazis' intensified prosecution of abortion providers—to take another example—was also not perceived as a problem requiring critical comment. Hans Harmsen, for instance, the president of Pro Familia, the German equivalent of Planned Parenthood, in 1953 openly celebrated National Socialist success in reducing abortion rates by (as he directly specified) introducing harsher sentences in 1933 and the death penalty for abortionists in 1943. In what can only be called an astonishing rewriting of reality in view of both the Holocaust and the thousands of abortions enforced on foreign laborers and prisoners of war, Harmsen declared that "under systematic and comprehensive care for the family in the time after 1933, in which every child was greeted as welcome, the number of abortions dropped dramatically."[149]

Just as noteworthy was the utterly unapologetic continuity in disdain for the disabled and embrace of eugenic perspectives. Self-described Christian Hans March in 1955 criticized the notion that "everyone has a right to love" and worried about the "racial-hygienic consequences" of free love, among them the "degeneration of a *Volk*." Explicitly suggesting that the Third Reich had been a good time for the health of the *Volk*, March said:

> Behind us lies an era that was filled with the demands and insights of the need for a conscious racial hygiene and scientific eugenics. In this context some prominent researchers mentioned the high responsibility of a marriage founded on love. Among these . . . [was] Hermann Muckermann [the influential Catholic eugenicist, who also opposed marriages between Jews and Germans], from whom we have the important comment that "only lasting monogamous marriage can be the racial-hygienic wellspring for the people of the future." There is no other way to keep the hereditary foundation pure. . . . Whoever also still today cares about the physical and psychic well-being of the *Volk* cannot insistently enough be reminded of the danger of experimenting in this area under the clanging slogan of progressive marriage- and sex-reform.[150]

The first seven or eight postwar years, in sum, were a time of libertarianism and of open possibilities. And they were a time that can aptly be described, in sociologist Y. Michal Bodemann's words, as "the late Nazi phase" (*spätnazistische Phase*).[151] The moment of admission of the non-normalcy and genuine difficulty of heterosexuality coincided with the mobilization of numerous conservative and restorationist efforts that experimented with different strategies in the effort morally to justify in new terms a very particular combination of misrememberings of Nazism and continuities with it.

CHAPTER THREE

Desperately Seeking Normality

THE CULTURE OF SEXUAL CONSERVATISM

Why would the Federal Republic of Germany, so soon after the end of Nazism and the Holocaust, direct so much moral energy to the reorganization of sexual relations? While the immediate postwar years were a time of remarkable sexual freedom and avid and open public discussion of sexual issues, the early to mid-1950s saw an abrupt shift toward far greater sexual conservatism. Within a short time, liberal commentators on sexual matters were on the defensive, and conservative politicians, religious leaders, journalists, and legal and medical authorities took an aggressive lead in promoting normative notions of sexual and familial relations. And these conservatives quickly won a series of significant victories at local, state, and national levels. Concerted church and political campaigns at the municipal and state level to shield adolescents from any exposure to nudity or sexually suggestive images led in 1952 to the passage of a national law that censored the display and sale of pornographic images and texts. After a brief postwar period of relative tolerance and uncertainty in legal decisions regarding men accused of homosexual acts, the 1950s witnessed an escalation of police persecution and punitive sentencing. In several states, the Himmler order of 1941 (banning the advertisement and sale of all birth control products except condoms) remained in effect, and efforts to decriminalize the marketing of birth control products failed; from the mid-1950s on, court decisions made access even to condoms more difficult in some regions. Meanwhile, an unusual convergence of efforts between more right-wing Christian Democrats in the Bundestag and otherwise more left-leaning Christian intellectuals had successfully defeated attempts to liberalize abortion laws.

Yet it was not only in the realm of law that conservatism was ascendant. The popular media, especially illustrated magazines, and marriage and sex advice books, were enormously influential in elaborating conservative ideas about gender roles, familial relations, and sexual mores. Politicians' and church leaders' rhetoric in favor of reestablishing female submission to male authority and children's deference to their elders, and popular magazines' idealization of a wife's selfless delight in pleasing and nurturing her husband, worked in conjunction. The conservative sex advice and pedagogical literature soon flooding the market in millions of copies emphasized the values of sexual purity, restraint, and fidelity, taught that premarital heterosexual sexual experiences would result in miserable marriages, and consistently treated homosexuality as a pathological condition. Some texts expressly instructed young people to fear and loathe male homosexuals (and to turn in suspected individuals to the authorities). In sharp contrast to the late 1940s and early 1950s, frank and detailed discussion in print of sexual practices—including sex within marriage—was heavily censored.

Vigilant monitoring by parents and neighbors intensified the restrictive atmosphere. As sociologist and sexologist Martin Dannecker would observe cuttingly in 2001: "When one looks at the early Federal Republic one really gets the impression that it had no other concern aside from putting sexual matters in order."[1] And, indeed, many who came of age in this climate would subsequently recall their childhoods as suffocating and claustrophobic and the 1950s as a time when external adherence to propriety was strictly enforced. The New Left writer and education professor Ulf Preuss-Lausitz would describe in 1989 what a 1950s adolescence had been like in this way: "The postwar child was *surrounded*, under the motto 'that just isn't done,' *with prohibitions and injunctions, with the compulsion to a fictive normality.* . . . The postwar German family (or what was left of it) was fixated on conformity, on not standing out." Children coming of age in the wake of the war were constantly confronted with the era's "restoration of prefascist 'apolitical' values, full of hostility to the body and sexuality."[2] Yet the "prefascist" tradition to which conservatives in 1950s West Germany sought a return was not the sex-radical tradition of Weimar. Nor was it the pre–World War I Wilhelminian culture either. Rather, it is more helpful to see 1950s conservatives as constructing a fantasized version of past security and stability—an era that had never existed, yet was represented as one of timeless value.

Scholarship on the 1950s in West Germany routinely acknowledges the decade's extraordinary sexual conservatism. Many simply assert or assume that this conservatism was an inheritance from the Third Reich. Others emphasize the significance of the negative counterexample of female "emancipation" in Communist East Germany; the pressure exercised by the East German government to make women work outside the home was taken to be yet another instance of the pernicious "Marxist" tendency to exploit female labor power and disrupt the private sphere of the family. When further explanations for the "yearning for normalization" or "search for 'moral' restabilization" are sought at all, these are identified as logical responses to the intensely disruptive experiences of war and its immediate chaotic aftermath.[3] Yet what remains unaddressed is how sexual conservatism served as a crucial strategy for managing the memory of Nazism and Holocaust.

The reasons sexual and familial relations became premier sites for memory management in 1950s West Germany are multiple, and the result was ultimately overdetermined. One powerful initial impetus for sexual conservatism in postwar Germany lay in the fact that incitement to sexual activity and pleasure had been a major feature of National Socialism. Turning against nudity and licentiousness in the early 1950s, especially in the name of Christianity, could, quite legitimately and fairly, be represented and understood as a turn against Nazism. The narrow emphasis on sexual morality to the exclusion of other moral concerns, within the version of Christian discourse that became politically dominant, was not merely a matter of political expediency but also one of deeply held belief. Restoring conservative sexual mores was important to Christians not only because sexual morality had for centuries been one of Christianity's major concerns and because sex had been a main element in Christians' specific conflicts with Nazis, but also because under Nazism sexual licentiousness and genocide had in truth become integrally linked.

At the same time, also many more secular postwar commentators shared Christians' convictions that Germany had experienced an unprecedented and cataclysmic spiritual crisis. There was a broad postwar consensus among intellectuals, politicians, and church leaders that what Germany desperately needed was to "turn back to the foundations of Christian-Western culture." Nazism was represented as "the falling away of the world from God." What Germany required was a profound "conversion"—away from Nazism and its "nihilism," "animalistic vitalism," and "practical atheism."[4]

In general, re-Christianization was a logical countermove to the secularization so manifestly furthered by Nazism. Insisting that there was a God in heaven who not only gave people strength in conditions of adversity but also made demands on human beings to be concerned with peace, justice, and care for the weak and vulnerable was a powerful moral claim to make in the wake of an era in which human beings had set themselves up as the lords of life and death, in which the so-called German race had treated itself as divine and the Führer had acted as though he was God, and in which every moral value had been perverted into its opposite. That believing Christians had been among the most articulate outspoken opponents of and courageous Gentile resisters against Nazism also added to Christianity's postwar moral stature. So too did the important solace and sustenance that both Christian churches had increasingly provided to ordinary Germans as they lost loved ones in the later years of the war.[5]

The move to re-Christianize postwar German culture also provided an unexpectedly effective way of adapting to the expectations of the American occupiers. Above all, the pressure from the rest of the West to come to some kind of terms particularly with the Judeocide cannot be underestimated as a key cause for the renegotiation of moral concerns that occurred in early 1950s West Germany. Shifting moral debate away from mass murder and onto sexual matters was one of the major tactics used by West Germans both in domestic politics and international relations.

For significantly, a main effect of "the normalization project of the 1950s" was precisely that the sexually inciting aspects of Nazism were largely forgotten.[6] Admitting to their children or to the rest of the world that they had had any particular pleasures during the Third Reich increasingly did not fit with one of postwar Germans' most successful strategies for dealing with guilt (whether internally felt or externally imposed) about the Third Reich: the tendency to present themselves as victims of Nazism rather than its supporters and beneficiaries. Stressing that familial and sexual conservatism were timeless German values that transcended political regime changes offered a way of hiding from view and subsequent memory one's own youthful departures from traditional norms, as these were facilitated by Nazism, and one's own enthusiasm for Nazism more generally. In other words, although the populace in many parts of Germany held not only anticlerical but also more thoroughly secularized views, also those not particularly involved with the churches had their own reasons for not challenging the ascendancy of sexually conservative rhetoric and laws.

Certainly, the dynamic whereby the moral crisis engendered by Nazism was resolved via enforcement of sexual conservatism had to do as well with the powerfully felt needs to repair individual partnerships and to reconstruct families to the extent that either was possible after the intense disruptions of total war and mass death. "Nesting" and reprivatization were completely reasonable responses both to years of wartime and postwar deprivation, separation, stress, and loss and to the Nazi state's aggressive invasion of the private realm alike. Yet as the psychoanalyst Sophinette Becker has pointed out, there was also a more insidious side to this withdrawal into privacy. Dating the onset of the move toward privatization already to the years when World War II was going badly for Germany while the war against the Jews was moving ahead with terrifying speed and effectivity, Becker sees in this privatization a strategy for denial of responsibility for and knowledge of mass murder.[7]

Moreover, the official re-Christianization of West German culture as it concretely ensued—as sociologist Y. Michal Bodemann especially has pointed out—itself needs to be seen as a way to manage the metaphysical crisis engendered by mass murder by casting questions of concrete German complicity in cruelty, expropriation, and genocide in deliberately universalizing (and hence no longer specifically German) existential categories of suffering, guilt, and redemption.[8] Re-Christianization too, then (and however perfunctory it might have been), became a way of avoiding responsibility. Many clergymen made this connection explicit when they argued angrily against the Allies' war crimes trials and denazification efforts that only God could judge human transgressions.[9]

Furthermore, and by a paradoxical though thereby no less crucial turn, postwar Christians' emphasis on cleaning up sexual mores also provided a convenient strategy for erasing from view and from popular memory both Christian churches' own very strong complicity with Nazism—not only with its anti-Bolshevism but also explicitly with its antisemitism. Meanwhile, in stressing the need to clean up sexual mores, postwar politicians and church activists speaking in the name of Christianity were—significantly—stimulating the very same punitive affects toward open or nonconventional expressions of sexuality that sexually conservative Nazis had originally, in the early 1930s, addressed as well and that had been absolutely central to Nazism's early political success (notwithstanding the regime's subsequently more complicated handling of sexual matters).[10] Indeed, it could be argued, however chillingly, that what was achieved in the 1950s was the realization of a promise originally made, but not kept, by the Nazis. The National Socialists had promised to set right again what Weimar had wrought, but instead they developed further major elements of Weimar trends and also drove the nation into catastrophic disaster. Now, in the postwar era, the "cleanup" was finally possible.

In addition, and in some ways even more disturbingly, the relentless emphasis placed by postwar Christian spokespeople on the moral requirement of premarital heterosexual chastity (this point indeed represented a manifest reversal of Nazi standards) functioned successfully to distract attention from the *continuities* between Nazis and postwar Christians in values relating to the issues of eugenics, birth control, abortion, and homosexuality. Stressing the importance of premarital chastity allowed postwar Christian commentators to delineate their difference from Nazism in especially stark terms, since Nazis had been so particularly eager to celebrate premarital sex and challenge the churches for their "prudery" on this matter. Yet the manifest postwar departure from Nazi values with respect to premarital heterosexual sex was often accompanied by unapologetic perpetuation of Nazi-era laws and attitudes especially as homophobia and eugenics both were refurbished and given renewed legitimacy under Christian auspices.

Meanwhile, some conservative laws and attitudes that had been promulgated during the Third Reich were experienced by the majority of young people as more directly oppressive in the 1950s than they had been before

1945. Key among these was the Nazi ruling prohibiting pimping (*Kuppel-eiparagraph*), which—although only infrequently formally enforced—still served in the 1950s as the backdrop against which parents, landlords, and hotel managers had reason to fear that neighbors might have them arrested if their children, renters, or guests received overnight visitors of the opposite sex. (By contrast, during the Third Reich parents had been exempted from the "pimping paragraph.") At the same time, the insistent hypervaluation in the 1950s of family life and self-sacrificial maternalism coupled with fierce hostility to women's emancipation (whether in the form of reproductive control or pursuit of work outside the home), the general climate enforcing petty bourgeois respectability and the secrecy and shame surrounding all sexuality outside of marriage, the prevalence of physical violence directed at children, and a general distinctive kind of animus toward anything deemed nonnormative were all experienced so viscerally in the 1950s that they seemed to many to be just as much evidence of failed denazification as the reappearance of former Nazis in positions of political and expert authority in every level of government and in all the professions.

Precisely this complicated combination of rupture and continuity between Nazism and postwar conservative politics, together with the sense that the hyper-preoccupation with sexual morality only thinly veiled some deeper entanglement in national guilt—as well as ongoing anger and resentment at the fact of that guilt—was unnervingly palpable to more critical young people coming of age in this climate. In 1983 the poet and art historian Olav Münzberg (born 1938) tried to express how it felt to grow up in post–World War II West Germany. Describing how parents who had lived through the Third Reich treated their postwar children, Münzberg observed: "One's own offspring did penance for Auschwitz with ethics and morality forcefully jammed into them, with notions of cleanliness that constantly broke against reality and had to break."[11] Few comments capture so well the double truth of the circuitous indirectness *and* the tangible intensity of postwar youth's relationship to the Holocaust. And yet at the same time the connections became difficult to decipher.

What many young people were left with was a profound sense that theirs was a society defined by hypocrisy. That the atmosphere was "stuffy" (*muffig*) and "philistine" (*spiessig*) was powerfully felt by many. What was perplexing was the disconnect young people experienced between official Christianization and popular disaffection, even disdain, for the churches. For the transition to a more Christianized culture was often only a superficial transition in an already partially secularized society (only one in four West Germans attended church regularly in the late 1940s, and these numbers dropped over the course of the 1950s), a fact that was not lost on many postwar observers.[12] As novelist Hermann Peter Piwitt (born 1935) would sardonically write many years later:

> After all, the churches were that which offered postwar Germans the most convenient solution for that which had happened. What had led to fascism? "Dearth of faith." "A turning-away from God." "After the collapse of the state to be embraced by the church" ([a comment from Protestant politician and longtime Bundestag president] Eugen Gerstenmaier), that was the yearning of many. And the business of selling indulgences went correspondingly well. Churches sprung up, as though there was nothing else to build, and every village architect developed the sweeping fantasy of a Corbusier. . . . But then it turned out that these churches did not function at all. They stood around like freshly dedicated train stations at tracks that have just been shut down. And the people made their jokes: "Soul-rocketing ramps." "Christ's power plant." Here too one had only "kept up appearances."[13]

Just as unnerving was the lingering sense that many older Germans were not really remorseful at all. Privately, vicious antisemitism was still routinely expressed. And an (only barely contained) aggressive sense of national pride and feeling of superiority toward the military occupiers was part of public discussion in the media and politics as well. Günter Grass, eight years older than Piwitt and a soldier in the Wehrmacht during World War II, was able to look critically on his own generation and those somewhat older from the perspective of 1980s hindsight: while some West Germans might subsequently have felt nostalgia for this decade of apparently successful democratization, integration into the West, and the "economic miracle," Grass reminded his cohort "how much Christian hypocrisy lay like mildew on the society," "how corrupt and full of lies it was," "how sassily the murderers stood among us," and "how it stank in the fifties so, it took one's breath away."[14] Not only was nostalgia completely inappropriate; it was itself a strategy of misremembrance.

The point here, then, is not to deny manifest continuities across 1945. Rather, as noted already in chapter 2, what requires critical attention is the complex and ever-shifting mixture between eras of continuity *and* rupture, of retrieval and reconstruction *and* new departure. Yet in many ways even more crucial, however, are the subtler dynamics of *redefinition* and *reinterpretation*, the development of new legitimations for old practices (in other words, a continuity presented as a change), as well as the opposite (something new introduced in the name of tradition). The ultimate success of the normalization strategies of the 1950s lay not least in one of their main long-term consequences: the construction of a wholly new version of the Third Reich, one on which parents and children, leftists, liberals, and conservatives could all agree, although for completely different reasons and with utterly divergent investments.

THE PROTECTION OF YOUTH

As the Federal Republic was just achieving sovereignty in 1949, one of the first moves made in the realm of sexual politics involved restricting the circulation of nude images. The ever-growing proliferation of cheap pornographic magazines and photographs displayed at newsstands all across the western zones was a major source of aggravation, puzzlement, and irritation to numerous observers in the late 1940s and early 1950s. No sooner had the currency reform of 1948 stabilized the economy than a flood of naked pictures became available for purchase. Most typical were pictures of females, breasts fully visible, with some object—a ball, a teddy bear—coyly held in front of their crotch, but some were full frontal shots. There were also others that pictured heterosexual couples engaging in intercourse, though these were not usually openly displayed. As much as freedom of the press was to be appreciated as a concept, one commentator lamented, surely these images were not what that concept had been intended to safeguard.[15]

Already in December 1949, the governing council of the Evangelical-Protestant Church in Germany took the initiative to develop a draft proposal for a federal law banning both the sale of pornographic products to youth and the open display of such products. Fines and jail terms were proposed for violators.[16] Under conflicting pressures from, on the one hand, some of the more conservative state governments (Bavaria, for example, was already formulating a similar state law in late 1949) and, on the other, the U.S. military occupiers (who were exceedingly dubious about permitting any infringement of freedom of expression in this nation only recently liberated from Nazi censorship), the Christian Democratic leaders of the fledgling Federal Republic initially sought to steer carefully, advocating the passage of a law constricting the advertising, sale, and display of pornography but framing the legislation as an urgently needed measure to protect Germany's vulnerable and morally disoriented youth.[17] Within two months, the text of the proposed law had become "one of the most controversial items in the session rooms of the Bonn parliament" and was being treated as "an affair of state of the first order."[18] Already by April 1950, five of West Germany's eleven states (specifically those in which the majority of the populace was Catholic) had either passed or were in the process of developing laws restricting the display and sale of sexually explicit materials.[19] The federal government was thus starting to face dilemmas of constitutional as well as moral authority: having barely come into existence, it was now confronting the possibility of profound divergences in the legal developments of the Federal Republic's component states, and it was being put in the awkward situation of having to appease conservative state leaders whose insubordination it was also striving to rebuke.

The law was popularly referred to as a law against "trash and smut" (*Schund und Schmutz)*, language already used in Weimar and earlier to describe the combination of pornography and lowbrow romance, adventure, and crime novels, and terms that the Nazis also adopted to describe any literature they deemed politically offensive. Yet precisely because of government defensiveness about censorship in view of Germany's recent past, it eventually acquired the supposedly less morally normative name of "Law about the Distribution of Youth-Endangering Publications" (Gesetz über den Vertrieb jugendgefährdender Schriften*)*. In this way the law was aligned with another passed at the end of 1951, the "Law for the Protection of Youth in Public," which provided police with the authority to scour park benches at night for young couples making out, ask minors to leave certain bars and even some street corners where sexually loose or deviant people (e.g., prostitutes) were known to gather, and in some cases turn in the names of arrested youth to the local social welfare offices for further supervision.

For the first three years of the 1950s, until the Law about the Distribution of Youth-Endangering Publications was finally passed and put into effect in 1953, its content and legitimacy were objects of recurrent debate in the West German press. Certainly opponents of the new law had every reason initially to be optimistic, for public opinion as well seemed generally opposed to the law, and numerous groups and individuals had risen to the defense of freedom of expression. Critically minded journalists and legal scholars, along with publishers' interest groups and writers' associations (under the courageous leadership of the liberal and pacifist poet and children's author Erich Kästner, who had suffered censorship under the Nazis), vociferously attacked the planned legislation. They pointed out that the antipornography law passed in Weimar in 1926 had been used to censor even canonized literature and that surely it was obvious that the Nazis' even harsher censorship law (which replaced the Weimar law in 1935 and shifted the emphasis away from sexual matters specifically to any publications which "endangered the cultural will of National Socialism") showed how frightening and abusable such loose terms as "the healthy sensibility of the *Volk*" (*das gesunde Volksempfinden*) were.[20] At first unable to believe that such censorship could possibly be instituted in a democratic society, but then increasingly aware that its passage was simply a matter of time, many liberals expressed repugnance at this renewed constriction of press freedom, now under the aegis of Christianity rather than Nazism. In light of this liberal pressure, the federal government continually modified the law and the justifications for it and ultimately, in mid-1952, adapted it to include not only sexually explicit materials but also (in a never adequately explained but quite indicative move to outflank left-leaning and liberal intellectuals and politicians on their own ground) any material "glorifying crime, war, or racial hatred."[21] The Bundestag debate of September 1952 about this proposed law made abundantly clear that the inclusion of racism and militarism had been appended by the Christian Democrats for strictly tactical purposes.[22]

Significantly, moreover, once it was passed, this provision of the law was rarely enforced. Not until 1960 were any books "glorifying war" censored.[23] Instead the law served above all to prohibit the advertisement and distribution of sexually explicit materials. Contemporaries remember how abruptly (and thoroughly) all nude images disappeared from public display after the law was passed.[24] In yet another odd and indirect but nonetheless definitive way, then, sexual issues in the postwar period were connected to issues of racism and mass murder. And this occurred even as, gradually, official discourses of morality got effectively diverted away from the racism and mass murder in the nation's immediate past to the perceived sexual conundrums in its present.

The law, going into effect in 1953, established a Federal Evaluation Office for Youth-Endangering Publications (Bundesprüfstelle für jugendgefährdende Schriften). Composed of representatives from the churches, youth welfare groups, and teachers' associations, as well as booksellers, publishers, artists, and writers, this office (which still exists) operated for most of the 1950s and well into the 1960s as the branch of government that censored sexual materials. Nor was it beholden to any superior judicial oversight. Some publications were directly censored and could not be sold to anyone; others were put on an "index," or blacklist, and they could not be sold to minors or advertised anywhere minors might see them. Serious scholarship on sexuality was affected as well. As late as 1963, for example, the Kinsey report could not be made available to a minor by a librarian without a notice of official permission.[25]

In the aftermath of the war, the very fact that liberals and Social Democrats were stunned when passage of the Law about the Distribution of Youth-Endangering Publications became inevitable showed how openended history had temporarily seemed. Initially unsure whether to mock the hypermoralism implicit in the proposed federal law and appeal to popular resentment against (or sense of superiority to) such moralism, or whether to emphasize forcefully the potentially grave dangers of censorship, some progressive commentators veered between both tendencies.[26] Others just treated postwar conservatives as buffoons. A writer in the *Frankfurter Rundschau*, for instance, made sarcastic fun of Bavarian minister of culture Alois Hundhammer's declaration that Bavarians needed to lead the way in the antipornography fight because the extant federal law only addressed "the coarser sexual literature, but not the more refined shamelessness": what exactly was "refined shamelessness," and how was it that people in the "lovely" and "tradition-rooted" Bavaria were so expert in identifying it?[27] Along related lines, although he also had more serious points to make, Erich Kästner noted that the appeal of the law for "reactionaries of every stripe" was to turn attention away from the society's real problems—among them catastrophic unemployment, widespread poverty, and a severe housing shortage—to a "pretend problem" which could be solved more easily: "Hocus pocus—finally, a law. Finally the youth have been saved! Now the poor little ones can no longer buy porn photos at the kiosk and instead carry their money to the bank!"[28]

A few liberals insisted on the grave dangers to freedom of art and literature caused by efforts to prohibit the representation of sex. Legal theorist and Social Democratic (SPD) Bundestag representative Carlo Schmid averred that the threat to democracy, if an antipornography law was passed, would be considerable. "There is simply no such thing as a democracy without freedom of art and scholarship, and this freedom is an extraordinarily fragile entity that can be attacked in numerous direct and very many more indirect ways."[29] And Kästner also declared that the whole aim of the law was not just a ridiculous effort to "force citizens once again to blush and to get outraged, where it used to be enough just to laugh or shrug one's shoulders." The real goal was absolutely to suppress art and literature, and the law constituted a deliberate assault on and the "infantilizing of modern human beings." Severe damage could be done by even the most patently foolish laws, Kästner asserted. However laughable Weimar-era censors might have appeared to be, they were the ones who had emotionally prepared the German people for Nazi censorship.[30]

But the evolving debate, as it played out in the pages of the media, and in the Bundestag itself, also revealed just how unimaginative and timid about sexual matters most representatives in the large opposition party, the Social Democrats, and in the minority liberal center party of Free Democrats turned out to be. Social Democrats in particular emerged as continually fearful of being associated with the sex radicalism of Weimar-era socialism. Instead of defending sexually explicit materials as either beneficial to youth and adults alike or as unfortunate and unpleasant but tolerable by-products of a free and open society, critics of the law tried to argue that it would be better to provide more high-quality literature for youth than to censor smut, or simply tried to suggest that there were matters more urgent for those who cared about Germany's youth (like young people's generally miserable economic prospects). Indeed, when they talked about sex at all, Social Democrats often confined their criticism of Christian Democrats to sarcastic exposés of Christian Democratic hypocrisy (e.g., citing various Christian Democratic municipal politicians who supported organized prostitution). The Social Democrats thereby reinforced precisely the conservative sexual values they might better have challenged.[31]

A mere handful of liberals assertively rejected the idea that sexual explicitness posed any social threat. It would be better, a writer for the *Frankfurter Rundschau* suggested, if Germans started worrying about protecting youth from the renewed rise of right-wing elements. These, he noted acidly, "may contribute far more to the moral degradation of youth than nudities have ever been able to do."[32] Another journalist pointed out that "the orgies of smut and trash" that had as their subject "the stupidest gossip about former Hitler cronies" was more worrisome and deleterious than nakedness to a young person's psychological health.[33] But aside from Kästner no one appeared to have the courage or wherewithal actually to defend nudity or literary pornography directly.

Not only did no politician on the left or in the middle of the political spectrum make progressive arguments either in favor of nude imagery or in defense of the naturalness of sexual activity with the earthy self-confident directness with which many Nazis had. But the very fact that Nazis had ever done this was itself thoroughly erased. Instead, and remarkably, conservative supporters of the law unapologetically echoed and repeated other far more aggressive elements of Nazi language. A raft of antipornography brochures published between 1950 and 1952 by conservative activists and youth organizations put forth in especially nasty and personal terms the case for suppressing sexual representations in print and image. In one 1950 brochure, for example, opponents of censorship were compared both to homosexuals and to murderers, with the suggestion that only criminals themselves ever opposed laws. Kästner was also denigrated directly; the brochure declared that his poetry was "far worse than smut and trash" and openly called for his writings to be censored once again.[34] These intimidating tactics were often quite successful.

The terms of debate shifted quickly and noticeably and most of even those who formally went on record against the law nonetheless implicitly endorsed the view that sexual images posed a threat to youth. Thus, for instance, a state prosecutor who opposed the law nevertheless spoke of the damage to young people's "character development" that resulted from "strong sexual stimuli."[35] Along related lines, the Protestant theologian Helmut Thielicke, another of the law's opponents, nonetheless concurred that some sort of antipornography activism was required, for it was important that "the erotic fantasy of our youth not be unnecessarily stimulated and intensified into the pathological through picture and print."[36] Even a newspaper as liberal as the *Frankfurter Neue Presse* still affirmed that kiosk displays with their nudes "solely fabricated for sexual purposes" were for youth "real poison."[37] Similarly, *Die Zeit* in 1952 in a strongly worded attack on "this miserable law" (after a first version passed the Bundestag), nonetheless opened its editorial this way: "That it is necessary to protect youth against the influence of indecent or shameless texts and pictures: on this point all conscientious quarters are in agreement."[38]

Although Protestant Church leaders had been the first to formulate an antipornography law, Catholic activists became increasingly important in moving the law through the political process. For example, in August 1950 the archbishop of Cologne wrote directly to the Bundesrat (Federal Council) urging swift passage of the Law about the Distribution of Youth-Endangering Publications.[39] The conservative media were influential as well. For the *Münchner Allgemeine*, for example, the prevalence of pornography in postwar Germany was an indication of "the lost state of human existence," and the government had every right to suppress it. Politicians, the paper averred, *must* "form their consciences in accordance with natural law and God's sacred revelation."[40] Even more influential were lay activists who took matters into their own hands: Catholic youth groups in Württemberg and the Rhineland set fire to piles of magazines or burned down porn-displaying kiosks on their own initiative.[41] In reaction, a Social Democratic newspaper in the Rhineland went on the offensive, asserting that it was "high time" that the government took "energetic measures" against such "bigoted moralists." Alluding to the color black associated with Catholicism, the paper declared: "This 'black terror' deserves the same contempt and stigmatization as the 'brown terror' of past years."[42] Yet Catholic conservatives were hardly deterred by such jabs. Bavarian CDU/CSU representative to the Bundestag Franz Joseph Strauss in 1952 demanded that the Bundestag representatives vote openly, one by one, for or against the law. "In this way it will become apparent who among the representatives of the people still has a Christian conscience."[43]

In the course of the process by which the law gradually became reality, liberals found themselves caught completely off guard. As one commentator noted in 1952, he found it "incomprehensible how a proposal that had already been declared half-dead can now cheerfully and even with the endorsement of the Federal Council be brought forward to the parliament."[44] Arguments that with this law West Germany would only embarrass itself, or that the law would inevitably be abused in order to control also the nonpornographic press, proved ineffectual. Within the parliament, efforts that insisted measures like support for quality youth literature would do more good than an antipornography law, or a move to keep organized nudist clubs' publications from automatic censorship when the law went into effect, did not gain widespread support. In September 1952 the law passed the Bundestag by a vote of 165 to 133 with 7 abstentions.[45] Chancellor Konrad Adenauer showed up in person to help ensure the government's majority. As one paper editorialized after the vote: "No one can deny that youth today, in the aftermath of National Socialism and the Second World War, is in more moral danger than before, and that therefore it needs to be protected more than before."[46] The transition from a morality concerned with the aftereffects of fascism to a morality concerned above all with the restriction of talk about and representations of sex was now well underway.

Even more significantly, and precisely via the campaign to suppress pornography, the rewriting of the memory and meanings of fascism also proceeded apace. A 1952 brochure for the censorship law, *Jugend in Gefahr* (Youth in Danger), made this task explicit: "We turn to all those who care about the future of the German *Volk* and who are prepared to help German youth in their search for new life-forms. Every German is convinced of the necessity of a clean spiritual guidance of youth so that the unhappy inheritance of our past may be overcome. We thus may not make ourselves guilty once more by being silent in the face of the attempt being carried out by profit-hungry smut publishers, and escalating constantly in extent and intensity, once again to assassinate the souls of our youth."[47] In this interpretation, the assault on youthful minds represented by pornography was no different from the "assassination" of souls undertaken by Nazism.

Throughout the remainder of the 1950s, the campaign against youth-endangering publications continued to rewrite the past. While the passage of the law effectively ended the circulation of sexually explicit materials, it proved less effectual in the suppression of cheap adventure and crime novels for adolescents. Over the course of the decade, in dozens of spectacular local campaigns, churches and conservative youth organizations announced that they would offer young people a trade: five (or ten) trashy books could be traded in for one "good" one. The "bad" books would then be buried in a mass grave (usually an old quarry) or burned in a public bonfire. Indeed, the organizers often unabashedly made the planned bonfire itself a titillating lure for youth. These events were well advertised, and pastors and priests often participated by delivering "anti-smut" sermons from the pulpit the Sunday before the trade-ins began. In this context too, the deliberate revision of the Nazi past and its import was crucial. In one well-publicized case in Frankfurt in 1957, for instance, opponents of censorship who criticized a planned bonfire (which had been heavily advertised) and who expressed horror that any book could ever again be burned on German soil, were in turn themselves accused of having been Nazis, who now wished to avoid a bonfire because it might stir unpleasant memories for *them*.[48]

Another effect of the censorship of sex-related materials, including sex advice magazines, was that conservative literature quickly came to dominate the sex advice market. These books and tracts—whether directed at adolescents or their parents or teachers—communicated several key messages. One was that girls were by nature less sexual than boys. Premarital chastity was necessary for both boys and girls, but for girls any lapse had even more ominous consequences than for boys; girls destroyed their chances at successful marriages if they were no longer virgins on their wedding day. Meanwhile, and this message was directed more at boys than at girls, masturbation was deleterious to one's emotional health and potential for long-term happiness. In general, youth were educated to self-restraint and alienation from their own bodies. Through their new-found dominant role in the market for advice literature and through their considerable influence on government policies and school curricula, conservative publicists were able to set the terms of public debate about sex in West Germany until well into the mid-1960s. Whether they themselves or their families were believers or unbelievers, young people could hardly avoid a climate where it was routine to hear that homosexuality and premarital sex were sins, or that masturbation had the most severe psychological consequences.

SEX EDUCATION FOR ADOLESCENTS

In endless variations, advice authors insisted that in their rejection of masturbation and premarital sexuality alike, they were only offering youth the latest in scientific insights. Restraint was not only a matter of morality but also of health. "Modern doctors and psychologists are of the opinion that every premarital sexual experience makes more difficult the lasting bond of a future marriage and the proper stance toward sexuality in general," one parenting advice writer argued in 1955.[49] Well-known expert Heinrich Oesterreich, director of the North Rhine-Westphalian State Working Group for the Combating of Venereal Disease and for Sex Education (Landesarbeitsgemeinschaft zur Bekämpfung der Geschlechtskrankheiten und für Geschlechtserziehung)—which supplied thousands of teachers with sex "enlightenment" materials for their own information and for classroom use—informed readers that "through strict moral guidance and influence youth should deny themselves sexual activities, so that they do not damage their future capacity for marriage."[50] Oesterreich admonished mothers and fathers to "never tire" of emphasizing to their "daughters especially . . . the value of untouched virginity and fulfilled motherhood. Encourage your sons to value that femininity which saves itself for marriage."[51] Another expert announced not only that to engage in premarital sex meant to "rip God's gift [of sex] greedily out of His hands" but also that marital sex would be enhanced by premarital abstinence.[52]

Meanwhile, although a range of experts in the Weimar and Nazi and early postwar years had emphasized not only the harmlessness of youth masturbation but even its value as a preparatory experience for later sexual relationships, the majority of 1950s experts with forcefulness and unanimity insisted on the opposite. The Protestant physician Erich Schröder devoted the bulk of his 1956 book, *Reif Werden und Rein Bleiben* (Becoming Mature and Staying Pure), to the importance of the individual's war against masturbation. The practice was addictive, he asserted, and this was cause for "highest alarm": "Here a dependency develops—reflexes that are conditioned by external circumstances, that are dangerous for later life. Someone who for years sought to satisfy himself, with all the fantasies that accompany that, can later only with difficulty make the transition to having sex with his wife in marriage."[53] For Catholic pedagogue Heinrich von Gagern, masturbation was an activity "in contradiction to the natural purpose of the sex organs." Female clitoral masturbation, moreover, made girls incapable, once they became women, of experiencing anything in their vagina and uterus in their marital relations—and these sites alone "contained in them the fullness of delight."[54] Another Protestant writer, although noting that "almost all boys (and numerous girls)" engaged in onanism, also declared it a "reprehensible practice" that should definitely not be tolerated; repeated masturbation could lead to the incapacity ever to love another human being. A young person must learn to do "battle" against temptation so as not to "demean" him- or herself into becoming a "slave to the deformed drive."[55]

The rhetoric of cleanliness and the restrictions on open speech about sexuality, and the lack of sex education in schools beyond the abstract descriptions of reproductive organs, had quite concrete consequences. As one boy who had been given a popular antimasturbation manual in early adolescence remembered decades later, "We were all *terrified*. We did masturbate, but we were sure our bodies would degenerate as a result. And even when we started to have sexual relations later, there was a lot of conflict in those relationships, a lot of anxiety that it was not acceptable to masturbate in addition to having the relationship; the women felt hurt, and the men couldn't justify it to them; it ended up being hidden, or a source of pain and confusion."[56] For girls, the situation was worse. The awkwardness and self-involvement of many of the boys, the misinformation even more than the absence of information, the fear of losing one's reputation, and above all a terror of pregnancy cast long shadows over many early sexual encounters.

In an extraordinary essay based on interviews conducted in the 1980s with men and women of the working and middle classes about their adolescences in the 1950s, Peter Kuhnert and Ute Ackermann painstakingly reconstruct the diverse ways people remembered negotiating the conservative climate of the 1950s. In these accounts, for many middle-class boys, girls were an intimidating other species. If one girl did finally permit coitus, often it either did not go well the first time (leading to insecurities about performance and further awkward encounters) or led to a situation in which boys absorbed the society's double standard about female sexuality. Girls who permitted coitus were somehow "yuck" (*bäh*), good enough for acquiring experience or releasing tension but not acceptable for loving or marrying or even treating well during (or after) sex; relationships with other, more parentally protected girls who had internalized the injunctions about virginity often did not work out either. Of the working-class boys, some hung out in male cliques and did not have sexual relations until their late teens, often marrying soon thereafter, though not always for love, either because a child was on the way or because they were looking for someone to take care of them. Other working-class boys, however, usually self-identified as "young toughs" (*Halbstarken*), as part of their larger rejection of societal norms, worked actively to develop a sexually confident style, which involved aggressive seduction techniques together with absolute refusal of romantic involvement. "The goal was somehow to develop a protective wall against the girls."[57]

And what was sex like for the girls? As one man retrospectively admitted, "we swung ourselves on and banged away in the most impossible positions, but really doing that with feeling and, let's say, really stimulating the woman, that was not part of it at all. Fucking and then falling off [of her] like a dead man. That was it. Or quick back on the moped and then onward." Condoms were intimidating to purchase, or perceived as too inhibiting of sensation to use. The girls were left on their own to keep track of the time of the month, or to seek out an illegal abortion if they got unlucky. Many middle- and working-class women recalled that as girls they had lived in fear not just of parental rage but also of acquiring a bad reputation. Middle-class girls in particular believed, or were afraid to be too skeptical of, the idea that giving themselves away to a boy would cause that boy to disrespect them. But the greatest fear of all, in this pre-pill world, was absolutely the fear of getting pregnant. "Then you've destroyed your life. It can happen so fast." This searing anxiety dominated the experience of sex; for many it ruined all possibility of pleasure. "This fear alone . . . one had such fear [of pregnancy], one always felt uptight [*verkrampft*]." Middle-class girls, feeling they had more to lose because they still hoped to pursue an education and perhaps even a career of their own, were often hesitant to attempt coitus at all, while those middle-class girls who did risk coitus were often, like their working-class counterparts, confronted with the misogyny of the boys and men with whom they slept. The men were so fixated on an unimaginative version of coitus and basically so preoccupied with themselves and their own masculine image, "that had nothing to do with tenderness." And again, because of a climate of shame and taboo surrounding sexual matters, it was difficult for young women even to talk with each other about their experiences.[58] None of these developments constituted especially encouraging preconditions for lasting and happy marriages.

MARRIAGE IN THE 1950s

Nevertheless, the romantic ideal of the mid-1950s was a marvelous and monogamous and moderately reproductive marriage where only the husband worked for wages and the wife was the nurturing homemaker. Yet this ordinary and traditional ideal actually represented a major shift for West Germany, given the many ways sex had escaped the familial framework already for the first half of the century—and then, more dramatically, in the years of war and its aftermath. The ideal was, crucially, also not widely realizable. Half of all women did work outside the home, millions of men had died, and many marriages—particularly for those couples separated during the war or during postwar imprisonments—ended in divorce. Significantly, moreover, the apparent innocence of elaborations of this ideal came together with laws enforcing women's dependence on husbands, psychologically and economically; strong ambivalence among experts about the use of birth control even within marriage; and utterly incoherent advice about achieving sexual happiness. Although equality between men and women remained anchored in the Basic Law, an assumption of gender difference permitted numerous exceptions in subsequent legislation. While a law passed in 1957, for example, was called the Equal Rights Law (Gleichberechtigungsgesetz), in reality it gave the father final authority to adjudicate decisions about the children whenever husband and wife disagreed. Although this ruling was declared unconstitutional in 1959, the ideal of the "housewife marriage" that undergirded marriage, divorce, and family law was not revised completely until 1977. Divorce became expressly more difficult to obtain with a law passed in 1961.[59]

The messages about sexual happiness within marriage in popular magazines and advice books, as in professional literature, were contradictory. On the one hand, advice literature continually raised expectations of the oceanic pleasures marital coitus (if based on true love) could provide. Allusions to the importance of women's orgasms appeared in a remarkably broad range of contexts. Indeed, the discussion of sex in the 1950s can be understood also as an important precedent for the celebration of sex so often associated with the 1960s; in this way, the sexual culture of the later 1960s might be interpreted not just as backlash against 1950s culture but also as an extension and expansion of several of its elements. On the other hand, the popular advice and professional literature relentlessly intoned that it was women who needed above all to transform themselves if marital bliss was to be achieved with their men. The feminist historian Hanna Schissler, building on the work of sociologist Norbert Elias, has accurately summarized the marital ideal of the 1950s as one of "harmonious inequality."[60]

Franz Josef Wuermeling, appointed minister of the family in 1953, and a Catholic, was explicit in his expectation that women needed to sacrifice themselves and to stand by their men. Wuermeling wished housework could be treated with more respect, but he never offered women a real choice: "*The mother-career is a main career like every other career and has a higher worth than any salaried career.* And nobody can do two main careers fully at the same time. . . . *Save our mothers for our families and our children! Their absence there can never again be rectified!*"[61] Protestant spokespersons made similar arguments. In 1957 the Protestant theologian Wolfgang Metzger, for instance, called just as forcefully for the idealization of faithful femininity and the need to "lead mothers back to the children."[62] In numerous lecture series and counseling services run by civic organizations and Protestant and Catholic churches, couples seeking guidance to improve or save their marriages were urged to ask God to help them forgive one another and to devote themselves more fully to each other. Even seriously depressed women were discouraged from speaking or acting out. A "few weeks of vacation" to restore themselves, and soon they could once again dedicate themselves to their families' happiness, or so they were instructed.[63]

Although it has received scant attention, what remains striking even now is not only how crassly commentators in 1950s West Germany appealed to female masochism but also how forthrightly they thematized the vulnerabilities and shortcomings of men. Wuermeling was quite blunt in his insistence that the wife's function was to compensate for any indignities experienced or insecurities felt by the husband at his workplace.[64] Popular advice magazines discouraged women from expressing opinions of their own but declared that a wife should learn to listen "when he tells you something, even if it seems boring to you."[65] A questionnaire printed in one of these magazines captured adroitly the ensuing pressures on women: "Are you a perfect wife?" The twenty tendentious questions included the following: "Are you free of petty jealousy and can you bear it—without immediately making a scene—if your husband occasionally admires another woman?" Also asked: "Do you attend to your clothing and your appearance as much as you did during your honeymoon?" But fully five of the questions underscored the requirement that women be more tolerant of male weaknesses: "When you have company or are visiting others together with your husband, do you see to it that you do not shine at your husband's expense and draw all attention on to yourself? . . . Do you succeed in holding back your anger if your husband makes a mistake or is clumsy? . . . Do you contain your own impulse to laugh about his fears and frailties . . . ? In order not to wound your husband in his sensitivity, can you hold back a sharp comment . . . ? . . . Do you carefully avoid at all occasions putting your husband in a bad light or making him look ridiculous in front of the children?"[66] Although the husband's potentially roving eyes are the only explicit reference to sex here, the general sentiment expressed—that if things were not going well, women should above all suppress their own needs and nurture their husband's ego more thoroughly—inevitably carried over into the bedroom as well.

At the same time, advice literature stoked a woman's desire to be overwhelmed by male strength and tenderness, while it held out hope for lifelong passion in bed. Simultaneously, however, Christian and secular literature alike continually elaborated normative notions that placed the blame for any sexual problems in a marriage on women. One common feature of this literature (as with the sex education materials directed at youth) involved disturbing descriptions of the consequences of premarital sex, declaring again and again that difficulties women encountered with their husbands were the result of their premarital experiences. Among other things, authors argued that women were permanently imprinted by their first sexual encounter and that, if this experience was with someone other than the future husband, the woman remained psychologically conflicted and unable to give herself fully to (and thereby enjoy raptures with) her spouse. Alternatively, if the woman had slept only with her future spouse, she nevertheless had sullied herself in his eyes and, by preempting what should only have occurred in the context of formal lifelong commitment (and thereby failing to train him to master himself), made herself responsible if he subsequently lost interest in her. Meanwhile, although lesbianism was rarely discussed openly (not least because it was not illegal), when it was addressed, it was most often represented as pathetic, a miserable substitute for heterosexual sex.[67] Yet popular marital advice, when addressing the possible sources of a woman's sexual unhappiness in marriage, listed female masturbation, lesbianism, or a general maladjustment to the female role (rather than male incompetence or selfishness) as its potential root causes.

A main theme especially in Christian advice literature, moreover, involved the absolute link between reproduction and marital happiness. Although "modern" (in the sense that it did not advocate childbirth every year, but rather suggested that the spacing of children was best for both mother and family), this literature insisted that no child or only one child was inadequate. Two or three children was the minimum number if the goal was proper joy. For instance, the postwar Christian advice book *Mann und Frau* (Man and Woman) expressly acknowledged the conflicts within marriages caused by years of wartime separation, by the long-term exhaustion of both partners, and by the weakness of men who were damaged by war and un- or underemployment. But *Mann und Frau* also invoked the biblical charge to be fruitful and multiply as it announced that there could be "no blessing" in childlessness. Even when they shared professional interests, childless couples easily ended up taking themselves too seriously, getting "all knotted up and hysterical." Nor would the sex be good. Without the "fundamental openness to the child" the "glorious tension between the sexes, which in accordance with God's will is a powerful force," became only a "shallow," "paltry self-purpose."[68]

As they made their case for procreation, postwar Christian commentators struggled particularly over how best to specify the differences between Nazi and Christian values. Thus, for instance, the *Frankfurter Hefte* already in 1946 had argued that, in contradistinction to Christian attitudes, the Nazi-encouraged "joy in children" was actually "the opposite of the true order of life, that is realized in humble acceptance and not in the goal-orientation of a state's hubris."[69] The prominent Protestant bishop Hanns Lilje ran into similar conundrums in 1954 as he attempted to articulate the distinctions between Nazi and Christian ideals. On the one hand, he pointed out that Nazism was ultimately about a "fundamental denial of the family . . . despite all wordy pro-family declarations." And he insisted that it must be self-evident that "it is the end of all ethics in this matter, when one wants to make a biological breeding institute out of marriage and family." On the other hand, however, he urgently wanted his readers to understand that having the "will to the child" (*Wille zum Kind*—a term frequently used in Weimar and even more in the Third Reich and which Lilje employed unselfconsciously) was a powerful act of Christian faith.[70] And also in 1954 a Catholic commentator in a "sexual-pedagogical lecture series" sponsored by the city of Bad Godesberg near Bonn made arguments for reproductive rather than "egotistical" marriage. Rejecting the models provided not only by Nazism but also by the Weimar Republic and the German Democratic Republic, his main purpose was to show that the Catholic Church's teachings not only had outlasted all political fashions but were essential for restoring healthy marriages in his present as well. Nazis had seen in sex only "the biological function . . . the breeding purpose." While this was offensive, reproduction *was* central to marital life; spouses fundamentally violated their bond "if they say no to the child."[71]

Another recurrent strand in Christian advice literature, indicatively often intertwined with remarks on the miseries of childlessness, involved the central importance of mutuality in bed. In this way commentators worked over and over to suture aspirations for lasting happiness, passion, and love to anxieties about nonnormative sexual practices and pregnancy prevention strategies. Anything directed solely at (what commentators regularly referred to as) "egotistic drive-satisfaction" was deemed unacceptable, both from the moral point of view and—crucially—also from the point of view of pleasure. Couples were informed that even intercourse in the missionary position, if one's thoughts were not completely focused on the spiritual bond with the partner, was little more than "reciprocal masturbation" (*gegenseitige Onanie*). But more than that, any emptiness a couple might feel, any vague sense of incomplete satisfaction or ambivalence about one another had its source in an inability fully to focus on the other person.[72] Christian advice givers styled themselves (in a manner that could be construed as protofeminist) as dedicated to women in their forceful insistence that men should never treat women like objects. But they also and repeatedly emphasized that women needed to give themselves fully, both in the sense of being selfless and in the sense of being receptive and open to the man. This openness (and hence real pleasure) was not possible if fear of pregnancy dominated sexual encounters. The solution, however, was seen in neither noncoital practices nor mechanical or chemical birth control products, but rather joyful receptivity to the possibility of procreation.[73]

BIRTH CONTROL AND ABORTION

Postwar West German culture was peculiarly inhospitable to open discussion of birth control products or practices. In comparison with the United States in the 1950s, for instance, there were in West Germany fewer family planning clinics, and sales of such objects as diaphragms or spermicidal jellies were proportionally lower; there was also less medical literature on the subject available to specialists, and of what literature there was, much expressed strong criticism of birth control.[74] There were several reasons for this hostility. One was that in a number of the Federal Republic's states, including North-Rhine Westphalia, the Rhineland-Palatinate, Bavaria, and (after a number of legal skirmishes) even the SPD-ruled state of Hesse, the Himmler order of 1941 banning the sale and advertisement of all birth control products besides condoms formally remained on the books. (Condoms had been exempted from the order during the Third Reich because of their usefulness in preventing the spread of venereal disease.) Yet another reason was that many doctors in postwar Germany had received medical training during the Third Reich and so had imbibed a fair amount of skepticism about birth control. In addition, there were also more subtle inherited forms of misogyny, and of unreflected anxieties about the declining German birthrate, that affected physicians' willing-ness to educate themselves or their patients about effective strategies. Meanwhile, when companies eager to market pessaries or contraceptive powders or gels sought to circumvent or challenge the law, some courts, openly defensive about reconfirming the validity of a ruling inherited from Nazi population policy, nonetheless at times repeated ideas that would be hard to distinguish from Nazi beliefs. Thus, for instance, a court in Frank-furt in 1955 argued that "not every legal measure that serves population growth has a National Socialist tendency. . . . For every healthy state . . . a growth in population is absolutely desirable."[75]

This resistance to fertility control among doctors, judges, and politi-cians was not solely an inheritance of Nazism, however. There was also the indirect, but no less powerful, impact of the conservative Christian backlash *against* Nazism's sexual incitements. For instance, condom vending machines had been fairly familiar aspects of the streetscape, of public toilets, and the backs of bars or barbershops in many German towns throughout the Third Reich and after the war—as soon as rubber was available again—also into the mid-1950s; symptomatically, however, the years from the mid-1950s into the early 1960s saw heated discussion among jurists and journalists over the desirability of these machines and their potential for corrupting the morals of youth. Even the neutral dis-play of condoms in vending machines could be interpreted—as some courts did—as an offense to "morals and decency" (*Sitte und Anstand*), a vague but for that reason all the more effective traditional legal category employed by conservative jurists in their efforts to deter youth (and inevi-tably also adult) access to fertility control.[76] Again, Catholic activists set the terms of the conversation. While in 1951–52 conservative Catholic youth organizations had demonstratively burned down kiosks that mar-keted pornography, in 1953 they initiated "actions" against condom vending machines. And, once again, far from being legally censured, this activism itself inspired conservative jurisdiction.[77] Yet it is crucial also to note that the major opposition party of Social Democrats did not provide much of an alternative to the Christian Democrats on sex-related issues but rather, into the 1960s, remained quite wary of challenging the churches. SPD politicians might vote against one or another repressive measure, but they did not offer an energetic defense of individual sexual freedom or self-determination.

Meanwhile, however, popular mores were decidedly at odds with offi-cial mores. This was true both with respect to Christian values more gen-erally and with respect to sexual morality per se. Germany was a more secularized society than either the United States or Great Britain, and Nazism had done its part to further that secularization. Meanwhile, even believers and churchgoers had their own opinions about sexual matters that diverged from both the churches' official stances and from those advanced by religious conservatives in the government; for example, popular mores, even in quite religious regions, could often make room for acceptance of durable nonmarital relationships. Moreover, in a survey conducted in 1949, also among regular churchgoers, fully 44 percent were of the opinion that premarital sex was acceptable.[78] Although the numbers admitting to and endorsing premarital coitus had dropped by approximately ten percentage points by the time the survey was repeated in 1963—and this was no doubt due precisely to the conservative cultural vigilance of the 1950s—numerous more informal estimates offered in the course of the 1950s and early 1960s suggested that anywhere between 80 and 90 percent of young people were practicing premarital coitus.[79] These numbers are much higher than the comparable figures for the United States or Britain. In short, in spite of all of the official and semiofficial rhetoric that adamantly insisted on female virginity before marriage, and which pleaded also for boys to desist from premarital experimentation, actual practices in Germany strayed sharply from formal norms. In no area of sex-related discussion was there so wide a gap between prescription and actual behavior, even as the prescriptions had profound consequences for how the sex people did have was engaged in and experienced.

Two national peculiarities, then, came together: a low level of information about and access to birth control and a high rate of premarital coitus. Yet another national peculiarity was crucial as well. Whereas American youth were internationally notorious for the practice of petting—mutual manual sexual play often leading to orgasm, a practice developed for the purpose of combining sexual intimacy and pleasure with pregnancy prevention (and the maintenance of technical virginity)—the conservative publicists who dominated the sex advice market in West Germany were tireless in their insistence that this form of sexuality, while seemingly offering "pleasure without regret" (*Genuss ohne Reue*), would nonetheless ruin the capacity for future sexual happiness in marriage. They were certain that girls who engaged in petting would prove to be frigid in their marriages.[80] Also more liberal German commentators found American petting practices bizarre. As one postwar journalist disapprovingly summarized the general attitude, "this 'petting' cannot possibly offer any sort of deeper satisfaction."[81] And, strikingly, although interviews with individuals who were adolescents in West Germany in the 1950s certainly reveal activity that could be defined as petting, it was almost always seen (by the participants themselves) as a brief transitional phase before the onset of coital activity and/or as a sad, even pathologically perverse, substitute for "real" sex. While in a study conducted in the early 1960s, for example, 72 percent of young men and 44 percent of young women between the ages of twenty and thirty admitted to having at some point engaged in petting, only a small minority voiced approval of the practice. Although it was "okay for the start of a relationship," they declared, it was also something basically "unnatural."[82] Even into the mid-1960s, when the sexual revolution was well underway, West German working-class youths in particular continued to feel that any sexual contact other than coitus was "perverse."[83] Here the advice givers and their public were in complete accord.

In sum, the messages could only have been experienced as contradictory and confusing. On the one hand, coitus was represented as the only natural sexual activity and all alternative or even supplemental practices were disdained or (more frequently) not mentioned at all and thereby treated as simply unimaginable. For example, with the exception of the sex advice magazine *Liebe und Ehe*—which had been shut down in 1951—no periodical in West Germany in the 1950s ever mentioned oral sex as a possible alternative to coitus. The contrast to Weimar era sex advice, when for instance the well-known physician Max Marcuse not only endorsed both oral and anal sex as pleasurable ways of avoiding pregnancy but also noted that their use was widespread, could not be more striking. Yet, at the same time, almost all advice writers treated female orgasm during coitus as an important desideratum. Indeed, some of the most sophisticated arguments put forward by medical doctors *against* birth control practices and products had to do with the idea that these practices or products would inhibit *female* pleasure. Simultaneously, however, the literature, whether Christian or secular, continually elaborated normative notions about gender. Even when the literature acknowledged that coitus, especially with a selfish man, might not always be a wonderful experience for a woman, it did not detail possible supplementary practices but rather declared that women simply did not like or seek sex as much as men did.

Aside from condoms, birth control products were difficult for unmarried people to procure. But birth control was not easily available for married people either. Access depended not only on the laws of the state in which couples lived but also on whether one lived in a big city or a little town, had a sympathetic and well-informed family physician or a local pharmacist from whom one could purchase spermicidal powders or jellies without embarrassment, and/or had the wherewithal to order birth control products and information from mail-order catalogs.

The *only* method in 1950s West Germany energetically endorsed by medical literature was the rhythm method, first discovered and refined during the 1930s. And although many doctors fiercely attacked the method as (variously) ineffective or unhealthy for a relationship, it was the sole form of birth control officially permitted believing Catholics.[84] A general familiarity with which days were likely to be "safe" and which were not was also fairly common knowledge among all strata of the population.

But so too was the knowledge that the method was not fully reliable, especially if one tried to "stretch" the days when coitus might be okay beyond a supersafe minimum, or if any untoward event (like stress or illness) threw the cycle off. Widely held beliefs that coitus during a woman's menstrual period was not normal or acceptable shortened the number of available days even more. And, again, the hostility to, or ignorance and utter lack of imagination about, possible alternatives to coitus on the "unsafe" days remained manifest in both the professional medical and the popular advice literature. Thus, for instance, a prominent physician analyzing the value of the rhythm method in 1953 could only recommend the method as a means of family planning "to that group of advice seekers who have at their disposal a considerable amount of conscientiousness and self-discipline," for (in his opinion) the period of "abstinence" required by the method could prove an "unbearable burden" on marriages.[85]

The single most widely used birth control in the pre-pill era, both before and within marriage, was withdrawal during intercourse (i.e., coitus interruptus). "My husband is careful" (*Mein Mann nimmt sich in acht*) was the standard way women phrased it when queried by a doctor about how they managed to space the births of their children.[86] And as a young man who grew up in 1950s West Germany remembered in 2001, speaking of himself and his girlfriend: "We thought this American petting business was *dumb*. We were in love; we talked about it. We decided to use withdrawal." (And when the girlfriend did get pregnant, this teenage couple married.)[87]

This last story points to a much larger phenomenon of premarital heterosexual activity among teens: *Frühehen* (early marriages), also colloquially called *Mussehen* (must marriages). Marriages among minors (which reached extremely high rates by the late 1950s) were almost always entered into solely because a child was "on the way." Among the approximate average of 500,000 marriages entered into annually in the early 1960s, 88,000 spouses per year were between the ages of sixteen and twenty; 20,000 brides annually were seventeen years old or less. Unsurprisingly, statistics showed that these marriages were also uniquely vulnerable to divorce.[88] But also among young couples who were no longer minors, unplanned pregnancy often led to a marriage that would otherwise have been delayed or not entered into at all. Numerous memoirs and oral history testimonies describe the social pressures within local communities that made rushed marriages the norm. At the end of the 1950s, it was found that approximately one-third of West German brides were pregnant on their wedding day. By the early 1960s, studies variously found that anywhere from 40 to 70 percent of firstborn children were conceived out of wedlock; more than 50 percent of all marriages and fully 90 percent of early marriages (with spouses between the ages of eighteen and twenty-one) were entered into solely because the bride was pregnant.[89]

Frühehen—or, if already married, another (sometimes only half-wanted) child—were, however, not the only consequences of a climate in which birth control products and information were not easily accessible to everyone. Many professional physicians' discomfort with or hostility to dispensing birth control information and products contributed not only to the popularity of coitus interruptus. It also resulted in an environment in which abortion, despite its illegal status under Paragraph 218, was nevertheless widespread.

In West Germany in the 1950s and early 1960s, the most prevalent method utilized to keep family size small—aside from withdrawal—was abortion. This was in stark contrast, as observers noted, to both France and Britain where there was much stronger public support for family planning.[90] As one doctor put it bluntly in 1953, Germany was in the midst of an "abortion epidemic," while still a full decade later another doctor matter-of-factly referred to "the abortion plague."[91] Over the course of the 1950s, estimates of abortion rates fluctuated and also varied by region, but there was general agreement among medical professionals that the rates remained extraordinarily high, or were even climbing. Midwives, quacks, and pregnant women themselves performed most of the abortions (sometimes using knitting needles or injections of soapy water or poisonous herbs or chemicals), but it was also no secret that there were doctors who were willing to break the law for a price. As some patients, when questioned gently by a trusted physician about what they had done in those instances when withdrawal had not worked, confided: "Well yes, a few times I did let myself get scraped out" (*na ja, ein paarmal habe ich mich ausschaben lassen*).[92] A frequently used technique was to go to a physician for a routine brief walk-in office visit, have him or her induce a miscarriage mechanically, and then be rushed to either a public hospital or a private clinic with "sudden" bleeding. In 1959 alone, 5,400 individuals were each sentenced to several years in prison for performing abortions.[93]

Experts assumed that for every case that came to the attention of authorities, either the police or a hospital (where women sometimes ended up not just because of induced miscarriages but also after botched operations or in instances of life-threatening complications), there were at least 100 abortions that went unrecorded. In a case that made national news in 1963, a doctor who had served time in prison a year earlier for the first time a woman in his care had died and was now committed to an insane asylum in the wake of his second fatality, admitted to having performed approximately 2,000 abortions over the prior decade.[94] Other ways of obtaining estimates involved asking women about their prior reproductive history, in confidential intake exams during visits to their gynecologists, and then extrapolating from this sample. Based on a total of between 10 and 11 million women of reproductive age in the Federal Republic between 1950 and 1957, estimates found that in any given year between 5 and 10 percent of all German women had an abortion. Experts repeatedly spoke of an average, for the duration of the 1950s, of anywhere between 500,000 to 1 million abortions in the Federal Republic each year. Some studies found a yearly ratio of 1 abortion to every birth; an oft-quoted 1953 study undertaken by a Hamburg gynecologist identified in his region an annual ratio of 3 abortions to every birth.[95]

By the early 1960s, the mainstream press and medical journals repeatedly referred to an annual average of anywhere between 750,000 to more than 1 million abortions. Some physicians even estimated 2 million abortions per year, and it also became routine for mainstream periodicals to note as common sense that there was an illegal abortion for every birth in the Federal Republic.[96] Contemporaries variously speculated that 1 of every 2 German women faced the decision of whether to abort at some point in her life, or indeed that every year 1 in 4 women was affected.[97] One prominent gynecologist interviewed in 1964 noted that abortions were available not only in every major city but also in the smallest villages, and that the methods used, also by nonprofessionals, had become so sophisticated (*geschickt*) that doctors had no chance of keeping track of the rates in their area.[98] While doctors had pointed out already in the 1950s that death rates from abortion were much lower than they had been in previous decades because of the widespread use of antibiotics, numerous observers in the 1960s still noted that health problems arising from illegal abortions were nonetheless widespread. This was so not least because the illegality made proper follow-up care unlikely, and there is no question that the furtive and not always clean conditions under which abortions were performed exacerbated the likelihood of both physical and psychological damage. Insurance records from the 1950s also reveal that, every year, an average of 10,000 West German women died from complications due to their abortions.[99] Only the invention and widespread dissemination of the birth control pill brought an end to this scandalous state of affairs.

SEXUALITY AND CRIME

To bring down the culture of sexual conservatism, however, it would take more than the medical-technological invention of the pill. The sexual liberalization of West Germany depended on three other crucial dynamics. One was the ever-intensifying use of sexual stimuli (including nude and seminude images and titillating narratives) in advertising and journalism—in other words, a dynamic largely intrinsic to economic processes.

The second dynamic, in complex interaction with the first, was a process of direct political mobilization against the official culture of sexual conservatism. This political mobilization, beginning in the late 1950s and escalating in ardor and strategic effectiveness in the first three or four years of the 1960s, involved both prominent liberal public intellectuals and younger, often left-leaning student activists. And there is no question that liberals and leftists, while on the one hand exceedingly critical of the commodification of sex and its role in consumer capitalism, also used the space opened by the manifest contradictions between conservative norms and sexualized marketing to press their own claims. Yet nothing was more important in helping liberals and leftists redirect the *moral* terms of debate about sex in West Germany than a third dynamic: the return with full force to public discussion of the Holocaust as its details were made public in the postwar trials of perpetrators. Preeminent among these was the trial of Adolf Eichmann in Jerusalem in 1961 and the trial, held in Frankfurt am Main from 1963 to 1965 of twenty-two SS men and one prisoner Kapo—all perpetrators in Auschwitz. Especially the Auschwitz trial provided a focal point for rewriting the memory and lessons of the Third Reich for liberal-left purposes and was a singularly important radicalizing event for the generation that came of political age in the later 1960s. Yet even before the Auschwitz trial began, the political mobilization against the culture of sexual conservatism had already gained considerable momentum.

A proposed reform of the Federal Republic's criminal code with respect to sexual matters served as an early occasion for the coordinated emergence of critical liberal voices. The development of a new criminal code had been underway since 1954, when a commission comprising of jurists and politicians had been established for this purpose. Medical and legal experts were consulted at various stages, and in 1960 a first draft was published, with a revised version of the draft appearing in 1962. This revised draft rapidly won approval from the cabinet of the Christian Democratic government and thereafter the Bundesrat. By 1963 discussion of the draft was immanent also in the Bundestag.

The 1962 draft was profoundly conservative. The draft expressly maintained the criminalization of adultery, as well as of pornography and mechanical sex aids. It constrained the advertising and marketing of birth control products and products designed to prevent the spread of venereal disease if this occurred in a manner that could be construed as offending "morals and customs." It criminalized both striptease and consensual partner-swapping (while noting that both were on the rise).

The commission's draft also recommended that male homosexuality remain a crime. It justified this recommendation on the grounds that the "overwhelming majority of the German population sees sexual relations between men as a contemptible aberration that is likely to subvert the character and destroy moral feeling." The commission averred that homosexual men affected by Paragraph 175 did not act from an "inborn disposition," but rather were "overwhelmingly persons who . . . through seduction, habituation, or sexual supersatiation have become addicted to vice or who have turned to same-sex intercourse for purely profit-seeking motives." The commission concluded that homosexuality was communicable and contagious. It argued that Paragraph 175 functioned as a successful and necessary deterrent to this threat, and it held that to decriminalize male homosexuality would result both in the further spread and ever-greater visibility of this aberrant condition. It also expressed the view that homosexuals should be in most instances capable, if they made enough of an effort, of suppressing their desires and hence living lives in accordance with the law. The commission also went so far as to announce that "wherever same-sex immorality has run rampant and grown to great proportions, the degeneration of the people and the deterioration of its moral strength has been the consequence." Once again, as advocates of Paragraph 175 had already done in the immediate postwar era, the commission underscored the special vulnerability of teenage boys and young men. Thus, the law served as a "barrier" especially to dissuade youth from the enticements of same-sex activities.[100]

Finally, and not least of all, the commission opposed the legalization of abortion. The only exemptions might be cases when the mother's life was in danger or there were incontrovertibly severe health risks to the mother if the pregnancy continued. The commission emphatically rejected any exemptions not only in cases of anticipated congenital disability or cases of anticipated hardship (whether economic or psychological) for the mother but also in cases when conception resulted from rape (because, in its view, a woman's rape claim could often not be proved, and thus there existed grave concern that exemptions in this regard would be open to abuse). Moreover, the commission felt that it was by no means a settled matter whether a raped woman might not after all develop maternal feeling for the child.

The commission sidestepped any reference to the Third Reich in its discussion of homosexuality, even though it had relied heavily on concepts and language drawn from Nazi homophobic policies. On the subject of abortion, however, the commission did address Nazism, albeit in contradictory ways. The commission emphasized the liberality of its own proposals in comparison with the more punitive laws of the Third Reich, which had instituted lengthy prison terms, as well as the death penalty, for some abortionists. By contrast, the commission urged jail time of three to five years for women who performed abortions on themselves or for abortionists who did not accept money for their services. (For paid abortionists, the commission set ten-year prison terms.) Yet the commission did little to distance itself from Nazi rhetoric to the effect that abortions impaired "the life-force of the German *Volk*." It also forcefully denounced Weimar-era campaigns to liberalize abortion laws. It held that Weimar-era liberalization efforts had been consistently insensitive to the supreme need to guard "life-in-the-making," and that the protection of "unborn life" was a matter of utmost importance "in the life of the individual, the family, and the *Volk*."[101]

Unsurprisingly, given both the content of and the legitimations advanced for these proposed reforms, older liberals and younger leftists alike condemned the commission's draft of a new criminal code. They criticized both the general world view upon which the draft was based and the positions expressed about birth control and abortion and especially about male homosexuality. The Frankfurt-based student newspaper *Diskus* referred to the commission's draft as taking "an undisguised restorationist approach" and described the draft as aggressive and affect-laden rather than informed by judicial impartiality and fairness.[102] The left-leaning Hamburg-based newsmagazine *Konkret* observed that the purpose of the so-called reforms was apparently to avoid any and all reform. *Konkret* argued that the commission's draft relied not on scientific research but rather on "a Christian-theological image of humanity as weighed down by guilt." And *Konkret* saw in the proposed "reform" not just misogyny and homophobia but also a "hostile stance toward everything sexual."[103]

The commission's defense of Paragraph 175 drew particular fire. The recommendation that male homosexuality continue to be criminalized was both found by critics to be the single most offensive aspect of the draft and seen as symptomatic of the commission's broader antisexual attitude. Critics of the commission repeatedly noted that this defense of ongoing criminalization directly bucked the tide of international Western developments. In Britain, both the Catholic Griffin Report of 1956 and the government-sponsored Wolfenden Report of 1957 had recommended decriminalizing sexual acts engaged in by consenting adults. Fifteen noncommunist European countries (including France, Italy, Spain, Belgium, the Netherlands, Denmark, and Sweden) criminalized male homosexuality only in the context of laws that addressed the protection of minors but left consensual adults free to do as they pleased in private. In general, a number of these countries, also predominantly Catholic ones, based their legal codes on the premise that the strictest of distinctions must be maintained between the realm of morality (the concern of religion) and the realm of crime (the business of the law).

The single most influential rebuttal of the commission's proposed criminal code was the 1963 anthology, *Sexualität und Verbrechen* (Sexuality and Crime). Although it included two contributors who tended toward more conservative views, the book brought together the reflections of more than twenty critically minded psychologists, medical doctors, jurists, theologians, and philosophers. *Sexualität und Verbrechen* appeared in an affordable paperback series with the popular Fischer press in Frankfurt; the book rapidly garnered nationwide notice, was widely reviewed, and was frequently quoted. Its inspirational impact especially on the emerging younger generation of New Left activists was considerable.

The anthology brought together Jewish reémigrés like Frankfurt School philosopher and sociologist Theodor Adorno and the jurist Fritz Bauer (soon to be the main prosecutor at the Frankfurt Auschwitz trial) with ex-Nazis like the head of the family planning association ProFamilia, Hans Harmsen, and the sexologists Hans Giese and Hans Bürger-Prinz, together with gentile non-Nazis like the liberal jurist Herbert Jäger. In so doing, the book itself provided a key instantiation of the intense cultural energy produced in postwar West Germany precisely by the mix of Jewish and ex-Nazi and non-Jewish liberal intellectuals.[104] It also demonstrated by example how *all three* of these constituencies were essential to the democratization of West Germany. (And at the same time, the enthusiasm with which young activists received this book opens an important window onto the intimate interrelationship between liberalism and New Leftism and the transgenerational affiliations that are often neglected in scholars' tendency to overemphasize intergenerational conflict in the 1960s.)

The most notable and oft-cited contributions to *Sexualität und Verbrechen* were those by Adorno and by the Berlin-based professor of education and psychotherapist Wolfgang Hochheimer. Hochheimer offered the most outraged condemnation of the commission. He pointed out that empirical reality in no way lined up with the commission's conservative ideals. The vast majority of West Germans—perhaps 90 percent—were not virgins when they married. Moreover, 40 percent of sexually mature individuals were not married at all. Nor did sexual behavior within marriage match normative expectations. Hochheimer also contended that homosexuality was a natural variant of human sexuality and far more prevalent, also among so-called heterosexuals, than either the extant law or the conservative commission acknowledged. Hochheimer was also appalled by the commission's presumptive position that women would develop maternal feeling for an unwanted child. Abortions, he said, had negligible negative impact on a woman's psychic state; on the other hand, legally to require that a woman carry a child to term against her will could cause grievous damage to both the mother and child. Invoking the Third Reich, Hochheimer made plain as well how offensive it was for the commission to justify its conservative opinions with repeated references to such concepts as "the moral sensibility of the people" (*sittliches Volksempfinden*). Hochheimer observed acerbically that "just yesterday" (i.e., during the

Third Reich), "the 'sensibility of the people' was addressed and unleashed quite differently . . . in order cruelly to annihilate 'those of a different nature' like 'insects,' 'lice,' 'devils,' 'animals,' 'subhumans.' Also the sexually 'abnormal' were expressly included here."[105]

Adorno also invoked Nazism and its legacies to promote the liberalization of contemporary West German sexual mores. Adorno did remind his readers that Nazism had sexually inciting aspects, as he noted the "breeding farms of the SS" and "the injunctions to girls to have temporary relationships with those who had declared themselves . . . as the elite." Yet he made clear as well that the Third Reich was no "kingdom of erotic freedom." Disgusted by the lack of courage evinced by so many otherwise progressive postwar German intellectuals whenever the subject turned to sex, Adorno decisively defended sexual freedom. "Precisely when it is not warped or repressed, sex harms no one," he wrote, adding that this view of sexuality "should also saturate the logic of the law and its application." But Adorno was also intent on pointing out how, specifically in the midst of both the growing commodification of sex and the increasingly popular attitude that coitus was natural and healthy, taboos against "perversion" (*Perversität*) and "sophistication" ([*Raffinement*) were intensified. This was bad for everyone, because this narrowing of what sex was and could be, this single-minded emphasis on "pure genitality" (*pure Genitalität*), made sex into a pitifully "shriveled" and "dull" thing. But these taboos were truly dreadful in the way that they fueled hostility to minorities like prostitutes and homosexuals. Just as bizarre but revealing was the fact that even though taboos against sexuality outside of marriage were becoming, in practice, so outdated, the taboos could still be mobilized at any moment. Sexually conservative, even aggressively punitive, messages still reached a wide audience—all the more reason to be suspicious that the one kind of nongenital sexuality that was not just permitted but actively cultivated in the society was voyeurism. And Adorno noted caustically that the sexual taboos that still prevailed in his postwar contemporary moment were a piece of the same "ideological and psychological syndrome of prejudice that helped to create the mass basis for National Socialism and whose manifest content lives on in a depoliticized form."[106]

Sexualität und Verbrechen did not singlehandedly defeat the commission's proposal for a revised criminal code. But it did provide opponents of the commission with new ways of thinking that would alter substantially how both sexuality and the memory of the Third Reich would be read and interpreted by a new generation of young West Germans. For now, and increasingly, rather than placing their emphasis on Nazism's sexual excess and inducements, as Christians had done in the more immediate aftermath of the war (and the ways these excesses had been connected with genocide), liberals and leftists began ever more frequently to stress Nazism's conservative and sexually repressive aspects. This collective move would deal a staggering blow to the commission's draft for the new criminal code and would finally cause the Bundestag first to set the matter aside—and fail eventually ever to return to it.

Among the groundswell of criticism that accrued around the commission's draft proposal, there were further contributions that deserve mention. Already in August 1962, for instance, *Diskus* criticized the persistence of sexual taboos in postwar West Germany. In this context, it noted that "without taboos there is no drive-denial, and without this there are no accumulated aggressions, which can, at the appointed moment, be directed against minorities or external enemies—Jews, capitalists, communists."[107] And in December 1962 the historian of religion Hans Joachim Schoeps, like Adorno and Bauer a Jewish reémigré, stressed the significance of his own Jewishness for having sensitized him to the German treatment of homosexuals. As Adorno was, Schoeps too was repulsed by the widespread cowardice evident among postwar German intellectuals when it came to taking a stand for homosexual rights.[108] Schoeps called for the abolition of Paragraph 175 and demanded that the members of the Bundestag closely examine their own conscience if they intended to continue to criminalize homosexuality:

> Since the persecution of the Jews during the Third Reich, in the eyes of the world the German people stands under the suspicion that it has a tendency to torment, persecute, and terrorize its minorities. Of course homosexuals are not an ethnic-religious minority, but certainly they are a biological-anthropological minority within the *Volk* as a whole. Since the gas ovens of Auschwitz and Maidanek burned . . . one should think twice, or three times, whether one also in the new criminal code wants to continue to treat the minority of homosexuals as people for whom there must be separate laws.[109]

Here then were new ways to theorize the relationship between sexuality and crime; in a reversal of the postwar formula that had linked sexual expression with cruelty and murder, now cruelty and murder were linked with sexual repression. Over and over again, West Germans began to argue that sexual repression was at the root of all evil.

Post-Holocaust Memory

It was in this context above all that liberal and leftist students, public intellectuals, and journalists increasingly highlighted the problem of conservatives' constriction of questions of morality to sexual matters and called attention to the far more profound moral ugliness of war and genocide. Youth magazines not only documented the concrete damages done by laws that criminalized consensual sexual activity and its consequences but also, and with increasing fervor, challenged what they saw as the hypocrisy of sexual conservatives and religious leaders the moment moral discussion turned to questions of racism and murder. It was the project of struggling to liberalize sexual mores in West Germany in the early 1960s that brought a different version of the Third Reich into public discussion. The convergence of debates about the Holocaust with debates about sex entered the mainstream media as early as 1963, when *Der Spiegel* approvingly cited a comment made by one of the prosecutors in the Frankfurt trial of Auschwitz perpetrators, to the effect that Auschwitz had been built by *Spiesser*—the term typically used by liberals and leftists to describe not only generally banal and conventional but also sexually uptight conservatives[110] (fig. 3.1).

Liberals and leftists also began to contend that the right to sexual activity was a fundamental human right and that the desire for sex was something for which no one needed ever again to apologize. Rather than having to argue defensively that sex was something people would engage in whether it was forbidden or not (the standard liberal strategy for most of the 1950s), in the early 1960s liberals started forcefully to assert that sexual pleasure was itself a moral good. Sick of a decade of talk when "pleasure craving" (*Genusssucht*) had been routinely treated as self-evidently morally repugnant, even when pursued within marriage, enraged at also the Social Democrats' "servile currying of the churches' favor," especially young left-leaning students increasingly declared that there was nothing wrong or sinful or indecent about pleasure—indeed, that the pursuit of pleasure was a genuinely just pursuit.[111]

The lesson that linked Nazism to sexual repression provided an especially important resource for turning the moral tables on conservatives. Already in 1964, for instance, *Konkret* railed against opponents of birth control, and especially against those who would deny the pill to unmarried women. The pill, conservatives posited, was morally unacceptable for casual "weekend relationships" and for the unmarried in general, because they did not have "the will to the child" (*Wille zum Kind*). *Konkret* sarcastically commented:

> Apart from the Nazi-racist origins of this concept what is revealed here is a contempt for human beings and [especially] for young people. . . . [Here there is] still the idea that sexual intercourse is a sin, only permitted for the purpose of making babies or (already very enlightened) for preserving the marital happiness that is necessary for raising children. . . . The pill is no good for a weekend relationship? Why on earth not? Since most do not want to get married, here the pill is especially suitable. What do they mean, young people who only seek pleasure? What else should they be seeking in this land?[112]

Tor zum KZ Auschwitz: Eine Stätte des Schreckens ...

... von Spießern erbaut: Auschwitz-Kommandant **Höß**, Bewacher

Figure 3.1. *Der Spiegel*, 18 December 1963, p. 47. The captions read: "The gate to the concentration camp Auschwitz: A place of horror . . ." ". . . built by philistines: Auschwitz-commandant Höss, guards." (Reprinted by permission of *Der Spiegel*, Höss photo reprinted by permission of AP/World Wide Photos.)

Similarly, in 1965, under the heading "Philistine Morality" (*Spiesser-Moral*), *Diskus* scathingly analogized between conservative campaigns like the mid-1960s effort of Christian Democratic politician Adolf Süsterhenn to "clean up" the film industry, the brutal "cleanup" that the United States was at that moment conducting in Vietnamese villages, and West German conservatives' efforts to scrub clean "the memory of even worse conditions in a filthy German past." *Diskus* expressed special repugnance at Süsterhenn's reliance on such notions as "the healthy sensibility of the *Volk*," as though this term had not been contaminated by Nazism.[113] Along related lines, also in 1965, *Konkret* pointedly juxtaposed pictures of topless and nude women (labeled "filth," "immoral," and "dangerous to youth") with antisemitic captions from the *Nationalzeitung*, a preferred venue of former Nazis (labeled "not filth," "not immoral," and "not dangerous to youth"). The aim, of course, was to underscore the hypocrisy of right-wing political views that found nudity more immoral than antisemitism.[114] But it was not just ex-Nazis *Konkret* abhorred. Increasingly, *Konkret* made a mission of exposing the persistence of popular antisemitism in postwar Germany—indeed, the *upsurge* of public expressions of antisemitism in the context, of all things, of the Eichmann and Auschwitz trials.[115] The magazine also documented in detail the entanglement of the Christian churches with Nazism and with Nazism's aggressive war on the eastern front.[116] All of this was intended rhetorically to ask: how could any conservatives in the older generation, and not least religious conservatives, possibly claim that they had the right to judge what was moral and what was not?

Conservatives did not give up easily, and would not immediately cede to liberals the right to reinterpret the significance of the Nazi past for the liberalized sexual politics of the 1960s. Incredibly, for example, the Christian Democratic politician Hermann Kraemer in 1964 denounced the brief incidents of masturbation and sexual intercourse shown in an Ingmar Bergman film as reflecting "the same spiritual stance" as "the concentration camp Auschwitz." Referring directly to the trial of Auschwitz perpetrators taking place in Frankfurt, he contended that "the degradation of the human is nowhere so clear at this moment than in this trial. This degradation of the human finds its continuation in the sexual acrobatics of the Swedish filmmaker."[117]

Yet a clear trend toward a reading of the Third Reich as above all marked by sexual repression proved unstoppable. The Marxist intellectual journal *Das Argument* in 1965 advanced the view that the insights of psychology were especially valuable for understanding fascism because what required investigation was "the connection between the suppression of sexual drives on the one hand and the antisemitic persecution mania and its raging in manifest cruelty on the other."[118] In 1966 *Der Spiegel* firmly

Sex-Kritiker **Hitler**
Erstickendes Parfüm

Figure 3.2. *Der Spiegel*, 2 May 1966, p. 58. The caption reads: "Sex-Critic Hitler: Suffocating Perfume." (Reprinted by permission of *Der Spiegel* and akg-images)

aligned itself with the side of sexual liberation and for this cause, crucially, it not only attacked the churches but also invoked Adolf Hitler as a negative counterexample of sexual self-repression and repressiveness. Offering a one-sided reading of *Mein Kampf*—which quoted Hitler's disgust with the "suffocating perfume of our modern eroticism" but did not mention that in the same sentence he had criticized "unmanly" prudery—*Der Spiegel* printed a photograph of Hitler demonstratively captioned "Sex-Critic Hitler"[119] (fig. 3.2). While in the early 1950s, Christians had been able to present themselves and their sexually conservative agenda as the antithesis of Nazism and its sexual politics, *Der Spiegel* here represented Christians and Nazis as comparable in their visceral hostility to sexual freedom. This rewriting of the past would prove remarkably durable.

From 1966 on, it was hard to find anyone who disagreed with an analysis of Nazism as inimical to sexuality. Philosopher Arno Plack, in his magnum opus of 1967 indicatively entitled *Society and Evil: A Critique of the Reigning Morality*, asserted: "It would be wrong to hold the view that all of what happened in Auschwitz was typically German. It was typical for a society that suppresses sexuality."[120] And the journalist Hannes Schwenger in his influential 1969 book criticizing the "antisexual" politics of the Christian churches, specifically identified the postwar churches' attacks on "free love, premarital intercourse, adultery, and divorce" as speaking "the language of fascism."[121] The New Left held these ideas of a thoroughly sex-hostile Third Reich quite dear, and these assumptions strongly informed New Left experimentations in communal living, nonmonogamy, and antiauthoritarian childrearing. But the New Left was hardly alone. These convictions were ubiquitous in West Germany by the late 1960s. They have rarely been challenged since.

Yet, and in all the ways I have been suggesting, the sexual conservatism of the mid- to late 1950s was itself a postfascist invention rather than inherited tradition. In its own way, this sexual conservatism was an attempt—and a remarkably successful one—to master the past. Coming of age, as they did, at a moment when liberals struggled to dismantle the hegemony of sexual conservatism in West Germany by linking sexual conservatism with Nazism and the Holocaust, politically critical young people in particular would be especially drawn to explanations of Nazism and Holocaust that found both phenomena rooted in sexual repression. And although the student movement that transformed the political landscape of West Germany after the mid-1960s would style itself as antifascist, it is crucial to understand it first and foremost as an anti*post*fascist movement, a protest against the postfascist settlement in West Germany, and postwar young people's own experiences coming of age among the suffocating pieties and claustrophobic philistinism of the 1950s.

The 1950s were a sexually conservative time also in other Western countries, and there, too, this decade was followed by student rebellions and sexual liberalization. But nowhere else was the insistence on sexual conformity and restraint experienced as so intensely hypocritical and inexcusable; nowhere else could a stifling sexual morality seem to the young such a patently obvious displacement of a deeper unresolved guilt. The New Left labor organizer and feminist activist Barbara Köster in the 1980s retrospectively summarized her own and her generation's coming-of-age in the 1950s this way:

> I was raised in the Adenauer years, a time dominated by a horrible moral conformism, against which we naturally rebelled. We wanted to flee from the white Sunday gloves, to run from the way one had to hide the fingernails behind the back if they weren't above reproach. Finally then we threw away our bras as well. . . . For a long time I had severe altercations with my parents and fought against the fascist heritage they forced on me. At first I rejected their authoritarian and puritanical conception of childrearing, but soon we came into conflict over a more serious topic: the persecution of the Jews. I identified with the Jews, because I felt myself to be persecuted by my family.[122]

This can be read for what it is: a disturbing and simplistic, even offensive, appropriation of the suffering of others. But it can also be read for what it also is: an important, urgent, even desperate flailing to free oneself from the cloying and everywhere inadequately acknowledged toxicities of the supposedly clean post-1945 period.

At the same time, this passage reveals as well the deeply held conviction about the "fascist" quality of the sexual conservatism and propriety pre-occupations with which Köster was raised. That there had been a displacement of the discourse of morality away from murder and onto sex was clear to critical young people in the early 1960s. What they were not, could not have been, aware of was how very recent the shift to sexual conservatism had been.

CHAPTER FOUR

The Morality of Pleasure

THE SEXUAL REVOLUTION

The sexual revolution arrived on the West German scene in the mid-1960s, escalating in extent and intensity throughout the remainder of the decade and into the early 1970s. The sexual revolution in all its dimensions demolished the postfascist culture of sexual conservatism. In making this revolution possible, the commercialization, liberalization, and politicization of sex were inseparable developments. While the sudden mass availability of reliable birth control in the form of the pill certainly contributed mightily to the change in sexual mores, it did not on its own create the revolution. Just as important was the thorough saturation of the visual landscape with seminude (and soon completely nude) images of women's bodies as well as the unabashed marketing of a multitude of objects via these images, together with an extraordinary boom in the market also of overtly pornographic pictures and narratives. This "sex wave," as West Germans called it, was joined by a broad liberalization of popular values around nudity and pre- and extramarital sex. What had previously been done surreptitiously and in hiding was brought out in the open and loudly defended. There was a far greater willingness to publicize liberal values and to attack sexual conservatism vigorously and directly. Finally, in the midst of these wider trends, there was also the emergence and rise to cultural prominence of a New Left movement as well as incipient feminist and gay and lesbian rights movements, each of which, albeit in divergent ways, sought radically to politicize questions and issues surrounding sexual relations. None of these phenomena was unique to West Germany. Rather, West German developments during the late 1960s and early 1970s moved in tandem with developments across the Western world, as throughout Western Europe and the United States youth countercultures and student rebellions exacerbated and spurred further already existing trends toward sexual liberalization.

Yet there were also crucial dimensions of the sexual revolution that were specific to West Germany. There was a distinctive force and fury to West German debates over sex and a heightened drama to the resulting social transformations. The new consensus developed in the early to mid-1960s by liberal intellectuals and New Left activists that the Third Reich had been not only brutally but also uniformly sexually repressive became so widely assumed as to seem incontrovertible. Furthermore, armed with the idea that there were strong equivalencies between Christian conservatives and Nazis on the subject of sex, liberals and radicals succeeded in putting powerful conservative publicists on the defensive and in redirecting completely the moral terms of debate about sex. Taking their cue from the groundswell of popular liberalization and the new moral arguments advanced by liberals and leftist activists, the Social Democrats, who joined the government in the Grand Coalition of 1966 to 1969 and then took over entirely in 1969, systematically worked to undo also the legal underpinnings of the postwar culture of sexual conservatism. Laws pertaining to adultery and divorce, male homosexuality, pornography, prostitution, and abortion were all in due course reformed.

By 1966 at the latest, it was abundantly clear that censorship of nudity or sex-related themes in the media had simply ceased to function. Pictures of scantily clad young bodies, revealed bellybuttons, and unclothed breasts (with only the nipples covered) blanketed billboards and magazine covers; advertisers proliferated erotically suggestive slogans to sell everything from cars to chocolate. Frank descriptions of sexual matters filled more (and more) space in periodicals and mass-market books alike. From the trashiest tabloids to the most highbrow journals and newspapers, print media sought energetically to cash in. Magazines now ran photos of young women topless at swimming pools and published essays on topics like nude dancing or the latest imported fashion from America: partner swapping (now popular at West German parties as well). Even when articles analytically and with self-reflexive intellectual detachment raised questions about West German culture's new addiction to voyeurism (or "sex as spectator sport," as *Der Spiegel* sardonically phrased it), these essays nonetheless became part of the same circuit of erotic explicitness they claimed to criticize.[1] Conservative commentators responded with horror at the barrage of provocative images and texts. Yet many people welcomed the sex wave. Certainly, once the door to titillating images and narratives had been opened, supply could scarcely keep up with demand. Meanwhile, the changes were not just in the realm of representations; it was clear that general popular attitudes were also shifting decisively in a more liberal direction.[2]

Adultery became a particular focus of nationwide fascination. As recently as 1963, the ideal of marriage, and also young and not just older people's devotion to the value of marital fidelity, had been celebrated in the media as *the* West German cultural common sense. At that time, fidelity had been at the top of the list of qualities most valued in a marriage partner, also among female and male youth.[3] But beginning in 1965, and within a few years spreading relentlessly also into the most mainstream of venues, adultery and its possible benefits for an individual *and* for a marriage became a much-debated media topic. From the left-wing youth magazine *Konkret* to the right-wing daily *Bild*, infidelity in general and threesomes in particular, though always two women with one man (not coincidentally a typical constellation in heterosexual pornography), received elaborate attention. Books like *Gruppensex in Deutschland* (Group Sex in Germany, 1968) became instant bestsellers; although they presented themselves as straightforward reportage, they also (and above all) served as narrative pornography.[4]

Meanwhile, sex in film broke all former taboos. In the early 1950s, a few seconds of female nudity on screen had sparked widespread popular protest; cinemas closed when distraught patrons threw stink bombs. For the remainder of the 1950s, a combination of film industry self-censorship and rigorous government control successfully kept all nude images out of movies. Only in 1964 did Ingmar Bergman's *The Silence* break with these restrictions (with two brief displays of sexual explicitness). The film drew ten million West German viewers, but it also caused considerable uproar, as conservatives reacted in outrage.

By the late 1960s, however, such a controversy seemed quaint and quite distant. Representations that would have been labeled absolutely shocking only two or three years earlier now appeared almost tame. For instance, pseudoscientific sex "enlightenment" films made for general audiences were released to tremendous commercial success and little real debate. Some of these new films—like the documentary *Du* (You, 1968)—involved prominent liberal professionals (among them Wolfgang Hochheimer, Hans Giese, and Hans Bürger-Prinz) interviewing prostitutes or sex criminals. Other films featured naked couples debating their sexual problems, while expert voice-overs assured people that marriages could be mended through open communication. In this new genre of soft-core "education," journalist and self-appointed sex apostle Oswalt Kolle clearly set the pace. The film versions of his popular article series and books on sexuality were smash hits. Kolle classics like *Das Wunder der Liebe* (The Miracle of Love, 1967) and *Dein Mann, das unbekannte Wesen* (Your Husband, the Unknown Being, 1969) revolutionized what West Germans considered acceptable cinematic fare. This was no revolution confined to the large metropoles; Kolle's films were shown also in schools (for anyone at least thirteen years old) even in the smallest towns.

As of 1969, the now SPD-led federal government was itself sponsoring nudity on film. Inspired by the ideal of an informed and sexually mature citizenry, the government gave Kolle financial backing to produce *Helga* (1969), which became the first German film ever to document childbirth on screen. Here also, as in most other Kolle films, the entire family went nude. And as with other Kolle films, it was completely unclear whether audiences went to be educated or rather just amused. Kolle himself was certain that he helped couples attain deeper intimacy and greater shared sexual pleasure. Yet there was something so programmatic and awkward about the way his protagonists spoke their parts that it seems more plausible to believe those of his contemporaries who say they learned nothing from his movies but just got a good giggle from the new chance to see so much naked flesh. At the same time, there is no question that Kolle's insistence that he was improving marriages contributed significantly to reversing conservatives' ability to monopolize the discussion of marriage, even as Kolle's own much-publicized marital infidelities again served both as titillating tabloid fare *and* as a focal point for West Germans' massive and quite earnest wrestling with the problem of monogamy.[5]

By 1970 at the latest, it was apparent to all that the already rather flimsy pedagogical apparatus for these quasi-documentary films was a farce. Yet even as the educational alibi fell away, the basic genre persisted; indeed, it achieved more commercial momentum while it grew ever more sexually explicit. The marketing of films as documentaries whose purpose was to inform citizens about sexual matters was now part of the gag. No film embodied the pseudopedagogical sexploitation nature of this genre with more aplomb and commercial success than Ernst Hofbauer's *Schulmädchen-Report: Was Eltern Nicht für Möglich Halten* (Schoolgirls Report: What Parents Don't Think Is Possible, 1970). As might be expected, this film (and its many sequels and many more rip-offs) witnessed nubile young women throwing off their clothes only to throw themselves at men (or one another) under many circumstances and for all sorts of reasons.[6] Purportedly based on "research" into the sexual experiences of young girls and women conducted by a Bavarian named Günter Hunold, *Schulmädchen-Report* was simply pornography. And it proved to be a financial bonanza. With the money he made from his schoolgirl movies, Hunold (who had received a degree in musicology) established an Institute for Sex Scholarship in Munich; naturally, Hunold appointed himself director.[7]

Fortunes flowed into (and were made in) this brave new marketplace of a sexually liberated West Germany. Even while there remained strong evidence that West Germans stayed evenly split over the desirableness of the new trends, all would concur that theirs—for better or worse—was a nation profoundly "obsessed with sex."[8] By 1968, for instance, West Germans reportedly purchased more naked and half-naked images than any other people in the world.[9] No longer was it a question of whether the flood should be stemmed; now the question was how best to capitalize upon it. Throughout the later 1960s and into the early 1970s, media and advertising just kept pushing further the boundaries of what was legally permissible and commercially palatable. And soon enough, sexual explicitness and nudity (including close-ups of penises and pubic mounds) appeared on television programs as well. As with cinema, while nudity on TV in the late 1960s had initially required a pedagogical excuse, by 1970 this was no longer necessary.

Meanwhile, the sex aids entrepreneur Beate Uhse expanded her already wildly profitable mail-order business when she opened sex shops all across West Germany. From her first major storefront in Hamburg in 1965 to twenty-six sex shops across West Germany in 1971, Uhse contributed substantially to making sex-obsession a respectable pastime, especially for the working classes. Uhse was a marketing genius with a keen grasp of social psychology. While 40 percent of her overall sales were in condoms, she had much else to offer. When patrons stepped into her playfully decorated stores, they received a discreet plastic sack—the better to conceal potential purchases from the prying eyes of others. The stores' loud music allowed customers to consult staff about intimate difficulties with no fear they might be embarrassed or overheard. And there on the shelves was just about every sex-related commodity one might desire, from "aphrodisiacs" (often consisting of vitamins and caffeine) to lingerie, from sex technique manuals to pornographic books (including Hunold's publications). By the early 1970s, Uhse's flagship store in Cologne alone sold between four thousand and six thousand Deutschmark worth of objects daily. At the same time, her mail-order business served two million customers. While at least seventy other mail-order businesses (and more than a hundred other sex specialty stores) competed with Uhse's company, this competition merely drove up demand.[10]

One did not need to enter a specialty store or do mail order to acquire pornography, however. By the early 1970s, and even though it was still illegal, soft- and hard-core pornography became available at neighborhood kiosks all over West Germany, and it sold extraordinarily well. The boom period lasted about two years from 1969 to 1971; afterward, several porn-producing companies went bust. By late 1971 the market stabilized—but at a very high level of turnover. And although this was not well known, quite a few respectable organizations across the ideological spectrum—including trade unions and the Social Democratic Party on the left, the more right-wing Axel Springer and Bauer publishing companies, and even some Catholic presses—turned a profit off this business in glossy nakedness, as printing machines did double duty producing both legitimate and illegitimate wares. Domestic manufacturers knew they faced tough competition from abroad; in 1971, West Germans spent 50 million Deutschmark annually on imported pornography (mostly hard-core magazines from Denmark and other Scandinavian countries). And yet more than twice that (or approximately 125 million) was spent on domestically produced pornography. Whenever a publisher was convicted of producing pornography, or if a particular magazine turned up on the federal government's index of youth-endangering literature, he launched a new periodical with a new name. Just to stay safe, some magazines simply changed their title every few weeks. For example, when the lesbian-targeting magazine *Bi* was shut down by the authorities (though whether it was purchased more by straight men than by lesbian women remains an open question), its editor simply started a magazine called *Tri*. Ever attuned to market niches that needed filling, providers (including Uhse, who took photographs of her own adolescent sons and sold them as "homophile" masturbation aids) responded to the 1969 liberalization of Paragraph 175 (which resulted in the decriminalization of homosexual acts between men over the age of twenty-one) by producing male homosexual pornography as well.[11]

Thus, mass demand became the key that unlocked and transformed social norms. As one owner of a sex-aids chain remarked, "the market forced us into porn—without it one cannot survive financially." Or, as the successful print pornographer Helmut Rosenberg, the owner of the Hamburg-based newspaper *St. Pauli Nachrichten*, put it as he described his phenomenal business success: "Live with porn, and you will arrive safely at your goal."[12] The government responded, first, by directing customs officials and police to be more lenient about pornography and, ultimately, by formally relaxing the antipornography law.

Scholarly experts on sexuality—among them medical doctors, sexologists, psychologists, pedagogues, and sociologists—were unsure what to make of the sex wave. They speculated variously that the proliferating opportunities for voyeurism were not actually changing people's sex lives very much; studies showed that the rates of marital coitus stayed about the same (two times a week) and experts surmised that, at best, Oswalt Kolle had given people the encouragement to try a few different positions or at least talk more openly with their spouses about their desires. One expert estimated that at most 3 percent of German couples ever practiced group sex. Fantasy lives had expanded, commentators suggested, but not actual practices. The incredible hunger West Germans were evincing for pornography, some argued, was simply a sign of how sexually frustrated most people were and of what serious damage had been done by the years of rigorous sexual repression. Beate Uhse's business acumen was widely admired, but no one quite knew how to feel about her customers. Were they being bamboozled by false promises of heightened sexual pleasure and intensity or were they heroically refusing to live bland and conventional lives? Also outside observers displayed perplexity. Thus, for example, the French magazine *Nouvel Observateur* in 1970 snidely summarized the new West Germany as preoccupied with "Sex über Alles," but also expressed a sense of relief: "Definitely, Germany has changed. Pink has replaced brown, the heavy breathing of orgasms covers over the muffled stomping of the legions. Vibrators, not cannons! It's quite reassuring."[13] The French, research soon revealed, were considerably more conservative in the bedroom than the Germans.[14]

Even as experts and outside observers remained puzzled over what was going on with married West Germans' sexuality, there was no uncertainty about the drastic shift in youth behaviors. With the protection of the pill taking away the fear of pregnancy, with the sex wave making premarital sex seem a matter not of shame but of pride, and with the rigidity of conservatives seeming not only hypocritical but simply laughable, the age at first coitus was dropping—and rapidly. As *Der Spiegel* wrote in 1971, summarizing the findings of sexologists, from the mid-1960s to the early 1970s, "within four to six years, the sexual behavior of German youth has changed as never before in this century." The "time between first kiss and first coitus" was getting shorter and shorter.[15] Many young people were starting to have sex three or four years earlier than even their own older siblings had done. As of 1971, a third of youth had intercourse by the age of sixteen or seventeen, and more than two-thirds of the women and three quarters of the men had done so by the age of twenty.[16] In the remainder of the 1970s, the age at first intercourse dropped even further.[17]

Numerous young people also strongly politicized the ideal of sexual liberation. High school students shocked school administrators by demonstrating in the nude for liberalized sex education. Some students not only called for distribution of the pill to teens, but handed out pills directly to their classmates; other student activists in all sincerity requested that "love rooms" be set aside within schools for those in the upper grades.[18] When school groups or youth organizations affiliated with the YMCA or with political parties like the Social Democrats went on vacation, the youth not only went into the ocean or coed saunas naked, they also— under the slogan "Asexual togetherness is hostile to life" (*Asexuelles Miteinander ist lebensfeindlich*)—demanded the right for boys and girls to spend the night with each other and have sex. And, remarkably, protests and lawsuits initiated by parents, teachers, and administrators were set aside by the courts.[19] Liberal sexologists' and psychologists' arguments that premarital heterosexual activity was not only normal but advisable were taken quite seriously and led directly to the reformulation of official norms. Once again, pressure from below forced policy changes.

Youth became fearless in spoofing the more uptight of their elders, even as the content of their activism suggests how profoundly they believed in the liberating power of sexual love. One story captures this doubleness of fearlessness and faith especially well. A much-disliked authoritarian high school principal (named Epting) in a small south German town arrived at school one day to find bold graffiti scrawled across his building: "*Fickt Epting?*" (Does Epting Fuck?), it said. However, the point of the story is not what one might think from the perspective of early twenty-first-century hindsight. These students were *not* engaging in any macho mocking or virility taunting. On the contrary, the students believed that the answer to their question was yes. The idea they had was that if only Epting would admit this truth, it would so transform him that he would voluntarily give up his power-hungry ways and become a better and more decent person.[20]

Challenging the Churches

In this climate, conservatives were caught off guard and rapidly lost their moral authority. Already in 1966, the Protestant campaign "Action Concern about Germany" (*Aktion Sorge um Deutschland*) warned that a "flood of demonic forces is overwhelming our people. Countless individuals are being lured into unrestrained pleasure and the living-out of their desires," while the archconservative Catholic campaign "Action Clean Screen" (*Aktion Saubere Leinwand*) under the direction of politician Adolf Süsterhenn denounced "sexual terror" and called for tightened censorship of film.[21] The Council of the Protestant Church in Germany called on pastors to preach from the pulpit against the "dictatorship of indecency," and the Catholic bishopric in Rottenburg attacked the "flood of slimy filth that ruins everything."[22] A Protestant pastor's wife condemned the female teenage editor of a school newspaper (who had criticized conservative and inadequate sex education) as "shitty, communist, and perverse."[23] Meanwhile, one Catholic theologian went so far as to praise Soviet communism for having stricter morals that the West.[24] In a signal act of cooperation, Protestant and Catholic church leaders together in December 1970 issued a statement of opposition to the sexual revolution.[25]

More moderate Christians strove to present themselves as by no means prudes but also emphasized how often feelings of anomie and insecurity had been generated by the sex wave, or took the tack that the sex wave was ruining sex. Thus, for instance, the Protestant theologian Helmut Thielicke declared the illustrated magazines to be "sex-blighting, because such a permanently sexual atmosphere is something unhealthy, that damages sex itself. [In this way] it loses its character as something unusual, something ecstatic, and becomes just ordinary."[26] Another Protestant author opined that the "orgasm discussion" in the media just made readers miserable and anxious. The rude tone with which "naked sexual facts" got handled by the press could not cover over deeper confusions and doubts people had about how to love or how to make love work for them. And teaching these things remained an appropriate role for the churches.[27] But the audience for both the conservative and the moderate appeals was dwindling.

More in step with the changing times was a liberal newsmagazine like *Der Spiegel*. It eagerly provided readers with pop history lessons about the Christian churches' problems with the joys of the body, observing among other things that the church fathers' "fear of sex became the trauma of a whole culture."[28] The magazine challenged the churches to admit their hypocrisy when they continued officially to prohibit premarital sex while quietly tolerating the one-third of all brides who came to the altar already pregnant.[29] It also reported that psychologist Hildegard Lange-Undeutsch, director of the first sex counseling center established at a West German university, the Free University in West Berlin, lamented how many of the suffering students who entered her office were above all victims of the "upholding by the churches of outdated sexual taboos."[30] But *Der Spiegel* was not alone in challenging the churches. The humor magazine *Simplicissimus* took a more tongue-in-cheek approach, publishing a cartoon of two Catholic schoolgirls listening to a priest give them conservative sex advice. One whispers to the other: "We need to go confess to him sometime soon—he sure is far behind with his well-meaning enlightenment."[31]

Not only did the most mainstream of venues increasingly engage in withering sarcasm about the Christian churches' discomfort with the sexual revolution and relentlessly press the point that Christianity was uncomfortable with sex in general. Christian conservatives were also so routinely compared with Nazis that conservatives felt preempted before they even opened their mouths or took pen in hand. They could hardly express hesitations about the direction West German society was taking or defend such notions as the "healthy sensibility of the *Volk*," or even argue in favor of such concepts as purity, chastity, fidelity, mother love, or family values, before immediately being accused of sounding like fascists, for each of these concepts was considered contaminated by Nazism. The Hamburg-based pedagogue and sexologist Friedrich Koch, a prominent liberal advocate of premarital sex for adolescents, brought this comparison to a very wide audience. While Koch was not consistently progressive (one of his arguments in favor of premarital heterosexual activity was that "repression of sexual wishes" and "ascetic build-up of the drives" led to "sexual neuroses, homosexuality, or intensified aggression"), he proved himself especially adept at documenting similarities between Nazi and Christian sex advice writings.[32] The journalist Karlheinz Deschner, who had already made a name in the early 1960s with a book demonstrating the Christian churches' support for Nazism, gained even more attention with his study, *Das Kreuz mit der Kirche: Eine Sexualgeschichte des Christentums* (The Cross with the Church: A Sexual History of Christianity, 1974). He not only scathingly quoted church leaders pleased by Nazi attacks on sexual immorality, but also cited example after example of postwar West German Christian spokespeople who, unfazed by the "millions of dead" in two world wars and in Vietnam, continued to act like sex, nudity, and pornography were the main moral challenges. As one post–World War II Catholic commentator cited by Deschner put it: "If there is a drive capable of pressing the human being down beneath the dignity of his reason and freedom, then surely that is the sexual drive." Incredulous that anyone "still takes this religion seriously!" rather than "making it the object of satire, of psychiatrists . . . [and] sticking its proclaimers among the comics, in courtrooms, in rubber cells," Deschner repeatedly underscored his central thesis: "The actual crime in 'Christian culture' is, precisely, absolutely not murder, but rather . . . sexual intercourse."[33]

Finally, however, conservative Christians were most stung by dissidents in their own ranks. Many progressive Christian activists also took up the call for sexual liberalization. For a notable development within the West German religious community of the late 1960s and early 1970s was that prominent theologians, clergymen, church officials, and activist laypeople adapted the Christian message to the new more permissive climate. In the late 1960s, a number of leading Protestant theologians called for liberalized divorce laws, more understanding attitudes toward premarital sex, and a heightened appreciation of sex within marriage. In this vein, for instance, the liberal University of Marburg theologian and sociologist Siegfried Keil, while still criticizing "masturbation and perversion, and also all forms of homosexuality and heterosexuality in which the other is not loved for his or her own sake but rather only serves as the object of one's own drive-satisfaction [*Triebbefriedigung*]," nonetheless forcefully defended nonmarital heterosexuality as long as it was loving and oriented toward a long-term partnership.[34] And in 1971 an official commission of the Protestant Church published a comprehensive statement entitled *Denkschrift zu Fragen der Sexualethik* (Memorandum on Questions of Sexual Ethics). Alluding to the changed social conditions and the widespread support in the populace for premarital heterosexual activity, the memorandum implied that as long as a couple intended eventually to marry, they could decide for themselves whether intercourse was morally acceptable also before marriage. The commission went so far as to recommend the use of birth control products during premarital intercourse.[35] Some Protestant pastors went further, for example, proposing that church youth organizations provide spaces for young people to have sex. Other pastors even openly challenged the biblical prohibition on adultery.[36] The liberal magazine *Der Stern* found the new openness to youth nudity and sex among pastors so comical it ran a cartoon showing a clergyman standing outside a church and calling through the door "Children, get dressed! The worship service is starting!"[37]

By the early 1970s, even notable Catholics in West Germany directly challenged the Catholic hierarchy and urged that church teachings liberalize in light of transformed social conditions, specifically the invention of the pill and the earlier onset of puberty (almost five years earlier, it was claimed, than at the beginning of the twentieth century). Progressive Catholic activists attending the Catholic *Kirchentag*, a big lay conference, already in 1968 had criticized Pope Paul and promoted the slogan "Yes to the Pill, No to Paul's Sex."[38] This mobilization by ordinary Catholics motivated theologians as well. Some Catholic commentators worried openly that the church's prohibition on premarital sex drove young people (and especially young men) away from religion entirely. Catholics like the Jesuit Roman Bleistein directly argued that the church had been overly fixated on confining sex only to marriage; like many Protestants, he emphasized the gradual development of a partnership, in which sexual intimacy naturally preceded marriage.[39] Above all, progressive Catholics warned that the Catholic Church needed urgently to revise its general centuries-old negativity about sex. For some, this involved reinterpreting the significance of New Testament passages, putting the Christian Bible's hostility to nonmarital sex in its proper historical context, and/or arguing that a negative attitude toward sex was not truly Christian but rather something absorbed from the Stoics or Gnostics. For others, this meant questioning whether biblical passages could even be applied to the contemporary moment. Were sexual activity and exclusive love *necessarily* bound to each other? In view of the new availability of reliable birth control, maybe sex and love had in fact become separable.[40] Yet others, like the former priest Hubertus Mynarek, confined themselves to attacking what they saw as the mendacity and duplicity inevitably caused by the church's prescription that priests remain celibate. In his much-discussed book on "eros and the clergy," Mynarek heaped on evidence of West German priests who had sex with their parishioners. Mynarek had little expectation that the church would change its rules; what he hoped for (he said) was a "revolt from below."[41]

While a minority of young people stayed in the churches and sought to liberalize them from within, most youth were not interested in listening to clergymen any longer, and working-class youths and university students alike had much harsher things to say about the churches than even their liberal elders did. Young workers interviewed in 1971 about the churches' prohibition on premarital activity responded with "it's nonsense" and "it's stupidity" and "they're insane." One young worker said: "If we want to have our fun in the evening and go pick up a babe, they should let us have our fun. We work hard all day long, the priests don't, at most they're fucking their cook during the day." In general, much resentment was expressed at the fact that clergymen got good salaries for cushy desk jobs. Young working-class women made yet other points. As one put it: "They should worry about their religious junk. . . . For me sexual intercourse has already done a lot of good, also without the church's permission." Speaking about Catholic priests, another said: "I feel sorry for them. If they had ever experienced the way one feels when one is making love, they would tell us something totally different."[42] Quite a few student activists shared this disdain for the churches' traditional denigration of sex. For instance, New Left–linked activists at the first nationwide gay rights demonstration, held in the strongly Catholic city of Münster in 1972, carried signs declaring that "chastity is no more a virtue than malnutrition is."[43] And the Frankfurt New Left student leader and sex rights activist Günter Amendt went so far as to characterize the authors of Protestant and Catholic sex advice manuals (because of the way they demonized sexual pleasure and stoked feelings of guilt and shame) as "sex criminals."[44]

READ WILHELM REICH AND ACT ACCORDINGLY!

The New Left was of singular importance in determining the trajectory of debates about sex in West Germany from the late 1960s on. As noted, from the explosion of pornography in all media and genres to the ways ordinary West Germans both young and old assertively declaimed to the press and to each other that they enjoyed sex and would not be made to feel guilty about it, the sexual revolution was manifestly a broader phenomenon than the New Left. The relationship between the sexual revolution in West Germany and the New Left student movement thus can certainly not be reduced to a simple equation. And yet it is no coincidence that in popular parlance "1968" is still often used as a shorthand to refer to both subjects.

For the influence of the New Left extended far beyond its own constituency. While the New Left student movement was never very large (actual activists numbered only in the thousands), its impact on West German values would be pervasive and profound. Not only was there considerable voyeuristic public fascination with such flamboyantly provocative experiments of the New Left as the (for a brief time) dedicatedly promiscuous left-anarcho Kommune 1 in Berlin (not least because supermodel Uschi Obermaier, fantasy object also for numerous less-leftist German men, had moved in), or the ventures in antiauthoritarian childrearing launched by the New Left *Kinderladen* movement in dozens of West German cities. Of crucial importance also is the way many of the notions articulated by New Leftists (or "68ers," as Germans call them) were taken up both by the mainstream media and by liberal professionals in the fields of medicine, sexology, psychology, pedagogy, law, sociology, and theology. All of this gave much greater legitimacy to New Leftists' sex-radical ideas, especially their challenges to the institutions of marriage and the family and their celebrations of nonmarital sex and antiauthoritarian parenting. In a mutually reinforcing dialectic of radical experimentation and expert liberal authorities' elaboration of the justifications for that experimentation, and with numerous of the student radicals themselves advancing to the status of experts as they published (often sophisticatedly theorized) articles and books on sexual topics, the terms of debate about sex in West Germany were increasingly set by the Left.

Among the West German New Left's liberal allies were many whose sex radicalism was just as fierce as New Leftists' own, and their status as degreed professionals allowed the new ideas to be promoted as scientific truth, and explicitly appreciated by the media as a contrast to religious mystification. For example, when the liberal psychologist Helmut Kentler (older than the generation of 1968 but an important inspiration and support for it) advocated that official organizations sponsoring youth group vacations provide spaces for premarital sex to occur, this was treated by *Der Stern* as informed and valuable guidance. When Kentler undertook a study of young West German marriages in which he treated adultery sympathetically, the middlebrow parenting magazine *Eltern* was proud to publish it.[45] When the young professionals assisting the esteemed sexologist Hans Giese at the Institute for Sex Research in Hamburg—Volkmar Sigusch, a medical doctor, and Gunter Schmidt, a psychologist—argued provocatively that the representation of sex per se did no damage to youth or children, and that the kind of pornography in which sex was actually "represented without prejudices as a pleasure-filled social activity . . . is exactly the kind that one could without worries give to children and adolescents," the West German mainstream took this most seriously.[46] Sigusch and Schmidt's arguments were known to be based on careful empirical research and counted as important insights; their studies on such matters as students' and workers' sexual attitudes and practices, or men's and women's reactions to pornography, were hailed in the press, and rightly so, as the best and most reliable work on the subjects. When the Protestant Church memorandum on sexual ethics was published, *Der Spiegel* invited and printed Sigusch's critical appraisal of it (including Sigusch's challenge to the ideal of monogamous marriage, based on his contention that sexual love depended "exactly on that which monogamous relationships to a large extent make impossible: unhemmed impulses and disobedient spontaneity").[47] Schmidt traveled to Münster and passionately defended homosexual rights against attacks on homosexuality made by Catholic bishop Heinrich Tehumberg. Yet it was Schmidt, not the bishop, who was treated by the nonchurch media as the competent and authoritative commentator. In Schmidt's view, homosexuality was simply unremarkable, just "*one* characteristic in otherwise thoroughly normal people" (ein *Merkmal bei ansonsten stinknormalen Leuten*).[48] As Sigusch remembered years later, speaking of himself and Schmidt: "We were constantly getting updates from the activists about what was going on in the streets, and we saw our research as complementary to their work."[49] Along related lines, when New Left activists Martin Dannecker and Reimut Reiche published their massive empirical study on the beliefs and behaviors of hundreds of West German homosexual men, *Der gewöhnliche Homosexuelle* (The Ordinary Homosexual, 1974), their findings provided the basis for sympathetic reports in the mainstream media.[50]

Precisely because the scientific research on sex in the 1950s had been so saturated with and distorted by normative notions of proper sexuality, the 1960s and 1970s turn toward empiricism—finding out what human beings were *actually* doing rather than what they supposedly *should* be doing—far from being at odds with progressive activism was in fact profoundly beneficial to it.[51] And by no means was this a simpleminded empiricism. Numerous New Left authors writing on sex clearly comprehended both the need for theoretically informed interpretation of evidence and the importance of critical self-consciousness about one's own standpoint and ways of framing questions.

At the same time, while the New Left understood itself, and was understood as, the vanguard of a certain kind of militant sex radicalism, it is also important to register that the New Left and its allies were often quite ambivalent about the mainstream sex wave booming all around them. The student movement was without question strongly motivated by sexual rebellion against the conformist culture of postwar West Germany. As New Left cultural critic Klaus Theweleit observed in retrospect, a "special sort of sexual tension was the 'driving force' of 1968" in West Germany.[52] Or, as the writer Peter Schneider put it, speaking of how he was drawn into New Left politics, "It was a new feeling for the body, a new way of moving, of speaking, and only then a new consciousness, that attracted me."[53] The New Left journalist Götz Eisenberg explained the "specific dynamite and radicality" of the student movement this way: "The antiauthoritarian movement was also a revolt of identity, a mutiny against the more or less awful consequences of authoritarian education in parental home and school, a detonation of the drilled bodies, senses, and wishes."[54] And yet many members of the New Left were also unnerved by the rapidity with which consumer-capitalist-driven sexualization took hold. The sociologist and political scientist Claus Offe remarked a bit cynically at the occasion of the thirty-year-anniversary of 1968: "They [the 68ers] demanded something that was happening anyway; they attacked only that which was already collapsing."[55] But the more important point is that the generation of 1968 knew this, indeed was acutely aware of this, and its members constantly struggled to specify the differences between what they were striving toward and what was going on more broadly.

The discomfort with the mainstream sexual revolution was strongly evident already in the earliest corpus of New Left publications on sex and family life, as these texts repeatedly included anguished or scathing attempts to explain—although always with different nuances—why the "bourgeois" sexual revolution was most definitely not the bodily and psychic liberation the students were yearning for. A classic sample of one typical approach—snatches of Marxism pasted together with inexpressible utopian longings—is provided by a book on antiauthoritarian child-rearing published in Berlin in 1970: "As long as the nuclear family survives—ultimately, for economic reasons—sexual freedom serves as a sad little palliative for daily surfeit and disgust." And: "Even if people humped around ten times more than ever before, it would not add up to real sexual liberation. For merely to amass orgasms, even if man and woman arrive at them simultaneously, cannot yet be seen as a satisfying form of sexuality."[56] Or as Dannecker and Reiche put it in 1974 as they directly criticized Oswalt Kolle: "Pleasure-filled sexual experience [lustvolles Sexualerleben] is as hard to achieve with the sexual techniques offered by the enlightenment industry as with the industry's . . . constantly changing recommendations for what is acceptable and what is not."[57] Günter Amendt's sex enlightenment book for teenagers, SexFront (his answer to the Christian manuals), mocked Kolle and Beate Uhse both as he announced that their recommendations for spicing up married couple's sex lives were nothing but gymnastic exercises that could not possibly recreate lost lust; marriage itself, he declared, was an oppressive institution.[58]

Frequently at odds with each other over whether fidelity was a bourgeois trap or (now that the bourgeoisie had given up on it also) actually an acceptable leftist value, what the activist students shared and what made their perspective on sex unique was not their advocacy of greater liberality per se but rather their insistence on connecting liberated sex with progressive politics. "No sexual revolution is possible without social revolution" is how Reiche put it in 1968 in Sexualität und Klassenkampf (Sexuality and Class Struggle). The mainstream sexual revolution, in his view, was all about maximizing "pseudogratification" so as to increase capitalist efficiency and minimize social conflict that could lead to social change.[59] Or as one gay rights placard carried frequently at demonstrations in the early 1970s put it: "Brothers and sisters / Whether queer or not / Combating capitalism / Is a duty we've got" (Brüder und Schwestern / Schwul oder nicht / Kapitalismus bekämpfen / Ist unsere Pflicht).[60] Achieving true sexual freedom, 68ers believed, was inseparable from broader struggles for social justice. As the Frankfurt School philosopher and sociologist Theodor Adorno, teacher to many of the leading New Leftists, had said already in

1963: "The liberation of sex in the present society is only superficial. . . . In an unfree society, sexual freedom is as unthinkable as any other."[61]

One impetus for New Left sex radicalism was the conviction shared by liberals and leftists that the Third Reich had been at its core sex-hostile and that the Holocaust was the perverted product of sexual repression. And there is no question that especially throughout the early phase of the sexual revolution, with its intersecting dynamics of rapid commercialization and liberalization, many liberals and leftists felt certain that sexual emancipation was itself an antifascist imperative. Members of the Kommune 1, on trial in 1967–68 for distributing leaflets against the Vietnam War (that allegedly also called for arson attacks on German department stores) sassily asked in response to prosecution witnesses' criticisms of the group's much-advertised advocacy of promiscuity: "If our antiauthoritarian stance . . . is a sign of constitutional abnormality, then is authoritarian behavior and National Socialism a consequence of the healthy normality of the Germanic race?"[62] As the New Left and feminist journalist Ulrike Heider later noted (in the course of her attempt to defend the gains of the sexual revolution against neoconservative ex-leftists and romantic maternalist ex-feminists), the early New Left proponents of the sexual revolution were convinced it was the sadomasochistic psychic structure produced by the petty bourgeois authoritarian nuclear family that had in the 1930s caused the Germans to become a people of racist murderers.[63]

Over and over, 68ers advanced the thesis that "un-lived-out sexual impulses" led to "aggression, indeed lust for murder," as Arno Plack put it in *Die Gesellschaft und das Böse* (Society and Evil, 1967). The image of the Holocaust perpetrator—repressed, conventional, family-values-oriented—emerging from the Frankfurt Auschwitz trials of 1963–65 functioned as exhibit A. Repeatedly Plack tried to put into words what clearly for many of his generation had been a profound and values-transforming revelation: those who had, as Plack put it, "celebrated true orgies of sadism" in the camp were seemingly, when outside the camp, so law-abiding and ordinary in every respect, people who had never run amok in even the slightest way. These apparently were individuals who, before and after their time in Auschwitz, were characterized by the most stereotypical philistine probity and petty bourgeois respectability. As one member after another of the generation of 1968 would subsequently testify, the similarity between the code of good behavior postwar society demanded of them and the model evidently exemplified by the executors of genocide sickened them deeply. But it is also clear that identifying this similarity helped them feel as though they could finally understand how "it" had happened, and it gave them something concrete to fight against in their present. Above all, it gave them a way to interpret what was for them one of the most puzzling aspects of older conservative Germans' attitudes: the way these elders acted as though sex was a horribly dirty matter even as they seemed to identify with Nazism and were clearly disinclined to support, or were even overtly hostile to, postwar trials of perpetrators. The perplexing thing, in Plack's words, was "the secret agreement of the society, that provides cover for the concentration camp murderer, but at the same time, for example, denounces the parents of a bride for the crime of pimping, if they allow the future son-in-law to spend the night."[64] This misplaced moral emphasis—treating sex among fiancés as somehow more alarming than genocide—was not just excruciatingly hypocritical. It also seemed to be based in the conservatives' own repressed sexuality.

Along related lines, 68ers were especially impressed with Freudian theories about fascism—like those of Erich Fromm from the 1930s—which suggested that Nazism was marked by a "relatively low degree of genital heterosexuality."[65] Thus, for example, already in 1965 when the Marxist journal *Das Argument* ran a series of special issues dedicated to retheorizing German fascism, one of the contributors summarized for readers the results of Freudian approaches to National Socialism and explained that the psychic structure of both Hitler and his followers was characterized by hate, guilt feelings, and hostility toward sexuality. The animus against sexuality marking the bourgeois family weakened heterosexual tendencies only to intensify "anal- and phallic-sadistic" tendencies and contribute to the production of individuals whose personality was "authoritarian-masochistic" or "ambivalent, sadomasochistic." This author suggested that in the sadistic subjection of and fear of the female purportedly evident among Nazis one could find the fear of sexual impulses in general, as he also pointed out that "the latent homosexual component among the Nazis" expressed itself in "the fanatic persecution of manifest homosexuality (like Jews and communists, homosexuals were sent to concentration camps)."[66] For Fromm, too, as Reiche quoted him at length in *Sexualität und Klassenkampf*, "the authoritarian-masochistic character" typical both of fascists and more generally of "petty bourgeois authoritarian types" was marked by an overabundance of pregenital and anal impulses evident in obsession with orderliness, punctuality, and thrift and also by a "curiously" split sexual orientation: "Physiologically, the average authoritarian man is heterosexual. . . . In his physical relationship to woman, in terms of satisfying bodily needs, he is potent. . . . But in terms of emotion he is homosexual and is hostile and cruel to woman." Although the latent homosexuality occasionally expressed itself in an overt homosexuality—as, in Fromm's view, Nazism had demonstrated—the more important phenomenon to note in Nazism was "the tender and loving masochistic relationship developed by a weaker man toward a strong one."[67]

To lend authority to their antiauthoritarianism, 68ers also frequently invoked the Frankfurt School more generally, and especially its leading members Theodor Adorno and Max Horkheimer. But while Adorno's and Horkheimer's essays on authority and the family contained quite nuanced assessments of the Third Reich's contradictory sexual and familial politics, and of the connections between sexual conservatism and political conservatism, what was evident in New Left writings from the late 1960s and early 1970s was their selective appropriation of Frankfurt School ideas. While Horkheimer, for instance, had expressly stressed that the Third Reich strove to dispense with the family as the mediating link between the individual and the state and had argued that the appeal of fascism had lain in part in the growing weakness of fathers, New Leftists tended to invoke only his notions about the psychological power of parents, the ways the very structure of the nuclear family inculcated submissiveness, and the ways in which hatred of overpowering parents, which could not be expressed directly, got repressed but then also aggressively turned on those more vulnerable.[68] And while Adorno et al.'s *The Authoritarian Personality* (1950), for example, explicitly noted that there was such a phenomenon as the politically reactionary but also sexually active person, 68ers drew exclusively on the study's findings about the links between the potential for fascism and sexual repression.[69]

"Fascist developments are facilitated by authoritarian character structures," opined the authors of a New Left childrearing text in summarizing *The Authoritarian Personality*, after having just specified that those character traits had their roots in strict toilet training and the suppression of child sexuality. And in their own eagerness to "smash the bourgeois nuclear family!" as the 1960s slogan went, the authors of the book ignored Horkheimer's premises about the Nazis' family-smashing aims and instead, in their concern to expose the damage done by liberal as well as conservative parents, quoted his remark from the 1930s that "whether parents are lenient or strict with the child is not important, for the child's character is influenced far more by the family structure than by the father's conscious aims and methods."[70] Another typical New Left childrearing text invoked Adorno as it summarily asserted that "the authoritarian personality" was characterized by "hostility to sex" and cited Horkheimer to explain how insecure people could become both brutal and overly submissive to authority. The same text then quoted Fromm's 1936 observations about parental authority being the mirror image, not the model for, social authority, only to conclude directly from there that "in the family the child is crushed, trained to be a subordinate, a faithful Christian, a sex-hostile future 'Mr. and Mrs. Clean,' an obedient worker."[71] The point is not that Adorno, Horkheimer, or Fromm did not say what they were quoted or summarized as saying; they did. The point is that the pieces of their work that got invoked ended up sounding a great deal like Wilhelm Reich.

For the communist Freudian Reich's influence on the New Left was unparalleled, and its members' felt need to reverse the lessons about proper behavior offered them by their own elders is the main reason for his immense popularity. No other intellectual so inspired the student movement in its early days, and to a degree unmatched either in the United States or other Western European nations. "Wilhelm Reich was probably bootlegged back then more than any other author," one former member of the West German SDS (*Sozialistischer Deutscher Studentenbund*, Socialist German Students' Federation) said in retrospect; it was "Wilhelm Reich up and down," as one New Left woman later remembered.[72] This had everything to do with Reich's central argument that sexual satisfaction and sadism were mutually exclusive—and that (as he phrased it) "cruel character traits" were evident among those "in a condition of chronic sexual dissatifaction," while "genitally satisfiable people" were notable for their "gentleness and goodness."[73] And it had a great deal to do with his insistence that child sexuality in particular needed to be not just tolerated but actively celebrated, if fascism and neurosis alike were to be averted—an idea repeated like a mantra in dozens of early New Left writings. Reprints of Reich's work from the 1920s to the 1940s, initially in bootleg copies, then formally published, were circulated widely in the late 1960s. No book display table on a campus was complete without Reich's *The Sexual Revolution* or *The Function of the Orgasm*, and *The Mass Psychology of Fascism* was, as one contemporary reported, read just as "breathlessly."[74]

It is indicative, too, that for a time in 1968 the outside wall of the cafeteria at the University of Frankfurt carried a graffiti slogan exhorting all passersby to "read Wilhelm Reich and act accordingly!"[75] While this was obviously both a humorously *and* seriously meant incitement to engage in more "free love," the issue that requires emphasis is the *moral* force of Reich's arguments. In rediscovering Reich, activists saw themselves as rescuing an aspect of the anticapitalist and sex-radical tradition of the interwar period that the Nazis had wiped out or driven into exile. But what they revered most about Reich was the way he helped them rewrite conventional wisdom about the relationship between pleasure and evil. Reich's concepts seemed to lend additional legitimacy to that ubiquitous 1960s slogan, Make Love Not War. For this slogan was not just a recommendation for a more decent and pleasurable activity than slaughtering other human beings while risking one's own life; it was also a theory of human nature, a deeply held conviction that those who made a lot of love simply would not be interested in hurting or killing others.

Reich's contention that the sexual repression of children within the family lay at the root of almost all human cruelty showed up in countless ways in the left-leaning literature of the late 1960s. New Leftists genuinely believed, as Ulrike Heider retrospectively summarized it, that "harmless, so-called well-behaved people had . . . been able to become sadistic SA henchmen and concentration camp guards because they had been tormented and sexually repressed by their parents."[76] As Dietrich Haensch put it in his key text, *Repressive Familienpolitik* (Repressive Family Politics, 1969), a particularly accessible cut-and-paste pastiche of Reich's main ideas, capitalist class relations, fascism, and brutality in wartime were all products of the "genital weakness" induced in those whose natural drives had been coercively distorted and repressed and who had been forced to develop "cramped-up" concepts of honor, duty, and self-control. Adolf Hitler's regime had only intensified already-existing petty bourgeois practices, and these, in turn, had outlived the Third Reich. "The tendency to sadism is maintained," Haensch bluntly informed his readers, "by diverting the libidinal energies away from the sexual drive and toward the drive for destruction and aggression; the necessary fixation on the enemy occurs by diverting the hatred produced by the ambivalent hate-love fixation on the sexual oppressor onto the military opponent."[77] Similarly, Dieter Duhm, in his much-discussed book, *Angst im Kapitalismus* (Fear in Capitalism, 1972), also found sexual repression at the source of "the murder orgies of the Third Reich." Duhm (in a series, incidentally, of poachings from Plack) underscored this message by suggesting that there was a direct connection between Gestapo chief Heinrich Himmler's Catholicism-induced sexual shyness and the pleasure in sadism Himmler evinced by traveling to Auschwitz specifically to observe the flogging of female prisoners there. And like Haensch before him, Duhm tied the potential for aggression to fear and hatred of repressive parents. Referring specifically to the Frankfurt Auschwitz trial, Duhm remarked that "The bestiality of these executioners sits deeply in all human beings who are raised with the instrument of fear and who because of their fear have no possibility of living out in any way their hatred against the oppressors (in the first instance the parents)."[78]

Yet the most profound reasons for Reich's tremendous appeal at the end of the 1960s lay in the complicated interrelationships between the 1940s and 1950s, between the decade of mass murder and the decade in which the future 68ers began to come of age. The extremity of the arguments advanced by sex radicals also, then, and above all, had its source in the more recent national past. For really, of course, it was the culture of the 1950s and early 1960s that the subsequent 68ers had personally experienced as repressive. The near-obsessive reference to the power of parents in writings that were supposedly theorizing Nazism suggests what else was being worked through as 68ers tackled the topic of sexual politics.

Many members of the West German New Left were preoccupied not just with loosening but with ripping to pieces the boundaries between the so-called public and private spheres. The now-familiar slogan "the personal is political" remains most usually associated with the women's liberation movements that grew out of and reacted against the various male-dominated New Lefts that had formed in Western nations in the late 1960s. But as New Left pronouncements on sex from the late 1960s and early 1970s make palpably clear, the urgent desire to transform both one's self and interpersonal relations was, at least in West Germany, very much a male New Left agenda as well. One would be hard pressed, for instance, to find as many examples in other Western countries as there were in West Germany of New Left activists demanding that private quarrels between lovers be worked through in group settings (as a Frankfurt collective put it, all its members "must attempt to uncover and analyze their sexual difficulties in all their autobiographical and whole-societal complexity" and they "must process this individual problem collectively").[79] One would also be hard pressed to find as many examples of activists airing in print their most intimate personal shames and hurts (such as publishing private letters from their parents, or sharing with mainstream news reporters the most painful and banal details of an unhappy student marriage). And, likewise, there is something worth noting about activists in Berlin's Kommune 1 deliberately removing the door to the bathroom from its hinges, or other Berlin antiauthoritarian childrearing activists (among them members of Kommune 2, Kommune 1's less promiscuous spin-off) publishing extended theoretical analyses of the dangerous political consequences of overly strict toilet training. None of this makes any sense except against the background of a postwar culture that idealized family values, overemphasized the importance of guarding family secrets, and treated the bodies of its young punitively. Only commune members sickened by the sentimental pieties of the culture in which they had been raised would suggest to their young children (as Kommune 2 did at Christmas 1969) that in an exemplary action they should burn down the Christmas tree.[80]

The 1950s in West Germany had been experienced by many as so utterly claustrophobic, and the sexual and familial conservatism advanced in that decade was interpreted as so wholly dishonest and reprehensible, that it seemed that only the strongest and most outrageous counterarguments and counteractions would do. Extremity appeared not only justified but mandated. The postwar tendency to present the concerns of morality as being above all about sex, not about murder—or in some cases even to present sex as being as bad as murder—could not fail to make a tremendous impression especially on socially critical young people. This is an important context to keep in mind when assessing the sexual activism of the late 1960s. In short, we need to remember just how dramatically overdetermined were the pressures to be morally righteous on that portion of the generation of 1968 that saw itself as politicized in a New Left sense.

Psychoanalyst Sophinette Becker once insightfully observed that West German New Leftists displayed an "overriding wish to be only good."[81] This wish is most comprehensible against the multiple backgrounds of the immense immorality in the nation's past *and* the obsessive moralizing about sex and proper comportment (but not mass murder) in the 1950s *and* young people's instinctive sense that this moralizing rhetoric was itself hypocritically veiling a deeper truth of entanglement with guilt. Only against these multiple backgrounds does the peculiar radicality of the generation of 1968's sexual activism on behalf of both adults and children make sense. And only against these multiple backgrounds can we understand the many difficulties New Leftists subsequently ran into, and the ultimately bizarre and troubling ways Nazism and the Holocaust would figure in their activism. It is specifically by looking at the seemingly most private and politically marginal documents of the New Left—the programmatic writings on child sexuality—that we can gain insight into that which otherwise seems inexplicable: the West German generation of 1968's contradictory mixture of intense emotional identification with, and supreme insensitivity to, the murdered Jews of Europe.

Educating for Disobedience

In December 1969 West German television aired a documentary entitled *Erziehung zum Ungehorsam* (Educating for Disobedience), made by the well-known television producer Gerhard Bott. The film presented a handful of recently launched experimental antiauthoritarian daycare centers for two- to five-year-olds organized by New Left activists in Frankfurt, Stuttgart, Berlin, and Hamburg. Called *Kinderläden* (children's stores) because they were initially often set up in abandoned storefronts, the centers had quickly spread throughout West Germany. From single centers founded in Frankfurt in September 1967 and Stuttgart in January 1968 and three started in Berlin in the spring of 1968, to eleven in Berlin in the early months of 1969, *Kinderläden* had been established in more than thirty German cities by late 1969.[82] The interest in *Kinderläden* can partially be explained by a generally acknowledged crisis in the availability and quality of preschool education, and the fact that they emerged at a moment of growing insecurity about the preparedness of West German parents for the task of childrearing (an insecurity both alleviated and exacerbated by the advent of new parenting advice magazines, and even beginning to be the subject of government investigations at both the federal and municipal levels). Above all, however, the *Kinderladen* movement represented a nationwide experiment to put into concrete practice theories about human nature gleaned from young radicals' rediscovery of the work of Wilhelm Reich and the Frankfurt School. The idea for the *Kinder-läden* in Berlin had first been advanced by the SDS-affiliated "Action Council for the Liberation of Women" specifically as a way to facilitate New Left–linked women's ability to get out of the isolation of the home and participate in political work. But already within a few months, although women remained involved in the centers both as parents and teachers, and occasionally as part of the authors' collectives writing about the centers, control over the movement was wrested away from the women by men eager to put their own theories into practice—even as, in so doing, the men revealed how utterly central the project of reconfiguring parenting in Germany was also for them.[83]

The alternative daycare centers became a flashpoint for debates about sex, politics, and the significance of the intergenerational and ideological tensions dividing West German society in the late 1960s. The *Kinderläden* in Berlin garnered especially hostile and mocking publicity in the mainstream press. A local Berlin newspaper, for example, complained of "the smell of stale food and unclean children" and the purportedly coercive indoctrination presented as "Mao ousts Little Red Riding Hood."[84] And in February 1969, *Der Stern* informed its five million readers that Berlin's *Kinderläden* were producing "Germany's most misbehaving children" (as the banner headline put it), "little leftists with big rights" whose environment was chaotic and filthy, whose parents engaged in wife swapping, and who were allowed to bash in each other's heads with blocks and splatter the walls of their centers with paint[85] (fig. 4.1). Yet this was hardly the end of the story.

Bott's film and the massive ensuing nationwide debate ultimately led to the founding of hundreds more antiauthoritarian childrearing projects. Antiauthoritarian methods (albeit stripped of their most radical implications) were also experimentally incorporated into numerous municipal and church-run preschools. And although by 1972 there were rumors that the *Kinderladen* movement had run its course and had become a victim both of the New Left's shift away from "subjective" concerns to various competing forms of more "objectivist" doctrinaire Marxism, *and* of the appropriation of reformist impulses particularly by liberal Social Democratic state governments into public preschool programs, these rumors proved premature. Not only were some of the earliest radical experiments still functioning in the later 1970s, but the modified yet still antiauthoritarian impulse also lived on in the *Kinderläden*'s more mainstream successors, the (frequently state-subsidized) "Parent-Child Groups."[86]

The *Kinderläden* and related experiments emerged as one of the West German New Left's major concrete accomplishments, and although the number of avidly theorizing radical activists remained small, the general notions associated with antiauthoritarian childrearing captured the

Figure 4.1. *Der Stern*, no. 9 (1969), cover page. The headline reads: "Germany's most misbehaving children." Protests from *Kinderladen* activists about the article's misrepresentations successfully achieved a court injunction forbidding further distribution of this issue. (Reprinted by permission of *Der Stern*)

imaginations and informed the practices of broad sectors of the generation of 1968, as well as many of its more liberal elders. The movement
transformed not only preschool but also elementary education in West
Germany, and affected parent-child relationships within countless families. American New Leftists on travels in Europe remember how stunned
they were in some of their first encounters with their West German counterparts. Young West German parents let their children, while covered in
dirt, walk the streets and ride streetcars. They allowed their children to
pummel them; they never slapped back. And when asked why they encouraged their children's disobedience, the parents answered simply:
"Because of Auschwitz."[87]

West German radicals saw their childrearing efforts in national terms.
They believed that German culture was especially *kinderfeindlich* (hostile
to children), and there is no question that they were trying (in a desperate
sort of neo-Rousseauian authoritarian antiauthoritarianism) to remake
German/human nature. It is also no coincidence that antiauthoritarian
parents grappled repeatedly with the widespread perception that human
nature might be innately evil, or that aggression between people might be
inevitable and solidarity in the long run simply impossible to achieve.
Precisely the ways in which the Nazi past functioned in *Kinderladen* literature, however, also helps us to see the anti*post*fascist elements of the New
Left. By taking seriously the intensity of *Kinderladen* activists' defenses
of child sexuality and critiques of the family and by examining the peculiar ways Nazism and the Holocaust were invoked in *Kinderladen* literature, we gain a deepened understanding of the West German New Left's
complexly *mediated* relationship to the Nazi past.

Gerhard Bott was yet another West German liberal professional quite
sympathetic to the young leftists, and like so many late 1960s liberals he
shared the New Left's ideas about Nazism. Framing his presentation of
the *Kinderläden* with contrasting images of the decidedly more authoritarian atmosphere in several mainstream, obviously miserably overcrowded and understaffed preschools, Bott openly justified the antiauthoritarian projects as crucial for both the prevention of individual
neuroses and the development of a properly functioning democracy carried by self-determining, nonsubmissive, and critically engaged citizens.
With a "scientific" psychologizing tone characteristic of much liberal argumentation of the day, the film's voice-over informed viewers that traditional childrearing techniques concerned with obedience and cleanliness,
and above all with the suppression of any expressions of child sexuality,
led to "unhappy and sick adults." This was a pressing cause for concern
because "the number of neurotics in the Federal Republic is estimated at
seven million!" More importantly, the film's narrator warned that a child
who was praised and rewarded for subordination would often "for the

rest of his life yearn for infantile dependence on authority, on a strong man. . . . Antiauthoritarian, noncoercive education . . . wants to break with this fateful tradition." Citing the (at that time much-discussed) research of Hamburg psychologist Annemarie Tausch, which found 82 percent of the remarks made by the more than two thousand kindergarten teachers she observed were either orders or directive questions, the film also showed unflattering footage of precisely such teacher behavior and argued that "this kind of education leads to people experiencing oppression as something natural and finally even as agreeable." As Tausch stated on screen in conversation with Bott, describing her own generation and that of most of the teachers, "we were in a certain sense raised for a dictatorship."[88]

Yet these framing issues were not what struck most viewers. What primarily proved controversial about the film was Bott's generous endorsement of the *Kinderläden's* commitment to permitting children, if they so wished, to go naked and freely touch their own and each other's bodies. The film included a brief scene from Stuttgart in which a little girl casually attached a cardboard penis to a cutout doll along with hair, nose, eyes and lips. It also incorporated a one-minute scene of "playing doctor" in Frankfurt in which one little boy painted in watercolor on another's erect penis while antiauthoritarian parents and educators explained the importance of not only tolerating but assertively affirming child sexuality. In Bott's view, these were moments of noncoercive learning, "tender play," and the development of an "un-cramped-up relationship to human sexuality."[89]

And it was these representations of child sexuality that offended and alarmed viewers. While the reception in the liberal press was—significantly—on the whole positive, conservative newspapers registered disgust, and much viewer reaction was also vituperative. After the documentary's first airing, the sponsoring television station received more than six hundred letters, only a small percentage of which expressed approval. One writer recommended the *Kinderladen* activists emigrate with their "naked babes" and "dirty little games" to warmer climates where people live in "mud huts," and another asked "whether these shots were really taken in Germany or in some 'corners' of some under-under-developed nations." Yet another outraged viewer referred to the doctor scene and asked: "Poor Germany, where are you headed. . . . 'Blacks' would be ashamed to do this sort of thing, for they honor moral laws." Meanwhile, a number of correspondents insisted that children had no sexual feelings of their own, that the little Frankfurt boy's erection had been forcibly produced by the adults (i.e., that the situation was akin to rape) and that in this and other ways the *Kinderladen* parents were acting "below the level of animals."[90]

Why did Bott's documentary film stir such strong negative reaction in a time when nakedness and overt displays of sexuality had become so routine? That the film provoked racism specifically in response to images of white children and that it elicited such visceral negativity in an era when nudity was commonplace not only in Kolle's sex enlightenment movies but also on television suggests that two things made the *Kinderladen* activists distinctive. One was the New Leftists' ideological stance in direct provocative opposition to their society. (By contrast, for example, Kolle's approach was far more conciliatory.) The second and more significant thing was the activists' emphasis not just on child nudity but also on child sexuality.

Indeed, aside from the general encouragement for children to be self- and peer- rather than adult-directed, the vociferous defense of child sexuality was precisely the heart of early *Kinderladen* activism. The activists did not just permit the children to run naked and play with their own and each other's bodies (fig. 4.2). They also applauded and publicized the most intimate details of the children's sexual explorations. The Berlin-Charlottenburg *Kinderladen* collective, for instance, dedicated an entire booklet to this issue. *Für die Befreiung der kindlichen Sexualität!* (For the Liberation of Child Sexuality! 1969) did not just criticize traditional punitive approaches to child masturbation but also mocked the verbal disapproval and strategic distraction techniques advocated by such supposedly more liberal and enlightened childrearing experts as Benjamin Spock or Kurt Seelman. As an inspiring contrast, the Charlottenburgers pointedly reprinted portions of a 1930s advice book by Annie Reich (wife of Wilhelm) in which she posited that every child was a sexual being and that child masturbation "never has any damaging consequences but rather, on the contrary, is an important preparation period for the later sexuality of the adult."[91]

There were also more flagrantly excessive moments. In the Charlottenburgers' pamphlet, and again in a June 1969 issue of the prestigious journal *Kursbuch*, members of the Kommune 2 (whose children attended one of the Charlottenburg *Kinderläden*) included a detailed description of a scene of (expressly adult-encouraged) genital touching between a little boy and a little girl within the Kommune 2, and another scene in which the same little girl attempted to fit an adult penis (which, after she had asked, she had been permitted to stroke to the point of erection) into her tiny vagina (it turned out to be, as she herself "determined resignedly, 'Too big' "). Throughout the account of this second incident, the authors emphasized the child's agency in initiating and developing the encounter. But the authors' main point was their special delight that the adult man's mature handling of this situation helped the little girl to realize on her own, *rather than via an adult prohibition*, that adult-child sexual relations

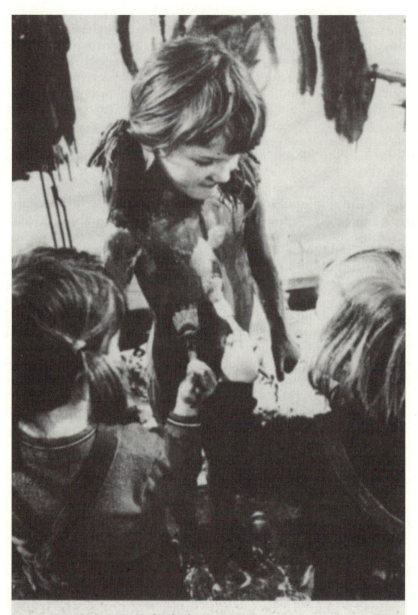

Antiautoritärer Kinderladen, 1971

Figure 4.2. Antiauthoritarian *Kinderladen*, 1971. A naked little girl is being painted by her classmates. From Kristine von Soden, ed., *Der grosse Unterschied: Die neue Frauenbewegung und die siebziger Jahre* (Berlin: Elefanten, 1988), p. 27.

were not feasible and that it was more "appropriate to reality" to satisfy her desires with peers.[92] Certainly some New Leftists were horrified and repelled by this and other Kommune 2 stories.[93] But it is also telling that after the *Kursbuch* essay appeared, the Frankfurt *Kinderladen* collective actively debated why it was that their preschool children were not seeking direct contact with adult genitals. Could it be, they surmised with hopeful pride, that the children in *their* school were free of the "fixation-constellations typical in families" and therefore were "able, as is reality-appropriate, to satisfy their sexual and genital needs in the children's collective with their peers?" Or, the Frankfurt adults worried, were their own unconscious hang-ups and insecurities inhibiting their children?[94]

Along related lines, the Stuttgart *Kinderladen* collective published the story of little girls and boys who tickled their female teacher under her clothes. Initially everything had been playful, but soon an overexcited little boy attempted frantically to pull off the teacher's underpants while the teacher tried first to say that it was cold and she did not want to undress, then that she would undress later when they all went swimming, but finally told the little boy to stop because he was hurting her by yanking on her pubic hairs. The story ended with another little boy, who had watched the proceedings, complaining to another female teacher that "sometimes my wee-wee gets all stiff and then it also often hurts." The teacher in turn recommended that he stroke it, and he replied, "Yeah, I've done that a lot."[95]

As these examples illustrate, the *Kinderladen* theorists sought to confront readers with the reality of children's desires. There was the evident compulsion to make public the most intimate details not only out of a presumed desire to shock, but also most likely out of a deeply held conviction that precisely what was most secret, shameful, or confusing could only be dealt with by engaging it openly and collectively. Stunningly, moreover, the teacher could find no other justifiable reason for defending her own bodily boundaries than physical pain. Finally, the activists, unable to imagine that children's emotional and physiological responses could be quite different from adults, instead projected their own assumptions about sexuality onto their children's behavior.

Meanwhile, however, and tellingly, far from recognizing the desire for sexual pleasure as some ineradicable drive in human beings, *Kinderladen* advocates instead stressed the drive's fragility and vulnerability. Enjoyment, too, was somehow not natural and inevitable but rather required strenuous cultivation. The *Kinderladen* collective in Frankfurt, for example, repeatedly pointed this out. "We are of the opinion that the tolerance of sexual activities alone is not adequate" to assist a child "toward a stable, positive development of its sexuality." It was necessary "fully and completely to affirm" such expressions of child sexuality as "masturbation, child exhibitionism, voyeurism, anal-erotic tendencies, sex games—father, mother, child—doctor games, etc." Yet at the same time, the Frankfurt collective was worried. "How can we, in view of our own problems, transfer to the children a positive attitude toward sexuality?" they asked, for "it is a fact that none of the adults in our fundamentally antisexual and pleasure-hostile society was able to develop an untroubled relationship to sexuality."[96] The *Kinderladen* literature, in short, was not just about children, but very much about the parents as well. The stories the activists chose to publish show how obsessed the parents were with demonstrating their lack of sexual hang-ups—even as they revealed precisely the existence of such hang-ups.

As New Left writer Peter Schneider would remark in pained amusement in the mid-1970s, antiauthoritarian parents "live out their own uncomprehended uptightness [*Verklemmtheit*] in front of their children, but view their children's every sexual expression with pious eyes as though it were something sacred."[97] Unquestionably, there was ridicule in this comment, yet Schneider's observation also communicates the urgency that many of his generation, and not just its main activists, had brought to the antiauthoritarian childrearing experiment. Over and over, antiauthoritarian parents pinned their hopes on their children. Because their libidinal focus was now the group and not the couple, maybe they could invent new ways to separate physical pleasure from emotional entanglement without psychic damage. Maybe they would find a way to meet each other's emotional and physical needs without overweening possessiveness, without boredom, without mutual pain. That at least was the dream. But above all, and most frequently, activists railed at the institution that they felt was responsible for their own crippling: the nuclear family.

Kinderladen activists' celebrations of child sexuality and lamentations about adult dysfunctionality were inextricably linked to a more broadly held New Left conviction that the nuclear family was a diseased and pernicious institution for which collective arrangements were the sole possible remedy. Declaring the nuclear family to be "rotten to the core," many *Kinderladen* activists not only rotated caregiving at the preschools, but actively worked to rupture what they called parent-child "fixations."[98] The deliberate rotation of caregivers within the *Kinderläden* was not just designed to reduce burdens on the grown-ups; the main aim was to give children many adult reference points rather than just one or two. And the insistence that children manage their own conflicts and that the adult caregivers avoid intervening if at all possible was yet another aspect of the *Kinderläden*'s efforts to destabilize children's dependence on parents; for even beneficent authority was still authority. Only in collective experiences, activists believed, could people develop attitudes of solidarity, overcome their fear of authorities, and develop shared strategies for resisting oppression. *Kinderladen* theorists (in a way that in hindsight seems quite astonishing) were thoroughly unconcerned about peer pressure. Grown-ups were always *the* problem. Even though the *Kinderladen* literature is rife with examples of parents and teachers admitting that aggression was the most difficult issue to manage in the preschools and a number of the Berlin groups gradually did get more interventionist in their approach to it, the *Kinderladen* activists were profoundly committed to the assumption that aggression was a transitory phenomenon whose existence could be traced back to some other, unfulfilled need for nurture or pleasure.

If anything, *Kinderladen* activists believed that children should direct aggression toward their parents and all authority figures. The obscenity of the traditional culture of child beating and the need to do away with it once and for all was a central motivating force of the antiauthoritarian childrearing movement. As New Left childrearing activist Lutz von Werder pointed out in the later 1970s, it was outrageous that West Germans allowed their dogs more room to play than their children, that the *Kinderschutzbund* (Federation for the Protection of Children) had only 80,000 members, while the *Tierschutzverein* (Association for the Protection of Animals) had 800,000, that beatings were still considered by many an acceptable pedagogical strategy, and that there were approximately 1 million cases of child abuse in the Federal Republic each year, including approximately 1,000 fatalities. In Werder's view, what was hidden behind these statistics was "an enmity toward children that has its source in the backwardness of the German conditions."[99] In the activists' view, the problem in the past was that the overwhelming power of the parents was such that the aggressions children actually felt toward their parents, and that also all adults still felt toward authority figures, could only be expressed downward, could only, in short, be directed toward those more vulnerable—toward, as the textbook-*cum*-document collection *Berliner Kinderläden* (1970) put it, "hippies, Negroes, yesterday Jews and today Arabs."[100]

As the reference to the Jews of "yesterday" already suggests, in the activists' efforts to explain the connections between overbearing parents, suppressed pleasures, and aggressions toward others, the Nazi past figured uneasily. The Third Reich was most frequently invoked when activists sought to demonstrate the broader political import and antifascist value of their pro-sex and antifamily values position. In their critique of even liberal sex education guides' tendency to downplay pleasure and emphasize the dangers of venereal disease, for example, the Berlin-Charlottenburg collective stingingly pointed out that "It is well known that the National Socialists combined their fascist racial theory with the irrational warning against the decadent Jews, because they were supposedly responsible for sexually transmitted diseases."[101] Moreover, the Charlottenburgers observed at another point, anyone who insisted on the "hallowed" importance of the mother-child bond was "simply confirming what clerics, National Socialists, and Christian Democrats have already for a long time been preaching from their moral pulpits about 'the smallest cell of the state—the family.' "[102] A father who worked in the Berlin-Neukölln *Kinderladen* informed a reporter from *Der Stern* with coy insolence that not only did the parents allow the children to masturbate and play sex games but also that "Many children were already toilet-trained. Now they shit in their pants again. They're repeating the anal phase. That's good. Did you know that most concentration camp guards had anal difficulties in their childhood?"[103] Members of the Berlin-Lankwitz collective, meanwhile, in the opening volley of their book, *Kinderläden: Revolution der Erziehung oder Erziehung zur Revolution? (Kinderläden*: Revolution of Education or Education for Revolution?, 1971), placed the anal phase and the Holocaust together at the center of political theory. Punitive toilet training, the authors contended, led to authoritarian personalities with sadistic fantasies who oppressed minorities; preoccupation with cleanliness was part and parcel of a mind-set that sent people "into the oven." And indicatively, although, as the Lankwitzers analyzed how abjected minorities were treated, they were clearly referring to Jews (and, above all, the way Nazis demonized Jews by associating them with sexual lasciviousness), they were *also* speaking about themselves. Thus, when they elaborated on how those who identified with authority projected their own forbidden wishes for pleasure onto "out-groups" and then took a substitute pleasure in aggressively persecuting those outsiders, the examples of outsiders they gave were also of "rebels," "troublemakers," and "radicals."[104]

But nowhere did the Holocaust function more awkwardly than in a brochure by the Charlottenburgers entitled *Kinder im Kollektiv* (Children in the Collective, 1969) (fig. 4.3). This booklet contained both the most sustained attack on the family form and on parent-child "fixations" of any *Kinderladen* document and the most direct and repeated references to the mass murder of European Jewry. The brochure was part of a series of annotated reprints of classics of literature on child development published under the auspices of Berlin's Central Council of Socialist *Kinderläden*. This particular brochure reprinted David Rapaport's 1958 article on collective childrearing in kibbutzim in Israel (the annotations revealed that the Charlottenburgers deemed this experiment inadequately radical) and Anna Freud and Sophie Dann's 1951 essay evaluating the psychological development and group dynamics of six child survivors of the concentration camp Theresienstadt, cared for in the postwar years in a British orphanage. What the Charlottenburgers so loved about Freud and Dann's depiction of the six German Jewish boys and girls, all orphaned shortly after birth because their parents had been deported and murdered in the killing centers in Poland, was the children's extra-

Figure 4.3. "Children in the Collective." Title page of *Kinder im Kollektiv*, ed. Zentralrat der sozialistischen Kinderläden West-Berlins (Berlin: Sozialistischer Kinderladen Charlottenburg I, 1969). Part of the series "Directions for a Revolutionary Education" edited by the Central Council of Socialist *Kinderläden* in Berlin. Contains: Anna Freud, "Children in the Concentration Camp"; David Rapaport, "Kibbutz-Education"; and Authors' Collective, "Education in the Socialist *Kinderladen*."

ordinary mutual solidarity and the way they directed their libidinal needs toward each other rather than toward adults. The Charlottenburgers saw the case of the Theresienstadt children as inspirational; they evidently believed that this case provided proof positive that an intense mother-child dyad in the early years was not necessary for a child's healthy emotional development.

The Charlottenburgers, however, were not only unreflective about their own romanticization of oppression. With breathtaking naiveté, they also compared the three- and four-year-olds in their own *Kinderladen* favorably with the Theresienstadt children. The work with the Charlottenburg children had demonstrated, they felt, that "new behaviors and more intensive relationships with each other" were possible also for children who had initially been raised in nuclear families. Meanwhile, the Charlottenburgers criticized Freud and Dann for being "bourgeois" researchers and for downplaying the Theresienstadt children's sexual activities, even as *Kinder im Kollektiv* juxtaposed Holocaust information with feminist observations. On the same page that documented the numbers of deportations from Theresienstadt to the death camps, for example, the Charlottenburgers also railed against the exclusion of women from societal life because of their childrearing duties within the nuclear family.[105]

Without question, this material is offensive. Rather than striving, as for example the Lankwitzers did, to make some sense of the ways sexual repression in childhood might contribute to the development of racist attitudes and violent impulses, the Charlottenburgers, while gesturing toward many of the same issues, treated the Holocaust more as a mundane event, a backdrop of sorts to what they appeared to see as the real drama, which was the Theresienstadt children's apparent ability to do without parents entirely. One possible reading of the comparisons and juxtapositions advanced by the brochure is that the Charlottenburgers simply exhibited exceptional insensitivity and thoughtlessness. For them, the facts of the fascist past and the Holocaust were not reasons to engage in antifascist childrearing; rather, a handful of child survivors of the Holocaust by complete coincidence happened to offer one of the best proofs that nuclear families were unnecessary. But another way to read what is going on in this brochure—for it cannot be coincidental that Rapaport's study on Israel is the other text discussed at length, and not any number of Communist collective experiments that could have been analyzed—is to see that *only Jews*, the New Left's parents' generation's primary victims, could offer morally acceptable evidence that parents were entirely dispensable, and that children were much better off without them. For if there was an unconscious wish expressed in this document, it was (as Reimut Reiche would point out in 1988) that the 68ers' own parents could be killed.

SEXUALITY MAKES YOU FREE

How can these contradictory invocations of the Holocaust by West German New Leftists be explained? On the one hand, numerous New Leftists were indisputably motivated to engage in antiauthoritarian childrearing precisely because they perceived the authoritarianism and conservatism with which they themselves had been raised as an extension of Nazism. They believed that to encourage a child's independence of spirit and lack of deference to authority enabled the development of a healthy selfhood. They were convinced that subservient, slavish, and insecure personalities made a democratic society impossible. They were also convinced, based on their readings of both *The Authoritarian Personality* and the writings of Wilhelm Reich, that racism and cruelty resulted from sexual repression. On the other hand, the Holocaust clearly functioned unevenly and selectively in New Left activism.

The fact of the Holocaust—as it had once again become so forcefully present in the West German cultural imaginary since the Auschwitz trial of 1963–65—gave New Leftists the single most important moral wedge against teachers, parents, and politicians perceived as corrupt. The Holocaust seemed to justify a rejection of practically the entire generation that had been adults during the 1930s and 1940s. That this older generation, with a few honorable exceptions, was "fascistic" became a frequently used shorthand to indicate New Leftists' revulsion at all personal or political conservatism.

Yet the 68ers were also quite confused about Jews, having absorbed fundamentally incoherent messages about them. The government took an officially philosemitic line, but individual politicians made antisemitic statements without embarrassment. Religious leaders made vague references to German guilt but advanced analyses implying that Jews were responsible for their own suffering. The Auschwitz trial had been accompanied not only by a heightened awareness of the details of the death camps but also a rise in open expressions of popular antisemitism, and suggestions that in the Weimar era Jews had "overreached" their place in German society and hence provoked their own destruction. Finally, New Leftists, with no genuine grasp of what it was like to be persecuted, or of how very gradually the process of marginalization had occurred, wondered why Jews had not rebelled sooner or more.

As Eberhard Knödler-Bunte, a member of the generation of 1968 and one of the coeditors of the influential New Left journal *Ästhetik und Kommunikation*, admitted in a retrospective essay written in the early 1980s, in his adolescent disgust with his family, he had unabashedly instrumentalized the Holocaust as he rejected the church and his parents. Yet in addition, his remarks reveal the ambivalence about Jews that he had as-similated from them as well: "From my parental home I knew only that one had sinned heavily against the Jews, and the pastor traced this back to the betrayal of our Jesus. More could not be gotten in a north Würt-tembergian small town in the fifties. . . . What remained palpable was the aura of innuendo and secrets that was as difficult to get at as the one surrounding sexuality." Knödler-Bunte confessed that, having learned about the Judeocide from a book in 1958, it became an ethical weapon for him:

> That the Germans could kill millions of human beings just because they had a different faith was utterly inexplicable to me. My whole moral world view shattered, got entwined with a rigorous rejection of my parents and school. If religion had not prevented this mass destruction of human beings, then it is no good for anything, then the whole talk of love of your neighbor and of meekness . . . was just a lie.

Meanwhile, as a preteen, Knödler-Bunte had fantasized himself rescuing the Jews from the concentration camps—as in a kind of cowboys-and-Indians game—although he also conceded that they had remained "face-less" to him. He had deliberately not educated himself much about the concrete details of the Holocaust: "I wanted the Holocaust abstract, an absolute fact for a morality that forgives nothing."[106] Solely to take offense at these remarks is to miss the significant truths they also tell, both about the quality of the postwar climate and about the ambiguities and resentments that intense but also incomplete awareness of the national past could engender.

Furthermore, New Leftists felt powerfully the superficiality of the official culture of philosemitism. They sensed the self-exculpatory ideological work that was ironically being done precisely by the ritual mea culpas annually proffered by government leaders, for example, at the occasion of *Kristallnacht* memorializations. One reason New Leftists so often evaded the centrality of the Holocaust to the Third Reich—and tended to treat it as an ancillary phenomenon to German fascism rather than its core—was due to the way conservatives had managed to monopolize the topic of the Holocaust, not only capturing the terrain of memorialization for themselves but also succeeding in treating the Holocaust as somehow disconnected from the rest of the Third Reich, and hence disconnected from the Germans and from history.[107] As Hermann Peter Piwitt put it in the New Left journal *Konkret* in 1978, with snarling sarcasm:

> Judeocide: the topic is and remains the great atonement market. Plant a little tree in Jerusalem and already the good German feels free inside to turn to new persecution of minorities and violence-agitation. . . . As long as fascism contin-

ues to be foreshortened into nothing but persecution of the Jews, these media presentations only over and over again allow the citizen the one conclusion: Nothing against National Socialism—just that business with the Jews shouldn't have been.[108]

And as this remark already suggests, New Leftists also sensed the anti-Jewish racism lurking just beneath the surface philosemitism. Yet New Leftists' almost kneejerk opposition to anything postwar conservatives supported only guaranteed that when conservatives were thrilled at the Israeli victory in the Six-Day War of 1967, the New Left (which had previously been strongly pro-Israeli, and especially inspired by the ideal of a socialist and democratic Israel) switched sides and became aggressively pro-Palestinian. To a degree that has not yet been fully explored, the excitement among West German conservatives at the Israeli victory appears to have something to do with the relief Germans felt at Jews no longer being victims.[109] A cartoon published in *Ästhetik und Kommunikation* captures well the doubleness of New Left reactions to this sense of relief. At one and the same time, the cartoon highlights the older generation's racism *and* communicates New Left suspicion and perplexity about how to feel about Jews having revealed themselves to be militarily adept: West German conservative elites are at a cocktail party chatting about the Israeli victory. Says one older man (apparently a military officer, thus by implication a former member of the *Wehrmacht*) to the others: "Honestly, I never thought that Jews could be such brave soldiers. Although, of course, there is much German blood in them."[110]

One of the most troubling features of the West German New Left is that despite its rebellion against so many values held dear by the older generation, and despite its awareness of the problems in that older generation's attitudes about Jews, it too advanced anti-Jewish ideas. But it would take more than a decade for New Left antisemitism to be discussed publicly and extensively in the West German media, and even longer before New Leftists acknowledged that this was a problem they had. Ultimately it would take Jewish members of the New Left—both German Jews and American Jews who lived in West Germany—to challenge their peers and get the issue taken seriously. When *Konkret* journalist Henryk Broder published his anti–New Left broadside in the major national newspaper *Die Zeit* in 1981, in which he recounted numerous instances of anti-Jewish remarks among West German New Leftists and feminists and charged that "you remain the children of your parents," it came as quite a shock.[111] Several other New Left–affiliated Jewish commentators soon offered related critiques.

Not until the late 1980s, however, did non-Jewish former members of the West German New Left attempt to disentangle their conflicting emotions, acknowledge the antisemitism in their erstwhile activism, and try to offer explanations for what had gone wrong in the late 1960s. While there had been earlier efforts to address the failures of the New Left, none of them had taken on the problem of New Left antisemitism. The year 1968 had marked both the high point of the antiauthoritarian student movement, and the moment when it had begun to unravel, and post-1968 history consisted of a whole set of delayed reactions. At each stage, New Leftists struggled to understand their difficulties through a different lens. The immediate aftermath of 1968 saw the retreat of some activists into depression about why the revolution had so quickly run aground. Others worked ever more frenetically to bring about that revolution, founding a profusion of (often rigidly authoritarian and mutually combative) Marxist-Leninist and Maoist splinter groups and hundreds of anticapitalist initiatives in working-class neighborhoods and on factory shop floors. By the mid- to late 1970s, New Left commentators wondered about their own relentless self-abnegation before a largely hostile working class. And it was in this context that New Leftists struggled to recall what had drawn them into anticapitalist activism in the first place. And yet references to the Holocaust are practically nonexistent in the retrospective reflections written in the 1970s. Indeed, the one time that Nazi mass murder is mentioned at all, the group being "gassed"—astonishingly but indicatively—is the German working class.[112]

Most scholars and popular commentators have understood this anticapitalism as an expression of disgust at the parents' generation and its postwar materialism. This interpretation makes sense not least because precisely the incessant economic activity of the postwar years—the busy rebuilding that created the "economic miracle"—did indeed serve as the parents' generation's alibi for avoiding its own confrontation with the Nazi past; demonstrating capitalist prowess had been one of many West Germans' primary ways of pretending to be democrats and of securing integration into the West. But in the late 1980s, the most thoughtful of the 1968 generation suggested that their own fierce anticapitalism may actually have represented an attempt to rescue the parents' honor and innocence.

In 1987 New Left writer Peter Schneider took the provocative position that the obsession with criticizing and combating capitalism was in fact a way of *absolving* the parents' generation of guilt. New Leftists' relentless insistence on rejecting all liberal and conservative analyses of Nazism—which tended to emphasize individual motivations and responsibility—in favor of Marxist interpretations that emphasized social and economic structures and processes did, he said, provide some insight. But it also and nonetheless had an exonerating effect:

As long as German fascism remains a "conspiracy" of a few powerful industrialists, then our parents, no matter what they may have done, were victims of this conspiracy. This historical lie spared us from having to come to terms with the concrete and personal guilt-portion of our fathers and thus also with our own entanglement as their sons and daughters.[113]

A year later, sociologist Claus Leggewie registered his own surprise at the perplexing phenomenon that, simultaneously, the New Left's emergence had been rooted in his generation's discovery of the Holocaust and yet New Leftists continually disavowed the Holocaust's German and Jewish specificities in a diffuse rhetoric of fascists versus antifascists. Leggewie noted: "About the burying of the initial impulses one can only speculate; it is possible that among those born after [Nazism] there was greater sorrow for the perpetrators, and namely one's own parents, than for the victims of the 'final solution.' "[114]

In a retrospective essay on the sexual revolution marking 1968's twenty-year anniversary, former New Left leader Reimut Reiche (now a professional psychoanalyst) put this case even more strongly. Reiche did not only contend that the 68ers' negative fixation on capitalism was actually the expression of an effort to locate the guilt for Nazism in a place external to their own parents. He went so far as to say that his reading of New Left documents from the later 1960s suggested to him that what was at work among 68ers was "a just as horrifying as it is devastating attempt to release the concrete Germans and thereby the collective parents of the 68ers from guilt and to project this guilt onto the 'capitalist means of production' . . . and on the Jews."[115]

Reiche sought to psychoanalyze his own generation and make sense of its conflicted impulses. In his view, a major though unconscious motivation for the 68ers was unbearable grief, rage, and guilt over the Holocaust. But he said as well that these emotions were not something the generation of 1968 expressed directly; rather it attempted to manage them both through incessant and exhausting political activity and by displacing the emotions onto the arena of sexuality. This premise was based on a particular reading of Sigmund Freud and of what Reiche understood as basic human nature: that depression and other painful affects can be held at bay through frantic sexual activity and a constant state of sexual arousal. Reiche thought the (preeminently but not exclusively male) New Left habit of compulsively multiplying one's sexual partners was an attempt to ward off crashing despair. Reiche's second premise was that the New Leftists both hated their parents and loved them. On the one hand, they were driven to avenge the Holocaust by, in a sense, murdering their parents. On the other hand, they were also desperate to absolve their

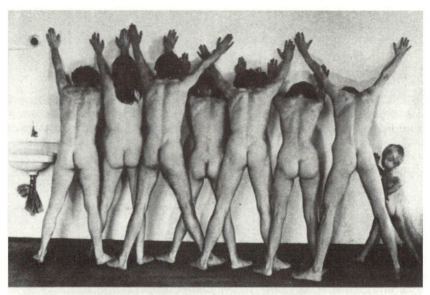

Kahle Maoisten vor einer kahlen Wand

Figure 4.4. *Der Spiegel*, 26 June 1967, p. 20. "Naked Maoists before a naked wall." Members of the Kommune 1 in 1967. From a self-promotional brochure. Photo reprinted and captioned (and the genitals erased) by *Der Spiegel*. (Reprinted by permission of Thomas Hesterberg and *Der Spiegel*)

parents. It was this doubleness of vengeance and reparations, this effort to invert *and* correct their relationships to their own parents that, in Reiche's view, was being acted out in turn on the children of the 68ers.

Reiche argued that the activism of Kommune 1 and Kommune 2 and the *Kinderläden* could not be written off as the work of anomalous extremists but rather was symptomatic of dynamics in the entire student movement. The activists' insistence on rupturing parent-child bonds, he thought, was a symbolic way to implement parricide. Their encouragement of shared sexual arousal between adults and children was a way again to reconcile the generations. "I do not hesitate to insist," Reiche declared, "that here a collective intergenerational trauma of the generation of the student movement is being acted out on the next generation." Reiche also commented critically on a famous photograph of the unclothed backsides of the Kommune 1—including one of the two children living with them—which had been distributed by the commune in a self-promotional brochure and circulated in the mainstream media in 1967 (fig. 4.4). The photo had become a major iconic image for the New Left, one that was routinely reprinted, usually in a spirit either of humor or nostalgia. Reiche thought the photo's popularity and its obsessive re-printing was no coincidence, for in his opinion no image more perfectly captured both the intensity of the struggle to overcome the terrifying past by sexualized means and the impossibility of doing so. Caustically, Reiche observed:

> Consciously this photo scene was meant to recreate and expose a police house search of the Kommune 1. And yet these women and men stand there as if in an aesthetically staged, unconscious identification with the victims of their parents and at the same time mock these victims by making the predetermined message of the picture one of sexual liberation. Thereby they simultaneously remain unconsciously identified with the consciously rejected perpetrator parents. "Sexuality Makes You Free" fits with this picture as well as "Work Makes You Free" fits with Auschwitz.[116]

Reiche's association of this particular photograph with the Holocaust was not just a retrospective or iconoclastic move. Already in 1967, when it first appeared in the media, Rudi Dutschke, one of the most earnest and charismatic of the New Left's leaders—and himself rather dubious about the Kommune 1's pursuit of promiscuity ("the exchange of women and men is nothing but the application of the bourgeois principle of exchange under the sign of pseudorevolutionism")—had a visceral reaction to the photograph. Labeling the commune's members "unhappy neurotics," Dutschke said that the group's naked self-display in the picture "reproduces the gas chamber milieu of the Third Reich; for behind the exhibitionism helplessness, fear, and horror are hidden."[117] Dutschke simply saw the New Leftists as taking the place of the Jewish victims of the Holocaust and did not have the more elaborate reading of their split identifications that Reiche provided in hindsight. This fit with Dutschke's belief that antileftism had in the 1960s come to substitute for Germans' erstwhile antisemitism. And it also no doubt had something to do with the way 1960s conservatives—from professors to construction workers—aggressively announced that New Leftists "all belong in a concentration camp," or shouted at student demonstrators "into the oven," "you should be gassed," or "under Adolf that wouldn't have happened" (*unter Adolf wär das nicht passiert*).[118] Yet that Dutschke had the specific immediate reaction he did above all suggests just how potently tangible was the sense already in the late 1960s, and not just with the benefit of hindsight, that sex was a key locus for young politically motivated West Germans' struggles with the national past.

Just as the sexual conservatism of the 1950s was not only about sex but served as well as a strategy for mastering the Nazi past, so too, albeit again in contradictory ways, the sexual revolution of the 1960s and 1970s became a major locus at which intergenerational conflicts over the events of the 1930s and 1940s were at once engaged and evaded. For finally, the disturbing ways references to Nazism and the Holocaust functioned within New Left and liberal writings of the 1960s and 1970s suggests not only how urgent was the felt need to reverse the sexual "lessons" of Nazism as these had been drawn in the 1950s, but also, and perhaps even more significantly, suggests something of the extraordinary difficulties of theorizing a sexual revolution—and, above all, of connecting pleasure with goodness, sex with social justice—in a country in which only a generation earlier pleasure had been so intimately enmeshed with evil.

More recent work on 1968 has ignored the insights generated in the later 1980s. Especially at the occasion of its thirty-year anniversary, 1968 was frequently represented as the moment when young New Leftists broke the postwar silence and angrily confronted an older generation compromised by Nazism. The more critical assessment of the 68ers' actually rather ambiguous relationship to the Holocaust has largely been suppressed and forgotten. At the very least, the fact of New Left antisemitism should be consistently integrated into the current retrospective assessments of 1968. Yet we can also move a step further toward explaining the otherwise perplexing coexisting tendencies to identification and disidentification with the murdered Jews by recalling how the New Leftists' antipostfascism shaped their antifascism. For this is what is missing in Reiche's otherwise brilliant reading. His implication that the 68ers initiated the displacement of intergenerational tensions about the Holocaust onto the arena of sex is not right, for that displacement had already long since been enacted by their parents.

Moreover, what requires attention are two distinctly related although seemingly incompatible aspects of the generation of 1968's experience. On the one hand, there was the oppressive proximity of the 1960s to the 1940s—in other words, the very real sense of threat still emanating from the older generation. As Klaus Theweleit strove to express it in 1990, it could be quite frightening to try to grow up in the wake of the Germans' "great lost/won war" (by which he meant that while Germans had lost the war against the Allies, to a large extent they had "won" the war against European Jews). It was, as he put it in almost hallucinatory stream-of-consciousness style, terribly scary and confusing to come of age knowing that many of the adults around one had been "Russian killers, Jew burners":

All these ground-beef faces . . . all these good warbling Germans, tears in the eyes at the sad melodies, blood in the mouth at the happy ones, and with rage and horror at the suspicion of anything sexual in the "little ones," . . . still not sated, still chewing, remains of the dead hanging out of all the holes in the sheared skull, lard from the occupied territories rotting in the yellow gaps between the teeth, the cold stench of tobacco in all the toilets, covering the past with stink. . . .

Theweleit recounted in revulsion "the sweaty pleasure of their celebrate-'em-as-they-come-parties, they came all the time and there was blood in the party punch [es war Blut in der Bowle], something about which I later, from about the age of fourteen on, informed about the extent of the murder of the Jews in the camps, could say: yes, that was *them*, who else."[119]

Yet we also need to keep in mind the misunderstandings about the past to which the generation of 1968 was subjected. For although the 1940s seemed in some ways unbearably close, on the other hand there was also an almost unbridgeable epistemological gulf separating the generations. The generation of 1968 had a profoundly distorted understanding of the national past, and precisely this faulty paradigm informed so many of the projects it pursued with such ardor. Taking seriously the obsessive reiteration of the damage done by the nuclear family and the provocative way references to the Holocaust sit in the midst of elaborations of the need for a more liberated attitude toward children's physical pleasures does not merely, then, help us to understand what motivated the student upheaval in the first place, and to understand the emotional and bodily wellsprings of the movement's very particular pathos and fury. It also helps us see how extraordinarily indirect, even circuitous—but therefore no less powerful—are the mechanisms by which the burdens of the past are handed down from one generation to the next.[120]

And finally, lest Reiche's incisive critique of his morally fervent former New Left comrades seem to absolve the rest of the sex-wave-obsessed West German populace, it is worth posing as a question—not least because the sex wave followed so rapidly upon the revelations of the Auschwitz trial and hit West Germany with such uncommon might—what possible psychological and ideological work in mastering the past and keeping massive depression and self-confrontation at bay was being done by the manic society-wide escalation of a culture of constant sexual invitation and arousal. Certainly the force with which the sexual revolution itself ultimately collapsed in West Germany (announcements that it was over would fill the media in the early 1980s) suggests that more—much more—had been at stake in it than the innocent pursuit of pleasure.

CHAPTER FIVE

The Romance of Socialism

Socialist Morality

If in West Germany the restoration of conservative Christian values with regard to sex, gender, and family relations was a primary means for dealing with the inheritance of Nazism, how did the self-styled antifascist regime of East Germany deal with the legacies of the Third Reich's sexual politics? In the Federal Republic of Germany, the Christian churches had considerable influence in shaping official sexual norms. How, by contrast, were sexual mores negotiated in the formally secularized German Democratic Republic? How were sexually conservative arguments advanced here without reference to God? And if the sexual liberalization of West Germany had depended significantly on market pressures, how in East Germany were liberal arguments put forth that nonetheless rejected the capitalist-driven sexual revolution in the West?

The unique situation of East Germany (post-Weimar, post-Nazi, but under Soviet-style communism) provides important and more generally relevant perspectives on the twentieth-century history of sexuality. This is not least because precisely the similarities with and differences from developments in West Germany foreground just how much social, political, and economic factors shape the seemingly natural realm of sexuality (as Marxist sexologists did not tire of pointing out; in this they were quite right). It is also because the particular trajectory of East German sexual politics lends new pertinence to Michel Foucault's shrewd observation that sexuality is "an especially dense transfer point for relations of power," a phenomenon that would be evident both in the way popular pressures forced concessions from the regime and in the regime's evolving efforts to woo its citizenry and solicit not only its compliance but also its love.[1]

Analyzing published writings about sex over the forty years of the German Democratic Republic's history gives us crucial insight into the GDR's "alternate modernity."[2] Such an examination also reveals new aspects of the complexities of interaction between regime and populace in a dictatorship. For although everything that made its way into print for public consumption was subject to control by the functionaries of the Socialist Unity Party (Sozialistische Einheitspartei Deutschlands, or SED), the perpetual struggles between regime and populace—and, indeed, often also the conflicts between different constituencies within the regime and the popu-lace—were everywhere in evidence in the printed record. The government ceaselessly sought to persuade citizens of its point of view, and thus tried strategically to make arguments it thought might be effective, and to take up and preemptively counter potential objections wherever it could. Moreover, because of the severity of the censorship, and the limited num-ber of permitted publications, social and political transformations can be clearly traced. The turn toward a socialist variant of sexual conservatism in the later 1950s and 1960s (part Stalinist, part ex-Nazi, part petty bour-geois) and the uneven but increasing liberalization from the mid- to late 1960s on and especially in the 1970s are evident in marriage and sex manuals, sexological articles and reference works, popular magazines, and sex education curricula. Both under Walter Ulbricht and (after 1971) Erich Honecker, the uppermost echelons of the SED regime were fairly conservative, even prudish, about sex. And so were a number of the ex-perts—physicians, jurists, psychologists, and pedagogues—who lent their authority to the promotion of conservative values. But there were also in every decade, and over time ever more, individuals within the upper reaches of the SED, as well as quite a few professional experts on sex, who found opportunities to make their case for sex-affirmative attitudes.

Like conservatives, liberal authors articulated their own arguments within the constraints of the approved Marxist idiom. But East German sex liberals also frequently used that idiom against itself and tried to stretch its boundaries. Among other things, for example, these more lib-eral commentators appealed to the regime leadership's professed atheism by highlighting Christianity's traditional hostility to sex, cited iconic so-cialists like August Bebel to the effect that sex should be stripped of shamefulness, or interspersed quotations from Karl Marx with tips for intensifying sexual pleasure. Eventually, moreover, the negative counter-example of Nazism, which initially had proved an awkward obstacle to the SED as it sought to justify its own determination to raise reproductive rates, could be used by progressive East German activists to advance more sexually liberal attitudes.

In the meantime, although East Germans found their regime's propa-ganda transparently hypocritical, and while also that portion of the intel-lectual elite which in the first two decades of the nation's history had iden-tified strongly with the antifascist and state-socialist project became over time decidedly disenchanted and alienated, both ordinary citizens and ac-tivist intellectuals shared many of the regime's announced values.[3] "Social-ist morality" (*sozialistische Moral*), as it was called, and which referred to much more than sexual mores but also explicitly incorporated these, was not just a strict set of injunctions imposed on a reluctant and cynical populace. The ideals of socialist morality and the "socialist personality" (*sozialistische Persönlichkeit*) were at once highly authoritarian concepts—mandating as they did certain character traits such as nonegoism and solidarity with others, personal responsibility and decency, nonmaterialism and commitment to progress—and terms subject to continual reformulation and contest, not only ones against which ordinary citizens could critically measure government initiatives but which they could make their own as well. Daily life in East Germany was profoundly affected by the pervasiveness of government monitoring of individuals' and groups' actions through the state security service, the Staatssicherheitsdienst (Stasi); the Stasi not only observed and reported on citizens' behavior and statements, but also—especially in the case of activists and intellectuals—maliciously intervened in private lives, spreading rumors, undermining individuals' self-esteem, and sowing mistrust between friends and even within marriages.[4] Yet mutual surveillance and punitive treatment of political dissidents and nonconformists also coexisted with considerable arbitration and compromises between government and citizens.[5]

"Socialist morality," then, also took on a life of its own and became a cluster of values that (notwithstanding privately expressed popular skepticism) all sides recurrently invoked, deployed, and argued over. It was no coincidence, for instance, that in the 1980s activists on behalf of sexual rights issues such as an end to discrimination of gays and lesbians succeeded precisely by putting their claims in the stiltedly pious terms preferred by the regime.[6] Indeed, and tellingly, one joke circulating in reunified Germany in the early 1990s was that only the supposedly thoroughly secularized East Germans, the *Ossis*, still adhered to the classic "Christian" values of nonmaterialism, care for others, and concern about social justice. The West Germans, the *Wessis*, had relinquished those values long ago.[7]

One thing that emerges with particular clarity from a reading of East German sexological and sex advice literature is further evidence that contemporaries did not consider Nazism particularly repressive with respect to sex. For example, and strikingly, commentators writing in the late 1940s and 1950s either treated developments during the Third Reich as being in unremarkable continuity with liberalizing processes underway since the early twentieth century (such as the prevalence of premarital sex, avid popular interest in sex technique books, and the acceptability of female initiative), or directly specified that Nazism had been sexually inciting. Thus, for instance, a prominent East Berlin gynecologist declared in 1956 that it was not just the war and its chaotic aftermath that had encouraged early premarital intercourse, for "we know from our own object lesson in the crucibles of the Third Reich [*Anschauungsunterricht in den Schmelztiegeln des Dritten Reiches*] (Hitler Youth, Labor Service, etc.) that also in Germany before the war the heterosexual activity of young people, especially of working-class youth, indicated a dissolution of the sexual order that was largely congruent with Kinsey's numbers (Kinsey could show that more than half of the 16-year-old boys and two-thirds of the 20-year-old men had such experiences!)"[8] And Friedrich Heilmann, a leading member of the East German Ministry of Education, in a 1956 medical journal essay also reminded his readers that "Nazism . . . after all, brought with it dissolution and disintegration in the sexual arena as well," even as he allusively gestured to the phenomenon of Nazi homoeroticism when he defended the GDR's commitment to coeducation. Heilmann suggested that "convents, military training schools, girls' boarding schools, prisons, and, in the extreme case, the male communities of the SS and SA" conclusively demonstrated that the atmosphere produced by sex segregation was "never healthy."[9]

Meanwhile, authors from the 1950s through to the 1970s regularly complained about the deleterious impact of Christian negativity toward sex and worried that also East Germans, especially those in the older generations, had not yet fully overcome this legacy. "No religion could say no to the sexual more awfully than Christianity has," opined Heilmann.[10] At the same time, however, writings from the 1950s onward suggest that especially premarital but also extramarital sex was quite routine in the GDR.[11] Conservative authors in the 1950s and 1960s thus struggled to find properly socialist arguments for delaying the onset of premarital sex and for containing sex within marriage. (Simultaneously, however—and despite Heilmann's reference to the stock antifascist cliché of the queer Nazi—cruel and pathologizing attitudes toward homosexuality were, as in the West, transplanted practically wholesale from Nazism.) Yet while the SED regime had always defended premarital heterosexuality with the expectation that it would be premarital in the technical sense (i.e., that it would lead to marriage), in the early 1970s the regime shifted and began enthusiastically promoting the very ubiquity of uncommitted youth heterosexuality which 1960s empirical studies had forced it reluctantly to acknowledge. This was read at the time by Western observers as a clearly desperate measure to raise birthrates in the wake of the introduction of the pill and the legalization of first-trimester abortions. But the East German context suggests that even more important than demography was the regime's abiding anxious desire to bind young people emotionally to the socialist project.

Reading the evolution of debates about sex in East Germany in turn encourages the revision of assumptions now standard among historians and other social scientists about gender relations in East Germany. The Western feminist master narrative of East German women as lamentably doubly burdened by work force participation and domestic chores despite the formally egalitarian rhetoric of the regime is complicated by attention to the history of sexuality. For instance, there is no question that East German women's growing economic independence from men profoundly affected heterosexual power dynamics. Taking sex seriously as a vital, consequential, and complex arena of human activity—as significant a matter as labor relations or political attitudes and, indeed, intricately interconnected with these—helps us see East German women as increasingly confident subjects with strong negotiating power vis-à-vis both their male partners and the state. It allows us as well to bring into view the distinctive egalitarian style of heterosexual masculinity developed among the younger generation in East Germany. Moreover, and crucially, as developments in the GDR in the 1970s and 1980s especially show, sex eventually became a crucial free space in this otherwise profoundly unfree society. Whether this indirectly strengthened the regime's control or should be read as a genuine democratic achievement is a question that remains open. Perhaps both are true.

Attention to the history of sexuality thus also alters our assessment of classic topics in East German historiography. It provides new insight into the divergent ways East and West Germany managed the Nazi past. It furthers our understanding of GDR citizens' gradual accommodation to life under SED communism. And finally, grasping the contours and the import of the sexual freedoms ultimately secured in the GDR helps to explain how the special sexual culture of the East would in the wake of German reunification become such an intense focus for East German nostalgia.

Recriminalizing Abortion

In the immediate aftermath of the war, in the Soviet zone of occupation, abortion was decriminalized. This development was the result of two main factors. One was the strong impulse to undo the harsh criminalization of abortion under Nazism. The other had to do with the extraordinary situation of chaos, crisis, and mass rapes of German women by Soviet soldiers, as well as hunger, homelessness, and generally wretched economic conditions. Permitting abortion under these circumstances was seen as a humanitarian imperative. Initially, the five eastern state governments reverted to the pre-Nazi German criminal code; abortion was technically still criminalized but far less brutally than it had been under the Nazis. Yet, at the same time, doctors were officially notified that abortions would be permitted also in cases of economic distress (the so-called social indication) and thus that they need not fear prosecution for performing abortions. In 1947 and 1948 this handling of the issue was formalized. Paragraph 218 was abolished in almost all Soviet-occupied jurisdictions.

It was common knowledge that abortion rates in the Soviet zone of occupation were exceedingly high. Those who could not find a doctor to perform a surgical abortion tended to rely on the (at once effective and dangerous) method of squirting soapy water through the cervix and thereby prompting a miscarriage.[12] While important work has been done by Atina Grossmann and others on the ways the one to two million rapes of German women by soldiers of the Soviet Red Army (far exceeding the numbers of rapes of German women by other Allied soldiers) contributed to the postwar authorities' willingness to tolerate abortions, this was not the full story as contemporaries interpreted it.[13] For while this explains why officials accepted abortions, it does not explain why so many women continued to seek them after 1945. And although the cataclysmic conditions of hunger and poverty were certainly mentioned by Soviet zone contemporaries, they did not suggest that this was the main cause for the heightened demand, either.

Some believed that it was the crushing defeat of Nazism that had caused massive emotional destabilization and moral disorientation. As one woman in Jena confided to her physician, so attached had she been to Nazism that "due to the war's outcome"—that is, the downfall of the Third Reich—she had experienced a "collapse of her entire way of looking at life." This had been accompanied by "lack of appetite, weight loss, life weariness," followed by "intimate acquaintanceship with a young man, abortion, and rupture of the relationship."[14] A physician in Leipzig was commenting as late as 1952 on the toll the experiences of war and military defeat had taken also on GDR citizens' private lives: "The wreckage field of the Second World War stretches into that region where interhuman relations are most frequently realized . . . namely into that of sexual life." Also among patients not physically traumatized by concrete injuries, "significant psychological problems" were often evident, and the incidence of sexual dysfunctions had grown substantially in the postwar years. "Not inconsiderable portions of the populace, with respect to their sexual lives," he averred, "have been cast into depression, helplessness, and . . . loss of moorings."[15] Yet other commentators simply tried to express, allusively but nonetheless with strong emotion, a generalized impression that the present they were experiencing felt like a kind of moral apocalypse.

Other contemporaries suggested either that the dynamics of total aggressive war or Nazi reproductive ideology itself had created conditions for a significant rise in casual sex and had spurred patterns of behavior that now continued after the war. One medical doctor, for example, remarking on the "frequently chaotic love relationships" evident all around him in the early GDR, explained the prevalence of postwar adultery with the observation that "in and after great wars, because of greediness for life and terror of death, sexual drivenness [*Triebhaftigkeit*] grows out of control."[16] Another Soviet zone doctor offered an at once Freudian and antifascist analysis, suggesting that the fault lay with Nazism and the psychopathology of the German populace that had made Nazism possible. For this observer, the puzzle was why German women were having so much unprotected sex and almost compulsively getting pregnant, even while they were simultaneously desperate to avoid procreating. Admittedly, the price of condoms had risen exponentially since the collapse of the Third Reich. But this could not be the primary reason. Germans, he suggested, really were at odds with themselves over whether to reproduce. They had coped with their own insecurities by projecting their innermost sense of self-worth onto the collectivity of the German "race" and were now unconsciously still unable to become fully individuated, or to separate themselves from the collective psychopathological patterns laid down under Nazism. This explained the reluctance to use any kind of planning in sexual encounters.[17]

At the same time, however, just as Paragraph 218 was in the process of being formally abolished in 1947–48, leading members of the SED had already begun to push for recriminalization. The effort to recriminalize was due not least to demographic concerns; there was a pervasive worry that the Soviet zone would rapidly experience an insupportable shortage of labor power. The drive to recriminalize was evidently also an accommodation to the decision (under Joseph Stalin in 1936) to reverse the decriminalization of abortion in the Soviet Union that had initially been implemented by the Bolsheviks in the wake of the Russian Revolution. And a key dynamic in the Soviet zone of occupation and the early GDR involved setting aside the more sex-liberal communist perspectives inherited from Weimar in order to promote decidedly more conservative Stalinist attitudes.[18]

Yet the drive to recriminalize abortion also posed some tricky ideological dilemmas for the SED leadership. First, the prospect of recriminalization evoked the specter of Nazism all over again. Second, because of its constitutive anti-Christianity, the SED had to find arguments against abortion that did not involve recourse to church teachings. This was all the more important in view of the fact that at this moment in the western zones Christian, especially Catholic, journalists, politicians, and doctors were mobilizing in an antiabortion campaign that would successfully prevent decriminalization in the West.

While initially in the Soviet zone the populace had been actively educated about the harshness of Nazi abortion policy and its links to racism, already by 1947 members of the SED had begun to formulate arguments for recriminalization. For instance, in 1946 the leading women's magazine in the Soviet zone, *Für Dich* (For You), had denounced the Nazis' preoccupation with procreation in no uncertain terms, making derogatory remarks both about the "poisonous" effects of "racial fanaticism" and the Nazis' treatment of women as no better than "baby-making machines."[19] But in 1947, state prosecutor Hilde Benjamin—later to become the much-feared minister of justice in the GDR—was already rejecting the slogan that had been advanced by communists and feminists in Weimar: "My body belongs to me" (*Mein Körper gehört mir*). Benjamin contended that the state absolutely had a right to intervene in women's lives, on the grounds that a society had a prerogative to "secure its progeny." Acutely aware that this sounded very much like Nazi rhetoric, Benjamin declared that the "misuse" of an idea under National Socialism was no reason permanently to discount its value. "After all, we still today speak of socialism, too!" she tartly observed. Meanwhile, however, Benjamin expressly rejected the Christian view that abortion was murder or that a fetus necessarily had a right to life. On the contrary, to criminalize abortion was to assure the right of "the polity as a whole" (*die Allgemeinheit*) to reproduce itself, and this polity could, in her view, be defined equally well as "the right of the society, the right of the [working] class, or the right of the people."[20] Precisely because the obsession with reproductivity had been such a central aspect of Nazism, the SED was forced openly to acknowledge the apparent similarities between fascist and purportedly antifascist demands and then to elaborate distinctions.[21]

The SED also, however, recognized that it had to make major concessions to women in return for depriving them of their reproductive freedom. The German Democratic Republic was founded in October 1949, and within less than a year, in September 1950, the GDR passed the "Law for the Protection of Mothers and Children and the Rights of Woman" (Gesetz über den Mutter- und Kinderschutz und die Rechte der Frau). This law recriminalized abortion, permitting abortion only in cases in which the mother's health or life was in severe danger ("medical indication") or in cases when an inheritable disease was likely to disable the child ("eugenic indication"). But it also guaranteed prenatal and maternity care and financial subsidies, removed all legal discrimination against unwed mothers, and announced the development of extensive state-run infant and childcare facilities. The unapologetically and openly expressed aim was to facilitate women's combined functions as workers *and* procreators; women's labor force participation was urgently needed, but so was their reproductive capacity. The SED well knew that the majority of women favored abortion rights. (As an internal SED document put it, "the mass of women sees [abortion] as morally a fully legitimate type of self-help, something understandable and self-evident.")[22] This consensus had to be countered. The text of the law boldly asserted that the law exemplified the full realization of women's equality. It also declared that the social order of the GDR secured "happy motherhood," that "children are the future of the nation," and that "care for the children, the strengthening of the family and the encouragement of wealth in children [*Kinderreichtum*] is one of the main tasks of our democratic state."[23]

In Minister-President Otto Grotewohl's bald-faced defense of the law, which was not only printed and circulated but also served as the basis for propagandistic instructions sent to all of the SED-affiliated women's committees to help them respond forcefully to anticipated public resistance, the law was again presented as a great advance for women's rights. Not only did Grotewohl assert that abortion could be fatal for women, and thus that it was in women's best interest to have it recriminalized. He also frankly noted that the GDR was a predominantly female society and that in the twenty-five- to thirty-year age bracket there were twice as many women as men. This "unhealthy" disproportion, he said, could be rectified with each new birth, and women should "consciously" make an effort to get pregnant more often. Every woman should have more than two children, and Grotewohl also had no qualms about saying that the reason for this was that the state needed more workers. But like Benjamin before him, Grotewohl also struggled to distance the SED's interest in raising reproductive rates from both Christian and Nazi antiabortion arguments. The state, Grotewohl said, should reject the religious prohibition on abortion, for such a religious prohibition constituted "an invasion of the personal freedom of the individual." And at the same time he declared that "there is no comparison between the population politics of Hitler and that of the German Democratic Republic. Fascist population politics served the war and catastrophic decline [*Untergang*]; our population politics serves peace and prosperity."[24] The overt aim of the 1950 law, in short, was to raise reproductive levels in the GDR; the most immediate effect of the law, however, was that 60 percent of all abortions were once again performed illegally.[25]

THE SEXUAL EVOLUTION

There would be no sexual revolution in East Germany. Unlike West Germany, where the mid- to late 1960s saw a liberalization of the social and cultural landscape so dramatic that to many observers it seemed as though it had happened virtually overnight, East Germany experienced a far more gradual evolution of sexual mores. By the late 1960s, West Germany had been inundated by the commodification of sex in every facet of existence—from highly sexualized advertising to easily available hard-core pornography, from a constant stream of news reportage about sexual matters to sex enlightenment films and curricula and a culturewide discussion of nudity, adultery, and group sex. Market-driven voyeurism had become an inescapable part of everyday life in the West. By contrast, and while East Germany entered a period of sexual conservatism in the 1950s and the first half of the 1960s in many respects comparable with the sexual conservatism of West Germany in those years, there were also already in the 1950s notable elements of liberality in the East which had no parallel in West Germany. These early liberal aspects of East German culture would have a decisive impact on the subsequent trajectory of sexual politics in the decades that followed.

In what did this liberality consist? One major difference between East and West Germany in the 1950s was not so much the extent of female labor force participation (since also in the West women worked outside the home to supplement the family's income, while in the East there were still numerous women, especially in the older generations, who were solely housewives), although it was indeed somewhat higher in the East. Rather, the difference lay in the combination of institutional structures and strong rhetorical support in the East that made women's work for wages not only possible but also much less guilt-inducing. The double burden of work for wages and household chores (or rather triple burden, if one added the demands of political participation in party- or workplace-linked organizations) did in the course of the 1950s influence East German women, too, to retreat to more part-time work. But there is no question that the psychological misery induced in so many West German women in the 1950s (and also later) by the idealization of faithful, home-bound femininity and self-sacrificing wife- and motherhood was much less evident in the East. East German women were continually told that they should improve and develop themselves through further studies, and men were enjoined to support this. Indeed, already in the 1950s, East German men were encouraged to participate in housework and child-rearing, a suggestion only intermittently voiced in 1950s West Germany (where the main message from the government and popular magazines alike was that a wife's whole purpose was to create a warm and nurturing home for husband and children and to tend to her husband's psychic wounds after his stressful day at work). The idea that a man might be the house-husband and care for the baby and assist his wife through her studies was familiar enough in the East already in the mid-1950s that one author approvingly noted the phenomenon had become so prevalent a part of the landscape one could "already recognize a certain type."[26]

Beyond these economic and social factors, there were also the SED regime's clear stances in defense of both premarital heterosexual activity and unwed motherhood. West Germany too had technically abolished legal discrimination against illegitimate children. But in the East, a push to end social discrimination and bring an end to the culture of shame surrounding illegitimacy was a genuine government objective. In the West, by contrast, with its officially Christianized political culture under Christian Democratic auspices, shaming was standard. Moreover, although in West and East alike premarital heterosexual intercourse was practiced by a large majority of the population, West Germany in the 1950s and early 1960s saw a major campaign against premarital sex. This campaign was not only promoted by the Protestant and Catholic churches through sermons and sex advice tracts running into millions of copies. Christian perspectives also informed government policy, teacher education, and school curricula, and popular West German magazines too reinforced the idea that good girls did not permit premarital sex and that a gentlemanly young man should respect this. Girls were told that if a boy really loved them, he would wait until the wedding day; the idea that girls might have desires of their own was simply not considered. Far from being a trivial matter, the postwar campaign to clean up German sexual mores was a core element in securing West German Christianity's antifascist moral authority, for during the Third Reich sexual matters had formed a main focus of conflict between the Nazis and the Catholic Church in particular and Nazis had continually ridiculed Christian prudery and opposition to premarital heterosexuality.

In the officially secularized East, by contrast, sex was not a main site for managing the legacies of Nazism because the East secured its antifascist status above all by emphasizing its anticapitalism. While fully aware of Nazism's encouragements to premarital sexual activity, the SED felt no particular need to break with this legacy, since it was congruent with popular values, which simply saw sex as the customary way to express love.[27] Instead, the main concern in the East was to bring some order into the postwar "chaotic love-relationships" by showing citizens that socialism provided the best conditions for lasting and happy love. (In fact, eastern authors frequently pointed out that sexual relationships really were more love-based and hence honorable in the East than in the West specifically because under socialism women did not need to "sell" themselves into marriage in order to support themselves.) In the East, then, discussion of sex was seen not so much as a means for mastering the past but rather as a means for orienting people toward the future—a future that was declared to be always already in the making, and which required all citizens' engaged participation. Socialism, it was constantly stressed, was steadily en route to perfection. And no sex advice text in the East was complete without reference either to the idea that only socialism provided the context for the most loving and satisfying marriages or to the notion that a couple's commitment to and struggle on behalf of socialism would enhance their romantic relationship.

While a number of East German doctors in the 1950s and 1960s counseled against premarital sex and/or cautioned that the East German government's support for illegitimate children should not be interpreted as direct encouragement to bear children out of wedlock, the overwhelming message from the government and from advice writers was that premarital heterosexual activity was both natural and normal. Medical doctor Hanns Schwarz, for example, in an SED-sponsored sex advice lecture delivered more than forty times throughout the East between 1952 and 1959 (and circulated in hundreds of thousands of copies), criticized promiscuity but otherwise energetically endorsed premarital sex and rejected "moralistic preachments" against it. "Sensuality," he told his listeners, "can be something glorious and positive," and should not be "branded as a sin by uptight people [*Mucker*]." All that mattered, according to Schwarz (as he revealed his heteronormativity) was that this sensual activity should occur between "two people of the opposite sex who in addition to physical attraction to each other are emotionally entwined, have similar ways of looking at the world, and have shared interests."[28] And in a book published in 1959, Schwarz again described sex as "the quintessence of being alive." Moreover, unlike more conservative East German writers who unreflectingly collapsed intercourse with reproduction, Schwarz declared forthrightly that "we as free people know that intercourse does not just serve the propagation of the human race, but also furthers pleasure very significantly."[29] A similar message was communicated by physician Rudolf Neubert's *Das neue Ehebuch* (The New Marriage Book, 1957), the single most popular East German advice book in the late 1950s and early 1960s. Although Neubert thought it advisable for teenagers between the ages of fourteen and eighteen to avoid "regular [*regelmässigen*] intercourse" (even as he was rather unclear what he meant by "regular"), he was completely in favor of premarital intercourse for the nineteen- to twenty-five-year-old set. "No one," he announced confidently, "will take moral offense if these matured people also love each other in the bodily sense." And this generosity extended also to nonmarital pregnancies. In Neubert's opinion, there was no need to rush into marriage. For as long as the child was "conceived and received in love, it is completely irrelevant when the parents marry."[30]

By the early 1960s, a government statement formalized the view that love made premarital sex permissible. The SED's memorandum on youth (*Jugendkommuniqué*) formulated in 1963 stated that "every true love between two young people deserves candid respect" and implicitly instructed parents and grandparents that they should be understanding of young couples' loving relationships also when these turned sexual. The GDR's gender egalitarianism and practice of coeducation, together with the incontrovertible fact that young people were simply experiencing puberty at an earlier age than previous generations had, it was held, made support for young love both sensible *and* ethical. The "morality of the convent" was anathema, "prohibitions, prudery, secrecy, and punishment" were inappropriate. Romantic happiness was inspiring and life-enhancing. "True love belongs to youth the way youth belongs to socialism," the memorandum announced, and "To be socialist is to help young people toward life happiness and not to create tragedies." At the same time, the memorandum emphasized, the government was definitely not advocating indiscriminate sexual experimentation. Love relationships, it advised, should be "deep" (*tief*) and "clean" (*sauber*).[31]

Yet despite the SED's consistent commitment to female economic independence and professional advancement and despite its apparent acceptance of premarital heterosexual intercourse, the GDR in the 1950s and 1960s also developed a distinctively socialist and in many ways quite oppressive brand of sexual conservatism. What needs to be grasped, as the 1963 memorandum's language already implies, is the double quality of the messages sent about sex in the 1950s and 1960s. There was in numerous texts, in all the sympathy expressed for the inevitability of premarital sex, nonetheless a strongly normative expectation that this sex would be entered into in the context of a relationship heading toward marriage and, ideally, that sexual relations would not start until "psychological maturity" had been attained. Numerous advice writers expended considerable energy emphasizing the importance of delaying the onset of sexual relations until this "psychological maturity" was evident, even as they variously associated this term with the capability for long-term commitment, a willingness to become parents in case contraceptives failed, or the attainment of a certain level of education and hence the capacity for economic independence from one's own parents.

A fundamentally conservative attitude was also powerfully evident in the SED's notions of socialist virtue, the suspicion that private bliss might draw citizens away from socialism rather than toward it, and a generalized skepticism about the pursuit of pleasure as potentially depoliticizing. This, then, was the grounds for hectoring injunctions that lasting happiness was only possible when human beings involved themselves in political struggle. As, for example, divorce court judge Wolfhilde Diehrl put it in 1958 in her especially tendentious attack on pleasure-seeking, "there is no fulfillment of existence in an idyll set apart from human society," and although she conceded that "a healthy marital life is generally not possible without the harmony of bodily union," she nonetheless drew on the authority of examples from her work encountering unhappy couples to argue that excessive sexual activity caused severe psychological and physiological damage. "An unmastered indulgence [*ein unbeherrschtes Geniessen*], a perpetual stimulation of the nerves so that pleasure can be achieved [*ein ständiges Aufpeitschen der Nerven zur Erreichung der Wollust*] and dissipation [*Ausschweifungen*] in sexual life," Diehrl declared in her frequently reprinted book, "rob people of joy, tension, and strength, drive them to perversities, cause bad moods and satiation. Such people show apathy in their dealings with others, enervation, indifference for one's own tasks and the problems of society." And to prove that lack of social concern also hurt the individual, Diehrl reinforced her point with a frightening tale of a couple that had had so much sex right after they were married that they became physically ill and also turned against each other. Only by redirecting them to their social responsibilities, she asserted, was the marriage rescued.[32]

Normativity made itself aggressively felt in other ways as well, as the recurrent rhetorical emphasis on "clean" relationships implied not only sexual fidelity but also a rejection of homosexuality. East German advice writers throughout the 1950s and 1960s did not only deem homosexuality a perversion, pathology, or deviance. They also often replicated the predominant Nazi analyses of homosexuality as they either asserted that most homosexuality resulted from seduction during the adolescent phase when sexual orientation was not yet fixed on the opposite sex and/or associated homosexuality with mental deficiency and crime.[33] In his book for young teens, for example, the oft-reprinted *Die Geschlechterfrage* (The Question of the Sexes, 1955), Rudolf Neubert pretended to be sensitive to the small minority of "true" homosexuals as he stated that homosexuality was sometimes caused by a "deformation of the inner glands" (*Missbildung der inneren Drüsen*) and went on to say that "these people are to be pitied just as much as those born with any other deformation." But Neubert also observed that even these congenital cases should be treated with hormone preparations, surgery (transplantation of "glandular tissue"), and above all psychotherapy (or, as he indicatively defined it, "pedagogic influencing by the doctor"). In addition, like Nazis before him and like so many in West and East Germany in the 1950s, Neubert insisted that while the number of true homosexuals was small, the number of those seduced in youth was larger. Yet even as he announced that homosexuality occurred primarily among "pleasure-addicted progeny of rich families" or "asocial elements from other social strata," Neubert also assured readers that the incidence of homosexuality was far less frequent in a "young, constructively developing" society like the GDR than it was in (presumably capitalist) societies in a state of "dissolution."[34]

In 1957 the SED quietly instructed police and judges no longer to prosecute or imprison adult men engaged in consensual homosexual activity, and this certainly marked an important contrast to the ongoing coordinated criminalization, replete with police raids and prison sentences, in West Germany.[35] And in 1968 the GDR abolished Paragraph 175, one year ahead of the FRG's modification of 175. Yet at the same time, a newly introduced law, Paragraph 151, under the guise of "protection of youth," criminalized same-sex activity for *both* men and women if it occurred between someone over the age of eighteen and someone under the age of eighteen. SED officials strenuously sought to avoid the topic of homosexuality altogether, in a double inability to acknowledge that homosexuality existed at all in a socialist society and to acknowledge that there could be within socialism "marginal" groups of any sort that could not be integrated seamlessly into the social whole.[36] Throughout the 1960s, what little was written about homosexuality continued to treat it as a "perversion." This term, for example, was chosen by Gerhard and Danuta Weber in their popular advice book *Du und ich* (You and I, 1965)—the advice book most frequently consulted by East German youth in the mid- to late 1960s—as they advised young women not to marry homosexual men.[37] And because the SED was always apprehensive and anxious to keep from international attention any empirical data that could possibly be used against socialism by its "enemies," it was no surprise that research that was able to demonstrate an especially low incidence of youth homosexual activity in the GDR was published.[38] The official tendencies to denigrate homosexuality and attempt to steer youth away from it and above all to force youth caught in homosexual encounters to undergo coercive psychotherapy remained disturbing features of East German life throughout the 1950s and 1960s and well into the 1970s.[39]

Meanwhile, and all through the 1950s and 1960s, East German sex advice writers also struggled to find imaginative arguments for frightening young people away from "too early" heterosexual activity. In gynecologist Wolfgang Bretschneider's view, for instance, premarital intercourse should preferably be avoided altogether, and in his advice book for parents of teens, he provided a battery of arguments against it. Not only could premarital intercourse disrupt the proper psychological maturation process. Nor did he only feel compelled to point out that, although the GDR had equalized the status of illegitimate with legitimate children, it was nonetheless exceedingly difficult to parent a child alone. He also strategically argued that the contraception that would likely be used to prevent unwed motherhood tended in almost all cases to inhibit sensation, and he warned readers that this inhibition of sensation in turn could cause lasting sexual dysfunction. He further said that long-standing use of contraceptives could cause female infertility. Moreover, he declared, the "abnormal" locations in which most premarital intercourse occurred—park benches, courtyard corners, behind the bushes—and the accompanying anxieties about fear of discovery, were not well suited to the development of female sexual responsiveness in particular (even as elsewhere he downplayed the importance of that responsiveness and declared that female orgasm really was not as important as many women seemed to think it was). At the same time, Bretschneider also adopted, with only the slightest modification, ideas from the Swiss Protestant (and devout Christian) advice writer Theodor Bovet, whose writings were enormously influential in 1950s West Germany. For example, Bretschneider's recommendations to men to help them distract themselves from the desire to indulge in masturbation were lifted directly from Bovet. And Bretschneider's ideas about the deleterious impact of masturbation on the potential for marital happiness were also indistinguishable from those advanced in West German Catholic and Protestant advice writings. Girls were warned that they would have trouble transitioning from clitoral stimulation to vaginal sensation during intercourse, while boys were informed that "masturbation is a pitiful substitute for real love," and that "one remains stuck in oneself."[40] Socialist sexual conservatism, in short, and despite the critical asides about Christian sex hostility in most East German sex advice texts, appeared quite compatible with Christian sexual conservatism.

In part, then, as noted, the conservative tendencies of the 1950s and 1960s had their source in the profoundly conventional views of the German communist leadership and the directives coming from the Soviet Union. The conservative tendencies of the 1950s and 1960s can also in part be ascribed to both the public's and the government's worries about the still fairly desperate state of the economy, and the atmosphere this created in which regime arguments about the need to concentrate energies on the basic daily task of survival could appear plausible.[41] Rationing, for example, was not ended until 1958. The "brain drain" of qualified technocratic and professional elites that continued unabated throughout the 1950s until the building of the Berlin Wall in 1961 not only increased regime paranoia but also exacerbated the difficulty of economic reconstruction after the combined devastations of wartime damage and Soviet appropriation of infrastructure, resources, and reparations payments. Basic consumer goods were frequently unavailable, and mismanagement and bad decisions in economic planning at the highest levels continually made production processes and their coordination uneven and unreliable.[42] The housing shortage remained acute well into the 1970s—even as, fascinatingly, a marriage book published in 1972 was still able to blame this on Nazism. (While encouraging its readers to have multichild families, the authors conceded that "there is without a doubt a contradiction between the demands of the society for larger families and the demands of families for larger living spaces." But alas, "after the terrible devastations of the fascist war our social means simply do not as yet permit us to offer every child-rich family anything like a four- or five-bedroom apartment—as much as we are making an effort to do this.")[43] Indeed,

there was hardly a sex advice text written that did not refer to the problems—self-consciousness, inadequate privacy—caused for young couples
by the inevitable need to continue living with parents even after they had
married (only once a child was born did most couples have a chance at a
tiny apartment of their own).

In sum, then, it is no surprise that the 1950s and at least the first half
of the 1960s in East Germany have been remembered by contemporaries
as the dark ages of an enforced fixation with conventionality and respectability. As one man put it, the atmosphere was "thoroughly sterile, there
was very little to delight the senses."[44] There was in that era "no public
discourse about many questions related to sexuality," but rather a "self-
disciplining morality, unfriendly to pleasure, chaste . . . ascetic or pseudo-
ascetic, uptight, interventionist," the leading East German sexologist Kurt
Starke recalled in the 1990s.[45] And the prominent West German sexologist
Volkmar Sigusch, who lived in East Germany until he fled to the West
in 1961, said "the climate in the East was horribly philistine [*furchtbar
spiessig*]. You couldn't get more petty bourgeois or philistine than that.
Ulbricht? Honecker? They were so narrow and provincial. All the liberal,
sophisticated people had gone to the West."[46] Starke and others recollect
a climate of intrusive supervision of private lives and public humiliation
for any departure from the expected narrow norms. This was especially
true for party members. Young people in party-run boarding schools were
forbidden from forming into couples ("*keine Pärchenbildung*"), student
dormitories were monitored at night to make sure no one was having sex,
and also after marriage the SED wanted its functionaries to maintain stable and conformist arrangements.[47] If married functionaries had extramarital affairs or one-night stands, they were expected to confess all, and
publicly castigate themselves and recommit to their spouses at a party
forum.[48]

Yet at the same time, and all through the 1950s and 1960s, popular
practices elicited significant regime concessions. Rates of illegal abortions,
unwed teen motherhood (only at age eighteen was it legal to marry in the
GDR), youthful divorces (especially among couples who had only married because a child was on the way), and even the strains on "student
mothers" struggling to juggle childcare and professional development all
caused consternation in SED circles and led the regime to reevaluate its
priorities. Empirical studies ordered to assess these issues turned up incontrovertible evidence that each was a genuine social concern.[49] The government responded, among other things, by directing doctors already in 1965
to handle abortion requests more leniently and to consider a woman's
psychological well-being in addition to her physical health.[50] And in a law
that went into effect in 1966, family, marriage, and sex counseling centers
were established throughout East Germany.[51] The experts involved in or-

ganizing these centers and coordinating continuing education for staff advanced some of the most progressive perspectives on sexuality in the GDR; they forged strong ties to the International Planned Parenthood Federation and sponsored conferences on sexuality that received respectful international notice. In turn, the issues that brought individuals and couples to these centers in ever-rising numbers—above all, worries about contraception and about sexual dissatisfaction within marriages—again created opportunities for professionals concerned with sexual matters to persuade the government that more expansive research, public education, and therapeutic services were needed.[52]

The second half of the 1960s saw a strong oscillation between conservative and liberal perspectives. On the one hand there were texts that explicitly reacted against what they found to be a too value-neutral tendency in early 1960s empirical studies and tried to find novel arguments for a return to sexual conservatism. (In this vein, for instance, experts warned of the deleterious impact especially on females of a sexual encounter experienced in a relationship not heading toward marriage. They used the idea that the female capacity for orgasm during coitus might be an acquired skill that took some practice as a reason to put off sex until a marriage partner had been found. Or they even declared outright that females under age twenty were simply unlikely to achieve sexual satisfaction so it was best not to try.)[53] On the other hand, in these years an increasing effort to present the German Democratic Republic as a desirable site for young romance was also evident. Sometimes both tendencies were combined, as for example when Heinrich Brückner proudly published his finding that more youth in the GDR than in the FRG felt that premarital abstinence was physically possible, even as he was also pleased to find that GDR youth had more sexological savvy than their Western counterparts.[54] A similar combination could be found in Klaus Trummer's 1966 advice book for young teens. While parents and teachers should never advance "the moral views of the convent," too-early intercourse would disturb an individual's psychological and intellectual development. At the same time, love was definitely better in the East, because "how people live together here is no longer determined by the laws of capitalism ('everyone is only looking out for himself')" and "love is not a commodity."[55]

Indeed, the comparison between East and West became a major motif in East German writings on sex after the mid-1960s—even as West Germans increasingly ignored the East. (This was an interesting departure from the powerful role anticommunist rhetoric had played in the West in the 1950s, as the West had sought to justify its efforts on behalf of female subordination and confinement within the domestic realm through constant rhetorical invocations of the purported horrors of female emancipation in the GDR.) It was almost as though now that the West was no

longer the stuffy place it had once been and had started to resemble a
pleasure palace in sexual terms, the East needed to stress the sexual advantages of socialism. What was most noticeable in the efforts to disseminate a new socialist message about sex was an apparently urgent—if
nonetheless also ambivalent—SED intention not to be perceived as overly
puritanical.

Thus socialist ethicist Bernd Bittighöfer in an essay on youth and love
from 1966 registered approval that more and more parents in East Germany were letting go of the remnants of bourgeois "prejudices" and "inhibitions." On the one hand, Bittighöfer declared himself in favor of "the
moral cleanness of our socialist way of life" and expressly criticized the
titillating material disseminated by West German radio and television.
The West was, in his view, purveying "imperialist ideology," propagating
"skepticism and anarchism in the realm of morality," encouraging "sexual excess" and "trivialization and brutalization of relations between the
sexes," and—as he awkwardly put it—"stimulating adolescents' natural
urge for recognition [Geltung] onesidedly in the sexual realm." Yet on
the other hand, and significantly, premarital chastity was not his recommendation. This idea, he said, was "antiquated." And he went on to contend that "the satisfaction of the sexual drive is . . . one of the most elementary needs of human life-expression," and he invoked August Bebel's
point that those who were prevented from satisfying drives that were so
"closely connected with their innermost being" would be damaged in
their development. "Fulfilling love," Bittighöfer concluded, "includes sexual union" and "is an essential element in personality development and
fulfilled existence."[56]

A similar kind of uncertainty marked the government's approach to
sex in literature. When the Central Committee of the SED met in 1965,
for instance, it considered the apparent problem that East German writers
increasingly included sex scenes that were not in tune with the regime's
notions of socialist morality. Rather than strictly censoring narrative representations of sexual acts and encounters, the SED described itself as
opposed to "prudery and prettification" (Prüderie und Beschönigungsten-
denzen). Once again, however, the message was mixed: such scenes should
only be allowed if they occurred in a proper partnership or, if not, the
narrative should in some way censure the characters' actions.[57]

In the face of the government's apparent disorientation through the
1960s and into the 1970s, progressive professionals concerned with sexuality, whether physicians or pedagogues, did their utmost to use the evidence of the populace's desires and difficulties as a wedge to influence
the SED and to redirect national debate on sexual matters. Collectively,
through their support for each other and through their publications, these
professionals—notable among them Lykke Aresin, Peter G. Hesse, Karl-

Heinz Mehlan, and Siegfried Schnabl—managed to make open discussion of sexual matters possible. Hesse was an early and eloquent advocate of more broad-based public education about contraception, rejecting worries about a declining birthrate and insisting on the "higher" morality of sex free from fear; he subsequently provided a major service by organizing and coediting a massive three-volume encyclopedia of sexological knowledge, the first of its kind in the GDR.[58] Mehlan was singularly important in the liberalization of abortion law.[59] And Aresin was enormously influential in making the birth control pill widely acceptable and available in the GDR. She and Schnabl were also pioneers in the treatment of sexual dysfunctions and marital disharmony; following the work of such American sexologists as William Masters and Virginia Johnson, they created individual and couple therapy in the GDR. (Strikingly, it must be noted that rather than seeing these centers as potentially invasive institutions, couples flocked to them.)[60] Schnabl also conducted the theretofore largest empirical study on sexual dysfunction and sexual practices within marriage, based on interviews with and anonymous questionnaires answered by thirty-five hundred men and women. Aresin's and Schnabl's work was crucial in making issues of sexual conflict within marriages an acceptable subject for public discussion. Schnabl's sex advice book of 1969, *Mann und Frau intim* (Man and Woman Intimately), based on his research findings, became a runaway best seller. His reassuring, no-nonsense recommendations for facilitating female orgasmic response were the centerpiece of his broader campaign to affirm the joys and the importance of heterosexual sex apart from its potential reproductive consequences.[61] By the GDR's end in 1989, this book (together with a guide on gardening) had the highest sales of any book in the nation's history.

Above all, however, GDR citizens plainly carved out their own freedoms. Nude bathing, for example (known as FKK, for *Freikörperkultur*), became an important part of GDR culture. Starting in the middle of the 1960s nude bathing became acceptable for growing numbers of GDR citizens and by the 1970s full nudity was clearly the norm at GDR beaches, lakeside or oceanside. Early attempts by municipal authorities to prevent this practice were simply overridden by the adamant masses, who stripped and would not move. Nakedness for the whole family also within the home became increasingly standard practice as well, especially for that generation that had grown up together with the GDR; for their children, nudism simply became the cultural common sense. As subsequent studies showed, homes in which parent and child nakedness were routine tended also to be those in which parents advocated progressive attitudes about sex and where there was generally warm, trusting, and open parent-child communication; this second GDR generation was raised with far more liberal and tolerant perspectives toward all aspects of sexuality.

In an interview published in 1995, the Leipzig sexologist Kurt Starke evocatively summarized the gradual transformation of the GDR's sexual culture in this way:

> At the latest in the 1970s the citizens in the GDR started to defy all kinds of possible constrictions with respect to their partner- and sexual behavior. They became FKK fans. They birthed illegitimate children in droves. They handed in divorce papers when love had faded. They casually got involved with a co-worker if they felt like it. At some point kissing couples lay on the grass in Leipzig's Clara-Zetkin-Park or female students sunbathed naked, and no police intervened. The few sex enlightenment books that appeared were not disdained but rather passed from hand to hand and by no means secretly. Often they provided the occasion for conversations between parents and their adolescent children. All of this came together with the improvement of living conditions, for example, the creation of more housing; after all, one needs a place for living and loving. . . . This process was also combined with a more positive valuation of sexuality. An affirmative attitude toward sexuality developed, very connected with family and with love. So: somehow a romantic ideal.[62]

Still, it would take another decade before the gains claimed by many in the GDR in the course of the 1970s became fully visible to all. Starke's own research, conducted under the auspices of the Center for Youth Research in Leipzig together with the center's director, Walter Friedrich, and in creative circumvention of the regime's monitoring efforts, would play no small part in helping GDR citizens see for themselves their own achievements. And by the early 1980s, when Starke published *Junge Partner* (Young Partners, 1980) and, together with Friedrich, published *Liebe und Ehe bis 30* (Love and Marriage until Thirty, 1984), it became apparent that East German women in particular had not only been special objects of their government's solicitude but had successfully reconfigured their private relationships as well.

FEMALE FANTASIES

Just as there had been no momentous or spectacular sexual revolution in East Germany, so too there would be no large-scale and dramatic feminist protest movement or development of a women-centered counterculture. While especially in the course of the 1980s, a number of women's organizations were founded in the GDR, their self-definition was rarely feminist. To a great extent, feminism in East Germany was simply perceived by East German women as a redundancy.

The hesitancy about feminism felt by East German women was due in part to the state-sponsored advantages East Germany offered them. So many of the desiderata West German feminists had to fight for in the 1970s—abortion rights, childcare facilities, economic independence, and professional respect—were things East German women by that point could largely take for granted. First-trimester abortions upon demand were legalized in 1972, an achievement never matched in the West. While West German women were continually encouraged to feel guilt if they placed their young children in daycare, and options to do so remained few and far between in any event, and while West German women constantly experienced motherhood and careers as conflicting, East German women increasingly tended to consider this combination fully manageable.

Another major impetus for the West German feminist movement was the pervasiveness of pornography and, more generally, the objectification of women's bodies in advertising and all media. Although available as contraband, pornography was illegal in the East; its distribution was severely limited. Whereas in the West, consumer capitalism functioned to a large degree via the (always distorted) representation of female sexuality, East German state socialism was not driven by this imperative. In East Germany, the populace did walk around naked, but nothing was being sold by this. Occasionally, products made in the GDR were advertised with a hint of sexual innuendo, and one popular magazine (*Das Magazin*) published a nude female centerfold every month, but these photographs were remarkably tame compared with representations in the West and generally lacked the lascivious look and the nonaverage bombshell bodies so prevalent in Western pornography. Meanwhile, the heterosexual male anxieties that both funded and were fostered by the pornography typically available in the West were not provoked in the same way in the East.

Yet another significant difference from the West was East Germany's state-sponsored insistence that men should respect women who were their superiors at work and that men should assist their female partners with household and childcare responsibilities. In both cases, and while the realization of these aims certainly remained imperfect, the standard set by the state had important consequences. East German women found themselves routinely in positions of authority and responsibility in work and public life. As the East German journal *Visite* (produced for Western visitors' consumption) exulted already in 1971, one-third of all judges in the GDR were female, "an impressive number that no capitalist country in the world can even approach." Every fourth school was run by a female principal. More than one thousand women were mayors—13 percent of all East German mayors (compared with less than one percent in West Germany). Hundreds of thousands of women held offices in unions; tens of thousands were members of production committees; thirteen hundred women were directors of industrial enterprises. And importantly, "sociological research shows that the majority of the workers take a female as their superior just as seriously as they would a man." The essay also emphasized that only men's help with the household and childrearing made this socialist female emancipation possible. And, of course, *Visite* did not fail to conclude sonorously that these amazing female achievements were no miracle but rather due to "the socialist relations of production that set free the creative forces of all people. Where the exploitation of the human being has been overcome, where the driving force of the society is no longer the striving after profit but rather the coincidence of individual and social interests, there is no ground in which egoism, self-glorification and oppression of woman could grow."[63] But for all the unwarranted self-congratulation, there was nevertheless a significant enough element of truth to these claims. For East Germany did develop its own distinctive standards of masculinity and femininity. The ideals propounded by the leadership were more than just empty phrases; they were also practically approximated in the daily interplay between social conditions and individual negotiations.

As the *Visite* item already makes clear, however, the SED's audience was always also the GDR's own citizenry, whom it continually strove to persuade of socialism's inherent advantages over capitalist culture. Discussions of gender relations became a major site for the SED both to address the East German female population's concerns and simultaneously to route East German women's loyalties back to socialism. Didactic instructions to the citizenry about what gender equality concretely meant were offered in a plethora of venues and a variety of genres. A classic technique was the coordinated representation of popular sentiment via the publication of readers' letters in widely read magazines. So, for example, the women's magazine *Für Dich* in 1974 printed a letter from a woman whose husband had stayed home with their ill child (so that the woman would not have to miss her work) and who was distressed that her husband's colleagues and supervisors had castigated him for this dereliction of duty to his own job. The ensuing outpouring of readers' letters, the vast majority of which supported this couple's handling of the matter and expressed outrage that the husband's co-workers harbored such "antiquated" sexism (How dare they accuse this woman of being "a bad mother"? How dare they act like men's careers were more important than women's?), showed how strongly ordinary citizens had internalized East Germany's constitutional guarantee of gender equality. But, of course, this "spontaneous" reaction was also being managed, and the framing of the letters with editorial comment shows how concerned the magazine (and by extension the government) was precisely about the tenacity of the double standard it so loudly claimed was steadily disappearing. And yet once again, despite the obvious choreography, the changing standards were clearly evident as well. As one letter writer recommended, the only solution to the lingering resistances to gender equality was to raise the next generation of boys "so that they will in their later marriage see equal rights as something self-evident and not feel like they are being heroes if they help out in the household."[64]

Just as important a strategy was the effort to connect fantasies of romantic fulfillment with engagement on behalf of socialism by rewriting the conventional love plot to incorporate notions of gender egalitarianism and a new ideal of socialist manhood. Along these lines, for example, the weekly magazine *NBI* in 1971 carried a feature story about a young married couple that perfectly expressed the efforts of the SED not only pedagogically to instruct citizens on properly socialist gender relations but also, and above all, to suture individuals' aspirations for happiness in love to their love for socialism (fig. 5.1). Under the unambiguous title, "Two Declarations of Love" (*Zwei Liebeserklärungen*), the magazine recounted the courtship of pretty seventeen-year-old bookkeeper Carola and twenty-one-year-old village high school teacher Helmut Nachtigall. Situating the story politically, *NBI* informed readers that Helmut's father, a farmer, had been "the red in the village" (i.e., a long-standing leftist) and hence "after 1945" (i.e., the end of the Third Reich) had been elected by his peers to be the village mayor. *NBI* also noted that all four parents had enthusiastically supported the young couple's romance and that a year after the marriage the couple's daughter Ines was born. But the main drama of the tale was the support that Helmut, the parents and in-laws, the villagers, and both his and her co-workers gave Carola in her determined battle for self-improvement (she wanted to become a kindergarten teacher).[65]

Socialism, the *NBI* story emphasized, made such opportunity for self-betterment available to all women as well as men. Also Carola's mother had gotten further education and said, "We could never have had it so good in the old system." And socialism was what made possible the solidarity that facilitated individual achievement; the other farmhands in Carola's mother's brigade did her farmwork on top of their own so that she could study. All the more devastating, then, that Carola brought home a "D" as her first grade in her class on Marxism-Leninism; how could she face her courageous father-in-law or her mother's self-sacrificial comrades? But with the constant support of Helmut and everyone else, Carola worked her way from a "D" to an "A." "The husband and history teacher [Helmut] did not only helpfully reach for the dish-drying towel and the shopping bag, he also asked his colleague Thieme, the specialist for state-citizenship studies and history, to come home with him whenever he thought he might not be able to explain a particular problem comprehensibly enough for his wife." Not only did Carola start learning more methodically, but the material also started to make real sense to her. "She recognizes, as she gets deeper into it, how important it is for the socialist society to develop wise, happy, hardworking people."[66]

Den Bund fürs Leben
zu zweit geschlossen:
Hochzeitsfoto 1961

Den Bund fürs Leben
mit Millionen geschlossen:
Carola und Helmut Nachtigall
erhalten von der Kreisleitung
der SED Halberstadt
im Lenin-Jahr 1970
ihre Kandidatenkarten.

Figure 5.1. "Two Declarations of Love," *NBI*, April 1971, p. 12. (Reprinted by permission of the Berliner Verlag)

Finally, the joys of individual achievement and of experienced community lead Carola and Helmut to decide they want to become SED party members. Nine years after they went to the town hall to get married, they went back in the same building to make another life-long commitment: "I have made another promise for life . . . a promise for thousands and more than thousands, for whom I will be comrade and trusted person . . . for a life that is ever more worth living." Soon after, Carola became a kindergarten principal and Helmut loved her even more: "my wife, comrade, indefatigable fellow battler . . . the mother of our vivacious, diligent daughter." The essay even managed the delicate issue of the perpetual housing shortage, recounting Carola's conversion from someone who angrily (and antisocialistically) did not comprehend why she was not being granted a larger apartment into someone thrilled—after she had become a party member—to be moving into a beautiful apartment in the same building as the kindergarten. Finally, the essay also incorporated the SED's endless refrain that things were perpetually in the process of getting better. As the essay concluded, "she [Carola] always has ideas for the future. For the future of the children in our city, our state. That is also a kind of declaration of love. To the society, in which we live."[67] Precisely the soap-operatic intricacy of the details was meant to facilitate readers' emotional involvement and identification, from the dream of nonconflictual cross-generational and neighborly relations to that of the ideal child. But the biggest appeal was "love." Readers might well have been disdainful of the SED's threadbare didacticism. But it would have been hard for many heterosexual females to remain unmoved by this vision of a smart and successful husband who loved a woman even more when she pursued her own career needs and goals—*and* who also shopped for dinner and cleaned up afterward.

This kind of strategic fantasy management was evident in full force a year later in *Für Dich*'s special issue on "Young Love." While the *NBI* story had emphasized romantic fulfillment while leaving the sexual aspects unspoken (although implied in the playfully affectionate photo portrait), *Für Dich* got right to the point. This special issue marked the moment when the SED officially endorsed a transformation in GDR youth culture that had been long since underway (figs. 5.2, 5.3). Premarital heterosexual activity, even if it was not heading toward marriage, was now deemed understandable and acceptable, as early as age sixteen. The issue included such items as responses to reader queries about relationship issues, treacly love poetry of the sort long favored by the East German populace and regime alike, a questionnaire readers could answer to figure out "who fits with each other," and an article praising sex education in East German (in contrast to West German) schools (among other things a West German pedagogue was quoted to the effect that "in the end our children know everything about male testicles and female ovaries. But they know nothing, really nothing at all, about love").[68] The issue included as well an article on the trials and tribulations of young marriages and their vulnerability to conflict and divorce, in which the expert commentator argued perceptively that precisely the fact that East German marriages were no longer a site for female economic dependence was what made these marriages so fragile. The high divorce rate among young East German marriages was thus recast as positive, because under socialism the maintenance of a marriage really had no other justification besides love.[69]

Figure 5.2. *Für Dich*, December 1972, cover page. Special issue on "Young Love." (Reprinted by permission of the Berliner Verlag)

Figure 5.3. *Für Dich*, December 1972, pp. 24–25. The free verse caption (very typical also of love poetry in other popular East German magazines like *Das Magazin*) reads: "Your room. And darkness outside. We two under the light, that is friendly to us, because it hides nothing. And very close your face. Was your thought my word, your word my thought? For born of two, love makes of us one." (Reprinted by permission of the Berliner Verlag)

Analyzing the "fundamental" differences in capitalism's and socialism's approach to sex, the key matter was female emancipation. The "class enemy" with its "sex wave," *Für Dich* declared, was intent on using the "sex bomb" as a "multipurpose weapon above all against equal rights." Women in the West were degraded to the status of "lust object for the man"; this manipulation of public opinion was also designed to distract people and displace attention away from "napalm and hunger, exploitation and oppression." Socialism, by contrast, was about "life-joy" in all its dimensions, and socialism recognized that "the capacity for sensual pleasure . . . erotic cheer and blissful twosomeness do not develop by themselves but are always connected with everything that excites and stimulates us in the world that we are changing, and which in the first place makes it possible for love to grow in all its beauty."[70] Socialism, in short, was not just about better love; it was about better sex.

Indeed, meticulous and elaborate attention to intensifying female pleasure became the most significant innovation in East German sexological writing in the 1970s and early 1980s. Nobody was more important in changing the level of public discussion on this matter than Siegfried Schnabl, not only through his accessible *Mann und Frau intim*, but also his companion guide for professionals, *Intimverhalten, Sexualstörungen, Persönlichkeit* (Intimate Behavior, Sexual Dysfunctions, Character, 1972) and through numerous articles in professional and popular journals. A movie version of his ideas was also made, sponsored by the Museum for Hygiene in Dresden, and shown in schools and at union gatherings. (In the key scene, a young couple is putting up wallpaper in their apartment and the husband asks the wife whether she has orgasms during sex with him. "An orgasm?" she says soberly, "rarely." The husband is crestfallen: "And all those years you never said anything?" The movie goes on to encourage couples to try different positions and above all to communicate about their desires.)[71]

Strikingly, Schnabl invoked the lessons of mid-twentieth-century German history to buttress his arguments for female sexual pleasure. For the first time, an East German sex advice writer broke with the assumption that the only kind of normal sex was penis-in-vagina penetration and that if contraceptives were used this would only be to space births and not to prevent conception permanently. Schnabl instead, and openly, rose to the defense of the very practices that so many experts had deemed problematic: not only "marital sex with contraception" and "nonmarital sex" but also, and explicitly, "heterosexual stimulation without intercourse . . . homosexual contacts, masturbation, etc." The inherited inhibitions of two thousand years of Christian indoctrination around these matters had caused so much damage, Schnabl said, it "cannot even be surveyed." And this is where German history proved so instructive; crucially, to lend extra moral force to his argument, and sounding very much like New Leftists and liberals in West Germany in the 1960s and early 1970s, Schnabl linked Christianity and Nazism. For Schnabl, Christianity and Nazism both advanced what he called a "stupid procreation-ideology" (*bornierte Zeugungsideologie*), based on a whole set of scientifically insupportable assumptions. Furthermore:

> German fascism found the ideology of fertility advanced by the religious communities quite useful, and it misused it for its predatory nationalism. The value of a woman was primarily measured by how many hereditarily healthy children she gave to "*Volk* and *Führer.*" She became a reproductive machine, the family was degraded to a breeding institute. In order to subdue the other nations within the framework of the "New Order in Europe," the "master race" needed soldiers and people who would settle in the place of the decimated and partially exterminated peoples. This is why for example research and publications about birth control were forbidden under the threat of punishment, and voluntary abortion was persecuted with inhuman harshness.

Thus, and for the first time since 1946, an East German author deliberately rewrote the early SED's analysis of the possible lessons of Nazism for postwar sexual politics. Rather than insisting that socialism too required women to reproduce for it and that this in no way was a continuation of Nazi attitudes, Schnabl strategically called attention to the mutual enmeshment of Nazi racism and a set of notions about heterosexual sex and challenged ideas inherited from the Nazi era about the supposedly mutually beneficial relationships between female orgasm and female fertility. As Schnabl put it, the main purpose of sex was "pleasure and delight," and he sought to make nonreproductive sex under socialism and even "noncoital varieties of satisfaction" morally acceptable and more widely practiced.[72] And in this aim, he proved enormously influential. "It was probably to Schnabl's credit that the orgasm rates for women in East Germany went up the way they did," one East German woman remembered a decade after the fall of the Wall.[73]

The popular success of Schnabl's books led to widespread imitation as the East German sex advice market boomed. Sexually speaking, things were never quite the same for East Germans after Schnabl. The dramatic shift in tone and content was captured perfectly, for example, in Wolfgang Polte's *Unsere Ehe* (Our Marriage), whose eighth edition, published in 1980, incorporated detailed excurses on sexual practices written by Schnabl and by the physician Karl Hecht and his wife Tamara Hecht, an officer in the Ministry of Health.

Here again, the emphasis was on intensifying and proliferating female orgasms. Schnabl recommended manual stimulation of the clitoris and more emotional involvement on men's part as well as finding coital positions that would facilitate clitoral stimulation. The Hechts seconded these opinions but took the campaign for more and better female orgasms even further. Readers were informed rather grandiosely (and on unclear evidence) that under turn-of-the-century capitalism, women may have had ten or more children, "but many, maybe most of them, did not even once experience . . . an orgasm." But the Hechts also energetically dispelled a number of durable myths, among them the notion that women's arousal curves were slower than men's and the idea that women's libido was less pronounced than men's. On the contrary, they asserted, men's and women's desires were quite similar; differences were *individual*, not gender-related. They also rejected the decades-old obsession with simultaneous orgasms and assured readers that sequential ones could be great too (especially if the woman had hers first). Above all, they effused about women's capacity for multiple orgasms, and enthusiastically described "male partners with a strong capacity for self-control who succeed in having their wife achieve a rapid series of orgasms before they themselves ejaculate." Almost all female dysfunction, they asserted, had its source in male "clumsiness or lack of erotic ability." And any disinterest wives evinced in sex, they slyly suggested, might be the result of exhaustion due to having to manage household chores alone in addition to their career and political engagement: "A man who does not help his professionally active wife either in the household or in childrearing need not be surprised if his wife displays disappearing levels of desire. A man would be just as disinterested if he was burdened in the same way."

Karl Hecht also raised directly—only to dismiss it—the inevitable concern that all this focus on the woman's pleasure might leave the man feeling stressed and unattended to. Does the man "gain nothing?" Hecht asked rhetorically. "Is he denying himself love-pleasure? On the contrary. It is not only that the man for a longer time himself moves continually at the border of a high blissful feeling; he also experiences with . . . joyful excitement the love gestures of his partner. Indeed, he experiences the togetherness in a different way, as a success experience, and his whole striving in the love act is concentrated solely on the beloved partner." With vintage SED-linguistic aplomb, moreover, and just in case any ordinary or official reader was on the verge of taking offense at the explicitness of his directives, Hecht abruptly segued into an extended discussion of Karl Marx's powerful affection for his wife Jenny, before once again returning to topic and providing specific tips for caressing the labia and rubbing saliva on nipples.[74]

This emphasis on heterosexual men improving their performance in bed was strongly assimilated in East Germany.[75] When Starke and Friedrich in 1984 published *Liebe und Sexualität bis 30*, based on extensive empirical research among East German youth, they not only found that young GDR women had their first orgasm on average at the age of sixteen or seventeen—and that already 70 percent of sixteen-year-olds had orgasmic experience—but also that two-thirds of all the young women surveyed had an orgasm "almost always" during sex, with another 18 percent declaring that they had one "often." In fact, the majority of informants—female and male alike—were very satisfied with their sex lives in general (and interestingly the authors found no differences in sexual experience or happiness between the Christian minority and the atheist majority). Moreover, the authors resolutely concluded that East German social conditions—"the sense of social security, equal educational and professional responsibilities, equal rights and possibilities for participating in and determining the life of society"—were preeminently responsible for the high rates of female pleasure. "The young women of today are in general more active and more discriminating, less inhibited and reticent, expecting to have their personality and wishes honored, striving much more self-confidently for higher sexual satisfaction," and "they are accustomed to demanding happiness in love . . . and to tasting it fully." These young women started having sex earlier, switched their partners more frequently, and enjoyed themselves more. And Starke and Friedrich were also convinced that whatever male ambivalence was still being expressed among the somewhat older men about this new state of affairs was just a passing phase of adjustment, since they found that such ambivalence had already disappeared almost entirely within the younger generation. Precisely those young men and women who had grown up in supportive families and in which the parents had been loving toward each other were the ones who were most secure in themselves and the most creative and experimental in their own love lives.[76] Nor were these conclusions contradicted by subsequent research. On the contrary, when the first comparative East-West German study of female students' sexual experiences was conducted in 1988, the results showed (to the Western scholar's amazement) that East German heterosexual women liked sex more (and experienced orgasms more frequently) than their West German counterparts.[77]

The East German experts' endless reiterations of the idea that socialism produced especially charmed conditions for mutually satisfying sex, in short, was not just a figment of their own fantasy lives. While Starke and Friedrich had also considered the introduction of the birth control pill as a key factor that made all this newfound female pleasure possible, the comparison with West Germany suggests that their argument about gender equality under socialism was far from insignificant. In the 1970s and 1980s, the West German feminist movement loudly proclaimed Western women's fury at heterosexual coital practices that left them cold and they made men's boorish and selfish behavior in bed a major public issue. During that same era, East German women made no such accusations; instead, they simply could (and did) break up with unsatisfactory men specifically because they possessed economic independence and because theirs was a social environment that treated singlehood, including single motherhood, as acceptable and feasible—and even a social norm. (By the end of the GDR, one in three children was born out of wedlock; in the FRG it was one in ten.)[78] Once East and West German women encountered each other more frequently after the collapse of the GDR, East German women could only roll their eyes and express astonishment at many West German heterosexual women's apparent lack of satisfaction with the men in their lives and at the fuss that Western feminists continued to make about sexual practices. "Those who enjoy it don't need to talk about it in public," one East German woman in her fifties said in exasperation in the 1990s, summarizing her feelings about her first experiences with West German feminists.[79] And also in the later 1990s a forty-something formerly East German woman proudly—almost patronizingly—announced: "East-women have more fun, everybody knows that [*Ost-Frauen haben mehr Spass, das weiss jeder*]. Orgasm rates were higher in the East, all the studies show that." And then (revealing a misconception some easterners still had about the West), she added: "After all, it was a proletarian society. None of this bourgeois concern with chastity until the wedding night."[80]

OSTALGIE

The collapse of the Wall in 1989 and the reunification of Germany under Western auspices in 1990 brought immediate change to the sexual culture of the East. The day after the Wall came down, entrepreneur Beate Uhse had her staff ship truckloads of sex toys and pornography into the five East German states; supply could not keep up with demand. Pornography shops proliferated, and easterners queued up for hours for a chance both finally to look and to purchase. "We felt like we'd been left out," one fortyish male East German librarian commented with both pathos and irony, and numerous comments made by easterners to West German reporters suggest much the same.[81] The long lines in front of pornography shops quickly became part of the standard self-congratulatory western narrative of communism's collapse, and western journalists gleefully seized upon each instance an East German articulated regret over a sex-commodity-deprived existence under socialism. Yet what got drowned out in these facile assumptions of Western superiority were more reflective East German voices that sought to articulate what had been valuable about East German sexual culture—as that culture itself began rapidly to dissolve.

There were indisputably gains made. It was not at all insignificant, for instance, that the collapse of East Germany helped liberalize major aspects of reunified Germany's sexual culture. While East German women's distress over the possible elimination of abortion rights was widely discussed in the media, some western feminists remained optimistic that the process of reunification might provide an opportunity for the West to adopt the more progressive East German arrangement. In large part, they were proven accurate. What resulted was a compromise; now all German women were granted first-trimester approval (standard in the East since 1972) if they agreed to preabortion counseling (as had been required in the West). Notably the process of reunification also provided the occasion for a new advance for gay rights, as—continuing a further legal liberalization implemented in the GDR in 1988—Paragraph 175 was finally abolished in all its dimensions in reunified Germany in 1994.

Yet for the most part, the former East German sexual culture found itself the object of condescending bemusement and ruthless ridicule as a cacophony of competing theories was promoted. The East German psychotherapist Hans-Joachim Maaz, for example, made a big name for himself with his book, *Der Gefühlsstau: Ein Psychogramm der DDR* (Emotional Congestion: A Psychological Diagnosis of the GDR, 1990), which caricatured his former fellow citizens as emotionally repressed and sexually deprived. "The GDR was a land with widespread sexual frustration," Maaz said, seeing this deficit of eastern life as a crucial symptom of a broader paranoia and psychic deformation induced by living under tightly controlled conditions and constant surveillance.[82] Contradictorily, others proposed that because there had not been much else to do in the East, and daily life had been so gray and monotonous, sex had emerged as a favorite pastime. Now, East Germans would have to learn to pull themselves together and acquire the work ethic necessary for success under capitalism. Rejecting as communist propaganda the notion that eastern women's reportedly higher orgasm rates might have their source in higher levels of female economic independence, for instance, the conservative tabloid *Bild* provided this countervailing analysis in May 1990: "Everywhere that human beings are offered nothing or very little—aside from much work and little pay—everywhere where there are few discos, restaurants, amusement parks, in other words few opportunities for entertainment—in all those places sex is practiced more frequently and more intensively."[83] Meanwhile, the East German habit of naked display at the beach was variously interpreted as quaint and odd, a trifle disturbing, or as (misplaced) compensation for easterners' lack of political independence. "Wasn't this FKK cult a kind of expression of your will to freedom?" a female reporter from Hamburg asked her younger East German colleagues, a question interpreted by the *Ossis* as yet one more exemplar of western snobbery and cluelessness.[84]

Above all, however, there was among easterners a profound sense of loss. The flood of Western pornography effectively demolished the eastern culture of nakedness. As West Germans rushed to stake out the beaches on the formerly East German shores of the Baltic Sea as they sought out cheap and beautiful vacation spots, they proceeded to take offense at the widespread nudity and insisted their children be spared the sight of guilelessly self-displaying *Ossis*. In effect, the West Germans achieved what the GDR police had failed to do decades earlier. Many East German women no longer felt safe going naked now that they were viewed with western men's "pornographically schooled gaze" (*pornographisch geschulter Blick*).[85] And they did begin to cover themselves. Indicatively, too, after they had sated their initial curiosity, many *Ossis* turned away in disappointment at the poor quality and (what they saw as) lack of genuine eroticism in the western porn products. (Already by 1995, two-thirds of the porn video shops that had opened in the formerly East German states shut their doors.)

Without a doubt, most devastating for the former East was a loss of economic security and the new idea that human worth would now be measured primarily by money. East German citizens felt enormous anxieties about the loss of jobs and social security, rising rents, and uncertain futures. Once it became clear that Germany would be reunified under western auspices (rather than developing some mutually worked out "third path") and once the full consequences of such westernization became apparent (it would not just mean easterners finally acquiring western goods and a strong currency and political freedoms, but a huge rise in unemployment and social instability), easterners scrambled to acquire new job skills and a whole new style of comporting themselves. These developments also had incalculable consequences on sexual relations. Many long-term East German relationships went into crisis; couples first clung together despite conflicts and then crashed as they struggled with varying degrees of success to reinvent themselves under new conditions.[86]

Little wonder, then, that the disappearing sexual ethos of the GDR quickly became an especially important site for *Ostalgie*—a popular coinage that joined together *Ost* (East) and *Nostalgie* (nostalgia). "In the East the clocks ran more slowly," the East German journalist Katrin Rohnstock remembered with retrospective longing in 1995. In the West, in her view, lust for capital had replaced desire for another person. With reference to capitalism's competitive climate, she said: "Eroticism feels with its fingertips, elbows destroy that. The pressure to achieve makes human beings sick and has a negative impact on sexuality."[87] Or as another formerly East German woman phrased it, as she explained that GDR sexuality was in some respects more emancipated than that of the West: "Money played no role. In the East, sex was not for sale."[88] The East German cultural historian Dietrich Mühlberg too emphasized in 1995 that "the cost-benefit analysis" so constantly employed in human interactions in the West "was largely absent" in the East and that this inevitably affected sexual relations and partnerships as well.[89] And the Magdeburg-based sexologist Carmen Beilfuss spoke of "the difficult path of love in the market economy."[90] Throughout the 1990s, and over and over, easterners (gay and straight alike) articulated the conviction that sex in the East had been more genuine and loving, more sensual and more gratifying—and less grounded in self-involvement—than West German sex.[91]

Whether these memories were fully accurate or not, there is no question that the GDR's sexual culture was remarkable, for it differed not only from capitalist West Germany but also from the rest of socialist Eastern Europe. While men in other Eastern European cultures were notorious for their "socialist machismo" (their patriarchalism and misogyny existing in counterpoint to gender-egalitarian Soviet bloc rhetoric), East German men's domesticity and self-confident comfort with strong women were both legendary.[92] Prostitution was relatively rare in the GDR, even while it was commonplace in Warsaw and Budapest. Homosexual men were thrown into prison in the Soviet Union and Romania up until the demise of communism; this had not occurred in the GDR since 1957. The Polish church was thoroughly homophobic; in the GDR, gays and lesbians—although certainly closely watched by the Stasi—were able to organize in the 1980s under church auspices.[93] In its rejection of prostitution and pornography, the GDR appeared prudish by Western standards. Yet precisely the absence of these two means of marketing sex allowed other liberties to flourish. The moralism and asceticism the SED tried to enforce was undermined by the very processes of secularization that the SED also fostered. In the end, there was something peculiarly *German* about East Germany, even if former East Germans did not necessarily recognize that. The easy relationships to nakedness and sexual matters had their source not least in a distinctive tradition going back to Weimar and even before.

Without a doubt, the West German sexual revolution had been perceived by the SED as a threat that needed to be countered. But the sexual liberalization in East Germany that happened from the mid-1960s on, and with growing force through the 1970s and 1980s, was *not* just an imitation of the West but took its own peculiar form not least because of a precursor liberalization that had already occurred in the otherwise so gloomy 1950s and early 1960s. While in West Germany the realm of sexuality repeatedly became the site for attempts to master the past of Nazism and the Holocaust, in East Germany the emphasis was always on what was yet to come—on the constant declaration that "the future belongs to socialism," a wishful prescription pretending to be a description.[94] Only once the GDR itself was a thing of the past did sexuality and memory in the GDR become firmly conjoined. All through the history of the GDR, there was in the SED the never-ending hope that the populace's affections might yet be won, if only the right formula of select consumer goods and managed freedoms were found. Love and sexuality became absolutely crucial elements in this struggle to win popular approval. The majority of the populace, however, never was taken in by the endlessly announced romance of socialism itself. Instead, it was the romance for which the GDR had indeed created important preconditions but which ultimately the people had simply claimed for themselves that became the eventual site for *Ostalgie*.

CHAPTER SIX

Antifascist Bodies

SEX RIGHTS ACTIVISM

What happened to the anticapitalist and antifascist impulse within the West? This chapter picks up the story of sexuality and memory after Nazism in the melancholic wake of the political upheavals of 1968 in West Germany. It is a story of the death of faith in the redemptive power of sexual love and of the dissolution of previously fiercely held beliefs about the inherent connections between sexual liberation and political struggle. At the same time, and however paradoxically, it is also a story that exemplifies once again the inextricability of conflicts over sexuality and the trajectory of other political developments. The sexual history of the 1970s and 1980s was nothing if not contradictory: spreading sexual liberalization coexisted with rising ambivalence about the sexual revolution, and heightened politicization of sexuality under the impact of gay, lesbian, and feminist activism occurred alongside recurrent pronouncements that sexual desire and intensity were in decline.

In the course of the 1970s, debates about sexuality initially came to be split off from debates about the lessons of the Third Reich, only to return in new forms in the context of the rise of—and backlash against—feminism. Only against this background of confusion over both the sexual revolution and feminism can we properly assess the significance of Klaus Theweleit's bestselling *Männerphantasien* (Male Fantasies, 1977–78), the now-classic text about sex and fascism. While most commentators over the decades (and certainly not incorrectly) have seen Theweleit's book as an intervention into debates about fascism—an effort to bring close attention to the subjects of gender and sex to bear on the problem of the Third Reich—when *Männerphantasien* is resituated in its historical context it becomes just as legible as an effort to bring the subjects of fascism and the Third Reich to bear on a set of problems West Germans were having with themselves about gender and sex in the 1970s. Theweleit's book, in short, was in its own way an effort to recapitulate and retrieve much of 1968's original impetus and to reestablish a strength of connection between sexuality, leftist politics, and the Nazi past that had started to become frayed. Increasingly, however, discussions of sexuality and of Nazism were carried out separately. Beginning in the 1980s and even more so once Germany reunited, a new historical touchstone for sexual conflicts came to supplant the Third Reich: 1968 itself.

The immediate aftermath of 1968 was saturated by a profound sense of loss, as West German New Leftists sought to come to terms with their own fading romance with socialism. Some held onto simplistic Marxist-Leninist or Maoist truisms with even greater determination the less they were able to admit that their dream of a complete social and political revolution was failing. Others engaged in intense debates over the inadequacy of Marxist and other political-economic analyses and activism, and the need for attention to subjective and personal matters. A generalized sense of disenchantment was widely articulated. Already by the mid-1970s, there was fierce controversy over whether the focus on the personal realm was a sign of depoliticization, a "drawing back into the private," or precisely part of the necessary "revolutionizing of the everyday" that Kommune 1, Kommune 2, and so many other New Leftists had initially wanted.[1] It was specifically the student movement's confidence in the absolute inseparability (and reciprocal beneficiality) of the personal and the political, as the writer Peter Schneider pointed out in 1977, that in the late 1960s had given the movement its original euphoric strength and revolutionary power. And it was exactly those "personal and political needs that later got separated into mutually hostile camps."[2] Only for a brief time in the late 1960s "everything"—sex, politics, hash, and Vietnam—"had seemed to hang together with everything else," as former SDS member Eckhard Siepmann put it, and then "everything" fell apart. What remained was "a desert, in which no one understood anyone else anymore, everyone was suspicious of everyone else, and no theoretical stone could still be found standing on top of another."[3]

Not all of this was immediately apparent to observers outside New Left circles, however. For in several respects, the 1970s also saw an extraordinary amplification and elaboration both of the society-wide liberalizing tendencies of the 1960s and of some of 1968's most transgressive and critical impulses. Popular receptivity to the loosening of sex-related law coexisted with, and created, opportunities in which the inventive activism of new militant groups could find a broader audience. Gay rights, lesbian rights, abortion rights, and the wider women's movement were all 1970s phenomena that initially emerged within and around the New Left. Simultaneously, young professionals in the fields of social work, psychology, education, journalism, and publishing, who had been active in the New Left and the broader "alternative scene" that grew out of it, popularized progressive analyses of sex-related issues and developed innovative sex education curricula. They often succeeded in securing government support, both nationally and at the municipal level, as they sought to counter conservative attacks on the sexual revolution and to provide teachers with classroom materials that would help young people to develop a sexual ethics based on consent and mutual pleasure, informed use of contraceptives, comfort with their own bodies, and acceptance of different sexual orientations.[4]

The dynamic interaction between broader trends toward sexual liberalization and the sustained activism of New Left–affiliated individuals and groups was decisive for creating the social transformations of the 1970s. The campaigns for gay rights and for abortion rights provide two key examples of this. For instance, the 1969 decriminalization of homosexual acts between men over the age of twenty-one (via the modification of Paragraph 175) made it possible for a gay pride movement to organize, even as it is unlikely that, without that gay pride movement, either the lowering of the age of consent to eighteen in 1973 or the gradual decline of homophobia in all social strata would have been achieved. Along related lines, without the openness of the Social Democrats (who acquired the reins of power in 1969) to reforming abortion law (through the modification of Paragraph 218), feminist activism would have had little chance of success in this area. Yet at the same time, the Social Democrats were so intimidated by the antiabortion campaign of conservative religious groups that they would clearly have let the matter drop had not the ensuing massive nationwide mobilization of women forced the government to come up with a compromise.

In the early 1960s, the ruling Christian Democrats' general disdain for sexual rights of any sort had triggered a counteroffensive of prominent liberal intellectuals and left-leaning students. As a result, the conservative 1962 draft of the criminal code was set aside by the Bundestag. A so-called Alternative Draft (*Alternativentwurf*) formulated by progressive jurists and finalized in 1968, became the basis for renewed discussions.[5] Yet decriminalization of homosexuality would not have occurred if the minority centrist party of Free Democrats and especially the conservative Christian Democrats (along with their smaller affiliate, the Christian Social Union) had not also gone through an unprecedented process of internal liberalization. In the reconfigured social and political climate of the later 1960s, under the quadruple impact of the "sex wave," the Social Democrats' ascension to participation in power in the Grand Coalition (1966–1969), the rise of the student movement, and the growing popular conviction that the morality of the Christian churches was hypocritical, there was far greater openness across the political spectrum to liberalizing sex-related law. Under these new circumstances, Christian Democratic politicians, while rejecting what they called "bleeding-heart liberalism" (*Humanitätsduselei*), acknowledged that, with respect to sex, their party needed "modernization" and "adaptation to the transformed views . . . of the twentieth century." Particularly with respect to homosexuality, the

CDU admitted that "the recognition of the inappropriateness of criminally punishing such things has won out." As a result, on May 9, 1969, the Bundestag decriminalized not only adultery (and the anachronistic transgression of "seduction through false promises") but also homosexual acts for men age twenty-one or older.[6] In short, rapidly changing attitudes about heterosexuality had created the grounds for a rethinking of attitudes about homosexuality.

While the first effect of decriminalization was a proliferation of publications directed at a homosexual market niche and the expansion of a homosexual nightclub scene, decriminalization was the crucial precondition for the rise of a gay rights movement. The prime impetus for this movement was the incendiary independent feature film, *Nicht der Homosexuelle ist pervers, sondern die Situation in der er lebt* (It's Not the Homosexual Who Is Perverse, but Rather the Situation in Which He Lives, 1971), codirected by the sex-radical film maker Holger Mischwitzky (better known by his pseudonym Rosa von Praunheim) and the gay activist, sociologist, and sexologist Martin Dannecker. Here gay male audiences encountered the slogan "Out of the toilets and into the streets!"[7] This movie was no plea for tolerance. It was a movie by homosexuals for homosexuals; but it was also a movie against homosexuals, in the sense of opposing the prevailing subcultural strategies of conformist passing and furtive anonymous sex. To publicize their cause, the filmmakers brought the film to every city and town in West Germany they could, and held open discussion forums after each showing. These forums then often resulted in the formation of local gay rights groups. Subsequently, the movie was shown on West German television, followed by a televised discussion. The significance of the film for West German gay activism can hardly be overestimated; the movie revolutionized many gay men's lives.[8] And while it did provoke homophobic outbursts (such as the taxi driver who reportedly said, "Now I know why Hitler gassed those faggoty pigs") as well as sneering condescension from the mainstream media (which attacked von Praunheim and Dannecker both for their leftism and for being "intellectual butt-sexualists [*Gesäßsexualisten*]"), and visceral resistance from more conservative homosexuals ("gay power within limits—okay!—but please no revolution of the fairies"), a national gay rights movement was soon a visible and much-discussed presence within West German political culture[9] (fig. 6.1). By 1978, when—in the popular newsmagazine *Der Stern*—682 men came out in a cover story entitled *"Wir sind schwul"* (We Are Gay) and permitted their names and, in many cases, also their photographs to be published, this marked the moment when the mainstream media (albeit still with considerable ambivalence) officially aligned itself with the demands of gay rights activists.[10]

Figure 6.1. *Der Spiegel*, 12 March 1973, p. 47. Gay rights demonstration in Münster, 1972. The posters say: "Homos come out of your holes!" and "Chastity is no more a virtue than malnutrition is." (Reprinted by permission. Photo: Kai Greiser)

The interplay between broader trends toward liberalization and tenacious activism was similar in the case of abortion rights. Abortion, indeed, was the issue that galvanized popular support for women's rights and turned what had been a fairly small New Left–linked feminist insurgence into a nationwide mobilization. The new government led by Social Democrats (together with the Free Democrats), in place since the end of 1969, had already in the summer of 1970 indicated an openness to abolishing Paragraph 218. Yet when conservative Catholics protested in outrage, Justice Minister Gerhard Jahn and the rest of the SPD retreated and rushed to reassure the public that they had no radical intentions. In response, women's groups organized all across the country to persuade the government that the majority of the populace did in fact want the abolition of Paragraph 218.

In hundreds of political actions—from street theater and mass demonstrations to speak-out "tribunals" and openly publicized bus trips to abortion clinics in the Netherlands—feminists exposed the violence, fear, and damage to women's health that accompanied illegal abortions and raised questions about church leaders who expressed sympathy about the moral dilemmas involved in killing in warfare but not about women's desperation in the face of an unwanted pregnancy. While widespread use of the birth control pill had reduced the number of abortions sought in West Germany each year from more than one million to several hundred thousand, to many women the criminalization of abortion simply crystallized the disrespect shown their sex in every realm of social existence; it seemed to foreground the experiential gulf between men's and women's worlds. With slogans such as "if men could get pregnant, abortion would be a sacrament!" and "the brood of gynecologists grows fat on our blood," and with images of a pregnant Justice Minister Jahn (". . . then he would have long since gotten rid of Paragraph 218!"), feminists worked to turn the moral tables on supporters of criminalized abortion.[11] Even women who had never had abortions or would never need them identified powerfully with the campaign. And also women affiliated with the churches supported the campaign to a remarkable degree; 80 percent of Protestant women and 40 percent of Catholic women favored the legalization of abortion. The campaign also got major support from liberal and New Left men and, crucially, from the mainstream media. The liberal newsmagazine *Der Spiegel*, for instance, declared Paragraph 218 to be "outdated," pointing out that "every two or three minutes . . . statistically speaking, an abortion is performed in the Federal Republic—that is five hundred each day." The humor magazine *Pardon* published a cartoon showing physicians and quack abortionists together demonstrating for the retention of Paragraph 218, because abortion's illegality was for many the basis of their livelihood. Could it be, *Der Spiegel* even implied, that the West German medical establishment's qualms about endorsing abortion rights had to do with the enormous amount of (untaxed) money made by physicians who performed abortions off the record?[12]

In reaction to this popular groundswell favoring abortion rights, conservative Catholics did not hesitate to invoke Nazism. "Murder remains murder, whether it is legalized by a National Socialist or a liberal socialist state," announced flyers distributed at the SPD party congress in 1973. Liberalizing abortion law would constitute "the most disturbing attack on the moral foundations of our society since 1945," the bishop of Essen announced. And Catholic physician Siegfried Ernst succinctly stated that the Social Democrats, by legalizing abortion, would be planning "the largest Auschwitz in European history."[13] Yet although reluctant to garner the churches' displeasure (the Protestant Church also announced its opposition to abortion, although in less extreme terms), the Bundestag—in view of the clear majority of public opinion favoring abortion rights—in 1974 voted to permit first-trimester abortions. Almost immediately, the Federal Constitutional Court issued an injunction that kept the liberalized law from going into effect, and in 1975 it formally declared the first-trimester ruling unconstitutional. Yet—and not least due to ongoing pressure from women's groups across West Germany—in 1976 a new law was passed. This new law permitted first-trimester abortions solely on the grounds of an appropriate "indication." Henceforth, women's ability to get legal abortions varied by region within West Germany, depending on how doctors in a particular area were willing to interpret a woman's "social indication"—that is, her anticipated difficulty raising a(nother) child under her current circumstances. And although incompletely satisfied with this outcome, feminists had every reason to see it as a major achievement.[14]

Women's shared sense of mission and experiences of collective action in the anti-218 campaign spawned numerous further projects, from women's bookstores and cafés to rape crisis and domestic violence shelters to feminist journals and publishing houses. In the course of the 1970s, in small towns and big cities alike, a female-centered public countersphere was created.[15] Sometimes tentatively and insecurely, sometimes boldly, women began to analyze every aspect of society from the point of view of gender and struggled to make better sense of their (often painfully competitive) relationships with each other and with men. Lesbians who had initially worked within both coed gay groups and the abortion rights campaigns developed organizations of their own, even as the wider and predominantly heterosexual women's movement (despite initial homophobic defensiveness) gradually also took the need to defend lesbian rights to heart and made the call to "end compulsory heterosexuality!" its own.[16] When, in a case that riveted the nation's attention in 1974, two women who were lovers, Marion Ihns and Judy Andersen, stood accused of having hired a man to murder Ihns's violently abusive husband (he had tried to kill Ihns with poison and had raped her repeatedly), many heterosexual women identified strongly with the accused. They protested vocally against the humiliation of all women that was expressed by (what turned out to be) a viciously lesbophobic outpouring in the courtroom and the press. Documenting and refuting in outrage the press' attempts to link lesbianism with criminality, feminists in the Frankfurt Women's Center compared the Ihns-Andersen case to the medieval persecution of witches and announced that in this case female sexuality as a whole was on trial.[17] "By the way: being a lesbian is beautiful," read a sign carried by two women at a demonstration supporting Ihns and Andersen[18] (fig. 6.2). Heterosexual women also avidly followed debates among lesbians over sexual practices.[19] Heterosexual women's efforts to learn from lesbian and bisexual women as they sought to repair what they felt were damaged

Demonstration gegen die Diskriminierung lesbischer Frauen im Prozeß in Itzehoe

Figure 6.2. "By the way: Being a lesbian is beautiful." Demonstration in support of Ihns and Andersen in Itzehoe, 1974. From Frankfurter Frauen, ed., *Frauenjahrbuch 1* (Frankfurt am Main: Roter Stern, 1975), p. 199.

relationships to their own bodies and make their sexual relationships with men more fulfilling became inseparably intertwined with the heightened emotional and physical closeness women were experiencing with one another within the women's movement.[20]

Yet even as gay and lesbian rights movements emerged as recognizable forces to be reckoned with and even as the women's movement became one of the largest and most influential social movements in West Germany, the New Left out of which these movements had grown was undergoing a period of exceptional crisis. Just as heterosexual feminists and gay and lesbian activists were refusing shame, secrecy, and self-hatred, celebrating nonnormative forms of sexuality, and demonstrating by example that human beings could in fact be united politically around issues of desire and pleasure, the New Left found itself in a state of serious political disorientation. The very success of the sex rights movements, embedded as they were in a broader social trend toward sexual liberalization, also coincided with a profound loss of left-wing faith that sexual emancipation could inevitably contribute to social revolution. Sexual liberalization was happening, and yet radical political change seemed as far away as ever. Maybe sexual politics and other sorts of politics did not, after all, have much to do with one another.

GENDER TROUBLES

The loss of political optimism on the New Left had significant consequences for how the relationship between sexuality and memory would be understood. The criminalization of male homosexuality and abortion had been two key areas in which postwar Christian Democrats—rather than returning to the liberalizing impulses of the Weimar Republic—had maintained, and refurbished in the name of Christianity, laws that had been in effect during the Third Reich. The 1970s liberalization of the criminal law in these two areas thus in many ways marked the conclusion of a long postwar process of undoing the inheritance of Nazism's sexual politics.

Yet one peculiar effect of the wider social consensus in favor of sexual liberalization that was forged in the course of the 1970s was that the Third Reich was no longer needed by liberals or leftists as a reference point in order morally to justify that liberalization. While conservative Catholics might invoke Auschwitz in order to resist the decriminalization of abortion, liberals did not even bother to counter this by pointing out that the Nazis had harshly criminalized abortion. In general, leftists and liberals were less likely to feel that Nazism was relevant in debates about sex in their present; the popular mood was on the whole so appreciative that repressive conservatism had been dismantled that it was easier just to criticize sexual conservatives directly. Only occasionally were references to the Third Reich made by more liberal commentators.[21] But these kinds of rhetorical moves were not common.

The New Left no longer required the use of references to Nazism as a kind of moral battering ram to advance sexual liberation. There were certainly recurrent setbacks for sex-liberal perspectives—for example, with regard to sex education in public schools, as local bureaucrats or vociferous parents sometimes took offense at one or another teacher's too explicit terminology or too cavalier perspective on the institution of marriage.[22] But the trend of the time was to move away from a generally repressive, anti-premarital sex message; those who tried to reintroduce repression could expect to be ridiculed.

This does not mean, however, that Nazism dropped away as a reference point for the New Left. On the contrary, the complicated political situation especially in the mid-1970s in West Germany made remarks about the purportedly "fascistoid" nature of the Federal Republic a common refrain in left-wing circles. The ruling Social Democrats, for example, while often happy to support initiatives for sexual liberalization, were also ruthless in pursuing such antileft initiatives as the *Berufsverbot*, which prohibited anyone with a communist party affiliation from pursuing a career in the civil service (this included public school teaching). And they were relentless in cracking down on New Left individuals and groups that had contact with left-wing terrorists of the Red Army Faction (RAF) and other far-left splinter groups intent on violent resistance against the state. Tapped phones and police house searches became familiar aspects of life for those with ties to the alternative scene. Police beatings of unarmed demonstrators also raised questions about the legitimacy of the state's monopoly on violence and furthered a felt sense of ongoing solidarity among leftists despite many New Leftists' discomfort with the RAF. Moreover, the West German government's ongoing alliance with the United States despite the U.S.'s cynical pursuit of war in Vietnam and Cambodia and support for brutal dictators around the globe made the state's claims to moral righteousness appear threadbare. In 1977, when the antiterror campaign was at its peak and a number of RAF terrorists died in Stammheim prison, presumably of suicide (although many believed at the time they had been murdered), despondency was pervasive. "From what point on is one allowed to call it fascism?" (*Ab wann darf man's Faschismus nennen?*) became a frequently debated question.[23] When one looked away from sexual politics and instead examined other aspects of politics, it was not clear at all that Nazism's legacies had been overcome.

Yet New Leftists often found themselves quite unable to deal effectively with the fact that the state turned out to be both more powerful and more flexible than they had imagined and that political transformation was not as easy to achieve as initially expected. "After all, if the revolution wasn't going to be happening in the next ten years, I wouldn't be participating. I will experience it," said one rather cocky New Left "chief" of a small political organization.[24] Others too remembered that they had felt "'the revolution is in front of the door'—we just need to figure out the right next step."[25] Or as another put it, he also had "truly believed for a while that a revolution was imminent in two, three years."[26] Starting at the latest in 1974, and increasingly over the next several years, a number of New Left men sought to reflect critically on the distinctive combination of machismo and masochism they had evinced as they exhausted themselves trying to convert a largely hostile working class to the cause of revolution. What on earth had they been thinking as they forced themselves to "rise at 4 A.M. to distribute leaflets" after they had stayed up all night reading and debating Marx's *Capital*?[27] In the late 1960s and early 1970s, the typical style had been to castigate oneself for still being too bourgeois, too inadequately attuned to the intricacies of Marx's insights, too preoccupied with "the problem of childrearing and the sexual crisscross relationships of the parents" rather than "the sole correct and necessary step toward revolution . . . namely the organization of the proletariat."[28] But by the mid- to later 1970s, the bigger puzzle was why it had apparently been so hard to find a balance, or at least mutually productive relationship, between basic concern for one's own well-being and commitment to social justice. As Peter Schneider sensibly proposed in 1977, "It's not the egoism that falsifies political activism but rather the attempt to hide it." Yet he too felt whatever subjective impulse was still motivating New Leftists was overwhelmingly "the egoism of despair."[29] And a year later three editors of the Frankfurt-based left scene paper *Pflasterstrand* confirmed this dour assessment: "Already years ago we had it up to here with the proletarians . . . now we apparently have it up to here with ourselves": "All we want to do is get away, just away, to Bologna, Barcelona." But even getting away would not do it. "Our age-old need for living out subjective radicality is now turned against ourselves. It is no longer the chains of factory work or parental home or university seminar that we need to burst open, but rather those within ourselves." The dream was that they could somehow "get back to a radicality that can move mountains." But in the meantime, "alcoholism is rising rapidly" and "pessimism, big-guy posturing, stereo systems . . . only begin to describe our backward slide."[30]

The conflicts between men and women that would so wrench the New Left and the wider alternative scene in the 1970s cannot be understood apart from this crisis of New Left masculinity, which was itself an expression of a crisis of New Left politics (both with respect to class relations and with respect to violence). Many men were clearly not happy with the kind of masculinity expected of them, and which they expected of themselves.[31] The spiraling murderous violence of the RAF and the state apparatus alike called also the far less destructive window-shattering, stone-throwing, and fist-fights-with-police kind of militancy into question. Joschka Fischer, for example, in 1977 in the journal *Autonomie*, called on his comrades to confront their preoccupation with virility:

> In our scene the same sexist mechanism as elsewhere has been at work and finally culminated in militantism. . . . What I mean is the flipping into a fundamentally destructive structure, one that has not been able to produce anything but death, madness, and a culture of collective suicide. . . . Brothers, there is no longer any other choice: either we, the big shots and violence dudes [*Macker und Gewaltmuftis*], succeed in making our way over to the other side of the barricade, to the women and children, or we will die from the schizophrenia between our own hopes for liberation and our predominant style of masculinity.[32]

But even as many men shared Fischer's rather patronizing attitude toward women, they did not all think that going over "to the other side of the barricade" was the best solution. Quite a few men were so enraged by the women's movement that it just prompted more misogyny from them rather than less.

The general treatment of women as second-class citizens within the New Left movement had been the spark that ignited the feminists' own revolution. And while young women had initially participated eagerly in the new opportunities for promiscuity and experimentation made available by the pill and the sexual revolution, within a few years it was apparent that there was considerable discouragement. That men arrogantly disdained women's intellectual abilities, that women's disproportionate burden of childcare and other household labor went unremunerated and unappreciated, that women were not considered equal political comrades—all of this became enmeshed with and articulated through conflict over sexual relations.

Misogyny had been woven into the very fabric of the sexual revolution. This was so not only in how women's bodies were used to market products as the "sex wave" took over the national media. It was evident as well, for instance, in the popular late 1960s antiauthoritarian male slogan "Whoever sleeps twice with the same woman, already belongs to the establishment" (*Wer zweimal mit derselben pennt, gehört schon zum Establishment*).[33] And it was expressed in some male commune members' harsh braggadocio about the acquisition of a new female member or groupie: "It's like training a horse; one guy has to break her in, then she's available for everyone."[34] But it was also expressed in more subtle ways.

Precisely because sexual liberation had been so extraordinarily important to the early New Left in West Germany, the difficulties subsequently encountered were all the more devastating. Transforming sexual relations was one of the most important tasks the New Left in West Germany had set itself. Indeed, Klaus Theweleit, formerly a member of the SDS in Freiburg, once retrospectively remarked that in West Germany, "the interest in the political was evident among many young people as an interest in the sexual. The bodies of young people in the early sixties were sexually charged in a wholly unusual way."[35] Or as the journalist Sabine Weissler summarily noted, after reviewing numerous New Left materials, the desire to change sexual relations was often *the* impetus for political activism. In the 1960s, she said, "the flood of articles, lectures, discussion events, and reading circles on the question of sexual enlightenment as a part of political emancipation was incredible." In school and student newspapers, "long before Vietnam, emergency laws, university reform, et cetera," sex was already "topic number one."[36]

Yet almost from the start, there was gender conflict. Complaining about the "laborious manipulations" demanded by contraceptive methods (aside from the pill), for instance, male students writing in the Berlin newspaper *FU Spiegel* in 1968 could not figure out why many female students were hesitant to take the pill. Did not these young women also want a "deproblematization of sexuality"? Didn't they too just want sex to be easier? The only conclusion the authors could reach was that young German women must still have considerable prejudices about and hostility toward sex.[37] In the fall of 1968, when activist women in Frankfurt published the first broadside of the incipient women's movement, they complained specifically about "socialist screw-pressure" (*sozialistischer Bumszwang*), and the ways in which women who did not cooperate got labeled "lesbian," or "frigid," or as suffering from "penis envy."[38] "Sure, we had lots of sex," one woman involved in the New Left later remembered, "and it was okay. But—and although this only dawned on us over time—was it really meeting our needs? Were these men actually interested in women's perspectives or feelings about sexuality?"[39] Verena Stefan's popular and influential 1975 novel *Häutungen* (Shedding), one of the key texts of the West German women's movement, apparently spoke to many women with such descriptions of heterosexual encounters as this one: "I make an effort, move everything properly, until he has an orgasm."[40]

Many New Left women expressed frustration that in coed New Left groups they had been treated only as objects ("suitable for screwing, nothing else").[41] Others pointed out that despite the sexual revolution, since women were still so economically dependent on men (because they did not have as salable skills, they needed ultimately to find a man who would support them), heterosexual sex was not really a free exchange. Female submissiveness was demanded: "The market value of the woman, like that of a breeding pig, is determined by age, weight, and the firmness of the flesh. . . . Since usually she has not learned much . . . she must therefore behave such that the man wants to fuck her."[42] Yet others sought to put into words what else seemed to be involved when two people had sex. One woman, writing a seminar paper on "sexual morality" in the early 1970s at the University of Frankfurt, for instance, noted perceptively that sexual intercourse was not just about the satisfaction of sexual drives; it was very much also about ego confirmation (and, in her view, this was especially so for men). Because in late capitalism (as she put it) sexuality was meant to function as a compensation for all existential insecurities induced in men by the experiences of daily life, especially at work, the fetishization of female bodies in the media and the recent efflorescence of rhetoric affirming also female sexuality—and the presentation of that affirmation as a victory for women's emancipation—really meant nothing but a coercion for women. There was now a constant compulsion for women "always and above all to be sexy . . . always and above all to be available for sex," and "the pressure voluntarily to identify with her role as sex object for men." The pill was constantly presented as *the* ticket to women's emancipation, but it came together with insistent duress, and frequent declarations that women were "neurotic, frustrated, or even repressive, if they do not want to sleep with someone."[43] Other women emphasized the baggage that both men and women brought to sexual encounters, often inherited from their own parents. As one woman put it in an early reflection, "Until recently I was involved with a man who had horrible fears about his potency and wanted to sleep with me very often, because he believed that otherwise it wouldn't work when he was older. I was rarely asked about my feelings and needs in this and was, at that time, also not really capable of expressing these often enough or of refusing him. I have after all also learned 'that a man just needs that' and 'that a woman should subordinate herself in this way' (quotes from my mother)."[44]

Certainly there had been rivalry between men within New Left groups not only over who could make the smartest Marxist statements or come up with the most militant plan of action but also over who got to sleep with the prettiest women.[45] Yet women were hardly the passive victims of this process. Within the first feminist consciousness-raising groups, for example, women too acknowledged that they had measured their own self-worth and expressed rivalry with each other by competing to "catch" the most impressive New Left leaders. "One likes sleeping with the famous comrades, because thereby one acquires higher status in the hierarchy."[46] At the same time, other women also acknowledged that women were sometimes the ones who held the erotic power in relationships with men, and that often it was the man, as much as if not more than the woman, who was the emotionally dependent one. "We were *not* a group of sexually frustrated women," one woman affiliated with the New Left recalled in 2002. Instead, she said, many marriages among New Leftists eventually broke up more because the couples had simply grown apart, or even because the women had outgrown their male partners.[47] Yet there was clearly often ambivalence on both sides. One woman put the problem poignantly in 1974: "I think the fear of being touched and the incapacity to touch others and to do so tenderly, passionately, is a general social phenomenon. It is hard, simply to approach people and hug them; the walls become higher all the time. But the worst thing is—I think—the way in which one tries to master this incapacity. After all, the need has not disappeared. So one does it aggressively, humiliates one another, separates emotionality and sexuality and 'bangs' on forcefully (like machines)."[48]

While the feminist campaign for abortion rights had garnered widespread support from men across most of the ideological spectrum, the women's movement that emerged out of that campaign elicited far more negative reactions. In particular, men's insecurities about their own attractiveness or potency and concerns about the loss of their formerly unquestioned dominance manifested themselves in a vituperative rage at feminism. The ensuing sense of catastrophe in gender relations extended far beyond the New Left. But it was also felt with particular acuity within the New Left.

SEX AND POLITICS NEVER DID WORK

Indeed, New Leftists dealt with the loss of their former confidence about the necessary link between sexual liberation and political revolution not least by interpreting the problem as an impasse between men and women. For a time, assumptions about irreconcilable gender differences became the framework through which all difficulties within and around the left-leaning scene were explicated. And although women in the U.S. and other Western European countries in the 1970s articulated comparable complaints about men (and would experience a similar antifeminist backlash), there was also a distinctive streak of venom in West German debates over heterosexual sex. This undoubtedly had to do with the crashing sense of political defeat (despite the measurable accomplishments in liberalizing so many areas of social and sexual life). And because of the extra burden sex carried due not least to the incompletely worked-through national past (transmitted via all kinds of circuitous familial and social mechanisms), the strains that were almost inevitable within individual partnerships took on magnified significance and expressed themselves in sometimes bizarre ways. The later 1970s were a moment when the 1960s sexual revolution and the 1970s feminist critiques of it were *both* felt to be in trouble. There were countless (often mutually incompatible) accounts announcing that promiscuity was not working, but coupledom was not working either, and that general romantic and sexual unhappiness was widespread. Not coincidentally, West Germans referred to their sexual partnerships as "relationship boxes" (*Beziehungskisten*). As one man summarily concluded in the pages of the Hamburg-based New Left newsmagazine *Konkret* in 1981: "Loving has become difficult. Certainly in this country it has."[49]

As a way to engage the broader sense of emotional emergency, in the late 1970s and early 1980s many of the leading New Left journals produced special issues on the topic of sexuality, and these issues were widely read and discussed—by all accounts sparking considerable conflicts in bars, workplaces, and bedrooms alike. In every case, the justification for such a publishing enterprise was formulated in terms of dissatisfaction with the reigning state of affairs in and between New Left bodies. As the editors of the *Pflasterstrand* put it in a tone of strategic self-deprecation in the wake of their special issue of December 1977, the reason the issue had sold out so rapidly had nothing to do with the quality of its contents. Rather, "the topic caught hold, because there is such a total deficit in the discussions around relationships, sexuality, and the women-men battle." Their only motivation, they claimed, had been "to provide something like a provocation, dragging the topic out of private drawers into the light of day."[50] Or again, as some members of the editorial collective put it, the goal was to "carry out [publicly] a discussion that otherwise always stays jammed up in the cogs of privateness."[51] The editors were worried that, among too many young people, "the same creepy dramas as went on in grandma and grandpa's bedroom still exist today."[52] In a related vein, the editors of *Konkret* announced in 1979 that they were bringing out a special issue, *Sexualität Konkret*, "because round about us we see the ruined sexual relationships and the helplessness in face of them."[53] Clearly, even as a number of contributors to the special issues complained (and rightly so) that (with few exceptions) no one was making themselves truly vulnerable, and even as members of the *Pflasterstrand*'s editorial collective, for example, expressed awareness that encouraging individual experiential contributions (or, as they put it, "subjective screw-experience-reports") could draw the rebuke that one was "solely grubbing around in one's own individual shit, rather than only even tentatively suggesting collective paths and perspectives toward liberation and transformation," part of the impetus for these projects was precisely the desire to make the private public (in some ways thus reclaiming one of the earliest impulses of the student movement).[54]

In this context, male bodies were called to a kind of visibility more usually reserved for women. Thus, for instance, *Pflasterstrand* coeditor

Daniel Cohn-Bendit responded to feminist criticism that male writers on matters sexual were all just "paper masturbators" by declaring that "I am not just a paper masturbator but rather a deeply committed masturbator with many fantasies and dreams that are neither all ugly nor all pretty."[55] Others ventured different forms of vulnerability (or exhibitionist self-exposure), whether sharing—as one man did—the self-derogatory information that he had so loved looking super-cool in his ultratight jeans ("pure insanity: for more than a decade I did that to myself, even though so often it made my balls and my stomach hurt"); or volunteering—as another did—that "I always come too early"; or revealing—as in yet a third case—that "I share with some men that I know the experience, in the course of screwing suddenly to be 5 kilometers away, separated from my penis, separated from the woman, totally alone."[56] If in the first half of the 1970s, women had sought to put into language what was bothering them about their relationships with men, the later 1970s was the moment when men started putting their feelings about their own bodies onto paper, whether they declared themselves as unapologetically macho *Chauvis* or as sensitive-guy *Softies*.

Discussions of politics and sexuality got thoroughly tangled. A whole series of issues on sex in the *Pflasterstrand* in late 1977 and early 1978, for example, consisted mainly of one long and embittered extended conversation about women's complaints about heterosexual practices and the related issue of New Left male resentment at feminism—and simultaneously one that provided an important forum for both male and female leftists to articulate their sadness and confusion about the state of leftist politics. Contributor after contributor remarked on "the political helplessness of the Frankfurt scene. Externally nothing succeeds anymore, internally we beat on each other."[57] Occasionally a call for a more utopian optimism broke through—as one "Micky" announced in February 1978: "I am not ready to sacrifice the visions of a liberated . . . world of revolutionary houses of lust and of laughing orgies."[58] But most contributors took the opportunity to remark on the growing confusion over what it meant to be leftist and over how exactly (or whether) leftist sexuality differed from the bourgeois version.

One New Left man, calling himself "a dinosaur," "a relic of the so-called Softie-era," generated particular consternation in the Frankfurt scene by confessing in 1977 that: "My most beautiful screw ever was on the morning when the news came over the radio of the deaths in Stammheim [announcing that three of the imprisoned terrorists from the Red Army Faction had committed suicide]. We were both for a long time completely numb. Then we fucked pretty brutally, then we were totally empty."[59] Responding to the outrage of the editors that he got pleasure from other people's suffering and thereby disengaged sex from politics in the most offensive way, the "dinosaur" tried to sort through his feelings once more. First he complained that the editors should not have accompanied their statement of disgust about him with such a hurtful caricature—as though what the "dinosaur" spent his time doing was masturbating while he fantasized about the suicides. The "dinosaur" accused the editors of imitating the influential antisemitic Nazi newspaper *Der Stürmer*. And the "dinosaur" also reflected further in self-critical anguish on his own and everyone else's confusions:

> The suicides in Stammheim did not get me horny. They made me feel rage, sadness, helplessness. In this situation I could—and that is first of all my brokenness, maybe—screw, specifically in this rage and mourning. I could screw AGAINST ALL THAT and was simultaneously driven by something outside myself, was a victim, okay, maybe I also turned the woman with whom I was having sex into a victim. In any case I was empty, and my body could speak, against the speechlessness, that we, I guess, all felt. Or didn't you feel it? With you apparently it's not like that. Sex must be integrated into a political reality, you say. That seems to work seamlessly for you. Not for me. Sex and relationships and politics, with me that's sometimes separate, sometimes opposed.[60]

This concluding perspective—that sex and politics, despite the 68ers' erstwhile fond hopes, were often fundamentally at odds—would be articulated even more directly two years later. The pseudonymous Gernot Gailer, in his sophisticated and much-discussed statement of (what one would now call decidedly politically incorrect) leftist pornographic fantasies, "A Dream Babe Undresses" (published both in the leftist Berlin daily *tageszeitung* and, in a longer version, in the intellectual-cultural journal *Ästhetik und Kommunikation*), connected the conflicts over feminism with the now-ruptured assumption that sexual liberation could further social justice. Gailer invoked the old 68er slogan "Pleasure, sex, and politics belong together," only to disagree completely. "Sex and politics," Gailer intoned, "never did work, do not work, and never will work." Moreover, Gailer asserted (after having, in the course of his essay, fantasized a rape): "After all, we are the truly oppressed ones. We men. Down with the women's movement. For more peepshows. That's no joke. Honestly. I am for the peepshow. The women's movement doesn't do anything for me."[61]

By no means were such tendentious sentiments confined to New Left men. To mock feminism in the most derisive terms had become commonplace. So had the frequently announced threat that men were losing desire for women as women asserted their own rights. The very moment—the mid-1970s—when female sexual response became a topic for nationwide discussion coincided almost exactly with ferocious (if incoherent) assaults against feminism and the call that West German women (also for their own sake) should "return to femininity."[62]

West German men across the political spectrum argued that feminism was bad for heterosexual sex. And they introduced evidence to prove that the incidence of male sexual dysfunction under heightened performance pressure was on the rise. As early as 1969, for instance, the enormously popular conservative tabloid *Bild* reported that men were sexually overtaxed. Until they turned twenty-five, the newspaper stated, German men wanted sex every day; after age thirty, however, husbands preferred the company of television after work and announced that they were "too tired."[63] But by 1977, precisely in the midst of major confusion about how to feel about feminist findings that female orgasms were easier to achieve through masturbation than through coitus, the subject of men's disinterest in sex with the women in their lives was almost constantly discussed. *Der Stern* printed a cartoon in which a woman compared a man's lack of energy in bed to nicotine-free cigarettes.[64] *Der Spiegel* declared that the performance pressure especially on middle-aged men was rampant, and it announced that "fear is the enemy of erection." Yes, it was unfortunate that men emphasized their work and let their sex lives slide. But to reverse this trend, what was required was an "especially sensitive female partner"; all too "rarely was this the wife."[65] Women who had discovered the joys of masturbation were only causing their men more grief, since it was well known that "militant masturbation . . . means man-hatred."[66] And women who expected ecstasy from their men every time ought to be appraised that for many men it was precisely these sort of "performance expectations" that "blocked sexual capacities the most."[67]

Male resistance left a lot of women just feeling underappreciated. One study in 1975 turned up desolate accounts of women's bad experiences with heterosexual sex; despite the pill and the pervasiveness of detailed sex talk, many women were finding themselves "just as frigid as before" (*noch genauso frigide*).[68] And a study done by a Hamburg research institute in 1978 found that "every third woman would be happy if she could at least regularly achieve an orgasm." Nor were women overly impressed when men claimed that feminist demands for better sex left them feeling anxious and overwhelmed. As one woman sarcastically summarized the dilemma: "The men are constantly calling for the hot-to-trot woman, who shows her desire openly—but woe if she actually shows up." (*Die Männer rufen ständig nach der scharfen Frau, die ihr Begehren offen zeigt—aber wehe, sie kommt wirklich.*)[69]

No one felt like they were getting anything like the pleasures they deserved. Typically, it was feminists who got blamed. "The women's movement has reduced our horniness to zero," summarized a man for *Der Stern* in 1982.[70] Sex had been fun for a while but no more, this was agreed; the sexual revolution was winding down. By the early 1980s, men and women were not having sex much more frequently than they had before the introduction of the pill just twenty years earlier. "After the rush of freedom comes the hangover?" asked *Der Stern* rhetorically about these sobering developments.[71] And it was sure that the root cause of these gender troubles was that the average German man had just gotten "fed up with the women's movement."[72]

It was in this pessimistic atmosphere that feminists and left-leaning male activists did also reach for the Third Reich as a negative reference point in their battles with each other over the terms and conditions of heterosexuality in West Germany. Yet rather than constituting any kind of attempt at theorizing Nazism, the aim on both sides was often just to be crude and ugly. The insults hurled all around became increasingly cliché and reductive.

Thus, for instance, in their attempts to score points against recalcitrant men, feminists decried Nazism's "masculinity madness" and "masculine ideology" or declared that "fascism was simply the expression of the worst kind of male dominance."[73] Men's attempts to defend pornography were linked with both fascism and Auschwitz.[74] When a man named Siegfried Knittel shared his particular misogynist fantasies in *Pflasterstrand* in 1978 (and the men in the editorial collective had inadequately distanced themselves from his remarks), forty enraged female staffers cosigned the following declaration:

> It is surely very regrettable, that the erstwhile SS bullies also did not have a pretty youth, [but] it is to be welcomed as well that they at least are not allowed to see the *Pflasterstrand* as their central genital. . . . Not even a concentration camp guard in the *National- and Soldiers-Paper* could report on his "self-emancipatory acts" with such freedom and ease. . . . We will not let the political frustration of the men be carried out on our backs and bellies.[75]

Feminists also drew parallels between the entirety of the sexual revolution and the Nazi period. Whereas in the 1960s, according to the feminist magazine *Emma*, young women had, together with leftist men, "gone on the street against rearmament, against the emergency laws, and Vietnam," these women who had "begun to take the pill and discuss the 'sexual revolution' " were now in the 1970s "slowly starting to realize that they were once again going to be betrayed," just like their erstwhile "brown [i.e., Nazi]" mothers had been. These daughters "no longer wanted to type and listen . . . and willingly spread their legs." Like their mothers, they too now awaited "the zero hour" (*die Stunde Null*, i.e., May 1945).[76]

Comments that did constitute attempts to offer analyses of Nazism had the effect of whitewashing women's complicity during the Third Reich. Antisemitism, it was declared, was preeminently "a male disease." And any antisemitic opinions expressed by females could be explained as the result not of their own views but rather the fear of losing an (antisemitic) man's love.[77] Meanwhile, conversely, it was proposed that "antifeminism" was "the hidden theoretical basis of German fascism," or that National Socialism was an "extreme form of patriarchy."[78]

It was not surprising, then, that men fought back with similar tactics. Henryk Broder, for instance, a well-known German Jewish commentator and self-described "Chauvi," could not resist the impulse to haul the Nazi past into his own hostile retort to feminist complaints. After he shared in the pages of *Konkret* that "when women have big boobs I automatically reduce my expectations of their brains," Broder went on to comment that the women's movement's slogan "all men are chauvinists" brought to mind the insidious antisemitic refrain that "all Jews are cunning."[79] Psychoanalyst and "masculinity specialist" Bernd Nitzschke, for his part, observed that feminists behaved like the Nazis when they articulated their opposition to pornography. Referring to the Third Reich in a presentation at a sexology conference, Nitzschke compared feminist criticisms of pornography with the Nazis' attacks on pornography and on its purportedly Jewish purveyors. Nitzschke sarcastically noted that "the dignity of the German woman was thoroughly protected back then, because the sex offenders were not sitting, as they supposedly are nowadays, behind trees at night, but rather . . . in the concentration camps."[80]

More generally, and for many women even more distressingly, the 1970s were also the decade when New Left men joined influential conservative male pundits in asserting that it had been "jubilant, hysterical" women who had "brought Hitler to power."[81] *Frankfurter Allgemeine Zeitung* editor and conservative historian Joachim Fest was particularly blatant; he argued that women under Nazism virtually achieved orgasm at the mere sight of Hitler.[82] If it had not been for the irrational in women, this line of argument suggested, the irrational in fascism would not have triumphed. Given the rising tide also of leftist antifeminism, New Left men increasingly found this explanation congenial as well.[83] As one feminist scholar remarked in annoyance, men's support for Hitler was always explained as the understandable result of the economic downturns and political instabilities of Weimar, whereas women were not granted such rational motivations. What was at work, she said, was apparently a wholesale "male attempt to shift the blame for Hitler onto the other sex."[84]

ANTIFASCIST FANTASIES

This was the contentious climate in which New Left cultural critic Klaus Theweleit was writing his major study on both sexuality and fascism: *Männerphantasien*. Published in West Germany in 1977–78, the book's two sprawling volumes constituted an extended treatise on the literature of the *Freikorps* (the semiorganized paramilitary gangs deployed in Weimar Germany and in the Baltics to crush potential popular insurgencies). It has generally been received as a study of the (proto)fascist male mind, not least because many members of the *Freikorps* ended up among Hitler's stormtroopers and/or as concentration camp commandants and guards. But it was also an exploration of the broader historical phenomenon of the "soldierly man" (*soldatischer Mann*), a term Theweleit used both to refer to military men in particular and to men socialized into self-discipline, aggression, and hardness more generally. Theweleit was a man who had absorbed the feminist perspectives on masculinity and Nazism alike. And perhaps even more importantly, Theweleit was an author who, even as he insisted on challenging older Freudian Marxist explanations of fascism, managed to rescue "the repressive hypothesis" of Nazism—the conviction that the Third Reich was not just characterized by but actually *explained* by sexual repression—that the New Left had held so dear.

Männerphantasien can be read as an energetic and imaginative last-ditch attempt at an optimistic reading of the relationship between the personal and the political. In contradiction to the building sentiment that pleasure, sex, and politics were at odds, *Männerphantasien* announced, resoundingly, that pleasure, sex, and politics *did* belong together. Indeed, *Männerphantasien* unabashedly proposed that sexual dysfunctionality was at the heart of the most significant and terrifying political events of the twentieth century—it brought, in short, both German fascism and the Judeocide explicitly back into the discussion West Germans were having with themselves over gender and sex—and it proposed that understanding the connections between bodily feelings and the propensity to violence in the past could show the way to a nonfascist future. And the book was a blockbuster success.

While some reviled it, most readers found Theweleit's book enormously persuasive and compelling. The book got cited constantly. It was not only widely reviewed, but also broadly appropriated, in both popular and scholarly venues. Rudolf Augstein, the editor of *Der Spiegel*, in 1977 deemed the appearance of the first volume "maybe the most exciting German-language publication of this year," while in the more right-wing but no less influential *Frankfurter Allgemeine Zeitung* in 1978, Lothar Baier (who found the book appalling and announced that its explanatory value "inclines . . . towards null") also noted that the two volumes had created a sensation, that the publisher was unable to keep up with the extraordinary demand, and that "in certain parts of the intellectual scene they are being almost maniacally devoured."[85] And in the pages of the opinion-making *Die Zeit*, Theweleit's tome was declared "the most productive contribution by a leftist theoretician to the fascism debate to date."[86] The review in *Pflasterstrand* actually said that the book could help heal the problems within the counterculture and "build bridges" between the estranged parties.[87] The impact was lasting. Almost two decades later, in an anthology on the history of masculinity, *Männerphantasien* once again would be hailed as a pathbreaking work, this time as *the* pioneering text in the history of masculinity in Germany and one that "surely now as much as ever counts as the best-known contribution" to that genre.[88] From the 1980s through to the present, Theweleit's analyses of fascism and masculinity remain frequently cited by scholars as impressive and self-evident truth. This enthusiastic response makes sense in the multiple contexts in which the book appeared: the increasingly depressed trajectory of the West German New Left, the fracturing of the sexual revolution under the impact of feminism, and the evolving ways the Third Reich and the Holocaust had been interpreted in the postwar era and the lessons that had been drawn from those interpretations.

Männerphantasien was the product of a 68er. In describing his parents, Theweleit (born in 1942) situated himself as similar to so many of his generation who felt that the aftereffects of Nazism had lingered throughout their adolescence in the 1950s: "The blows [my father] brutally lavished as a matter of course, and for my own good, were the first lessons I would one day come to recognize as lessons in fascism. The instances of ambivalence in my mother—she considered the beatings necessary but tempered them—were the second."[89]

But *Männerphantasien* was also a *post*-1968 book. Rather than simplistically adopting Wilhelm Reich's dictums about the relationships between sexuality and fascism in the way New Leftists had in the late 1960s, Theweleit was constantly at pains to criticize and go beyond Reich. Moreover, rather than assuming that to triumph over the Right would be easy, *Männerphantasien* assumed a world in which leftists were disoriented as they struggled to understand what made conservatism so appealing to "the masses," as well as a world in which there was tremendous puzzlement about the relationship between the personal and the political. And finally, far from assuming that all antifascists' sex lives were going smoothly, *Männerphantasien* engaged directly the challenges brought by feminism as well as the general sense of dissatisfaction with the sexual revolution. *Männerphantasien* was above all an intervention in two conversations: the one that the New Left and West German society as a whole were having with themselves about gender relations; and the one (less openly thematized but no less pressing) that West Germans had intermittently been having since the end of the Second World War about the relationship between pleasure and evil.

Männerphantasien was an attempt to make sense of the (proto)fascist male mind above all by consulting protofascist and fascist men's own writings. Theweleit examined over 250 *Freikorps* memoirs, supplemented by the writings of such men as Nazi propaganda minister Joseph Goebbels and Auschwitz commandant Rudolf Höss. In addition to this extensive source base, Theweleit engaged a broad array of theoretical works and issues. Although resolutely anticapitalist and committed to understanding human psychology, Theweleit was repeatedly critical of Marx, Freud, and the Freudian Marxist Frankfurt School alike. Instead, *Männerphantasien* drew eclectically on various non-Freudian analytic theories. It was particularly influenced by Gilles Deleuze and Félix Guattari's notions of the unconscious as a "desiring-machine" and by Margaret Mahler's insights into how acts of aggression provided "self-maintenance strategies" for children suffering from psychosis, particularly children who, being (as she put it) "not fully born," had never acquired the necessary sense of bodily boundedness to relate libidinally to other bodies. Theweleit was convinced fascist men had this same problem. One of *Männerphantasien*'s largest arguments had to do with what it found to be the fascist man's fear of the feminine—especially of imagined hordes of Bolshevik females—and of anything wet, muddy, red, or gushing, as well as the fascist man's fear of his *own* body's potential for pleasure. Theweleit's contention was that his own cohort had not yet overcome these problems either. He was convinced that heterosexual men were hurting themselves by being afraid of female fluids or of a merging of bodies and loss of ego boundaries.[90] Theweleit's message to the heterosexual men of his own generation was that they should not resist feminism. To transform sexuality would transform politics: "It no longer suffices simply to demand more frequent and more pleasurable orgasms. . . . Instead, the very notion of the orgasm as the sensation of *one* person has to be dissolved, abandoned. If human beings were to begin to achieve release through orgasms in which they experienced the other, the diverse, and the different as equal, they might well become nonfascists."[91]

Yet as he dug deep into the messy details of the past, Theweleit ran into considerable difficulties. Repeatedly, for example, he appeared unable to decide whether fascism offered its supporters pleasure or not. This was true whether he discussed the appeal of fascism for the general public, for the warrior on the battlefield, or for a perpetrator in a concentration camp.

Theweleit's contention throughout the book is that "the fascist never experiences the existence of a body capable of release. . . . [his is] a body incapable of the experience of pleasure in any form." On the other hand, however, Theweleit intuits that fascism had been successful in Germany not least because of its "refusal . . . to relinquish desire" (albeit "desire in its most profound distortion"), while—according to Theweleit—communists and socialists in Weimar had "never so much as intimated that there might be pleasure in liberation." Theweleit, in trying to break from a

1970s Marxist analysis that the German populace turned to fascism because it promised economic recovery, argues instead that "what fascism allows the masses to express are suppressed drives, imprisoned desires." Or at another point: "Fascism never expropriates the owners of the means of production. . . . The only thing it 'liberates' is perverted desire—which it then turns loose on human beings."[92] However, and even as he repeatedly challenges the New Left's economistic interpretations of fascism, Theweleit never fully lets go of a conviction that fascism simply was sexually repressive.

Thus, when he turns to the battlefield, and even as he invokes the notion of "the orgasm of killing," Theweleit nonetheless emphasizes the absence of sexual pleasure. For the "soldierly man," Theweleit writes, "heroic acts of killing take the place of the sexual act." Soldiers took pleasure in killing, but it was not a sexual pleasure. According to Theweleit, the pleasure offered by killing was the pleasure of *averting* sexual desires in one's own body by destroying the bodies of others. Soldierly men tried to escape or transform their own sexuality, "which they perceive as a force that will engulf and destroy them." Or most explicitly, as Theweleit puts it at another point: "It seems increasingly doubtful that terms such as hetero- or homosexuality can usefully be applied to the men we are studying. . . . These men seem less to possess a sexuality than to persecute sexuality itself—one way or another."[93]

The conundrum of potential pleasure in evil presents itself most acutely in Theweleit's discussion of cruelty within concentration camps. In one extended section, for example, Theweleit ventures an interpretation of a phenomenon observed by the author of *Die Männer mit dem rosa Winkel* (The Men with the Pink Triangle, 1972), a homosexual survivor of the concentration camps of Flossenbürg and Mauthausen, who said he had witnessed "on more than thirty occasions" an SS camp commander masturbating while prisoners labeled as homosexuals were publicly flogged on their buttocks. In Theweleit's interpretation, the public masturbation needs to be understood in multiple ways: as a deliberate reminder to the prisoner-spectators of their utter disempoweredness; as a celebration of the torturer's own aliveness in the face of those condemned to death; as a torture specifically intended to diminish the victim's capacity as a sexual being; and also—and here we get to the heart of Theweleit's problem— as the masturbator's act of sexual repression against himself. Theweleit implies that whatever orgasms the perpetrators experienced, they were somehow not the best kind. And in trying to reconcile his own conviction that fascists were incapable of genuine pleasure with the horrifying empirical evidence to the contrary, Theweleit presumes to know that the public masturbator at the floggings absolved himself of the requirement that he fantasize in order to get pleasure. Masturbation releases him absolutely from his threatening interior since this now takes the externalized form of the victim at the whipping post. His interior is severed from his body. . . . he is now able to repress the "desire to desire," the very existence of his unconscious. And the more he can substitute external perceptions for those of the interior, the more successful repression will be.[94]

Theweleit encounters serious complications also when he seeks to address the mass murder of European Jewry. For far from ignoring the Jewish question, as has been surmised, simply because Jews were not a major concern for the *Freikorps* men that provided Theweleit with his main source base, Theweleit instead repeatedly and deliberately invokes the Holocaust ("concentration camps," "Auschwitz," "gas chambers") in order—it starts to seem—to give his arguments about sex an impact and weight they would not have had if the Holocaust went entirely unmentioned.[95] Theweleit has been criticized for being inattentive to the various levels at which his argument operated: the level of the fascism-loving masses, the level of the soldierly man, the level of the dyed-in-the-wool Nazi, or the level of Western bourgeois men in general—a problem he engages quite openly himself, only in order to dismiss it.[96] What has not been noted is that the level of the Holocaust is in fact present as well; and precisely the ensuing ambiguity is what gave Theweleit's argument, in his time, its power.

Indeed, the second volume of *Männerphantasien* opens with the problem of trying to explain Nazi antisemitism. Here Theweleit perceptively points out the limitations of traditional leftist analyses in which antisemitism was above all explained as a technique for diverting anticapitalist impulses among the masses toward Jews. Theweleit stresses that this point was "secondary." He adds: "What we find at the core of German antisemitism is instead a coupling of 'Jewishness' with a 'contagious' desire for a better life." But quickly, in comments both before and after this particular one, it becomes apparent that once again, for Theweleit, fascism is about the fear of the female and the fear of bodily delight. Thus he underscores that the fascistic soldierly male has within him "a concentration camp, the concentration camp of his desires." And at another point, Theweleit states: "I do not believe it is at all exaggerated to claim that [Auschwitz commandant Rudolf] Höss and his contemporaries treated concentration camp internees in precisely the same way as they treated their own desires, the productive force of their unconscious: for both they had nothing to offer but incarcerations, the labor of dam-building, and death." It is on this basis that Theweleit could once more conclude confidently that "the core of all fascist propaganda is a battle against everything that constitutes enjoyment and pleasure."[97]

So, then, as for the earlier 68ers—although with more attendant angst and interpretive contortions—mass murder turned out primarily to be the result of sexual repression. Theweleit's book gave evidence of an earnest and heartfelt effort to update and refine the old 68er notion that sexual repression was the root of all evil. But what the book wound up doing was circling around this problem, stumbling over it, trying to put the same point in endlessly various ways, and yet running up against obstacles and inconsistencies at each turn. What the book ultimately, in its hundreds of pages, once again made apparent was that the shards of evidence left behind by the Nazi past just did not fit neatly together with a conclusion that sexual pleasure and cruelty were incompatible.

Remembering 1968

In the wake of the collapse of communist East Germany in 1989 and German reunification in 1990, Nazism lost its power as a reference point for discussions of sexuality. It no longer mattered so much to Germans what the Nazis had believed or done about sex or what their sexual politics might have been. Although while Germany was still divided, West Germans in particular had frequently grappled with the many relationships between sexuality and politics by routing their discussions of sexual matters through constructed memories of Nazism, this was much less the case after reunification. This is not to say that sex no longer had its referent in politics; it is to say that a new referent started to take the place of the Third Reich. That new referent was "1968," and all the many contradictory things that year was thought to have represented.

The terms of the relationship between sexuality and memory changed. On the one hand, conflicts over sexual politics in the 1990s became split off from conflicts over the memory and meaning of the Third Reich—even as, in the course of the 1990s, Holocaust memory culture expanded in Germany as never before (and even while annoyance over its expansion remained an ever-present and sometimes explosive contrapuntal factor of German political and cultural life as well). On the other hand, debates about late twentieth-century Holocaust memory culture and about late twentieth-century sexuality—these two now largely independent areas of social and ideological conflict—*both* increasingly got worked out via retrospective references to 1968. In the process, what 1968 stood for underwent significant change.

With reunification, not only democratic capitalism as a political and economic system but also West Germany as a historical entity accrued a moral legitimacy they had not previously had. All the corruption, falsehood, and hypocrisy of West Germany that New Leftists and others had criticized, all the continuities with Nazism and persistence of antisemitism and other forms and aspects of racism, were dramatically relativized in importance as the superiority of the West appeared proved. Leftists' challenges to West Germany's immoralities (which had depended on invocations of Nazism) no longer seemed pertinent. A new past of dictatorship and totalitarianism—East Germany's—now demanded to be worked through and mastered. And in their eagerness to distance themselves from a leftism in retrospect tainted by association with apologetics for communist repression (a stain that seemed difficult to remove despite the numerous New Leftists who all along had opposed the Stalinist kind of socialism that existed in East Germany), many former New Leftists outdid themselves in announcing their conversion to neoliberalism and a belief in free-market systems. Few managed to take the time even to mourn the loss of their former anticapitalist values, even as, by an odd twist, they often felt free to upbraid *Ossis* for not having rebelled sooner.[98]

The new triumphalist social consensus of democratic capitalism required the antifigure of 1968, but in contradictory ways. Among other things, the argument was made that what 1968 had been about, in truth, was the modernization of capitalism, despite the overlay of Marxist jargon. Bringing blue jeans and rock 'n' roll to the masses, and thereby making capitalism more fun, was the real outcome of 1968, even though the 68ers had not been aware of that at the time. For neoliberal commentators, this was an especially pleasing historical turn.[99] Alternatively, 1968 was treated as a moment of immature, even infantile, rebellion that had not just brought with it the revitalization of consumer capitalism but also a disturbing amount of violence. New Leftism had not only been inane; it had also led both to blindness about Soviet bloc socialism's cruelties and to the bloody terrorism of the Red Army Faction within West Germany. Far from ironic, the lesson here was that leftism was inevitably pernicious and that there was a fairly straight line between antiauthoritarian street demonstrations and the RAF's premeditated execution of bankers and politicians.[100] Yet a third strategy, prevalent among some ex–New Leftists, involved a self-congratulatory endorsement of both the hedonist and the morally righteous impulses of 1968 (and a basking in the glow of once having been a courageous idealist), often accompanied by an attestation to the greater maturity and realism one had acquired since.[101]

In all three approaches, it was apparent that antileftism had largely outlived leftism in reunified Germany. Retrospectively, 1968 became so important not least because it signified the moment of moral self-criticism *within* the West. This moment remained (and still remains) an irritant for the smooth functioning of the evolving present; this is perhaps why its meaning continues constantly to be reworked. The evolution of Holocaust consciousness and the trajectory of the history of sexuality have provided yet further occasions for reimagining 1968.

In the 1990s the Holocaust became a major theme for national discussion in Germany and an inextricable component also, or maybe even especially, of non-Jewish German national self-definition, but the mood of the early twenty-first century appeared more opposed to than encouraging of further attention to the Holocaust. Just as new studies about the collaboration of numerous nations in making the Holocaust possible were being published and these nations (including Austria, Switzerland, Belgium, France, and the Netherlands, as well as Poland) were paying delayed-reaction attention to the need to confront their complicity in the crimes of the Nazis, and a number of political scientists and politicians were proposing that the Holocaust could usefully serve as a negative touchstone for an increasingly politically and economically unified Europe—*the* reference point that could help orient Europe morally toward an ever-vigilant defense of democracy and freedom—concern with the specificities of the Holocaust was once again going out of focus.[102] There were several reasons for this. They could be found precisely in the growing political and economic integration of Europe and the accompanying decline of the relevance of the nation-state and of nationalism. They could be found in the increasingly multiethnic and multicultural nature of Germany itself. (Should young Turkish Germans or Afro-Germans, for instance, feel any particular sense of national obligation to remember the crimes of National Socialism?)[103] They could also be found in the United States' precipitous fall from moral high ground due to its military intervention in Iraq in 2003, an intervention strongly opposed by the majority of Germans. And they could be found in long-standing and now once again flourishing patterns of (often resentment-laden) German memory management strategies.

Among these long-standing memory management strategies was an insistence also on the extent and intensity of non-Jewish German suffering and a recurrent complaint that it had been taboo to discuss that suffering (even while assertions of the taboo's existence have repeatedly provided occasions for breaking it). For example, the turn from the twentieth to the twenty-first century saw special attention paid to the hundreds of thousands who experienced the Allied bombing raids on cities like Dresden and Hamburg (which turned entire districts of these cities into infernos), the millions of German refugees driven out of the eastern territories by the Soviets at war's end, and, more generally, the *longue-durée* psychic toll of the violence and losses of World War II not only on those who were adults at the time but also on those born during it and growing up in its wake.[104] It has been a delicate matter even for the most thoughtful of commentators to negotiate the moral imperative of acknowledging the enormity of this pain and suffering in view of the immediacy with which, in the wake of the war, emphasis on non-Jewish German suffering was preemptively invoked against any expectation that non-Jewish Germans should feel remorse for what had been done to Europe's Jews.[105]

There are further strategies closely connected with, although developed in uneven relationship to, the self-exculpatory discourse of equivalent victimizations. They involve what can only be called a hyperpreoccupation with Jewish imperfection (which slides easily into antisemitism) and the complementary complaint that there is a surfeit of Holocaust memory, that "too much" emphasis has been placed on Jewish suffering, and that—as the writer Martin Walser memorably put it in 1998—Germans had a right to be sick of the "moral cudgel" which the Holocaust had become.[106] All through the postwar period, and despite the official government philosemitism, aspersions were cast on Jewish morality. Thus, for example, in the 1950s Christian Social Union (CSU) politician and minister of finance Fritz Schäffer nastily remarked (in the context of debates over "restitution" payments to survivors) that "if the Jews want money, then they should raise it themselves by arranging a foreign loan."[107] Or, for instance, in the 1960s, the anti-Nazi Protestant clergyman Heinrich Gruber made the outrageous suggestion that everything that happens is God's will (and hence perhaps also the Holocaust had been divinely ordained); he coupled this with a plea to a visiting American Jewish dignitary to help discourage the few Jews living in Germany from being so prominently involved in the nightclub business (because this just made it harder for good Christians to combat German antisemitism).[108] In such moments, old antisemitic clichés of Jewish greed or sexual indecency were revitalized. Similarly, in a more recent debacle, the Social Democratic mayor of Hamburg, Klaus von Dohnanyi (son of the anti-Hitler resister Hans von Dohnanyi), could unabashedly insult Jews in 1990s Germany to challenge themselves "whether they would have been so much more courageous than most other Germans, if after 1933 'only' the disabled, homosexuals, or Roma had been dragged off to the extermination camps." In so doing, von Dohnanyi revived stock antisemitic notions not only of Jewish cowardice but of the selfish Jew as well (also advanced in prior postwar decades) that all along have functioned as a means to disavow self-interestedness among non-Jews.[109] Along related lines, the unusually avid attention paid in Germany to Middle East politics and more recently, to the Israeli military's violent response to the second Intifada, constantly slips into off-the-record but loudly made remarks that "Jews are just making capital from their victimization"; that there are also strenuous and agonized debates among Jews all over the world over Israeli politics is missed in such unapologetically generalizing claims as "when I think Jewish point of view, I think Ariel Sharon."[110] All of this makes it hard to disagree with Israeli psychoanalyst Zvi Rex's wry 1990s observation that "the Germans will never forgive the Jews for Auschwitz."[111]

What was distinctive about the 1990s discussions in Germany was that they foregrounded, more than had ever been done before, the massive extent of participation of ordinary Germans in the social exclusion, persecution, torture, and murder of Jews in the 1930s and 1940s. While Daniel Jonah Goldhagen's *Hitler's Willing Executioners* (1996) was furiously attacked by leading German historians, it had the unexpected effect also of creating a space in which both the prevalence of antisemitism and the voluntarism and even pleasure in cruelty toward Jews could be acknowledged in ways they never had been before.[112] So too did the photograph and document exhibit *Verbrechen der Wehrmacht* (Crimes of the Wehrmacht), launched in Hamburg in 1995, against initial vehement resistance, rupture the long-standing postwar myth of a "clean" army and generate the necessity for conversation between the generations in which admitting the entanglement of ordinary soldiers both in antipartisan warfare and in genocide became possible.[113]

So profound were the ensuing transformations in what counted as common sense about the Third Reich that the historian Hannes Heer, one of the coorganizers of the Wehrmacht exhibit, could speak of the exhibit's effect as "the victory of history over memory."[114] By this he meant that finally the historical facts of ordinary Germans' participation in the Holocaust had been able to displace the various strategies of memory management that postwar Germans had used so successfully to veil their own enthusiasm for Nazism and complicity in marginalizing and harming those targeted by the regime (even as, simultaneously, and significantly, more touchy issues such as the potential "traumatization" of the perpetrators could be broached as well, and more productively than they had been in the past). The 1990s and early 2000s also brought the publication of important new studies on such diverse issues as the murder of the disabled, the involvement of medical professionals and social workers in the involuntary sterilization programs and persecution and imprisonment of so-called asocials, and the torture and murder of Sinti and Roma and of homosexual men. In addition, there were crucial studies on the greed and nepotism characterizing the "aryanization" process of the German economy, the treatment of Jewish Germans by their non-Jewish neighbors, as well as (often facilitated by sources newly available in the archives of the formerly communist East) the behavior of military and civilians in the vast swath of territories occupied by Germany during World War II.[115] In addition, the 1990s and early 2000s saw the publication of pathbreaking studies on the postwar handling of Nazism, the successful postwar careers of numerous perpetrators, and the combination of amnesties, active repression, and misrepresentation of the Nazi past and integration of former

Nazis that characterized the early Federal Republic.[116] But just as new clarity was being achieved, new incarnations of old obfuscatory techniques appeared as well.

As historian Atina Grossmann has pointed out in her discussion of the success of Goldhagen's book in Germany, the postwar period has seen "a continual oscillation between the drive to forget . . . and the injunction to remember," and a constant "swinging between anxious remembrance and resentful denial." Grossmann, along with others, has diagnosed in postwar West Germany a kind of "repetition compulsion," an endlessly recurring series of "guilt occasions" that morph into media scandals during which ugly charges and countercharges are exchanged with ritual regularity and unclear results.[117] Moreover, as the New Left journalist Klaus Hartung pointed out already in 1987—in one of the most perceptive autocritiques written by a non-Jewish German—it would be much too facile to try to make sharp distinctions between "the enlighteners" and "the repressers." In Hartung's account, perhaps maybe especially for the New Left, "confronting fascism was inextricably tied up with avoidance, exposing with blinding, sensitivity with hardening."[118]

Reunification in 1990 permitted the consolidation of a rewriting of 1968's relationship to Holocaust memory that had been already partially underway since the mid- to late 1980s. By the mid-1990s, many of those who before reunification had still identified with the New Left began formally to declare their conversion to liberalism. In this process, they advanced a new narrative of 1968 in which they downplayed their erstwhile anticapitalism, taking credit instead for having brought democracy to West Germany and forced the culture to shed its lingering authoritarianism.[119] In styling themselves as having courageously broken the postwar silence about Nazism and having decisively challenged their parents' generation to confront the crimes of the past, they conveniently erased the rather more ambiguous attitudes about Jews that accompanied their Marxism.[120] The years immediately preceding the collapse of the East, 1987–88, marked the highpoint in the West of thoughtful self-criticism for having so long been insensitive to Jewish suffering.[121] Simultaneously, however, those very same years saw the beginnings of an interpretation of 1968 as having been "too" strongly concerned with Nazi crimes and too fixated on accusing the parental generation rather than trying to understand it; this second interpretation ascended rapidly after reunification.[122] This second interpretation of the New Left as inadequately sensitive to its parents' sufferings did not only neglect the New Left's own antisemitism but also ignored the remarkable extent to which New Leftists had in fact not been all that accusatory toward their own parents—for example, numerous New Leftists had represented the German populace as victims of Nazism rather than its beneficiaries. And what is most striking about the 1990s is the vehemence with which 68ers were themselves chastised for once having taken an accusatory stance toward their elders.[123] The effect was to undercut any ability to take a critical stance on postwar German behavior. In this version of history, then, 1968 stood for inappropriate hypermoralism.

Meanwhile, and as though they were happening on another planet, debates about sexuality in the 1990s were continually routed through references to 1968 as well. As with Holocaust memory, so also with sex, the narratives of sexual history produced in the 1990s and early twenty-first century, and the place of 1968 within them, were already starting to take shape in the 1980s. In these accounts, 1968 stood for the beginnings of the sexual revolution that was in the early 1980s falling into disrepute.

The eruption of the HIV/AIDS epidemic in the early to mid-1980s, and the initial panicked popular and media response, abruptly revived the specter of Nazism. As West German sexologist Volkmar Sigusch noted sadly in 1986 in *Sexualität Konkret*'s special issue on AIDS, also the self-defined liberal press participated in fanning mass hysteria: "The exclusion of persecuted minorities, [the press's] goading of an already thudding and rumbling 'healthy' sensibility of the *Volk*, is devastating. As if we needed proof that racism is still alive and well among us, and not just in latent form—AIDS has provided that proof."[124] A year later, the influential CSU/CDU politician Peter Gauweiler and others called for quarantining HIV-positive individuals, forced testing, and contact-tracing. It was not least because of the inescapable echoes with the Third Reich this call evoked that Gauweiler was forcefully rebuked.[125] His CDU colleague Rita Süssmuth, minister for youth, family, women, and health, became one of the foremost government spokespeople for a pragmatic response to HIV/AIDS, for Safe Sex/Save Sex campaigns coupled with the protection of individual rights.[126] Also in East Germany, while fears were initially high that panic over HIV/AIDS would undo the tiny successes achieved by gay and lesbian rights activists in the early 1980s and lead to a revitalization of homophobia, the epidemic actually had the opposite effect and there too provided the occasion for a major government-sponsored campaign for tolerance toward sexual minorities.[127] While HIV/AIDS certainly did not alone lead to the end of the sexual revolution, not least because a more general conservative retreat had already been in evidence beforehand, the reality of HIV/AIDS did nonetheless change sexual attitudes and practices among hetero-, homo-, and bisexual individuals, and did spur wider changes in what counted as sex.[128]

The collapse of the sexual revolution in the 1980s paradoxically coexisted with ongoing sexual liberalization, however. These liberalizations can be seen in such a phenomenon as the recent legalization of lesbian and gay unions (approved by the European Parliament in 2003)—which could be read (and often is) as a domestication of that which once was thought to hold transgressive potential and yet also marks a victory for decades of dedicated activism on behalf of human dignity.[129] Or these continuing liberalizations could be located in the rise of an "exhibitionist society" in which "anything goes" and in the routineness with which every sort of predilection that was once deemed a perversion and was nourished in secrecy is now assertively presented in magazines or on television as a major constituent of individual identity.[130] (As one commentator put it, "the shame barriers are sinking, the vulgar TV talk show rules.")[131] Or, alternatively, the ongoing liberalizations could be located in the success of feminist activism as manifested in the ascent of a sexual culture that places a high premium on the values of negotiation and consent.[132]

At the same time, something *did* end in the late 1970s and early 1980s, only to be gradually supplanted by something new, which does not yet have a name but might now in retrospect, from the vantage point of the late twentieth and early twenty-first centuries, be called "the neosexual revolution."[133] The term, coined by Volkmar Sigusch, is an attempt to capture a range of historical changes in the very essence of what sexuality is and might mean. This neosexual revolution can be recognized in diverse phenomena—the pharmacologization of sex (with its ability to split the capacity to perform from the experience of desire), the intensification of a culture of incessant voyeurism (in which it becomes unclear whether one is making love with a partner or more with oneself or with the images crowding in one's head—a phenomenon only escalated by the advent of phone sex and cybersex), a tendency to find the "ego trip" of narcissistic self-display at least as exciting as the physiological sensation of orgasm, and an attempt to optimize the time investment in sexual encounters so as to make them less disruptive of the pursuit of career achievement.[134] The Berlin sociologist Alexander Schuller has described the new state of affairs as "the onanization of sexuality."[135] But the point is also that the sex that occurs between two bodies is changing. When the Pfizer company in 2002 in its German-language ads for Viagra could declare provocatively that "Every fifth man in Germany has *erectile difficulties.*—You too?" (and then answer its own question by directing men to "Speak with your doctor. Love is worth that!"), it was clear that problems that were once more likely to be deemed psychological or social were now being refigured as chemical in ways that reshape not only the relationships between emotions and glands but also those between selves and others.[136] And various companies' eagerness also to invent female sexual dysfunction as a clinical category as they work to develop and market a "female Viagra" has to be seen as a rather ambivalent result of and response to feminists' efforts to question standards of "normal" sex and to foreground issues of attitude and practices.[137]

As critical observers seek to articulate what they see as a de-dramatization and banalization of sexuality in the early twenty-first century, 1968 functions as the key counterpoint. In the late 1960s, as sexologist Gunter Schmidt points out, the New Left student movement and the distraught religious conservatives that vociferously opposed it *both* believed in sexuality as an earth-shaking force. Radicals tried to liberate it; conservatives tried to contain it. But both believed in its power. Schmidt finds this somewhat quaint. What he and many of his colleagues have documented in Western societies since the 1980s is a decline both in felt desire, and a decline in belief that desire is an unruly force, erupting either from within individuals or between them. Instead, what consumer capitalism has wrought is an endless circuit of stimulus and arousal, display and looking, a continual search for thrills rather than for any kind of conclusive satisfaction. People out themselves in all their multivalent glory, declare themselves as fetishists, perverts, bi-, hetero-, or homosexual, describe their preferences in exhaustive public detail. And yet the studies keep showing that many people are bored. Arousal is everywhere present as the most risqué clothing and the most sexually suggestive advertising are pushed inescapably into every individual's line of vision. But bodies don't even react; nothing stirs. As Schmidt succinctly notes, "The concept of 'passion' is nowadays as obsolete as the concept of 'sexual sin.' "[138]

Other observers too have tried to make sense of the coproduction of hypersexualization and widespread "desirelessness" (*Lustlosigkeit*). Psychoanalyst Micha Hilgers, for instance, noted in 2000 that while not only advertising but also nudity in magazines and "especially the Internet" offered countless "masturbation-aids and voyeuristic opportunities," sex with a partner and "lust that is shared" were on a steep decline. Also for Hilgers, the sexual revolution of the late 1960s and the 1970s provided this telling contrast: back then studies showed 8 percent of women and 4 percent of men complained of low libido and disinterest in sex; by the 1990s it was 58 percent of women and 16 percent of men. Hilgers saw depression and low self-esteem, the heightened stress of daily life, and fear of unemployment as key sources for the lowered libidos.[139] The women's magazine *Freundin* (Girlfriend) directly identified the pervasiveness of explicit sexual imagery on television and in advertising as the source of heightened insecurity and unhappiness in bed, while the *Frankfurter Allgemeine Zeitung* reported in 2002 that sexual activity had dropped precipitously since the early 1980s; serial monogamy was in and fidelity was valued, but partners lost sexual interest in one another much more quickly than they had in prior decades.[140] "Every fourth couple," the *Frankfurter Neue Presse* reported, "only does 'it' once a month.[141] Some observers were convinced that even when bodies still directly connected with one another, the nonrelationality and the detachment of physiological response from emotions had become so acute that orgasms functioned more as self-reassurance and as trophies in a battle with the other body than as the pleasant effects of sexual encounters in the context of a powerful attraction to another, specific human being. In this dystopian vision, sex became nothing but "two people somehow manipulating around on each other."[142] In this context of listlessness and malaise, 1968 is remembered as the moment when prohibitions still made sex thrilling.[143]

But references to 1968's role in the evolution of the history of sexuality have yet another purpose beyond fights about sex per se: they also offer opportunities to criticize or mock more generally the moral-political ambitions of the generation of 1968. The New Left's sexual activism thus plays several roles within accounts of 1968. For instance, for those who tend to the view that 1968 was about nothing so much as the modernization of capitalism, the student rebels are usually genially given some credit for loosening up the stuffy postwar atmosphere. But even as their playful antics are subsumed into a broader story of victorious sexual liberalization, their critical insights on the coercive aspects of the consumer capitalist sexual revolution are smirkingly dismissed. Young people at the start of the new millennium define themselves as "a pragmatic generation" and distance themselves both from 1968's sexual and political ideals and its strenuous efforts to "connect sex and liberation." For these "young mellow ones," highly aestheticized self-display and masturbation are both fun, but "sex is overrated" and "rebellion is an empty gesture."[144] In yet other accounts the New Left sex rights movements are more affectionately spoofed. So, for example, the gay cartoonist Ralf König (born 1960)—much beloved also by straight readers—in a thirty-years-after-1968 cartoon showed two fortyish gay men, about to be interviewed by gay teens about the beginnings of the gay pride movement, confessing to each other that actually they never were all that revolutionary. All they could really remember from their own teenage years were the young men on whom they had had crushes and who had permitted them to give blowjobs (including in one case a twenty-year-old communist— "is *that* political?") and, above all, how wonderful, in those glorious pre-HIV days, sperm had tasted.[145] Increasingly, however, the ardent agitation of early gay and lesbian and feminist activists is treated as cranky and misdirected, even often by the very constituencies that have benefited most from it.[146]

Simultaneously, other commentators emphasize what they see as the dangerous aspects of New Left sex rights struggles. *Kinderladen* teachers and other antiauthoritarian pedagogues, for example, are variously accused (in the face of all empirical evidence to the contrary) of having been pedophiles or—because they succeeded so thoroughly in liberalizing elementary education in West Germany—of being responsible, through their failure to "set boundaries" for children, for the rise in right-wing radicalism among youth in the 1980s and 1990s.[147] And numerous younger people, perplexed and put off by the apparent nostalgic fixation of their 68er elders on the heady heyday of the sexual revolution, often venture the opinion that the 68ers have never really grown up. As one younger Green Party politician, aggravated by the now-aging New Leftists' condescension toward his generation, observed sarcastically in the late 1990s, the only "achievements" of 1968 were "street battles, sexual liberation, communal horninesses." He asked: "Must we really dive around in this murky little basin for treasures, if we want to become mature politically?[148] That the (however problematic) sexual activism of the late 1960s ever had anything to do with the legacy and memory of Nazism or the Holocaust has been almost entirely forgotten.

References to the sexual activism of the generation of 1968 provide key occasions for trivializing its political activism. In a 1997 thirty-years-after retrospective series on the student rebellions of 1967–68, *Der Spiegel*—still to this day Germany's premiere liberal newsmagazine—reprinted a photo from the 1960s (fig. 6.3): a topless Uschi Obermaier, professional model and major object of desire for the young (and old) men of West Germany, together with her lover, Rainer Langhans, well known at the time as one of the leading members of the Kommune 1. The caption that *Der Spiegel* added was notable. It was a quote (also from the 1960s) that read: "All of them belong in a concentration camp" (*Sie gehören alle ins Konzentrationslager*).[149] Elsewhere in the article one learns that the quotation came from an unnamed professor who made this crude remark about some unnamed New Left students, not about Obermaier and Langhans. What possessed *Der Spiegel* in the 1990s to jumble this comment and this picture together?

The surface reading is easy: by juxtaposing what most of its readers could be presumed to consider quite harmless nudity with the shocking allusion to Nazism—and even (albeit indirectly) the Holocaust—*Der Spiegel* was styling itself both hip *and* morally righteous. It simultaneously mocked and exposed as grotesquely inappropriate the hysterical uptightness displayed in the late 1960s by conservative opponents of sexual liberalization. The 1990s move is really not so surprising since *Der Spiegel* pulled similar moves already in the 1960s, when the sexual revolution was just getting underway. Back then, after all, *Der Spiegel* had trumpeted its own support for the sexual revolution by running a photo of Adolf Hitler with his legs daintily crossed above a caption that described the Führer as a repressed "sex-critic."[150]

But there is more going on here. For with this 1997 combination of caption and picture, it is not only conservatives who are mocked. The

Kommunarden Obermaier, Langhans
„Sie gehören alle ins Konzentrationslager"

Figure 6.3. *Der Spiegel*, 2 June 1997, p. 109. "They all belong in a concentration camp." Obermaier and Langhans in the 1960s. (Reprinted by permission of *Der Spiegel* and Studio Bokelberg)

image of Obermaier's breasts would certainly stir nostalgic associations for many an ex-68er (by this point themselves in their fifties and sixties)— among them memories of innocent adolescent fantasies, of one's own erst-while transgressive aspirations, of the overall feeling of excitement at the rapid liberalization of West German culture and the sense that one was participating in a transformation of world-historical proportions. And that nostalgic recuperation is in fact dignified, and its moral significance under-scored, by the addition of the caption, with its implicit reference to mass murder. Yet at the same time, the choice of photo itself undermines any message of moral seriousness. For precisely the presence of Obermaier— as anyone who lived through the late 1960s would have known, since she was at that time a media celebrity—undercut 68er claims to moral virtue. Obermaier was notoriously apolitical, given to declaring nonchalantly that she was far more interested in drinking Coca-Cola than in reading Marx, and that she could not have cared less about the commune's political goals; she just enjoyed hanging out with Langhans. In addition, Obermaier's cover-girl modeling gigs were at times the only income the Kommune 1 had; that they, as avowed anticapitalists supposedly disgusted with the brainwashing manipulations of the mass media, accepted her money, made them seem to many like hypocrites. Moreover, that Obermaier was also a sex icon for bourgeois men was just one more uncomfortable reminder that perhaps there was nothing special about New Leftists' sexual politics. In short, although offering former New Leftists opportunities for cozy re-membrances, *Der Spiegel* also poked fun at them. And certainly, the broader context of the series in which this image was included indicated that the barbed message was intentional. While in the late 1960s, *Der Spiegel* had very much sympathized with Kommune 1 and with the New Left as a whole, by the mid- to late 1990s the magazine had taken the neoliberal turn and missed few opportunities to ridicule leftism. The article made no effort to theorize or explain the potential relationship between picture and caption, and its overall effect was to undermine the moral earnestness that had once been so important to the West German New Left. What remained was only the faintest trace of a once so powerfully felt connection between the 68ers' sexual activism and their struggles to undo the legacies of the Third Reich.

Conclusion

FROM THE PERSPECTIVE OF THE HISTORY of sexuality, a notable conjunction of continuities and discontinuities characterizes each of the standard demarcation lines in twentieth-century German history. Neither Germany's entry into World War I in 1914 nor its defeat in 1918, for example, marked the onset of sexual liberalization; rather the aftermath of defeat saw an exacerbation of trends already underway as the century began. Organized homosexual rights activism existed as early as the middle of the first decade of the century; so too did a profusion of physicians' commentaries on the loosening of premarital heterosexual mores and the use of contraceptive strategies also within marriage. Yet after 1918, distressed contemporaries immediately began to *construe* the sexual liberalization as an effect of military defeat and "Marxist" government. Meanwhile, although the hectic years of the Weimar Republic have been retrospectively imagined as the heyday of sexual experimentation (an image Nazis played no small part in creating), already before Weimar ended there was a concerted conservative countermovement against the perceived excesses of the era.

When the Nazis came to power in 1933, they frequently presented themselves to the public as the restorers of traditional sexual morality (although this stance was also contested within the party leadership quite early on). And yet, as the Third Reich unfolded, a wholly new and highly racialized sexual politics emerged. While sexually conservative appeals continued to be promoted to the very end, it became clear that under Nazism many (though certainly not all) preexisting liberalizing trends would be deliberately intensified, even as, simultaneously, sexual freedom and happiness were redefined as solely the prerogatives of "healthy" "Aryan" heterosexuals.

In the wake of Nazism's defeat, Nazism's sexually inciting aspects were first thematized in elaborate detail and then gradually forgotten. Within the western zones and then the Federal Republic of Germany, a postfascist conservatism came to political prominence that drew its antifascist moral authority not least from its emphasis on the restoration of those traditional sexual, gender, and familial mores that Nazism had first loudly avowed and then so aggressively despoiled. Yet precisely the departure from Nazism with respect to premarital heterosexual activity was conjoined with an evident continuation of both eugenic and homophobic impulses and (an, if anything, even exaggerated) suspicion both of contraceptive use and of women's work outside the confines of the home.

At every point, then, the *interpretations* of the immediate and the more distant past proffered by contemporaries were a significant factor in the legitimation and contestation of the sexual politics of the evolving present. (This was as true in East Germany as it was in the democratic capitalist West; communists were as preoccupied with specifying their differences from Nazism as postfascist westerners were, and they got into similar difficulties.) In addition, and frequently, the combination of persisting trends and new departures was accompanied by unabashed redefinitions of what might constitute a continuity or a discontinuity (with innovations justified in the name of timeless virtues while continuities were styled as novelties).

Recurrently, there was also recourse to modes of thinking that had been tried in earlier times. Thus, for instance, and although those Nazi theorists of sexual orientation who were most successful in the Third Reich presented their emphasis on the fluidity of sexual identities as a resolute contrast to (what they deemed to be) Weimar activist Magnus Hirschfeld's stress on constitutionally determined sexual orientations, they in fact were not just suppressing the complexity of Hirschfeld's work but also building on earlier theories of sexual variability that had been promoted at the turn of the century by some homosexual rights activists as well.[1] Similarly, West German conservatives in the 1950s, unable to admit their continuities with Nazism and unwilling to reconnect with the more progressive impulses of either Weimar or late Wilhelminian culture, resorted to an imagined past of pre-twentieth-century bourgeois values when they sought to realign gender and familial relations. Or, in yet another variation on this theme, when New Left–affiliated students in 1960s West Germany sought to lend moral force to their assault on the postwar culture of sexual conservatism, the resources they reached back to recover were specifically the writings of (often Jewish) Weimar-era sex rights activists. In short, threads dropped decades earlier could be rewoven into the tapestry of sexual debates and could even become the newly dominant motifs.[2]

Yet it is not just a more nuanced periodization, or a deepened insight into the apparent complex mutual entanglement of different eras in German history, that close attention to the history of sexuality can provide. What the history of sexuality also shows us is the remarkable, indeed often determinative, significance of meaning-making processes. The point is not to prioritize interpretations or representations over that which we might variously—and always inadequately—refer to as "social conditions" or "lived reality," but rather to register the mutual constitutiveness of interpretations and conditions, representations and reality.[3] Or, to put it in other terms: how people understood the world has had tremendous consequences for how they acted in the world. Conflicts over sexuality provide a particularly salient example of this wider phenomenon.

At the same time, the twentieth century provides us innumerable object lessons in the broader political pertinence of sexual matters. In the course of the century, sexuality became not only a prime arena of social and cultural conflict but also a motor of economic development, a focus of heightened personal significance, a locus of government-citizen negotiation, and a space for working out a remarkable range of matters that (on the surface) would seem to have little to do with sex. There was not only an ever-increasing publicity surrounding sexuality. Concern with sexuality also appeared to spill over into ever more other areas of life. The dynamic transformations in the functioning of economies and the mutual accommodation between governments and citizens both seemed to provoke a (continually recalibrated) synthesis of stimulus *and* regulation of sexuality, phenomena that were as evident under East German state socialism as they were under Nazism or Western democratic capitalism.

The intrinsic interest of the history of sexuality, then, lies not just (though also) in its content per se. The value of the history of sexuality lies just as much in what it can teach us about how meaning-making happens in quite diverse political circumstances—and how it is shaped by and shapes those circumstances. For it is not least because of the pressing epistemological questions (about the interrelationships between psyches, bodies, beliefs, and social contexts) that sexuality inevitably raises *and* because of the ever-growing popular concern and political importance that sexual matters have accrued in the course of the twentieth century (to which conservatizing and liberalizing impulses have both contributed) *and* because of the way sexual politics are inevitably inflected by conflicts over other relations of power that controversies over sexuality, like few other subjects, provide us with an extraordinary opportunity to think about the workings of ideology. This is not just a general observation but has special historical relevance for thinking about the Third Reich and its (ideologically bifurcated) aftermath. Understanding how ideologies work, how they take hold of individuals, how they construct subjectivities, where the possibilities for resistances are—these were obsessions in the 1930s and 1940s for Nazis and anti-Nazis alike. And they were of grave concern for conservative, liberal, and leftist postfascist Germans in West and East as well. Strikingly, for Germans living both under and after Nazism, discussion of sex proved to be an especially privileged site for pondering the puzzles of human nature and the powerful—but never complete—purchase that social forces seemed to have on individual souls.

Among other things, then, what we can learn is that ideology works *through*, not despite, contradictions. So, for instance, the seemingly incompatible claims made about the generation of 1968 in the wake of communism's collapse in 1989—too ascetically morally rigorous, too hedonistically self-indulgent—both contributed to easing the transition away from anticapitalist critiques and commitments in the 1990s (even as these claims simultaneously effected an erasure of the memory of 68ers' ambiguous attitudes about Jews). Or, to take a different example, quite secular-minded individuals invested in downplaying their own pleasurable experiences under Nazism and conscientiously antifascist Christians hoping to reawaken moral sensibilities could both contribute to the consolidation of a sexually conservative climate in the 1950s. Or, in a more subtle but therefore no less significant form of contradiction, in the immediate aftermath of Nazism, acknowledgment and banalization of Nazism's crimes coexisted—and indeed facilitated each other. Or, to take perhaps the most important example, in the Third Reich it was both the antisex and the pro-sex arguments that *together* reinforced an utterly hallucinatory—but indisputably consequential—antisemitism. And while it might be argued that for many Germans, antisemitic rhetoric was hardly sincere but rather a language that was adopted cynically and instrumentally, such a perspective misses the crux of the problem, which was the language's effect. As Theodor Adorno and Max Horkheimer put the matter with devastating eloquence already in the late 1940s, the "horror is that the lie is obvious and yet it persists."[4]

While there is much that consideration of the history of sexuality in twentieth-century Germany can teach us, there are also new questions opened up that will require transnationally comparative research. Among the enigmas we have hardly begun to explore, at least four implicate some of historians' most deeply held beliefs about causation and the frameworks and language we use for explaining change over time. First, there is the question of secularization in the twentieth-century West. Charting the drops—and sporadic renewed rises—in church (and synagogue and mosque) attendance is an important but insufficient activity, for what we still need most to understand are such matters as the changing *content* of beliefs about divinity and transcendence as well as the manifest inextricability (although always again differently configured) of religious and political commitments. We also need to understand much more about the activism of the laity in reshaping what counted as religiosity. Among the matters that will need most attention is the liberalization that took place *within* the postwar churches from the 1960s onward, and the (perhaps paradoxical but nonetheless apparent double corollary of reduced church affiliation and revitalized spirituality in conjunction with left-leaning projects).[5] Another matter that might best be approached through transnational comparisons is the relationship between secularization and changing sexual mores. That resistance to church teachings on sex was a major motive of anticlericalism was well understood by contemporaries all through the twentieth century (although many historians have yet to start telling the twentieth-century histories of religion and sexuality in conjunction with one another).[6] But that the churches in the West themselves became spaces for emancipatory and not just constrictive thinking about sex has yet to be researched in depth.[7]

Second, a major puzzle that demands transnational reflection has to do with the incontrovertible recurrent appeal not just of sexual liberality but also of sexual conservatism. Historians' plausible and sensible gestures toward the apparently mutually reinforcing dynamics of Cold War anticommunism and familial, gender, and sexual conservatism still beg the question of why Cold War culture, across so many different Western nations, manifested itself in sexual conservatism.[8] There is no necessary link—only a historically produced one—between sexual conservatism and political conservatism (they can also be unlinked, as the history of Nazi Germany so clearly suggests).[9] Initial national and transnational analyses indicate that there was something in the cataclysmic experience of World War II itself that provoked a conservative counterimpulse; clearly, across all Western cultures, a strenuous effort to reconstitute something resembling "normality" followed the apocalyptic violence of the 1940s.[10] Yet there is more to explore. Investigating how contemporaries in various nations—with divergent relationships to fascism—explained the appeal of conservatism to themselves and each other might be a good starting point. This would mean not only thinking about the role of sexual conservatism in securing a populace's governability and thus tracing the potential additional functions served by certain versions of sexual conservatism (displacement of moral emphasis?, reassurance in a time of instability?, scapegoating of minorities?). It would also mean taking seriously contemporaries' reflections on issues of love and durability of attachment as well as variety and excitement. Pursuing these different aspects might also help us think about the more recent resurgence of sexual conservatism especially (though not exclusively) in the United States.

Third, we continue to have difficulty interpreting the sexual liberalizations of the 1960s and 1970s. What exactly were the interrelationships between loosening popular mores, the engaged struggles of activists, intergenerational conflict *and* cooperation, government policies and laws, and the more impersonal processes of economic and technological development? In some cases, legal innovations preceded activism, while in other cases they spurred it; arguably, in some cases, a shift in which political party held the reins of government occurred at least in part also because of changing sexual mores. How did these complicated interrelationships differ in post-Nazi (Catholic) Austria and (Protestant and Catholic) West Germany and postoccupation (Catholic) France? Were long-standing juridical traditions more important than predominant religious affiliation and more important than what happened in a particular country during World War II? (For example, homosexual acts between consenting adults in private had not been illegal in France since the French Revolution. While under Vichy, an adult who had sex with someone of the same gender under the age of twenty-one was subject to prosecution and this legal innovation remained in effect into the 1970s, adult homosexuality was simply not criminalized in postwar France or in most predominantly Catholic European countries.[11]) So was religion a decisive factor? (But then how would we explain the divergent trajectories in Scandinavia, the Netherlands, and Britain?) Simultaneously, we need to ask ourselves why such phenomena as gay rights movements emerged in different locales at around the same time even though they were initially unaware of each other. (The West German gay movement, for instance, began without its organizers knowing about the Stonewall rebellion in the United States.)[12] And how can we explain the simultaneity in the emergence of the French and West German gay movements, even though the histories of criminalization of homosexuality in those two cultures were so distinct?[13]

Comparisons with communist-ruled Eastern Europe would also be helpful. In Eastern European countries, for instance, abortion rights were introduced without nationwide activist campaigns (even though popular pressures may well have played a role). But perhaps most interestingly, sustained comparisons with Eastern Europe would usefully bring into focus the significance of sex for regimes in societies in which the majority of the populace had to be held in place with an Iron Curtain. Why did the East German government not just permit but actively encourage a loosening of sexual mores in the 1970s and 1980s, even as surveillance of dissidents and restrictions on mobility were rigidly maintained? In retrospect, the formerly East German sexologist Siegfried Schnabl suspected that the encouragement had been deliberate, a way of containing and dissipating political discontent.[14] And yet the specific sexual culture that evolved in East Germany was without question also the populace's own creation.

A fourth source of perplexity has to do with memory. This book has traced the political effectuality of numerous kinds of misrememberings. The most significant were the many permutations in the misrememberings of Nazism. But the book has also considered the misrememberings of other times in twentieth-century Germany, including the pre–World War I era, Weimar, the 1950s and 1960s in West Germany, the 1970s and 1980s in East Germany. This book has not fully resolved what to make of these misrememberings. In some instances (Nazism being only the most obvious one), adjudication of right and wrong, while not completely possible, is nonetheless fairly straightforward—even as we guard against the simplistic self-righteousness that comes with the benefits of hindsight and of personal, temporal, and geographic distance. But in other cases conclusive assessment is more challenging. A key instance, discussed in chapter

3, involves the dismantling in the 1960s of the most punitive and oppressive aspects of the conservative sexual culture consolidated in West Germany in the 1950s, and the ultimately successful collective efforts of liberal and leftist intellectuals, jurists, and activists to intercept the passage of what would have been a severely constrictive criminal code. This effort, in its time, depended on the continual invocation of a profoundly distorted image of Nazism as thoroughly sexually repressive. That it was ultimately a false version of history that produced conditions for progressive and humane social change is something historians may wish to meditate on further.

"I do think that in a society that was more free about sexuality, Auschwitz could not have happened."[15] Thus argued the eminent liberal jurist Herbert Jäger in 2003. Jäger is the last living coeditor of *Sexualität und Verbrechen*, the 1963 anthology that did so much to redirect moral debate about sexuality in West Germany. This book has been written in refutation of the view summarized by Jäger. It has provided a countervailing reading of the Third Reich's sexual politics, one that has emphasized the historic links between incitements to sexual activity and murderous racism (while also attending to the contradictions and complexities in Nazism's sexual politics, which later made opposing interpretations of those politics possible). In subsequent chapters, this book has also critically investigated the complicated mechanisms of post-Nazi memory management in Germany that allowed perspectives like Jäger's to become plausible to a broad segment of public opinion both in Germany and elsewhere in the postwar West. A goal throughout has been to *historicize* the construction of memory. And yet, one of this book's larger aims will be missed if it is not also read as a tribute to the intensity of conviction that animated Jäger's particular interpretation of his nation's past and the urgency of his effort, and that of so many others, to think critically and earnestly about the possible relationships between pleasure and evil.

Notes

INTRODUCTION

1. Arno Plack, *Die Gesellschaft und das Böse: Eine Kritik der herrschenden Moral* (Munich: Paul List, 1967), p. 309.

2. Anton-Andreas Guha, *Sexualität und Pornographie: Die organisierte Entmündigung* (Frankfurt am Main: Fischer, 1971), pp. 126–27.

3. Michael Rohrwasser, *Saubere Mädel, Starke Genossen: Proletarische Massenkultur?* (Frankfurt am Main: Roter Stern, 1975), p. 9.

4. Leonore Tiefer, *Sex Is Not a Natural Act and Other Essays* (Boulder: Westview, 1994).

5. Important contributions include Norbert Frei, *Adenauer's Germany and the Nazi Past: The Politics of Amnesty and Integration* (New York: Columbia Univ. Press, 2002); Geoff Eley, ed., *The "Goldhagen Effect": History, Memory, Nazism—Facing the German Past* (Ann Arbor: Univ. of Michigan Press, 2000); Jeffrey Herf, *Divided Memory: The Nazi Past in the Two Germanys* (Cambridge, MA: Harvard Univ. Press, 1997); Anson Rabinbach, *In the Shadow of Catastrophe: German Intellectuals between Apocalypse and Enlightenment* (Berkeley: Univ. of California Press, 1997); Y. Michal Bodemann, ed., *Jews, Germans, Memory: Reconstructions of Jewish Life in Germany* (Ann Arbor: Univ. of Michigan Press, 1996); Omer Bartov, *Murder in Our Midst: The Holocaust, Industrial Killing and Representation* (New York: Oxford Univ. Press, 1996); Michael Geyer, "The Politics of Memory in Contemporary Germany," in *Radical Evil*, ed. Joan Copjec (London: Verso, 1996); Kathrin Hoffmann-Curtius, "Feminisierung des Faschismus," in *Die Nacht hat zwölf Stunden, dann kommt schon der Tag: Antifaschismus—Geschichte und Neubewertung*, ed. Literaturwerkstatt Berlin (Berlin: Aufbau, 1996); Jürgen Danyel, ed., *Die geteilte Vergangenheit: Zum Umgang mit Nationalsozialismus und Widerstand in beiden deutschen Staaten* (Berlin: Akademie-Verlag, 1995); Heinz Bude, *Das Altern einer Generation: Die Jahrgänge 1938 bis 1948* (Frankfurt am Main: Suhrkamp, 1995); Geoffrey Hartman, ed., *Holocaust Remembrance: The Shapes of Memory* (Oxford: Blackwell, 1994); Saul Friedlander, ed., *Probing the Limits of Representation: Nazism and the "Final Solution"* (Cambridge, MA: Harvard Univ. Press, 1992); Atina Grossmann, "Feminist Debates about Women and National Socialism," *Gender and History* 3 (autumn 1991); Silke Wenk, "Hin-weg-sehen oder: Faschismus, Normalität, und Sexismus," in *Erbeutete Sinne: Nachträge zur Berliner Ausstellung "Inszenierung der Macht, ästhetische Faszination im Faschismus,"* ed. Klaus Behnken and Frank Wagner (Berlin: NGBK, 1988); Anson Rabinbach and Jack Zipes, eds., *Germans and Jews since the Holocaust* (New York: Holmes and Meier, 1986); and Lutz Niethammer, ed., *"Die Jahre weiss man nicht, wo man die heute hinsetzen soll": Faschismuserfahrungen im Ruhrgebiet* (Berlin: Dietz, 1983). On

the "layerings" of memory, see Dagmar Herzog, "'Pleasure, Sex and Politics Belong Together': Post-Holocaust Memory and the Sexual Revolution in West Germany," *Critical Inquiry* 24, no. 2 (winter 1998), pp. 118–19.

CHAPTER ONE
SEX AND THE THIRD REICH

1. The "will to know" is not just a term coined by Michel Foucault, but rather was already in use in the immediate aftermath of Nazism; as used then, the term was clearly meant also to convey a violent aspect in the drive for comprehension. See the comments on Nazi doctors' criminality, dilettantism, and overweening "will to know" (*Wissenwollen*) in Otto Bernhard Roegele, "Wertloses Leben?" *Rheinischer Merkur*, 30 Aug. 1947, p. 2. Roegele was a prominent western German Catholic publicist. But see also another postwar (Soviet zone) commentator's insistence that Nazi doctors, although indeed criminals, were *not* motivated by "the passionate urge for knowledge and understanding, that characterizes true research"; they were not genuine intellectuals but rather "workmen, who have learned nothing but the application of the routine and practice of experimentation." See Kühne, "Der Nürnberger Ärzteprozess," *Das deutsche Gesundheitswesen* 2, no. 5 (1 Mar. 1947), p. 145.

2. For example, see G. Schubert, *Die künstliche Scheidenbildung aus dem Mastdarm nach Schubert* (Stuttgart: F. Enke, 1936), reviewed by W. Stoeckel in *Zentralblatt für Gynäkologie* 60, no. 45 (7 Nov. 1936), p. 2672; H. R. Schmidt-Elmendorff, "Künstliche Scheidenbildung durch vernix-caseosa-Tamponade und Follikelhormon," *Zentralblatt für Gynäkologie* 61, no. 45 (6 Nov. 1937), pp. 2602–3; F. Beetz, "Über die von den weiblichen Geschlechtswerkzeugen auslösbaren Empfindungsqualitäten," *Archiv für Gynäkologie* 162, no. 1 (1936); U. Hintzelmann, "Über das Sexualtonikum 'Effecton-Dragées,' " *Deutsche medizinische Wochenschrift* 61 (1935), pp. 379–80; H. Ritter, "Über Erfahrungen und Erfolge mit Hypophysenvorderlappenpräparat bei Impotentia coeundi et generandi," *Dermatologische Wochenschrift* 105, no. 45 (1937), p. 1467; Paul Schmidt, "Zur Behandlung der männlichen Impotenz," *Die Medizinische Welt* 12, no. 22 (1938), pp. 783–84; B. Belonoschkin, "Weibliche Psyche und Konzeption," *Münchener medizinische Wochenschrift* 88 (1941), pp. 1007–9; Carl Clauberg, "Nachweis der Wirkung von künstlich zugeführtem Corpus luteum—Hormon am Menschen," *Zentralblatt für Gynäkologie* 57, no. 32 (12 Aug. 1933), pp. 1895–96; Carl Clauberg, "Das Wesen der weiblichen Sexualhormone," *Schriften der Physikalisch-Ökonomischen Gesellschaft zu Königsberg* 68 (1935), p. 205; Carl Clauberg, "Die Stimulierung der männlichen Geschlechtsdrüse durch weibliches Sexualhormon (Tierexperimentelle Untersuchungen)," *Zentralblatt für Gynäkologie* 60, no. 25 (20 June 1936), pp. 1457–64; and Carl Clauberg, "Konzeptionsoptimum," *Deutsche medizinische Wochenschrift* 69 (July 1943), pp. 548–49. On the genital, reproductive, and hormonal experiments as forms of torture, see Olga Lengyel, "Scientific Experiments," in *Different Voices: Women and the Holocaust*, ed. Carol Rittner and John K. Roth (New York: Paragon House, 1993); Jörg Müllner, "Heimkehr des Monstrums," *Die*

Woche, 6 Oct. 1995, p. 10; and Ernst Klee, *Auschwitz, die NS-Medizin und ihre Opfer* (Frankfurt am Main: Fischer, 1997).

3. Liliana Cavani quoted in Hartmut Schulze, "Was ist so sexy am Faschismus?" *Konkret*, Apr. 1975, p. 41. Cavani also confessed that she personally found SS uniforms to be "very erotic." See "Was ist am Faschismus so sexy?" *Der Spiegel*, 17 Feb. 1975, p. 126. Referring to French and German films indulging in nostalgic and decadent representations of the 1930s and 1940s as well as movies made by the Italian directors Cavani, Pier Paolo Pasolini, Luchino Visconti, and Bernardo Bertolucci, *Der Spiegel* noted that "these films were all made by people who call themselves Marxists" and hypothesized that the 1970s turn toward a fascination with highly aestheticized sadomasochism and deviant sexuality as an explanation for fascism and Nazism had a great deal to do with the political and cultural defeat of the New Left (pp. 123–24). On these and related matters, see as well Karl W. Pawek, "Im Dritten Reich der Sinne," *Konkret*, Aug. 1978, pp. 44–45; Lucy S. Dawidowicz, "Smut and Anti-Semitism," in *The Jewish Presence: Essays on Identity and History* (New York: Holt, Rinehart and Winston, 1977); Saul Friedländer, *Reflections of Nazism: An Essay on Kitsch and Death*, trans. Thomas Weyr (New York: Harper & Row, 1984); Alvin H. Rosenfeld, "The Fascination of Abomination," in *Imagining Hitler* (Bloomington: Indiana Univ. Press, 1985); Joan Smith, "Holocaust Girls," in *Misogynies: Reflections on Myths and Malice* (New York: Fawcett, 1991); Linda Mizejewski, *Divine Decadence: Fascism, Female Spectacle, and the Makings of Sally Bowles* (Princeton: Princeton Univ. Press, 1992); and Lynn Rapaport, "Holocaust Pornography: Profaning the Sacred in *Ilsa, She-Wolf of the SS*," *Shofar* 22, no. 1 (fall 2003).

4. For a devastating documentation and critique of the tendency of British and American (and some German exiled) commentators to locate the source of Nazism above all in a (defensively denied, repressed, and repudiated) latent homosexuality, see Carolyn Dean, "Who Was the 'Real' Hitler?" in *The Fragility of Empathy after the Holocaust* (Ithaca: Cornell Univ. Press, 2004). For an acute analysis of American commentators' obsessive insistence on continually relinking Nazism with homosexuality rather than with the murderous homophobia that became Nazism's far more defining feature, see Paul Morrison, "Lavender Fascists," in *The Explanation for Everything: Essays on Sexual Subjectivity* (New York: New York Univ. Press, 2001), pp. 140–61.

5. For a good introduction to the case and its ramifications, see Eleanor Hancock, " 'Only the Real, the True, the Masculine Held Its Value': Ernst Röhm, Masculinity, and Male Homosexuality," *Journal of the History of Sexuality* 8, no. 4 (1998).

6. See especially Gert Hekma, Harry Oosterhuis, and James D. Steakley, eds., *Gay Men and the Sexual History of the Political Left* (New York: Haworth, 1995); Andrew Hewitt, *Political Inversions: Homosexuality, Fascism and the Modernist Imaginary* (Stanford: Stanford Univ. Press, 1996); and Anson Rabinbach, "Van der Lubbe—ein Lustknabe Röhms? Die politische Dramaturgie der Exilkampagne zum Reichstagsbrand," in *Homophobie und Staatsräson: Zur Entstehung der Idee des Homosexuellen Staatsfeindes in Deutschland 1900 bis 1945*, ed. Susanne zur Nieden (Frankfurt am Main and New York: Campus, 2004).

7. Geoffrey J. Giles, "The Institutionalization of Homosexual Panic in the Third Reich," in *Social Outsiders in Nazi Germany*, ed. Robert Gellately and Nathan Stoltzfuss (Princeton: Princeton Univ. Press, 2001). See also the important reflections in Harry Oosterhuis, "Medicine, Male Bonding and Homosexuality in Nazi Germany," *Journal of Contemporary History* 32, no. 2 (1997).

8. On the difficulties—and yet also value—of trying to find a language to express the repudiated-but-palpable homoerotic elements of some forms of heterosexual male rivalry and bonding without simultaneously either reinforcing homophobic assumptions or relying more generally on (both empirically and conceptually untenable) notions of sexual "normality," see the debates between Martin Dannecker and Randall Halle over how to interpret Frankfurt School theorists Theodor Adorno's and Erich Fromm's at once deeply problematic but not completely unperceptive comments about homoeroticism and totalitarianism. Randall Halle, "Zwischen Marxismus und Psychoanalyse: Antifaschismus und Antihomosexualität in der Frankfurter Schule," *Zeitschrift für Sexualforschung* 9, no. 4 (1996); Martin Dannecker, "Die Kritische Theorie und ihr Konzept der Homosexualität: Antwort auf Randall Halle," *Zeitschrift für Sexualforschung* 10, no. 1 (1997); and Randall Halle, "Wer ist hier Don Quixote? Antwort auf Martin Dannecker," *Zeitschrift für Sexualforschung* 10, no. 3 (1997). Theodor Adorno's much-debated remark (written 1944 and published 1951) that "totality and homosexuality go together" is in *Minima Moralia: Reflexionen aus dem beschädigten Leben*, in *Gesammelte Schriften*, vol. 4 (Frankfurt am Main: Suhrkamp, 1980), p. 51. See in this context also the discussion of the coexistence of homophobia and homoeroticism and of the homoerotic elements in misogynist sexual violence in Peggy Sanday, "The XYZ Express," in *Fraternity Gang Rape: Sex, Brotherhood, and Privilege on Campus* (New York: New York Univ. Press, 1990).

9. For outstanding analyses, see Manfred Herzer, "Hinweise auf das schwule Berlin in der Nazizeit," in *Eldorado: Homosexuelle Frauen und Männer in Berlin 1850–1950—Geschichte, Alltag, Kultur*, ed. Berlin Museum (Berlin: Frölich und Kaufmann, 1984); and Manfred Herzer, "'Die entsetzlichsten Homosexuellenpogrome der Neuzeit'—Wie werden die Massenmorde an schwulen Männern im NS erklärt?" *Capri: Zeitschrift für schwule Geschichte*, no. 32 (June 2002). For further valuable introductions to the pertinent issues, see Erik N. Jensen, "The Pink Triangle and Political Consciousness: Gays, Lesbians, and the Memory of Nazi Persecution," *Journal of the History of Sexuality* 11, nos. 1–2 (Jan.–Apr. 2002); and Burkhard Jellonek and Rüdiger Lautmann, eds., *Nationalsozialistischer Terror gegen Homosexuelle: Verdrängt und ungesühnt* (Paderborn: Ferdinand Schöningh, 2002).

10. For important examples, see zur Nieden, *Homophobie und Staatsräson*; Stefan Micheler, "Selbstbilder und Fremdbilder der 'Anderen': Eine Geschichte Männer begehrender Männer in der Weimarer Republik und der NS-Zeit" (Ph.D. diss., University of Hamburg, 2003); John C. Fout, "Homosexuelle in der NS-Zeit: Neue Forschungsansätze über Alltagsleben und Verfolgung," Claudia Schoppmann, "Zeit der Maskierung: Zur Situation lesbischer Frauen im Nationalsozialismus," and Angela H. Mayer, "'Schwachsinn höheren Grades': Zur Verfolgung lesbischer Frauen in Österreich während der NS-Zeit," all in Jellonek and Lautmann, *Nationalsozialistischer Terror gegen Homosexuelle*; Geoffrey J. Giles,

"The Denial of Homosexuality: Same-Sex Incidents in Himmler's SS and Police," *Journal of the History of Sexuality* 11, nos. 1–2 (Jan.–Apr. 2002); Joachim Müller and Andreas Sternweiler, eds., *Homosexuelle Männer im KZ Sachsenhausen* (Berlin: Rosa Winkel, 2000); Andreas Pretzel and Gabrielle Rossbach, eds., *Wegen der zu erwartenden hohen Strafe: Homosexuellenverfolgung in Berlin 1933–1945* (Berlin: Rosa Winkel, 2000); Claudia Schoppmann, *Verbotene Verhältnisse: Frauenliebe 1938–1945* (Berlin: Querverlag, 1999); and Cornelia Limpricht, Jürgen Müller, and Nina Oxenius, eds., *"Verführte" Männer: Das Leben der kölner Homosexuellen im Dritten Reich* (Cologne: Volksblatt, 1991). See also the testimony on the gang rape by Soviet and French POWs (ordered by the SS) of lesbian prisoners in a German concentration camp (Bützow in Mecklenburg) in Ina Kuckuc, *Der Kampf gegen Unterdrückung: Materialien aus der deutschen Lesbierinnenbewegung* 2nd ed. (Munich: Frauenoffensive, 1977), pp. 127–28.

11. For a recent example of this approach in an otherwise highly interesting analysis of Hitler's relationships to women and of many German women's attraction to the Nazi movement, see Jutta Brückner, "Politik und Perversion: Die Frauen und das Unbewusste des 3. Reichs" (paper to be presented at the Goethe Institut, New York, 11 Nov. 2004). (Brückner is relying for this point on the work of French psychoanalyst Jeanine Chasseguet-Smirgel.) For a critique of Chasseguet-Smirgel, see Morrison, "Lavender Fascists," p. 148.

12. For sharp critical analyses of the tendency of both more recent observers and postwar commentators to feminize fascism and thereby displace responsibility for Nazism away from men and onto women, see Eva Sternheim-Peters, "Brunst, Ekstase, Orgasmus: Männerphantasien zum Thema 'Hitler und die Frauen,' " *Psychologie Heute* 8 (1981); Silke Wenk, "Hin-weg-sehen oder: Faschismus, Normalität, und Sexismus," in *Erbeutete Sinne: Nachträge zur Berliner Ausstellung "Inszenierung der Macht, ästhetische Faszination im Faschismus,"* ed. Klaus Behnken and Frank Wagner (Berlin: NGBK, 1988), pp. 17–32; Kathrin Hoffmann-Curtius, "Feminisierung des Faschismus," in *Die Nacht hat zwölf Stunden, dann kommt schon der Tag,* ed. Claudia Keller (Berlin: Aufbau, 1996); and Elizabeth D. Heineman, "Sexuality and Nazism: The Doubly Unspeakable?" *Journal of the History of Sexuality* 11, nos. 1–2 (Jan.–Apr. 2002), pp. 25–33. For examples of texts that do assume a peculiar predilection of women to be aroused by Hitler, see Joachim Fest, *Das Gesicht des Dritten Reiches: Profile einer totalitären Herrschaft* (Munich: R. Piper, 1963); and Maria Macciocchi, *Jungfrauen, Mütter und ein Führer: Frauen im Faschismus* (Berlin: Wagenbach, 1976). See also the important reflections in Jane Caplan, "Introduction to Female Sexuality in Fascist Ideology," *Feminist Review* 1, no. 1 (1979). On female perpetrators being represented as the epitome of Nazi evil, see Claus Füllberg-Stollberg et al., eds., *Frauen in Konzentrationslagern* (Bremen: Edition Temmen, 1994); Insa Eschebach, "Interpreting Female Perpetrators: Ravensbrück Guards in the Courts of East Germany, 1946–1955," in *Lessons and Legacies V: The Holocaust and Justice,* ed. Ronald Smelser (Evanston, IL: Northwestern Univ. Press, 2002); Alexandra Przyrembel, "Transfixed by an Image: Ilse Koch, the 'Kommandeuse of Buchenwald,' " *German History* 19, no. 3 (2001); and Lynn Rapaport, "Holocaust Pornography."

13. For a good recent summary of scholarly findings on the contributions Nazism made to the modernization of women's roles, including a critical assessment of earlier scholars' faulty assumptions of pervasive female oppression and victimization under Nazism, see Hans-Ulrich Wehler, *Deutsche Gesellschaftsgeschichte*, vol. 4 (Munich: C. H. Beck, 2003), pp. 752–60. Yet note that Wehler too makes a problematic assertion about the purported "orgiastic" expression on women's (but apparently not men's?) faces at the sight of Hitler (p. 758).

14. Essen-based historian Alexander Geppert is currently writing a scholarly book on the hundreds of love letters sent by German women to Adolf Hitler. For public fascination with this phenomenon, see H. J. Vehlewald, "Forscher untersuchen Liebesbriefe an Nazi-Diktator Hitler: Süsser Adolf, ich bin zu allem bereit," *Bild*, 13 Feb. 2004, available at Bild.T-Online.de. For a recent attempt to theorize the swooning crowds of men and women, see Christoph Kühberger, "Sexualisierter Rausch in der Diktatur: Geschlecht und Masse im italienischen Faschismus und deutschen Nationalsozialismus," *Zeitschrift für Geschichtswissenschaft* 51, no. 10 (2003).

15. On both the shreds of available evidence and on contemporaries' and subsequent commentators' fantasies about Hitler's personal sexual eccentricities, see Ron Rosenbaum, *Explaining Hitler: The Search for the Origins of His Evil* (New York: Random House, 1998); Dean, "Who Was the 'Real' Hitler?"; Hoffmann-Curtius, "Feminisierung des Faschismus"; Brückner, "Politik und Perversion"; and Vera Laska, "Sex," in *Women in the Resistance and in the Holocaust: The Voices of Eyewitnessess* (Westport, CT: Greenwood, 1983).

16. Rapaport, "Holocaust Pornography," p. 79; see also p. 71. See also Jean-Pierre Geuens, "Pornography and the Holocaust: The Last Transgression," *Film Criticism* 20 (fall—winter 1996); and the comments on Holocaust imagery in pornography in Israel in the interview with Susie Bright, in Andrea Juno and Vivian Vale, eds., *Angry Women* (San Francisco: Re/Search Publications, 1991), pp. 201–2. On the seemingly arousing but actually ultimately soothing and reassuring qualities of pornography, see also Silke Wenk, "Rhetoriken der Pornografisierung: Rahmungen des Blicks auf die NS-Verbrechen," in *Gedächtnis und Geschlecht: Deutungsmuster in Darstellungen des nationalsozialistischen Genozids*, ed. Insa Eschebach, Sigrid Jacobeit, and Silke Wenk (Frankfurt am Main: Campus, 2002).

17. The classic statement on the use of Nazi paraphernalia for erotic purposes is Susan Sontag, "Fascinating Fascism," *New York Review of Books*, 6 Feb. 1975. The most recent round of public fascination with actual pornographic films produced during the Third Reich—and with what the fact that they were produced during the Third Reich might suggest about the Third Reich more generally—was triggered by the announcement that German writer Thor Kunkel's novel *Endstufe* (Final Stage) had been rejected by the press, Rowohlt, that had paid him an advance for it and had widely advertised that it was forthcoming. Apparently concerned that the Holocaust was referenced in the novel with inadequate sensitivity, Rowohlt extricated itself from its arrangements with Kunkel. The Eichborn press in Berlin will be publishing a revised version of the novel. See Luke Harding, "Porn und Drang," *Guardian*, 12 Feb. 2004; and Volker Weidermann, "Die Nackten und die Toten," *Frankfurter Allgemeine Sonntagszeitung*, 1 Feb. 2004. On the real films on which Kunkel's fiction is based, see Daniel

Kothenschulte's interview with film collector Werner Nekes, "Professionell: Der Sammler Werner Nekes über Pornofilme aus der Nazizeit," *Frankfurter Rundschau online*, 7 Feb. 2004.

18. In this context, see also the perceptive reflections in Omer Bartov, "Kitsch and Sadism in Ka-Tzetnik's Other Planet: Israeli Youth Imagine the Holocaust," *Jewish Social Studies* 3 (winter 1997).

19. Joachim Hohmann, *Sexualforschung und -aufklärung in der Weimarer Republik* (Berlin: Foerster, 1985), p. 9; Sabine Weissler, "Sexy Sixties," in *CheSchah-Shit: Die Sechziger Jahre zwischen Cocktail und Molotow*, ed. Eckhard Siepmann et al. (Berlin: Elefanten Press, 1984), p. 99; Christian de Nuys-Henkelmann, "'Wenn die rote Sonne abends im Meer versinkt . . .': Die Sexualmoral der fünfziger Jahre," in *Sexualmoral und Zeitgeist im 19. und 20. Jahrhundert*, ed. Anja Bagel-Bohlan and Michael Salewski (Opladen: Leske & Budrich, 1990), p. 109; Scott Spector, "Was the Third Reich Movie-Made? Interdisciplinarity and the Reframing of 'Ideology,' " *American Historical Review* 106, no. 2 (April 2001), p. 472.

20. This prevalent argument is summarized in (and given some endorsement by) Erich Goldhagen, "Nazi Sexual Demonology," *Midstream*, May 1981, p. 11.

21. Friedrich Koch, *Sexuelle Denunziation: Die Sexualität in der politischen Auseinandersetzung* (Frankfurt am Main: Syndikat, 1986), p. 60.

22. Udo Pini, *Leibeskult und Liebeskitsch: Erotik im Dritten Reich* (Munich: Klinkhardt and Biermann, 1992), pp. 9–11. See also Stefan Maiwald and Gerd Mischler, *Sexualität unter dem Hakenkreuz: Manipulation und Vernichtung der Intimsphäre im NS-Staat* (Hamburg and Vienna: Europa Verlag, 1999): "The total state leaves no room in German beds for self-determined sex. The subjects of the NS-state have to forfeit their sexuality unconditionally to the regime" (p. 57).

23. Mayer, " 'Schwachsinn höheren Grades,' " p. 84.

24. Annette Miersch, *Schulmädchen-Report: Der deutsche Sexfilm der 70er Jahre* (Berlin: Bertz, 2003), p. 69.

25. Jeffrey Herf, "One-Dimensional Man" (review of Herbert Marcuse, *War, Technology and Fascism*), *New Republic*, 1 Feb. 1999, p. 39.

26. George Mosse, *The Image of Man: The Creation of Modern Masculinity* (New York: Oxford Univ. Press, 1996), pp. 175–76. For the ongoing resonance of Mosse's perspectives, see also John Borneman, "*Gottvater, Landesvater, Familienvater*: Identification and Authority in Germany," in *Death of the Father*, ed. Borneman (New York: Berghahn Books, 2004).

27. See George L. Mosse, "Beauty without Sensuality: The Exhibition *Entartete Kunst*," in *"Degenerate Art": The Fate of the Avant-Garde in Nazi Germany*, ed. Stephanie Barron (Los Angeles: Museum Associates, 1991), pp. 25–31.

28. For example, see Hans Dieter Schäfer, *Das gespaltene Bewusstsein: Über deutsche Kultur und Lebenswirklichkeit 1933–1945* (Munich: Carl Hanser, 1985); Detlev Peukert, *Inside Nazi Germany: Conformity, Opposition and Racism in Everyday Life*, trans. Richard Deveson (New Haven, CT: Yale Univ. Press, 1987); Peter Reichel, *Der schöne Schein des Dritten Reiches: Faszination und Gewalt des Faschismus* (Munich: Carl Hanser, 1991); Shelley Baranowski, *Kraft durch Freude—Strength through Joy: Tourism, Leisure and Consumerism in the Third Reich* (Cambridge: Cambridge Univ. Press, 2004); Norbert Frei, "Wie mo-

dern war der Nationalsozialismus?" *Geschichte und Gesellschaft* 19 (1993); Peter Fritzsche, "Nazi Modern," *Modernism/Modernity* 3, no. 1 (1996); Jeffrey Herf, *Reactionary Modernism: Technology, Culture, and Politics in Weimar and the Third Reich* (Cambridge: Cambridge Univ. Press, 1984).

29. For example, see Hans von Hattingberg, *Über die Liebe: Eine Aerztliche Wegweisung* (Munich: J. F. Lehmanns, 1936), p. 10; Matthias Laros, *Die Beziehungen der Geschlechter* (Cologne: Staufen-Verlag, 1936), p. 167; Paul Habermann, "Zur Frage der Sexualpädagogik," *Kinderärztliche Praxis* 16, nos. 9–10 (1948), p. 288.

30. For example, see Benno Chajes, "Die Ehe des Proletariers," and Adolf Gerson, "Die Ursachen der Prostitution," both in *Sexual-Probleme*, Sept. 1908, pp. 524–25, 541; Hans Albrecht, "Ueber Konzeptionsverhütung," *Münchener medizinische Wochenschrift*, no. 9 (27 Feb. 1931), pp. 347–50; Johannes Ehwalt, *Eheleben und Ehescheidung in unsrer Zeit: Aufzeichnungen eines Rechtsanwaltes* (Berlin: Germania, 1936), pp. 4–5; Gerhard Reinhard Ritter, *Die geschlechtliche Frage in der deutschen Volkserziehung* (Berlin and Cologne: A. Marcus und E. Weber, 1936), p. 28; and Dr. Wollenweber, "Das Gesundheitswesen im Kampfe gegen den Geburtenschwund," *Der öffentliche Gesundheitsdienst* 5 (1939–40), p. 447. See also the interesting survey conducted in 1932 of doctors' perceptions of the pervasiveness of premarital sex: "Erhebung über Sexualmoral," in *Studien über Autorität und Familie: Forschungsberichte aus dem Institut für Sozialforschung*, ed. Max Horkheimer (Paris: Félix Alcan, 1936). On significant class differences in experiences of premarital sex (girls in that minority of the population that was middle or upper class tended to wait longer, while in the working class premarital sex was the norm), see the summary of research conducted between 1925 and 1930 in Johannes Dück, "Virginität und Ehe," *Archiv für Bevölkerungswissenschaft und Bevölkerungspolitik* 11 (1941), p. 306.

31. See Julia Roos, "Backlash against Prostitutes' Rights: Origins and Dynamics of Nazi Prostitution Policies," *Journal of the History of Sexuality* 11, nos. 1–2 (Jan.–Apr. 2002), pp. 67–78; Julie Stubbs, "Rescuing Endangered Girls: Bourgeois Feminism, Social Welfare, and the Debate over Prostitution in the Weimar Republic" (Ph.D. diss., University of Michigan, 2001); Derek Hastings, "Between Church and Culture: The Rise and Crisis of Progressive Catholicism in Munich, 1900–1924" (Ph.D. diss., University of Chicago, 2004); and Tim Kaiser's dissertation on Protestants in Weimar (University of Michigan). See also the periodization of mores suggested by B. van Acken, S.J., "Prüderie—Distanzhalten," *Theologisch-praktische Quartalschrift* 92 (1939), pp. 77–78.

32. For example, see John S. Conway, *The Nazi Persecution of the Churches, 1933–45* (London: Weidenfeld and Nicolson, 1968); Wolfgang Gerlach, *Als die Zeugen schwiegen: Bekennende Kirche und die Juden* (Berlin: Institut Kirche und Judentum, 1987); Ernst Klee, *"Die SA Jesu Christi": Die Kirchen im Banne Hitlers* (Frankfurt am Main: Fischer, 1989); Victoria Barnett, *For the Soul of the People: Protestant Protest against Hitler* (New York: Oxford Univ. Press, 1992); Robert P. Ericksen and Susannah Heschel, "The German Churches Face Hitler: An Assessment of the Historiography," *Tel Aviver Jahrbuch für Deutsche Geschichte* 23 (1994), pp. 433–59; Wolfgang Stegemann and Dirk Acksteiner, eds., *Kirche und Nationalsozialismus* (Stuttgart: Kohlhammer, 1997); Robert P. Erick-

sen and Susannah Heschel, eds., *Betrayal: German Churches and the Holocaust* (Minneapolis: Fortress Press, 1999); David Kertzer, *The Popes against the Jews: The Vatican's Role in the Rise of Modern Antisemitism* (New York: Knopf, 2001); Daniel Jonah Goldhagen, *A Moral Reckoning: The Role of the Catholic Church in the Holocaust and Its Unfulfilled Duty of Repair* (New York: Knopf, 2002); Michael Burleigh, "The Brown Cult and the Christians," in *The Third Reich: A New History* (New York: Hill and Wang, 2000); Wehler, *Deutsche Gesellschaftsgeschichte*, 4:795–818; Jochen-Christoph Kaiser and Martin Greschat, eds., *Der Holocaust und die Protestanten* (Frankfurt am Main: Athenäum, 1988); Doris Bergen, *Twisted Cross: The German Christian Movement in the Third Reich* (Chapel Hill: Univ. of North Carolina Press, 1996); Richard Steigmann-Gall, *The Holy Reich: Nazi Conceptions of Christianity, 1919–1945* (Cambridge: Cambridge Univ. Press, 2003); Gerhard Besier, *Die Kirchen und das Dritte Reich: Spaltungen und Abwehrkämpfe 1934–1937* (Munich: Propyläen, 2001); and Manfred Gailus, review of Besier, *Die Kirchen und das Dritte Reich*, in *Die Zeit*, 27 Mar. 2002.

33. For example, the head of the official Nazi women's organization, Gertrud Scholtz-Klink, organized a letter-writing campaign of women's clubs against the pornographic style of the antisemitic Nazi newspaper *Der Stürmer*. See Ingke Brodersen, Klaus Humann, and Susanne von Paczensky, eds., *1933: Wie die Deutschen Hitler zur Macht verhalfen. Ein Lesebuch für Demokraten* (Reinbek: Rowohlt, 1983), p. 38.

34. Venereal disease prevention expert Bodo Spiethoff, quoted in Annette F. Timm, "Sex with a Purpose: Prostitution, Venereal Disease, and Militarized Masculinity in the Third Reich," *Journal of the History of Sexuality* 11, nos. 1–2 (Jan.–Apr. 2002), p. 230.

35. R. Hunger, "Grundgedanken zur Sexualerziehung der deutschen Jugend," *Dermatologische Wochenschrift* 105, no. 5 (Oct. 1937), p. 1344 (Flex's comment is the epigraph); P. Orlowski, "Zur Frage der Pathogenese und der modernen Therapie der sexuellen Störungen beim Manne," *Zeitschrift für Urologie* 31, no. 6 (1937), p. 380.

36. August Mayer, *Deutsche Mutter und deutscher Aufstieg* (Munich: J. F. Lehmanns, 1938), p. 31; Fritz Reinhardt, "Frühehe und Kinderreichtum im nationalsozialistischen Staat," *Neues Volk* 5, no. 7 (1937), pp. 22–24.

37. Martin Staemmler, *Rassenpflege im völkischen Staat*, 2nd ed. (Munich: J. F. Lehmanns, 1933), pp. 61, 64.

38. A good example of the conservative pedagogical literature is Walter Hermannsen and Karl Blome, *Warum hat man uns das nicht früher gesagt? Ein Bekenntnis deutscher Jugend zu geschlechtlicher Sauberkeit*, 4th rev. and exp. ed. (Munich: J. F. Lehmanns, 1943). In general, the series on "Political Biology" published by the J. F. Lehmanns press in Munich (in which also more than thirty thousand copies of Hermannsen and Blome's book were printed) served as a steady source of sexually conservative views.

39. For one doctor's account of the "consistently positive, sometimes enthusiastic" resonance he achieved among those considered "the fully valuable" (*Vollwertigen*) among his female patients when—in order to encourage them to desist from the use of contraceptives and bear more children—he flattered their figures

or expressly contrasted their good health with those "mentally ill and disabled persons . . . who after all are being sterilized," see Wollenweber, "Das Gesundheitsamt," pp. 454–55. Incidentally, Wollenweber had no objections to premarital sex. "From a population-political standpoint I cannot see it as a tragedy if a young man in the city or in the countryside, in the youthful rush of love, takes his girl in his arms and has sexual intercourse with her" (p. 452).

40. Herbert Marcuse, *One-Dimensional Man: Studies in the Ideology of Advanced Industrial Society* (Boston: Beacon Press, 1964), p. 56. The idea, as Reimut Reiche concisely summarized it, was that "sexuality is given a little more rein and thus brought into the service of safeguarding the system." Reimut Reiche, *Sexuality and Class Struggle* (London: NLB, 1970), p. 46.

41. The poster is reprinted in Klaus Theweleit, *Male Fantasies*, vol. 2 (Minneapolis: Univ. of Minnesota Press, 1989), p. 9.

42. The cartoon (from the *Deutschvölkische Monatshefte* in 1923) is reprinted in Christina von Braun, "Und der Feind ist Fleisch geworden: Der rassistische Antisemitismus," in *Der Ewige Judenhass: Christlicher Antijudaismus, Deutschnationale Judenfeindlichkeit, Rassistischer Antisemitismus*, ed. von Braun and Ludger Heid (Berlin and Vienna: Philo, 2000), between pp. 192 and 193.

43. See Arthur Dinter, *Die Sünde wider das Blut: Ein Zeitroman* (Leipzig: Matthes und Thost, 1920); and the discussion of Dinter in E. Goldhagen, "Nazi Sexual Demonology."

44. Adolf Hitler, *Mein Kampf* (Munich: Franz Eher/Zentralverlag der NSDAP, 1943), p. 357.

45. Max Marcuse, *Der Präventivverkehr in der Medizinischen Lehre und Ärztlichen Praxis* (Stuttgart: Enke, 1931), pp. 4, 65–66, 91, 103–4.

46. See Manfred Herzer, *Magnus Hirschfeld: Leben und Werk eines jüdischen, schwulen und sozialistischen Sexologen* (Frankfurt: Campus, 1992).

47. For example, see Max Hodann, *Bub und Mädel: Gespräche unter Kameraden über die Geschlechterfrage* (Rudolstadt: Greifenverlag, 1929). On Hodann's significance, see Kristine von Soden, *Die Sexualberatungsstellen der Weimarer Republik 1919–1933* (Berlin: Hentrich, 1988), pp. 72–74; and Atina Grossmann, *Reforming Sex: The German Movement for Birth Control and Abortion Reform, 1920–1950* (New York: Oxford Univ. Press, 1995), pp. 122–26. Grossmann notes that Hodann was considered far more important by his colleagues than the somewhat "crazy" Wilhelm Reich, who would in the later 1960s become so immensely popular with the West German student movement. Above all, Grossmann provides an incisive critical assessment of the limitations of the Weimar-era sex reform movement, including among other things its imbrication with eugenics, its tendency to normativity, and its inconsistent attention to women's perspectives on sex.

48. See Grossmann, *Reforming Sex*, pp. 81–84; and Cornelie Usborne, "Representation of Abortion in Weimar Popular Culture" (paper delivered at the German Historical Institute, Washington, DC, 26 Oct. 2002).

49. Georg Schliebe, "Die Reifezeit und ihre Erziehungsprobleme," in *Wege und Ziele der Kindererziehung unserer Zeit*, 3rd ed., ed. Martin Löpelmann (Leipzig: Hesse and Becker, 1936), p. 148.

50. Walter Tetzlaff, "Homosexualität und Jugend," *Deutsche Jugendhilfe* 34 (1942–43), p. 5.

51. "Die Rolle des Juden in der Medizin," *Deutsche Volksgesundheit aus Blut und Boden* (Aug.–Sept. 1933), reprinted in *"Hier geht das Leben auf eine sehr merkwürdige Weise weiter . . .": Zur Geschichte der Psychoanalyse in Deutschland*, ed. Karen Brecht et al. (Hamburg: Verlag Michael Kellner, 1985), p. 87.

52. Chemnitz-based pediatrician Kurt Oxenius, quoted in Martin Staemmler, "Das Judentum in der Medizin," *Sächsisches Ärzteblatt* 104 (1934), p. 208.

53. "Homosexualität—keine Erbkrankheit," *Deutsche Sonderschule* 5 (1938), p. 663.

54. Quoted in Koch, *Sexuelle Denunziation*, p. 62.

55. Text of book-burning speech reprinted in Brodersen et al., *1933*, p. 34.

56. According to Hunger, "Jewish psychoanalysis" worked "*individualistically-autistically,*" while, by contrast, "*German psychotherapy*" (*Deutsche Seelsorge*) was more oriented toward the "*holistic coherence of the soul and the community that creation intended.*" Heinz Hunger, "Jüdische Psychoanalyse und deutsche Seelsorge," in *Germanentum, Judentum und Christentum*, vol. 2, ed. Walter Grundmann (Leipzig: G. Wigand, 1943), pp. 314, 317, 332, 339.

57. For example, see Johannes H. Schultz, "Die Bedeutung der Psychoanalyse im Kampfe mit uns selbst," *Jahreskurse für ärztliche Fortbildung* 24, no. 5 (1933), pp. 8–18; Rudolf Allers, *Sexualpädagogik: Grundlagen und Grundlinien* (Salzburg and Leipzig: Anton Pustet, 1934), pp. 45–47; von Hattingberg, "'Chemische Liebe' (der Irrtum Freuds)," in *Über die Liebe*, pp. 25–30; H. Eymer, "Zur Frage der Scheidenspülung," *Deutsches Ärzteblatt* 72 (1942), p. 320; and Joachim Rost, "Sexuelle Probleme im Felde," *Medizinische Welt* 18 (1944), pp. 218–220.

58. Staemmler, "Das Judentum in der Medizin," p. 210.

59. See ibid., p. 208; and "Dreht sich alles um die Liebe?" *Das schwarze Korps* (hereafter *DSK*), 25 June 1936, p. 7.

60. See Alfred Zeplin, *Sexualpädagogik als Grundlage des Familienglücks und des Volkswohls* (Rostock: Carl Hinstorffs, 1938), p. 31.

61. Alfred Rosenberg, *Unmoral im Talmud* (Munich: Franz Eher, 1943), p. 19. The book was originally published in 1933.

62. Staemmler, "Das Judentum in der Medizin," p. 208. Or as Staemmler remarked elsewhere, lambasting Max Marcuse in particular, that there was "no longer anything sacred in the intercourse between the sexes" was a consequence of the "prominent role played by the Jew" in the development of "the new sexual morality." Staemmler, *Rassenpflege*, pp. 59, 61.

63. "Die Rolle des Juden in der Medizin," p. 87.

64. For example, see "Der Kastrierjude," *Der Stürmer* 10, no. 43 (Oct. 1932), p. 2.

65. See von Soden, *Die Sexualberatungsstellen*, pp. 148–49, 156; and the important reflections in Grossmann, *Reforming Sex*, pp. 136–37.

66. See Ute Frevert, *Women in German History: From Bourgeois Emancipation to Sexual Liberation* (Oxford and New York: Berg, 1989), pp. 230–32. See in this context also Cornelia Usborne, *The Politics of the Body in Weimar Germany: Women's Reproductive Rights and Duties* (Houndmills and London: Macmillan, 1992).

67. See Harald Focke and Uwe Reimer, *Alltag unterm Hakenkreuz: Wie die Nazis das Leben der Deutschen veränderten*, vol. 1 (Reinbek: Rowohlt, 1979), pp. 122–23.

68. Frevert, *Women*, p. 232. See also the statistics in Jill Stephenson, *Women in Nazi Germany* (Edinburgh: Pearson, 2001), p. 24; and Dörte Winkler, *Frauenarbeit im "Dritten Reich"* (Hamburg: Hoffmann und Campe, 1977), p. 193; as well as the discussions in S. L. Solon and Albert Brandt, "Sex under the Swastika," *American Mercury*, Aug. 1939, p. 431; Gisela Bock, "Racism and Sexism in Nazi Germany: Motherhood, Compulsory Sterilization, and the State," *Signs* 8 (spring 1983), pp. 400–421; and Robert Proctor, *Racial Hygiene: Medicine under the Nazis* (Cambridge, MA: Harvard Univ. Press, 1988), p. 126. While the overall birthrate rose from approximately 970,000 in 1933 to 1.4 million in 1939 (it sank again during the war to just over 1 million births annually), scholars have also suggested that in many cases a woman's decision to have another child could be read as less a response to regime propaganda than a strategy to avoid conscription into the labor force once the regime switched course and decided, against its earlier attempt to put women back into the home, that it needed women's labor power.

69. For example, see Weinrich, "Randbemerkungen zum Ehe-Problem," *Monatsschrift für Pastoraltheologie* 30 (1934), pp. 278–79; Theodor Haug, "Die Sexuelle Frage in der Seelsorge," *Zeitwende* 15 (1938–39), pp. 609, 614; and "Oesterreich erwache!" *DSK*, 25 Feb. 1937, p. 6.

70. Conversations with G. C., 2002, and R. W., 2004.

71. Johannes H. Schultz, *Geschlecht-Liebe-Ehe: Die Grundtatsachen des Liebes- und Geschlechtslebens in ihrer Bedeutung für Einzel- und Volksdasein* (Munich: Ernst Reinhardt, 1940), p. 111.

72. Report on conditions for foreign laborers in Nazi Germany prepared by the French Catholic Workers' Youth Movement, quoted in Pieter Lagrou, *The Legacy of Nazi Occupation: Patriotic Memory and National Recovery in Western Europe, 1945–1965* (Cambridge: Cambridge Univ. Press, 2000), p. 145. Furthermore, as historian Gabriele Czarnowski remarked with respect to condom use in the Nazi era, "one medical officer [she is referring to Dr. Wollenweber, who was based in Dortmund] noted that, especially after weekends, large numbers of them could be seen in the drains of the municipal sewage facilities." Or, as historian Robert G. Waite found, residents of Dachau complained about how the benches and grass at a park adjacent to a nearby military base were filled with teenage girls and Wehrmacht soldiers and that the park "was littered with used condoms." So strong was the regime's apparent commitment to condom production that at one point during the war, a group of mothers even complained that rubber (in increasingly short supply not least because of its use for the tires of military vehicles) was being used more for the production of condoms than for making baby bottles. It was not during the Third Reich, but rather in the *aftermath* of its defeat, that the price of condoms "quintupled." See Gabriele Czarnowski, "Hereditary and Racial Welfare (*Erb- und Rassenpflege*): The Politics of Sexuality and Reproduction in Nazi Germany," *Social Politics* 4 (1997), p. 129; Robert G. Waite, "Teenage Sexuality in Nazi Germany," *Journal of the History of Sexuality* 8, no. 3 (Jan. 1998), p. 451; Pini, *Leibeskult und Liebeskitsch*, p. 326; Kühne, "Geburtenkontrolle," *Das deutsche Gesundheitswesen* 2, no. 23 (1947), pp. 746–47.

73. See Gunter Schmidt, "Weshalb Sex alle (Un)schuld verloren hat," *taz-magazin*, 24–25 Apr. 1999, p. v.

74. See Wollenweber, "Das Gesundheitsamt," p. 451. In 1941, the regime—incoherently—ordered that the advertisement and sale of contraceptives inserted in the vagina (both spermicidal products and diaphragms and cervical caps) be outlawed entirely (in the Himmler ruling of January 1941) *and* that these items be available only in pharmacies and only with a doctor's prescription (in the Conti ruling of March 1941). Conti was the head of the Reich Medical Office. See Hans Harmsen, "Mittel zur Geburtenregelung in der Gesetzgebung des Staates, unter besonderer Berücksichtigung des neuen Entwurfes eines Strafgesetzbuches," in *Sexualität und Verbrechen*, ed. Fritz Bauer et al. (Frankfurt am Main: Fischer, 1963), p. 179. Even after Himmler's ruling went into effect, magazines continued to carry advertisements for mail-order contraceptive devices (of "hygienic rubber"), with only minimal veiling of their meaning. See Heineman, "Sexuality and Nazism," p. 46, n. 81. On the popularity also of intrauterine devices (IUDs) and their continued availability in the early years of the Third Reich (from doctors, medical and rubber supply stores, and door-to-door saleswomen), see V. Ohnesorge, "Gefahren der intrauterinen 'Schutzmittel,' " *Zeitschrift für Gynäkologie* 59 (13 Apr. 1935), p. 875.

75. Contrary to many postwar commentators' assumptions, information about the rhythm method was not censored during the Third Reich (though the method's effectiveness was certainly contested); doctors discussed in print how to use and interpret the calendars and at least as late as 1942 calendars could be purchased by mail order from Vienna. Hermann Knaus, the Austrian who had, contemporaneously with the Japanese physician Kyusaku Ogino, developed the method, continued to publish updated information on the use of the method, even as his critics published their counterarguments as well. See, for example, Hermann Knaus, "Die periodische Frucht- und Unfruchtbarkeit des Weibes," *Zentralblatt für Gynäkologie* 57, no. 24 (17 June 1933), pp. 1393–1408; Alfred Greil, "Der optimale Konzeptionstermin," *Zentralblatt für Gynäkologie* 58, no. 34 (25 Aug. 1934), pp. 2002–6; Ernst Rumpf, "Praktische Erfahrungen mit der Konzeptionstheorie nach Knaus-Ogino," *Zentralblatt für Gynäkologie* 61, no. 27 (1937), pp. 1589–92; F. Besold, "Ovulation und Orgasmus," *Zentralblatt für Gynäkologie* 65, no. 48 (1941), pp. 2111–12; and Hermann Knaus, "Was versteht man unter dem Knaus'schen Ovulations– bezw. Konzeptionstermin?" *Medizinische Welt* 16 (25 Apr. 1942), p. 428. Strikingly, moreover—though also logically—Catholic advice writers were the most active in promoting the method during the Third Reich, both to priests, continually burdened by the anguish of the couples they counseled in their offices and in the confessional, and directly to married couples. Thus, for instance, one Catholic advice writer (whose book, when reprinted in 1938, had already sold fourteen thousand copies) explained matter-of-factly to women how to monitor themselves for several months to identify their own unique variations in cycle, and also noted that as a rule of thumb the first five to seven days after the end of menstruation were safe for intercourse, then twelve days of abstinence were necessary, but that then the remaining days in the cycle were fine for having sex as well. See Hans Wirtz, *Vom Eros zur Ehe: Die natur-*

getreue Lebensgemeinschaft (Heidelberg and Innsbruck: F. H. Kerle, 1938), pp. 249–54.

The information on the rhythm method was no closely guarded secret kept from ordinary family physicians or from wives or even from unmarried women but rather appears in some circles to have been common knowledge. During the war, for instance, it was known that the military encouraged soldiers to take their leaves to see their wives during the days when conception was most likely. See Rita Thalmann, *Frausein im Dritten Reich* (Frankfurt am Main: Ullstein, 1987), p. 154. Also see how a medical doctor educated his colleagues about women's cycles (again so as to assist soldiers on short leave in maximizing the possibility for conception) in Schröder, "Konzeptionsoptimum . . . Frage 2," *Deutsche medizinische Wochenschrift* 69, nos. 29–30 (July 1943), p. 549. But unmarried young women could be familiar with enough of the information basic to the method to use it effectively. As one former junior Wehrmacht officer remembered, when asked about how pregnancy prevention worked in the Third Reich, "All of them knew about the rhythm method—doing the math with the days. After all, those were intelligent girls." (*Alle wussten von Knaus-Ogino—Tage berechnen. Das waren ja intelligente Mädchen.*) Conversation with G. C., 2002. And also postwar medical literature made clear that unmarried women had relied on the rhythm method in order to avoid pregnancy; what doctors remarked on was the way that the disruptions in cycles caused by dislocations due to work in the Reich Labor Service or to war caused unplanned conceptions. On the other hand, what also requires attention is the mental world of many young girls, in which eagerness to have sexual experiences (and the active seeking of these) coexisted with ignorance of anatomy and the process of conception; also an otherwise sophisticated girl could easily believe a boy or man who assured her "don't worry, I know what I'm doing, nothing will happen to you"—even as the girl did not know enough about bodies to be sure in retrospect whether her partners had in fact practiced withdrawal or not. Conversation with R. W., 2004.

76. Claudia Koonz, *Mothers in the Fatherland: Women, the Family and Nazi Politics* (New York: St. Martin's, 1987), p. 186. The rate of illegal voluntary abortions was still so high in 1943 that the regime instituted the death penalty for abortionists in an effort to suppress the practice. See also Robert G. Waite's informative essay, " 'Eine Sonderstellung unter den Straftaten': Die Verfolgung der Abtreibung im Dritten Reich," in *Nationalsozialistische Gewaltverbrechen und Strafverfolgung nach 1945—Forschung, Lehre und politische Bildung* (Berlin: Haus der Wannsee Villa, 2004).

77. The classic statement of Weimar Germany's uniquely open discussion of sexual response and clamorous preoccupation with the problem of female frigidity is Atina Grossmann, "The New Woman and the Rationalization of Sexuality in Weimar Germany," in *Powers of Desire: The Politics of Sexuality,* ed. Ann Snitow, Christine Stansell, and Sharon Thompson (New York: Monthly Review Press, 1983). Contrast the far greater discomfort with discussions of female pleasure in contemporaneous Great Britain in Susan Pedersen, "National Bodies, Unspeakable Acts: The Sexual Politics of Colonial Policy-Making," *Journal of Modern History* 63 (Dec. 1991). On the discussion in Weimar, see also von Soden, *Die Sexualberatungsstellen,* pp. 102, 128–33; and Anson Rabinbach, " The Politiciza-

tion of Wilhelm Reich: An Introduction to 'The Sexual Misery of the Working Masses and the Difficulties of Sexual Reform,' " *New German Critique* 1, no. 1 (winter 1974), pp. 93, 96. Evidence of the double reality of widespread dissatisfaction and growing popular conviction that mutual pleasure was achievable pervades medical doctors' writings across the ideological spectrum, from both Jewish and Gentile leftists and liberals in Weimar to Christians and Nazis in the Third Reich. For some typical Nazi-era discussions of diverse strategies (including hormonal and psychotherapeutic) for enhancing female orgasmic response, see F. Siegert, "Die Behandlung der weiblichen Frigidität," *Medizinische Welt* 12, no. 31 (July 1938), pp. 1094–98; the summary of Kemper, "Zum Frigiditätsproblem," in *Zentralblatt für Gynäkologie* 64, no. 45 (1940), pp. 1930–31; and F. Besold, "Beiträge zum Problem der Frigidität," *Zentralblatt für Psychotherapie und ihre Grenzgebiete* 12 (1940), pp. 249–56. As Besold reported, while working-class women would not use the word "orgasm" (*Orgasmus*), that was certainly what they meant when they used such terms as "being satisfied" (*befriedigt werden*), "coming to the end" (*zum Ende kommen*) and "getting done" (*fertig werden*) (p. 254). Siegert's essay provides a classic example of Nazi-era reconfigurations of preexisting pro-sex impulses; the text mentioned that female frigidity rates might be as high as 50 percent of all women, included intricate diagnostic analysis of different forms and aspects of frigidity, made careful distinctions between libido and orgasm, specified erogenous zones with precision, and carefully assessed the complex possible interrelationships between emotions and physiology, but also suggested that "racial differences" between partners—because they might lead to "psychosexual conflicts"—could be the source of female frigidity (p. 1096).

78. Staemmler, *Rassenpflege*, p. 61.

79. Ferdinand Hoffmann, *Sittliche Entartung und Geburtenschwund*, 2nd ed. (Munich: J. F. Lehmanns, 1938), pp. 13, 21, 24–25, 34.

80. Ibid., pp. 16, 30, 49–50, 55.

81. On the notion that Jewishness could have become internal to Germanness, see also the military officer who admonished his noncommissioned officers (NCOs) in 1942 not only that they needed to choose "squeaky clean" women as their brides but also that any German man still attached to a sexual double standard needed to expel the "poisonous substances of the Jewish moral perspective . . . sitting in his bones. Out with them!" Maj. Dr. Ellenbeck, "Der deutsche Unteroffizier und das Thema 'Frauen und Mädchen,' " *Die Zivilversorgung*, 15 Oct. 1942, pp. 281–82. Along related lines, see also Heinz Hunger's complaint in 1942 about the "*Jewification*" (*Verjudung*) of non-Jews influenced by sex-obsessed Jewish psychoanalysts. Hunger, "Jüdische Psychoanalyse," p. 323.

82. Paul Danzer, "Die Haltung zum anderen Geschlecht als unentbehrliche Grundlage völkischen Aufbaus," in *Streiflichter ins Völkische: Ausgewählte Lesestücke für deutsche Menschen aus dem "Völkischen Willen"* (Berlin: Rota-Druck, 1936), pp. 5–6.

83. Hans F. K. Günther, *Führeradel durch Sippenpflege*, quoted in Hermannsen and Blome, *Warum hat man uns das nicht früher gesagt?*, p. 120. Günther, an avid antisemite already during the Weimar Republic, became one of the most influential "race experts" in the Third Reich.

84. Knorr, "Eine noch nicht genügend beachtete weltanschauliche und bevölkerungspolitische Gefahr," *Ziel und Weg: Organ des Nationalsozialistischen Deutschen Ärztebundes* 7, no. 22 (Nov. 1937), p. 570.

85. Wollenweber, "Das Gesundheitsamt," p. 451.

86. Orlowski, "Zur Frage der Pathogenese," p. 383. Orlowski's message to men was that "If Nature has denied a gift, then you are not obliged to force it through practices that are damaging to you." Men's struggles to extend the duration of coitus, he warned, led to "a weakening of the ejaculatory centrum" and even to the dangerous condition of "colliculitis, in some cases a colliculus-hypertrophy."

87. On the "top secret" directive to the BDM from the Information Service of the Reich Youth Press Office, see Michael Kater, "Die deutsche Elternschaft im nationalsozialistischen Erziehungssystem," *Vierteljahresschrift für Wirtschafts- und Sozialgeschichte* 67, no. 4 (1980), p. 489. On the contrast between the BDM's official conservative rhetoric and its loose reputation in popular parlance, see also Martin Klaus, *Mädchen im Dritten Reich: Der Bund Deutscher Mädel (BDM)* (Cologne: Pahl-Rugenstein, 1983), pp. 119–20.

88. Victor Klemperer, *I Will Bear Witness: A Diary of the Nazi Years, 1933–1941*, trans. Martin Chalmers (New York: Random House, 1998), p. 137. I thank Maria Hoehn and Anson Rabinbach for calling this passage to my attention.

89. *Deutschland-Berichte der Sozialdemokratischen Partei Deutschlands (Sopade)* (Salzhausen and Frankfurt am Main: Petra Nettelbeck/Zweitausendeins, 1980), report of Aug. 1937, p. 1070. See also an earlier (1935) report by the Social Democratic Party in exile, to the effect that the so "coarsely" presented "propaganda for racially pure offspring" was leading youth to engage in "uninhibited sexuality." Quoted in Pini, *Leibeskult und Liebeskitsch*, p. 85.

90. See Clifford Kirkpatrick, *Nazi Germany: Its Women and Family Life* (Indianapolis: Bobbs-Merrill, 1938), p. 36.

91. Herbert Marcuse, *Technology, War and Fascism: Collected Papers of Herbert Marcuse*, vol. 1, ed. Douglas Kellner (London: Routledge, 1998), pp. 84–86, 90, 162–63.

92. Excerpts from Walter Gmelin's essay "Bevölkerungspolitik und Frühehe" (published in the *Deutsche Ärztezeitung*) reprinted in "Mütterheim Steinhöring," *DSK*, 7 Jan. 1937, pp. 13–14.

93. Excerpt from Rudolf Bechert's essay (published in *Deutsches Recht*, nos. 23–24 [15 Dec. 1936]), in "Mütterheim Steinhöring," p. 14.

94. Carl H. Csallner, *Das Geschlechtsleben, seine Bedeutung für Individuum und Gemeinschaft* (Munich: Otto Gmelin, 1937), p. 10.

95. Zeplin, *Sexualpädagogik*, pp. 12, 24. Zeplin blamed the Christian "sinfulness dogma" for all manner of social ills, from hypocrisy and overweening self-righteousness to the proliferation of perverse fantasies, venereal diseases, abuse of alcohol, and lack of sexual harmony within marriages (pp. 22–23).

96. Von Hattingberg, *Über die Liebe*, p. 16.

97. Frommolt, review of F. Kuenkel, *Charakter, Liebe und Ehe*, in *Zentralblatt für Gynäkologie* 57, no. 22 (3 June 1933), p. 1326.

98. Schultz, *Geschlecht-Liebe-Ehe*, pp. 60, 77, 82.

99. See especially the work of Ute Benz, "Brutstätten der Nation: 'Die deutsche Mutter und ihr erstes Kind' oder der anhaltende Erfolg eines Erziehungsbuches," *Dachauer Hefte* 4 (1993), pp. 144–63; and Sigrid Chamberlain, *Adolf Hitler, die deutsche Mutter und ihr erstes Kind: Über zwei NS-Erziehungsbücher* (Giessen: Psychosozial-Verlag, 2000). Contrast Schultz, *Geschlecht-Liebe-Ehe*, pp. 62–66, 81.

100. Johannes H. Schultz, "Nervöse Sexualstörungen und ihre Behandlung in der allgemeinen Praxis," *Therapie der Gegenwart: Medizinisch-chirurgische Rundschau für praktische Ärzte* 78 (June 1937), pp. 252–55.

101. Schultz, *Geschlecht-Liebe-Ehe*, pp. 47, 74, 77, 82–83.

102. Notably, a recent dissertation on sexuality research under Nazism found that strategies for achieving female orgasm were more openly discussed by doctors in the Third Reich than in 1950s West Germany. See Marc Dupont, "Sexualwissenschaft im 'Dritten Reich': Eine Inhaltsanalyse medizinischer Zeitschriften" (Ph.D. diss., Johann Wolfgang Goethe-University, Frankfurt am Main, 1998), pp. 29–42; Dupont observed as well that Nazi medical professionals concerned with sex felt quite free to cite "Jewish sexologists" like Magnus Hirschfeld or Sigmund Freud, and he documented Nazi physicians' recommendations for clitoral and anal stimulation.

103. O. Albrecht, "Ars amandi in matrimonio," *Wiener klinische Wochenschrift* 55, no. 22 (1942), pp. 423, 425–26. German readers were also treated to translations of English-language essays on sex. Thus, for example, in 1938 German readers could learn what one Frederick Harris, late editor in chief of the official newspaper of the Young Men's Christian Association (YMCA), had thought about "sexual adjustment" in marriage. According to Harris, "complete mutuality" was the goal; "both should reach the climax that is absolutely necessary for spiritual and bodily well-being." Castigating those husbands that did not even know whether their wives had ever had an orgasm, and admitting that he was well aware of "the difficulty," Harris nonetheless reminded readers that "We talk about nature as the proper guide. But the kind of sexual intercourse of which I have spoken is by no means 'natural.' It is as unnatural as streetcars or a Beethoven symphony. It is the result of human patience, intelligence, skill. . . . Mutuality in sexual relationships is an artistic achievement, and artistic achievements don't just happen." Frederick Harris, "Sexuelle Beziehungen in der Ehe," *Die Auslese* (Berlin) 12 (Feb. 1938), pp. 156–59. The essay had first appeared in the *Reader's Digest* in 1937.

104. Schultz, *Geschlecht-Liebe-Ehe*, p. 113; "Frauen sind keine Männer!" *DSK*, 12 Mar. 1936, p. 1.

105. Within a few years of its founding, 500,000 copies a week were being printed; by 1944 the total was more than 750,000. See Norbert Frei and Johannes Schmitz, *Journalismus im Dritten Reich* (Munich: Beck, 1989), pp. 71, 101–4; and William L. Combs, *The Voice of the SS: A History of the SS Journal "Das Schwarze Korps"* (New York: Peter Lang, 1986). By the paper's own report, although it was very much a "men's paper," "hundreds of thousands of women" read it as well, and the paper repeatedly opened its pages to female columnists. Editorial note to "Wie eine Frau es sieht," *DSK*, 13 July 1944, p. 4. See also the detailed discussion of *Das Schwarze Korps'* rhetorical strategies in Claudia

Koonz, *The Nazi Conscience* (Cambridge, MA: Belknap at Harvard Univ. Press, 2003), pp. 238–52.

106. For example, see "Es gibt keine katholische Fruchtbarkeit," *DSK*, 24 Oct. 1935, p. 9; and "Witzecke für Schwachsinnige," *DSK*, 14 Nov. 1935, p. 17.

107. "Anstössig?" *DSK*, 16 Apr. 1936, p. 13.

108. Hans Lüdemann, "Neues Stadium der Frauenbewegung?" *DSK*, 19 June 1935, p. 10. Lüdemann is criticizing Marie Joachimi-Dege's essay in Will Vesper's journal *Neue Literatur*. For another statement from this time about ancient "Germanic" customs with respect to sex—among other things advancing the notion that among these ancient peoples "fidelity" was a racial concept (not just male but also female fidelity was above all owed to the purity of "*the Nordic race*" and had nothing to do with sexual fidelity per se, which was not especially honored)— see R. Walther Darré, *Das Bauerntum als Lebensquell der Nordischen Rasse* (Munich: J. F. Lehmanns, 1935), pp. 384–85. A similar view on the complete disinterest in female virginity demonstrated by the "old Germanic" peoples—in contrast to the Christian preoccupation with it—is reported in Dück, "Virginität und Ehe," p. 302.

109. " . . . Unzucht in der Soldatenzeit," *DSK*, 5 March 1936, p. 6.

110. "Homosexualität—keine Erbkrankheit," p. 663. (While this author was convinced that "it is not justified to label an immature boy a homosexual on the basis of a few incidents of this sort," because the whole goal was to "return" such a young man to "normal sexual sensibility," he was quite concerned that if the "mostly Jewish" sex experts in Weimar had had their way, the result would have been "appalling" and homosexuality could have become a "mass phenomenon.") For another elaboration of the idea that orientation was fluid in many young men, that only a minority were truly "sick," and that men could "step by step" be awakened to "love for the other sex," see Haug, "Die Sexuelle Frage in der Seelsorge," p. 609.

111. Fritz Mohr, "Einige Betrachtungen über Wesen, Entstehung und Behandlung der Homosexualität," *Zentralblatt für Psychotherapie* 15 (1943), pp. 1, 13.

112. See the important discussions in Peter von Rönn, "Politische und psychiatrische Homosexualitätskonstruktionen im NS-Staat," part 2: "Die soziale Genese der Homosexualität als defizitäre Heterosexualität," *Zeitschrift für Sexualforschung* 11, no. 3 (Sept. 1998); and Jellonek and Lautmann, *Nationalsozialistischer Terror gegen Homosexuelle*.

113. Schultz's comments were printed in the *Zentralblatt für Psychotherapie* 12 (1940), p. 113, quoted in Ulrich Schultz, "Autogenes Training und Gleichschaltung aller Sinne," *Die Tageszeitung*, 20 June 1984. In the 1990s, some psychiatrists and psychologists still defended Schultz as "apolitical." See "Bluthaftes Verständnis," *Der Spiegel*, 27 June 1994, pp. 183–86.

114. Johannes H. Schultz quoted in "Bluthaftes Verständnis," p. 185; and in U. Schultz, "Autogenes Training." The exposé of J. H. Schultz's role in the Third Reich that appeared in *Der Spiegel* in 1994 seems largely to have been based on the pioneering polemic by Ulrich Schultz (now Schultz-Venrath, no relation to the Nazi Schultz) that was published in *Die Tageszeitung* in 1984; Schultz-Venrath built on the important foundational research done by Regine Lockot in her dissertation, which was published as *Erinnern und Durcharbeiten: Zur Geschichte der*

Psychoanalyse und Psychotherapie im Nationalsozialismus (Frankfurt am Main, 1985). For J. H. Schultz's own presentation of the homoerotic stage in adolescence and of his notion that fully "four-fifths" of all self-presenting homosexuals were really not constitutionally homosexual but rather had acquired homosexuality due to a developmental disturbance or a kind of (curable) fetishism, see his *Geschlecht-Liebe-Ehe*, pp. 56, 96–97, 103–4. Here he claims that the Göring Institute could take credit for the successful cure of "several hundred of these severely sick people" (p. 104).

115. See " . . . Unzucht in der Soldatenzeit," p. 6; and "Frauen sind keine Männer!" *DSK*, 12 March 1936, p. 1. For further comments on the prevalence of "lapses in puberty" (*Pubertätsentgleisungen*)—that is, homosexual incidents among youth—see Tetzlaff, "Homosexualität und Jugend," p. 9; and "Homosexualität—keine Erbkrankheit," p. 663. For a fuller elaboration of the notions both that homosexual activity could be a natural precursor to heterosexuality and that homosexuality represented a flight from, or inhibited capacity for, heterosexuality, see Ritter, *Die geschlechtliche Frage*, pp. 235, 238, 241.

116. "Was sag ich meinem Kinde?" *DSK*, 15 Apr. 1937, p. 6.

117. "Das sind Staatsfeinde!" *DSK*, 4 Mar. 1937, pp. 1–2; and "Ächtung der Entarteten," *DSK*, 1 Apr. 1937, p. 11.

118. "Ist das Nacktkultur? Herr Stapel entrüstet sich!" *DSK*, 24 Apr. 1935, p. 12. The strategy of displaying images of nude women while chastising the Weimarera media for their sexual sensationalism was hardly restricted to *Das Schwarze Korps*. The same double maneuver can be found, for instance, in Karl Eiland, "Deutsche Frauenschönheit," *Neues Volk* 10, no. 9 (Sept. 1942).

119. For example, see "Ehestifter Staat," *DSK*, 26 Mar. 1936, p. 11; "Kinder— ausserhalb der Gemeinschaft?" *DSK*, 9 Apr. 1936, p. 5; "Das uneheliche Kind," *DSK*, 9 Apr. 1936, p. 6; and "Mütterheim Steinhöring," p. 13.

120. "Frauen sind keine Männer!" p. 1.

121. For a fascinating analysis of the racial implications of nudism in Weimar and Nazi Germany (a phenomenon that also repeatedly challenges our contemporary assumptions about what might constitute eroticization or deeroticization), see Chad Ross, "Building a Better Body: Nudism, Society, Race and the German Nation, 1890–1950" (Ph.D. diss., University of Missouri, 2003). See also the discussion of the regime's reversal of its initial resistance to the nudist movement in Matthew Jefferies, "Naturism, Nudity, and the Nazis," *German History* 23, no. 4 (2005).

122. Aside from landscapes, no subject was more frequently painted in the Third Reich than female nudes. See Berthold Hinz, *Die Malerei im deutschen Faschismus* (Munich: Hanser, 1974), p. 87; Christian Gross and Uwe Grossmann, "Die Darstellung der Frau," in *Kunst im Dritten Reich: Dokumente der Unterwerfung*, ed. Georg Bussmann (Frankfurt am Main: Frankfurter Kunstverein, 1974), p. 182; and Wenk, "Hin-weg-sehen," p. 21. On sculpture, see Klaus Wolbert, *Die Nackten und die Toten des "Dritten Reiches"* (Giessen: Anabas, 1982). As Wolbert observed in the 1980s, "the Nazi sculptors pretty much exclusively—leaving aside for the moment eagles, lions, and horses—produced figures of naked women and men. Wherever one looked in the Third Reich, all architectural areas built or planned for state-representative purposes were covered by naked figures; in city

squares, at fountains, at memorials, monuments, or state buildings stood—usually cast in bronze, less frequently chiseled from stone—nudes, generally of remarkable size." Photos of statues of female nudes were circulated nationwide on postcards and in newspapers, and photos of both paintings and statues of female nudes were frequent features also of periodicals designed for Wehrmacht soldiers. See Klaus Wolbert, "Die figurative NS-Plastik," in *Faszination und Gewalt: Zur politischen Ästhetik des Nationalsozialismus*, ed. Bernd Ogan and Wolfgang W. Weiss (Nürnberg: Tümmels, 1992); and Silke Wenk, "Aufgerichtete weibliche Körper: Zur allegorischen Skulptur im deutschen Faschismus," in *Inszenierung der Macht—Ästhetische Faszination im Faschismus*, ed. Klaus Behnken and Frank Wagner (Berlin: NGBK, 1987). On the postwar mainstream and leftist media's repetition compulsion in declaring that Nazi art was "not true art" or "complete kitsch" or "justifiably forgotten" while simultaneously reprinting some of the most titillating samples of that art, see Wenk, "Hin-weg-sehen." The effect of both the mainstream and alternative press strategies, Wenk proposed, was to allow the (mostly male) commentators to engage in a practice of "looking-away-at" (*Hin-weg-sehen*), that is, they were able to enjoy the voyeuristic pleasures of gazing at attractive and well-proportioned nude women while distancing themselves from those same nudes by declaring them to be both politically contaminated and bad art.

123. See "NS-Kunst—Ende der Berührungsangst," *Der Spiegel*, 12 Aug. 1974, pp. 86–88.

124. "Schön und Rein," and "Geschäft ohne Scham," *DSK*, 20 Oct. 1938, pp. 10 and 12.

125. "Sie Meinen: Apart und lustig," *Frauenwarte* 8, no. 16 (Feb. 1940).

126. See Hartmut Lehmann, "Hitlers protestantische Wähler," in *Protestantische Weltsichten: Transformationen seit dem 17. Jahrhundert* (Göttingen: Vandenhoeck und Ruprecht, 1998), pp. 136–39.

127. Guenter Lewy, "Pius XII, the Jews, and the German Catholic Church," in Ericksen and Heschel, *Betrayal*, p. 130. On the compatibility of Nazism and Catholicism already before 1933, see also Derek Hastings, "How 'Catholic' Was the Early Nazi Movement? Religion, Race, and Culture in Munich, 1919–1924," *Central European History* 36, no. 3 (2003).

128. Susannah Heschel, "When Jesus Was an Aryan: The Protestant Church and Antisemitic Propaganda," in Ericksen and Heschel, *Betrayal*, p. 81.

129. Walter Künneth, Walter Michaelis, and Gerhard Kittel paraphrased and quoted in Besier, "Kirche und NS-Rassenpolitik," in *Die Kirchen und das Dritte Reich*, pp. 810–11.

130. See Steigmann-Gall, *The Holy Reich*, pp. 10, 13–50.

131. Joseph Lortz, *Katholischer Zugang zum Nationalsozialismus*, Reich und Kirche, vol. 2 (Münster: Aschendorff, 1933), pp. 9–10.

132. Sellmann quoted in Hans-Georg Stümke, *Homosexuelle in Deutschland: Eine politische Geschichte* (Munich: Beck, 1989), p. 92.

133. See Roos, "Backlash," pp. 81–83; and Jefferies, "Naturism, Nudity, and the Nazis."

134. *Kirche im Volk: Monatsschrift für die katholische Pfarrgemeinde*, Jan. 1934, p. 31, quoted in Joachim Braun, "Lustprinzip und Sexualität in der Wahr-

nehmung der Nationalsozialisten" (Diplomarbeit, Freie Universität Berlin, 1991), p. 107.

135. "Der frische Zug im neuen Staat," *Volkswart* 26 (1933), pp. 170–71, quoted in Roos, "Backlash," p. 83. Roos argues persuasively that the early Nazi self-presentation as intent on cleaning up the sexual landscape of Germany was directly motivated by the party's effort to reverse the German Catholic leadership's initial skepticism and hostility toward Nazism (p. 81).

136. Weinrich, "Randbemerkungen zum Ehe-Problem," pp. 274–75, 278.

137. See John Connelly, "Catholic Opponents of Nazism and the Jewish Question: Vienna in the 1930s" (paper presented at the conference of the American Historical Association, 9 Jan. 2004); the quotations from Muckermann are from his *Volkstum, Staat und Nation eugenisch gesehen* (Essen: Fredebeul und Koenen, 1933).

138. Hermann Muckermann, *Grundriss der Rassenkunde*, 2nd ed. (Paderborn: Ferdinand Schöningh, 1935), p. 122.

139. *Weisses Kreuz*, 15 Apr. 1935, pp. 20–22, quoted in Braun, "Lustprinzip," p. 111.

140. Archbishop of Freiburg in *Kirche im Volk: Monatsschrift für die katholische Pfarrgemeinde*, Mar. 1935, no page, quoted in Braun, "Lustprinzip," p. 110. For an indication of the (situational but also self-imposed) constraints that kept the highest-ranking church leaders from attacking the regime's encouragements to extramarital sex more directly, see in this context also Walter Brockman, "Illegitimacy in Germany," *Current History* 46, no. 4 (July 1937), p. 70.

141. Ehwalt, *Eheleben und Ehescheidung*, p. 16. Also see the discussion of Ehwalt's views in "Ausverkauf der Liebe," *DSK*, 1 Apr. 1937, p. 6.

142. See Franz Gillmann, "Zur christlichen Ehelehre," *Archiv für katholisches Kirchenrecht* 116 (1936), p. 92.

143. Renate Schmid, "Zum Problem der geschlechtlichen Erziehung: Betrachtungen einer Mutter," *Zeitwende* 13 (1936–37), p. 45.

144. The story is reported in "Anstössig?" p. 14.

145. The story is reported in "Was ist schamloser?" *DSK*, 20 Jan. 1938, p. 8.

146. Ernst Krupka's remarks in *Der Weg zum Ziel*, no. 18 (1935), quoted and discussed in "Pikanterien im Beichtstuhl," *DSK*, 26 June 1935, p. 5. For a moving and telling testimonial to the kind of mental compartmentalization and single-minded focus on freedom for Christian witness that could permit a Christian missionary to believe as late as 1937 that Hitler and the SA were supportive of Christian values, while simultaneously being repelled by the overt anti-Christianity and "inhumane, murderous tendencies" of the SS, see Ernst Krupka's reminiscences in Maria-Luise Krupka, ed., *Lebensauftrag: Evangelist. Ernst Krupka, Sein leben und Sein Wirken* (Bad Liebenzell: Verlag der Liebenzeller Mission, 1986), pp. 62–63.

147. See "Ist das schon 'Das Wunder des Lebens? Grundsätzliche Betrachtung zur Ausstellung am Kaiserdamm,'" *Katholisches Kirchenblatt* (Berlin), 31 March 1935, p. 10, as well as the ferocious critique of this essay and effusive defense of the exhibit in "Offene Antwort auf eine katholische Kritik," *DSK*, 17 Apr. 1935, pp. 1–2. Among other things, *Das Schwarze Korps* described the photographs of the handicapped as a "train of horror," photographs of the "hereditarily less

valuable, whose fathers unfortunately were *not* sterilized in time," and *Das Schwarze Korps* challenged the *Katholisches Kirchenblatt* whether it really believed "that these figures of horror represent the will of the Creator?" Playing on anxiety and confusion about disability formed a major element in *Das Schwarze Korps's* campaign to drive a wedge between Germans and the Christian faith. By 1937 *Das Schwarze Korps* was advocating not just sterilization but also euthanasia. Not coincidentally, the tactic used was to criticize Christianity for cruelly endorsing pain and suffering. *Das Schwarze Korps* printed a letter purportedly written by a father of nine children, eight of whom were vibrantly healthy, one of whom was severely disabled and had lived in excruciating agony for a decade before dying. As the father wrote, "Which love is greater: that which let the little child suffer ten long years, let it suffer without pity, or that which would have saved it from its undeserved agonies through a quick death?" The father was especially angry about what his erstwhile pastor had said: " '*It's a pity, it's a pity,*' he said when he saw the little child, '*but,*' he added smiling, '*there you also have something to remind you of God.*' " With great bitterness and sarcasm, the father remarked on this and other Christian counsels to accept suffering as God's will: "Really, that's a nice God . . . you've got!" See "Was ist 'humaner'?" *DSK,* 1 Apr. 1937, p. 13.

148. Schmid, "Zum Problem der geschlechtlichen Erziehung," p. 40.

149. *Klerusblatt,* quoted in Beth A. Griech-Polelle, *Bishop von Galen: German Catholicism and National Socialism* (New Haven: Yale Univ. Press, 2002), p. 110; Martin Rade in *Christliche Welt,* 1 Nov. 1935, quoted in Gerlach, *Als die Zeugen schwiegen,* p. 161.

150. Conversation with R. W., 2004. This memory of an individual (who had connections to those members of the Confessing Church who risked themselves to care for "non-Aryan" Christians), is in keeping with the historical record. While courageous individual Protestant theologians and activist laypeople (e.g., Dietrich Bonhoeffer, Karl Barth, Rudolf Bultmann, Marga Meusel, Elisabeth Schmitz, Martin and Marianne Albertz, Ernst Lohmeyer, Wilhelm Freiherr von Pechmann, Gerhard Jasper) took stands on their own, they were unable to move the church's official organizations to make public pronouncements in defense of Germany's 500,000 Jews or even in clear defense of the approximately 116,000 Christians of Jewish heritage (90,000 of which were Protestant, the rest Catholic). On disputes in the Protestant Church over whether or how to take a public stand on Nazi abuse of Jews, see Besier, "Kirche und NS-Rassenpolitik," pp. 809–14, 827, 843–49; and Wehler, *Deutsche Gesellschaftsgeschichte,* 4:798–809. The anti-Nazi Confessing Church did not take a formal public stand against Nazi antisemitism either, despite a few of its members' efforts. On the contrary, some leading members of the Confessing Church—as a police report of the time noted—even "fundamentally affirmed the stance of the state on the Jewish question." Bielefeld police report to Berlin Gestapo office, 4 Sep. 1935, quoted in Klee, *"Die SA Jesu Christi,"* p. 123; see also more generally Klee's discussion, pp. 121–26; as well as Gerlach, *Als die Zeugen schwiegen,* pp. 152–59; Barnett, *For the Soul of the People,* pp. 122–54; and Manfred Gailus, *Protestantismus und Nationalsozialismus* (Cologne: Böhlau, 2001). See also the retrospective remarks of theologian Eberhard Bethge: "We were against Hitler's church policy, but at the same time we were

antisemites." Bethge interviewed in *The Restless Conscience* (1993, dir. Hava Kohav Beller).

151. Erwin v. Kienitz, "Katholische Sexualkasuistik und Sexualmoral," *Schönere Zukunft* 11, nos. 12–13 (24 Dec. 1935), p. 310.

152. Laros, *Die Beziehungen der Geschlechter*, pp. 11–12, 15, 34, 70, 166–67. Laros both described the hedonistic culture in the Germany of his day as an especially dangerous form of "Americanism" (*Amerikanismus*) and tried to use the Nazis' own concepts against Nazi sexual mores, insisting that "ur-Aryan inheritance" and the "original source of Germanic essence" were in the process of being ruined (pp. 20, 24).

153. Wilhelm Stapel, "'Neuheidentum.' Ein Brief und eine Antwort," *Deutsches Volkstum: Monatsschrift für das deutsche Geistesleben*, Apr. 1935, p. 293; and see "Ist das Nacktkultur?" p. 12.

154. Wilhelm Stapel, "Aphoristisches zur Judenfrage," in *Das neue Deutschland und die Judenfrage*, ed. Gottfried Feder et al. (Leipzig: Rüdiger, 1933), p. 172.

155. Wilhelm Stapel, *Die literarische Vorherrschaft der Juden in Deutschland 1918 bis 1933* (Hamburg: Hanseatische Verlagsanstalt, 1937).

156. See the extended discussion in Adolf Köberle, "Unter den Studenten," in *Christus lebt! Ein Buch von fruchtbarem Dienst in Lehre und Leben*, ed. Hans Dannenbaum (Berlin: Furche, 1939), pp. 325–26.

157. Adolf Allwohn, "Zu unseren Beiträgen," *Seelsorge* (Dresden) 15 (1939), p. 67.

158. See "Geschlechtliche Erziehung und paulinischer Geist," *Katholisches Kirchenblatt* (Berlin), 14 Apr. 1935, p. 13; the neopagan essay criticized and quoted by the *Katholisches Kirchenblatt* appeared in *Flammenzeichen*, 6 Apr. 1935.

159. Thus, for instance, Catholic priest Laros in 1936 complained both of "the fairy-tale of the body-hostility of Christianity" and of how "most people smile and mock Christianity." Laros, *Die Beziehungen der Geschlechter*, pp. 27, 96. See on this point as well the Catholic publicist and historian Friedrich Heer's cutting retrospective observation that Christians themselves were to blame for the lacunae in their moral texts with respect not only to such themes as "global responsibility," "brotherliness" and "humanism," but also specifically "love" and "sex" (*Sexus*): "Whoever looks into the theological tracts, into the handbooks of moral theology, . . . will become aware of a huge gaping space that Hitler—without resistance, indeed not infrequently invited by the theologians themselves—could occupy." Heer quoted in Werner Reichelt, *Das braune Evangelium: Hitler und die NS-Liturgie* (Wuppertal: Hammer, 1990), p. 170. See also the thoughtful reflections in James Bernauer, S.J., "An Ethic and Moral Formation That Are Repentant: Catholicism's Emerging Post-Shoah Tradition—The Case of the Jesuits" (paper presented at the conference "Remembering for the Future: The Holocaust in the Age of Genocide," Oxford and London, 16–23 July 2000). Bernauer meditates on "how Nazism successfully exploited a strong religious alienation from the body and, thus, Christianity's estrangement from its own incarnational tradition." Bernauer goes on to say that "In that endless searching after the reasons for why the Jews were so victimized by the Nazis, for why so many collaborated

in their murder, and especially for why so many stood aside and failed to do what could have been done, I propose that this issue of sexuality gives an essential answer. Before the Jews were murdered, before they were turned away from as not being one's concern, the Jew had already been defined as spiritless, on the one hand, and sexually possessed, erotically charged on the other hand." I thank John Connelly for calling Bernauer's paper to my attention.

160. Haug, "Die sexuelle Frage in der Seelsorge," pp. 542, 609, 614.

161. Theodor Bliewies, "Mädchen in Not: Eine Fragestellung zur geschlecht-lichen Aufklärung," *Der Seelsorger* 14 (1938), p. 212.

162. Hermann A. Krose, S.J., "Die Ursachen der neuzeitlichen Ehezerrüttung," *Stimmen der Zeit* 133 (1937–38), p. 364. This is a review of Roderich von Ungern-Sternberg's *Die Ursachen der neuzeitlichen Ehezerrüttung* (Berlin: Georg Stilke, 1937). Ungern-Sternberg defended premarital sex, as he also made a case for the close interrelationship between the decline of religiosity and loosening sexual mores.

163. A. Eberle, "Über die Versuchung," *Theologisch-praktische Quartalschrift* 94 (1941), p. 232.

164. Van Acken, "Prüderie—Distanzhalten," pp. 73–74, 77–79.

165. Himmler quoted in Felix Kersten, *The Kersten Memoirs, 1940–1945* (London: Hutchinson, 1956), p. 177.

166. Himmler order reprinted in Josef Ackermann, *Heinrich Himmler als Ideo-loge* (Göttingen: Musterschmidt, 1970), between pp. 240 and 241.

167. See Kersten, *The Kersten Memoirs*, pp. 176, 179.

168. Hitler, 23 Apr. 1942, quoted in Henry Picker, *Tischgespräche im Führer-hauptquartier, 1941–42*, ed. Gerhard Ritter (Bonn: Athenäum, 1951), pp. 301–2. According to Picker, Hitler said that Christianity "kills joy in that which is beautiful." In this respect, "a certain Protestant philistinism is even worse than the Catholic Church"—for the Catholic Church at least permitted the faithful to sin during carnival. Hitler, 1 Dec. 1941, in ibid., p. 347. Both Picker's compilation of Hitler's daily remarks and the compilation by Hermann Rauschning have re-cently come under attack by scholars as being potentially inaccurate; no one, how-ever, has challenged the representation of Hitler's views on sex. See (on Picker) Richard C. Carrier, "Hitler's *Table Talk*: Troubling Finds," *German Studies Re-view* 27, no. 3 (Oct. 2003); and (on Rauschning) Steigmann-Gall, *The Holy Reich*.

169. Hitler quoted in George W. Herald, "Sex Is a Nazi Weapon," *American Mercury* 54, no. 222 (June 1942), pp. 656–65. Herald's source is Rauschning.

170. See Marianne Regensburger and Klaus Scholder, *30 Jahre Deutschland und die Kirche* (Munich: Chr. Kaiser Verlag, 1964), pp. 52–53.

171. Endres quoted in Herald, "Sex Is a Nazi Weapon," p. 661.

172. Just as more sexually conservative Nazi moralists had done before him, so too did Rost try to blame Jews for non-Jews' interest in sex. Rost argued that, despite the "gratifying progressive development" initiated in 1933 one could not, of course, expect such a habit-forming belief that "everything that is pleasing is permitted" would be overcome overnight. See Rost, "Sexuelle Probleme," pp. 218–20.

173. See "Das Eherecht in der neuen Gesetzgebung," *Die deutsche Frau* (sup-plement to the *Völkischer Beobachter*), 12 Feb. 1939. See also Burleigh, *The Third Reich*, p. 231; Frevert, *Women in German History*, pp. 236–37; and Stephenson,

Women, p. 29. While Frevert notes that the Weimar women's movement had (in vain) fought for a liberalization of divorce laws, other scholars emphasize the disproportionately deleterious effects of the new legislation on women. See Thilo Ramm, "Eherecht und Nationalsozialismus," in *Klassenjustiz und Pluralismus: Festschrift für Ernst Fränkel*, ed. Günter Doeker and Winfried Steffani (Hamburg: Hoffmann und Campe, 1973), pp. 158–59; and Norbert Westenrieder, *"Deutsche Frauen und Mädchen!": Vom Alltagsleben 1933–1945* (Düsseldorf: Droste, 1984), p. 32. Notably, the new legislation was also used to pressure non-Jews living in mixed marriages to divorce their spouses (and thereby facilitate their deportation and murder). See Marion Kaplan, *Between Dignity and Despair: Jewish Life in Nazi Germany* (New York: Oxford Univ. Press, 1998), p. 89. In this context see also a classic example of the kind of pseudoscholarship produced under Nazism: a legal expert's call for greater empathy for those "German-blooded" spouses in mixed marriages who had been reluctant to divorce their Jewish partners "as a consequence of their entanglement in Jewish thought patterns" but who now should be encouraged to proceed with divorce in view of their "in the meantime matured recognition of their *völkisch* obligations." Werner Klemm, "Die Lösung deutsch-jüdischer Mischehen," *Deutsches Recht* 9 (1939), p. 1899. Another indicative essay discussing the ramifications of the new divorce law for Jews—replete with remarks about the biologically determined psychological instability of "mixed-race" offspring—and for those with mental illness in the family is Konrad Ernst, "Psychiatrisch Wichtiges im Neuen Ehegesetz," *Klinische Wochenschrift* 18, no. 44 (4 Nov. 1939), pp. 1405–8.

174. See Rudolf Paulsen, "Ein Kapitel über die Ehe," *Die deutsche Frau*, 7 June 1933, p. 2; "Ehe und Persönlichkeit," *Die deutsche Frau*, 27, 28, 29 May 1939; and the discussion in Hannelore Kessler, *"Die deutsche Frau": Nationalsozialistische Frauenpropaganda im "Völkischen Beobachter"* (Cologne: Pahl-Rugenstein, 1981), pp. 52–53 and 88–89.

175. See Walter Menzel, "Ehebruch und ehewidriges Verhalten als Dienststrafvergehen," *Wirtschaft und Recht* 9, no. 6 (15 June 1942), pp. 61–62. (This was a supplement to *Der Deutsche Erzieher*, the official journal for schoolteachers.)

176. All quotations from Karlheinz Deschner, "Krieg und Kirche," *Konkret*, Jan. 1963, pp. 8–9.

177. Bishops' telegram quoted in Regensburger and Scholder, *30 Jahre*, p. 52.

178. Marahrens quoted in Deschner, "Krieg und Kirche," p. 9.

179. Burleigh, *The Third Reich*, p. 724.

180. Prayer quoted and discussed in Regensburger and Scholder, *30 Jahre*, pp. 54–55.

181. Conversation with R. S., 1999.

182. Conversation with G.-L. L., 2000.

183. See Saul Friedländer, "The Wehrmacht, German Society, and the Knowledge of the Mass Extermination of the Jews," in *Crimes of War: Guilt and Denial in the Twentieth Century*, ed. Omer Bartov, Atina Grossmann, and Mary Nolan (New York: New Press, 2002), pp. 24–28. As Friedländer observes (in noting also that the NSDAP's Winter Aid program and the "Jew markets" (*Judenmärkte*) in large cities, respectively, distributed for free or sold the personal belongings of murdered Jews "at dirt-cheap prices . . . often without the original tags having been removed"): "Whether under these circumstances one can speak of the nor-

mality of everyday life under National Socialism is a moot question. Differently put, the everyday involvement of the population with the regime was far deeper than has long been assumed, due to the widespread knowledge and the passive acceptance of the crimes, as well as the crassest profit derived from them. A massive repression of knowledge, if it existed at all, took place after 1945, and probably much less so beforehand" (pp. 27–28). For an autobiographical statement testifying to having knowledge of the mass murder of Jews before 1945 and "losing" that knowledge afterward, see Ursula von Kardorff, "Zeit der Feigheit, Zeit der Gewalt: Beim Durchblättern eines Tagebuches," *Konkret*, Feb. 1964, p. 7.

184. The literature on these subjects is vast, even as there is still far more research that needs to be done. The best scholarship includes Angelika Ebbinghaus et al., eds., *Heilen und Vernichten im Mustergau Hamburg: Bevölkerungs- und Gesundheitspolitik im Dritten Reich* (Hamburg: Konkret Literatur Verlag, 1984); Gisela Bock, *Zwangssterilisation im Nationalsozialismus: Studien zur Rassenpolitik und Frauenpolitik* (Opladen: Westdeutscher Verlag, 1986); Gabriele Czarnowski, *Das kontrollierte Paar: Ehe- und Sexualpolitik im Nationalsozialismus* (Weinheim: Deutscher Studien Verlag, 1991); Kaplan, *Between Dignity and Despair*; Müller and Sternweiler, *Homosexuelle Männer im KZ Sachsenhausen*; Pretzel and Rossbach, *Wegen der zu erwartenden hohen Strafe*; Christa Schikorra, *Kontinuitäten der Ausgrenzung: "Asoziale" Häftlinge im Frauen-Konzentrationslager Ravensbrück* (Berlin: Metropol, 2001); Patricia Szobar, "Telling Sexual Stories in the Nazi Courts of Law: Race Defilement in Germany, 1933 to 1945," *Journal of the History of Sexuality* 11, nos. 1–2 (Jan.–Apr. 2002); Jellonek and Lautmann, *Nationalsozialistischer Terror gegen Homosexuelle*. For an excellent critical survey of much of this scholarship, see Heineman, "Sexuality and Nazism."

185. For a thoughtful elaboration on these issues with respect to World War I, the first "total war," see Elizabeth Domansky, "Militarization and Reproduction in World War I Germany," in *Society, Culture and the State in Germany, 1870–1930*, ed. Geoff Eley (Ann Arbor: Univ. of Michigan Press, 1996), pp. 427–63.

186. See the chapters "Die Verrohung greift um sich" and "Grausamkeit und Sadismus als Kriegsprodukt" in Magnus Hirschfeld and Andreas Gaspar, eds., *Sittengeschichte des Ersten Weltkrieges*, 2nd ed. (Hanau: Verlag Karl Schustek, 1966), pp. 463–518. The first edition was completed in 1929 and based on the collaborative work of an international panel of physicians and scholars.

187. See Bartov et al., *Crimes of War*; and Hannes Heer and Klaus Naumann, eds., *Vernichtungskrieg: Verbrechen der Wehrmacht 1941–1944* (Hamburg: Hamburger Edition, 1995).

188. "Practically necrophiliac" is Omer Bartov's term for the incidents he discovered in military archives; Ulrich Herbert found similar incidents in the course of his research. Conversations with Bartov, 1998, and Herbert, 2001. On rapes in the killing fields, see Birgit Beck, "Vergewaltigung von Frauen als Kriegsstrategie im Zweiten Weltkrieg?" in *Gewalt im Krieg: Ausübung, Erfahrung und Verweigerung von Gewalt in Kriegen des 20. Jahrhunderts*, ed. Andreas Gestrich (Münster: Lit, 1996), pp. 34–50; and Doris Bergen, "Sexual Violence in the Holocaust: Unique and Typical?" in *Lessons and Legacies VII: The Holocaust in International Perspective*, ed. Dagmar Herzog (Evanston, IL: Northwestern Univ. Press, forthcoming). On sadism in the ghettos and camps, see Lengyel, "Scientific

Experiments"; Joan Ringelheim, "Women and the Holocaust: A Reconsideration of Research," in Rittner and Roth, *Different Voices*; Andreas Gaspar et al., eds., *Sittengeschichte des Zweiten Weltkrieges: Die tausend Jahre von 1933–1945* (Hanau am Main: Schustek, 1968); Vera Laska, ed., *Women in the Resistance and in the Holocaust: The Voices of Eyewitnesses* (Westport, CT: Greenwood, 1983); Heinz Heger, *The Men with the Pink Triangle* (Boston: Alyson, 1980); and Wolfgang Sofsky, *The Order of the Terror: The Concentration Camp* (Princeton: Princeton Univ. Press, 1997). On how "fond of promiscuity" and of "drinking and whoremongering" were the SS officers and guards working in that "paradise of shirkers," the concentration camps, see Eugen Kogon, *The Theory and Practice of Hell: The German Concentration Camps and the System behind Them* (New York: Berkley Medallion, 1968), pp. 285–86. On sexual licentiousness among perpetrators who killed the handicapped, see Henry Friedlander, *The Origins of Nazi Genocide: From Euthanasia to the Final Solution* (Chapel Hill: Univ. of North Carolina Press, 1995), pp. 193–94, 237.

189. Letter from Obersturmführer Karl Kretschmer in Kursk to his wife and children, 15 Oct. 1942, reprinted in *"The Good Old Days": The Holocaust as Seen by Its Perpetrators and Bystanders*, ed. Ernst Klee et al. (New York: Free Press, 1991), pp. 167–68. Earlier letters to his wife indicated that "the sight of the dead (including women and children) is not very cheering. . . . Here in Russia, wherever the German soldier is, no Jew remains," and "There is no room for pity of any kind. . . . we are mopping up where necessary. . . . There are no Jews here any more" (Kretschmer letters, 27 Sept. 1942 and date unknown, pp. 163, 165).

190. Nini Rascher's letter to Heinrich Himmler reprinted in *Concentration Camp Dachau 1933–1945*, ed. Barbara Distel and Ruth Jakusch (Brussels: Comité International de Dachau, 1978), p. 147. Note too that hundreds of wives and children of SS men stationed at Auschwitz lived there as well and that wives also visited husbands who were involved in the mass shootings of Jews on the eastern front. See Sybille Steinbacher, *"Musterstadt" Auschwitz: Germanisierungspolitik und Judenmord in Ostoberschlesien* (Munich: Saur, 2000), pp. 184–88; and Gudrun Schwarz, *Eine Frau an seiner Seite: Ehefrauen in der "SS-Sippengemeinschaft"* (Hamburg: Hamburger Edition, 1997).

191. Beck interviewed in the film *Paragraph 175* (2000, dir. Rob Epstein and Jeffrey Friedman).

192. Conversation with B. W., 1999. See also the remark of Arthur Maria Rabenalt, to the effect that sex under the bombing raids deserves a history of its own. Arthur Maria Rabenalt, *Film im Zwielicht: Über den unpolitischen Film des Dritten Reiches und die Begrenzung des totalitären Anspruches* (Munich: Copress-Verlag, 1958; reprint, Hildesheim: Olms, 1978), p. 29.

193. Conversations with H. F., 1998, and R. P., 2002.

194. Conversation with A. D., 2003. See also Catrine Clay and Michael Leapman, *Master Race: The Lebensborn Experiment in Nazi Germany* (London: Hodder and Stoughton, 1995); Georg Lilienthal, *Der "Lebensborn e.V." Ein Instrument nationalsozialistischer Rassenpolitik* (Stuttgart: Fischer, 1985). On the jokes, see Pini, *Liebeskult und Liebeskitsch*, pp. 111, 327. See also how *Das Schwarze Korps* felt obliged to deny the rumors: "Nobody thinks of improving the race in a laboratory, as it were, and of 'pairing' humans with each other ac-

cording to some theory of producing 'Nordic supermen' progeny." " 'SS.-Voll-blut'?" *DSK*, 25 Mar. 1937, p. 12. Richard Grunberger does find some evidence of deliberate breeding via intercourse and not just artificial insemination. See his *The 12-Year Reich: A Social History of Nazi Germany 1933–1945* (New York: Holt, Rinehart and Winston, 1971), pp. 246–47. For a different interpretation—that the Nazi regime had *not* organized "Aryan" mating sessions in the Lebensborn homes but that there were German women who nonetheless volunteered themselves for such sessions—see Brückner, "Politik und Perversion."

195. For example (on parents), see Solon and Brandt, "Sex under the Swastika," p. 428; and Brockman, "Illegitimacy in Germany," pp. 67–69. Or, as one woman remembered decades later: "In my Hitler Youth generation, on the whole, piggish things [*Schweinereien*] were said about sex, decidedly piggish things. People did it [had sex] secretly, and for me that was repugnant and disgusting." Lothar Steinbach, *Ein Volk, Ein Reich, Ein Glaube: Ehemalige Nationalsozialisten und Zeitzeugen berichten über ihr Leben im Dritten Reich* (Berlin and Bonn: Dietz, 1983), p. 78.

196. For example, see the comments of Christa Meves in Margarete Dörr, *"Wer die Zeit nicht miterlebt hat . . .": Frauenerfahrungen im Zweiten Weltkrieg und in den Jahren danach*, vol. 2 (Kriegsalltag) (Frankfurt am Main: Campus, 1998), p. 152.

197. See Birthe Kundrus, *Kriegerfrauen: Familienpolitik und Geschlechtsverhältnisse im Ersten und Zweiten Weltkrieg* (Hamburg: Christians, 1995). Already by 1941 jurists and the regime were actively debating how to handle the proliferation of adulterous behavior on the home front of the wives of men enlisted in the Wehrmacht. For example, see Brinkmann, "Ehebruch und Beleidigung vom Standpunkt des Staatsanwalts aus betrachtet," *Deutsches Recht* 11, no. 38 (1941), pp. 1987–88.

198. Gudrun Schwarz, "Männer und Frauenmoral in der SS," paper presented at conference on "Moral im Nationalsozialismus," Institut für Sozialforschung, Hamburg, 4 June 2002. See the discussion in Harry Nutt, "Die Gewalt der Ehre: Moral im Nationalsozialismus—eine Hamburger Tagung," *Frankfurter Rundschau*, 11 July 2002.

199. See Maiwald and Mischler, *Sexualität unter dem Hakenkreuz*, pp. 141, 144–49; and Ebba Drolshagen, *Nicht ungeschoren davongekommen: Das Schicksal der Frauen in den besetzten Ländern, die Wehrmachtssoldaten liebten* (Hamburg: Hoffmann und Campe, 1998).

200. Military doctor Rost, for example, openly discussed the difficulties officers encountered convincing men that Nazi racial laws prohibited sex with women in the occupied nations. Potential sex partners, he admitted, were "of course easy . . . to find, especially among the *population of the occupied country*," and the men challenged their officers to let them have their fun with enemy civilians, repeatedly bantering—as Rost summarized it—"that the relations of the sexes are international law and therefore have nothing to do with the war." On the other hand, Rost also shared with his medical colleagues the news that in trying to convince military men to desist from sex with racially inappropriate civilians the tactic of making racist arguments (about "the dangerous fertility of the East and the growing black subversion from the West") was more effective than warning

them about the potential risks to their own health from venereal disease. Rost, "Sexuelle Probleme."

201. See Pini, *Leibeskult und Liebeskitsch*, pp. 326, 353, 357.

202. Letter to the editor of *Stern*, quoted in Christoph Boyer and Hans Woller, "'Hat die deutsche Frau versagt?': Die 'neue Freiheit' der Frauen in der Trümmerzeit 1945–1949," *Journal für Geschichte*, no. 2 (1983), p. 36.

203. Conversation with E. I., 1994.

204. Memoirs of G. C.

205. Conversation with R. W., 2004. For further discussion of the climate encouraging extramarital (sometimes also nonconsensual) sex in the Reich Labor Service, see Brockman, "Illegitimacy in Germany," pp. 67–69.

206. All three quotations from Kundrus, "Forbidden Company: Romantic Relationships between Germans and Foreigners, 1939–1945," *Journal of the History of Sexuality* 11, nos. 1–2 (Jan.–Apr. 2002), pp. 206–7, 210. On the sexual liberties taken on the home front during the war, see also Erich Kasberger, *Heldinnen waren wir keine: Alltag in der NS-Zeit* (Hamburg: Ernst Kabel, 1995), pp. 94–98.

207. On the relationship between these two different forms of taboo breaking, see also Sophinette Becker, "Zur Funktion der Sexualität im Nationalsozialismus," *Zeitschrift für Sexualforschung* 14, no. 2 (June 2001).

208. For example, under the caption, "Contraception—Still a Stepchild in Germany," a medical journal announced in 1965: "Who could still be surprised that marital counseling in Germany, the enlightenment about planned conception, is still in its infancy? . . . Germany's reigning generation of medical professionals still comes from the era in which maintaining the reproductive capacity of the German woman was the most noble task, the thought of birth planning a heresy worthy of malediction and death. Whoever went through medical training between 1933 and 1945, was cut off from all information about these problems and thoroughly weaned of any mental confrontation with family planning." See "Die Antikonzeption—in Deutschland noch ein Stiefkind: Symposium der Pro Familia in Berlin," *Berliner Ärzteblatt* 78, no. 2 (1965), pp. 73–74, 77. (Hans Harmsen, the head of the West German Pro Familia, an affiliate of the International Planned Parenthood Federation, not only endorsed Nazism but was responsible for coordinating the sterilization of handicapped individuals living during the Third Reich in the institutions of the Protestant Church's Inner Mission.)

209. For example, the eminent sociologist Helmut Schelsky in his widely read 1955 book on the "sociology of sexuality" mentioned National Socialism in only one context. Obviously alluding to the avowedly homosexual leader of the SA, Ernst Röhm, and some of his associates, although not mentioning that Hitler had Röhm murdered in 1934, Schelsky noted: "The consciousness of being able to live beyond the bounds of the rules regulating the lives of ordinary citizens surely contributed to the maintenance of homosexual relations among the leading political mercenaries of the early National Socialist time of struggle, even if the formation of these relations can probably be traced to earlier social constellations like the isolation [from women] during the army time and wartime." Moreover, and while Schelsky neither mentioned his own former Nazi Party affiliation, nor bothered to note that tens of thousands of homosexual men had been imprisoned and thousands murdered by the Nazis, Schelsky spent an entire chapter endorsing

ideas about homosexuality developed under Nazism. Relying especially on the work of his friend Hans Bürger-Prinz, a psychiatrist who had been instrumental in providing innovative social constructionist scholarly "legitimations" for the expanded Nazi persecution of homosexuals, Schelsky "explained" what was wrong with homosexuals and why homosexuality could never be equalized with heterosexuality. Homosexuals, in Schelsky's view, could not be culture bearers at all. They could not, in truth, be real citizens; their level of personhood was simply not high enough. Homosexuals suffered from a "failure to build up a complete opposite-sex partner relationship." Homosexuals' "solipsism," this "staying with one's own body," "locks these individuals away from the start from the originary access to sociability." They never even reached the level of behavior at which sexual moral norms could be productively developed. They remained stuck at an "autistic" level, in a "sexuality only of pleasure-seeking." The idea that homophobic prejudice caused difficulties for homosexuals' acceptance in society reversed cause and effect, Schelsky thought. "The abnormals are not condemned to an outsider role only through some arbitrary norm-placement of society. . . . Rather, the normative verdict constitutes the assessment of a culture that these groups are not capable of reaching the higher states of being." See Helmut Schelsky, *Soziologie der Sexualität: Über die Beziehungen zwischen Geschlecht, Moral und Gesellschaft* (Hamburg: Rowohlt, 1955), pp. 62, 71–73, 82–83.

210. Conversations with R. G., 1997, and V. J., 1999.

211. Furthermore, in contrast to those who might dismiss all accounts of a pro-sex Third Reich as based on an extrapolation from the "chaos" of the war and immediate postwar years, Rabenalt emphasized the opposite, saying that if it had had any effect on German sexual politics at all, World War II had brought with it the first hesitations about the overarching trend toward liberalization, because of the concern that incidents of adultery on the home front, or even the perception that they might be occurring, could be damaging to the Wehrmacht's morale. Rabenalt, *Film im Zwielicht*, pp. 26–29.

CHAPTER TWO
THE FRAGILITY OF HETEROSEXUALITY

1. Johannes Leppich, "'Thema 1,'" in *Pater Leppich Spricht: Journalisten hören den "roten" Pater*, ed. Günther Mees and Günter Graf (Düsseldorf: Bastion, 1952), p. 43.

2. For example, see Richard Gutzwiller, "Die Überwindung der sexuellen Krise," in *Gesundes Geschlechtsleben*, ed. Franz Xavier von Hornstein and Adolf Faller (Olten: F. Pittet, 1950), p. 436; and Franz Hubalek, "Die Sexualnot unserer Tage," *Der Seelsorger* 20 (1949–50), p. 276.

3. Walter Dittmann, "Die Krisis der Ehe: Die Ansicht des Geistlichen," *Nordwestdeutsche Hefte* 2, no. 10 (1947), p. 36. See also Franka Schneider, "'Einigkeit im Unglück'? Berliner Eheberatungsstellen zwischen Ehekrise und Wiederaufbau," in *Nachkrieg in Deutschland*, ed. Klaus Naumann (Hamburg: Hamburger Edition, 2000), pp. 206–26.

4. Theodor Hartwig, *Die Tragödie des Schlafzimmers: Beiträge zur Psychologie der Ehe* (Vienna: Rudolf Cerny, 1947); Gerhard Fechner, *Die kranke Ehe* (Hamburg: Grupe, 1949), p. 10.

5. Dr. K, "Was halten Sie vom Frauenüberschuss?" *Liebe und Ehe* 2, no. 2 (1950), p. 12.

6. Hans Bürger-Prinz, "Über die männliche Sexualität," *Zeitschrift für Sexualforschung* 1, no. 2 (June—July 1950), pp. 108–10.

7. H. Schürmann, "Promiskuität—Zeichen der Zeit," *Liebe und Ehe* 3, no. 9 (1951), p. 385.

8. Peter Schult, "Anarchy in Germany," in *Keine Zeit für gute Freunde: Homosexuelle in Deutschland 1933–1969*, ed. Joachim Hohmann (Berlin: Foerster, 1982), pp. 74–77.

9. Erich Langer, "Die Bedeutung der Geschlechtskrankheiten," in *Sexuelle Erziehung in Elternhaus und Schule*, ed. Winfried Schimmel and Karl-Heinz Grothe (Berlin: Berliner Medizinische Verlagsanstalt, 1954), p. 153.

10. Placards quoted in ibid. See also Petra Goedde, "From Villains to Victims: Fraternization and the Feminization of Germany, 1945–1947," *Diplomatic History* 23, no. 1 (winter 1999), p. 9.

11. Siegfried Häussler, "Ehenot und Ehehilfe in der ärztlichen Praxis," *Neubau: Blätter für neues Leben aus Wort und Geist* 5, no. 9 (1950), p. 358.

12. A typical story recommending mutual forgiveness for wartime adulteries is Wolfgang Fix, "Das Geständnis," *Die Wochenpost*, 21 July 1946, p. 5.

13. "Politisches ABC," *Neues Abendland* 2 (1947), p. 91.

14. See Rüdiger Proske, "Die Familie 1951: Eine Beschreibung ihrer wichtigsten Merkmale," *Frankfurter Hefte* (Apr. 1951), pp. 272–74.

15. Walter Hemsing, "Der Heimkehrer und seine Ehe," *Wege zum Menschen* (1949–50), p. 245.

16. August Brunner, S.J., "Über den Sinn der Ehe," *Stimmen der Zeit: Monatsschrift für das Geistesleben der Gegenwart* 139 (1946–47), p. 436.

17. Dittmann, "Die Krisis der Ehe," p. 36.

18. See Petra Lund, "Zwei Frauen? Mir Reicht's!" *Constanze* 1, no. 20 (1948), p. 7.

19. For example, see Dr. K, "Was halten Sie vom Frauenüberschuss?" p. 12.

20. K. Bier, review of Theodor Bovet's *Die Ehe, ihre Krise und Neuwerdung* (1946), *Zeitschrift für Sexualforschung* 1, nos. 3–4 (1950), p. 305.

21. See John Willoughby, "The Sexual Behavior of American GIs during the Early Years of the Occupation of Germany," *Journal of Military History* 62 (Jan. 1998), p. 160; and Goedde, "From Villains to Victims," p. 9.

22. See Maria Hoehn, *GIs and Fräuleins: The German-American Encounter in 1950s West Germany* (Chapel Hill: Univ. of North Carolina Press, 2002), pp. 135, 148–51.

23. Klaus-Dietmar Henke, "Fraternization," in *Die amerikanische Besetzung Deutschlands* (Munich: R. Oldenbourg, 1995), p. 194. Henke provides a nuanced and well-documented explanation for the mutual attraction (see pp. 185–204).

24. Richard Joseph with Waverley Root, "Why So Many GIs Like the Germans Best," *Reader's Digest* 48, no. 287 (March 1946), pp. 6–7. Similar perceptions of the contrasts between French and German women are described in a letter to the

editor of the *New York Times*: "In Germany, naturally, the GI finds the best deal. . . . In France the deal is different. The GI doesn't find the all-out bootlicking of Germany." Theodore Singer, letter to the editor of the *New York Times*, 30 Nov. 1945, p. 12, quoted in Willoughby, "The Sexual Behavior of American GIs," pp. 166–67. For another contemporary convinced that postwar German women's easy sexual availability had its source in Nazi encouragement to extramarital sex and reproduction, see the scathingly condescending remarks in Judy Barden, "Candy-Bar Romance—Women of Germany," in *This Is Germany*, ed. Arthur Settel (New York: Sloane, 1950), pp. 161–65. A far more tempered analysis of German singularity suggested that GIs were delighted by German women because they were, on the one hand, "less bound to strict convention" than women of Romance lands like France, and yet, on the other hand, they had been "raised with more of the fear of God" than their "ethnically related" (*stammverwandte*) English counterparts. Thus they were able to offer to GIs "the illusion of an at once 'free' and yet also virtuous . . . love." W. E. Süskind, "Bilanz der Fraternisierung," *Frankfurter Hefte* (Aug. 1946), p. 9.

25. Quoted in Christoph Boyer and Hans Woller, "'Hat die deutsche Frau versagt?': Die 'neue Freiheit' der Frauen in der Trümmerzeit 1945–1949," *Journal für Geschichte* 2 (1983), p. 34.

26. Dittmann, "Die Krisis der Ehe," p. 34.

27. Laszlo Hamori, "Die rationalisierte Sexualität," *Aktion* 8 (1951), p. 48.

28. H. Hesse, "Welche Rolle spielt das Sexualproblem in der Ehe?" *Liebe und Ehe* 2, no. 1 (1950), p. 5.

29. See Petra Lund, "Muss Liebe amtlich beglaubigt sein?" *Constanze* 2, no. 1 (1949), p. 3.

30. See Udo Undeutsch, "Comparative Incidence of Premarital Coitus in Scandinavia, Germany, and the United States," in *Sexual Behavior in American Society: An Appraisal of the First Two Kinsey Reports*, ed. Jerome Himelhoch and Sylvia Fleis Fava (New York: W. W. Norton, 1955), p. 362. Undeutsch was drawing on the same *Wochenend* survey that Friedeburg relied on, just emphasizing different numbers.

31. A. Pauly, "Soll die Verlobung eine Probeehe sein?" *Liebe und Ehe* 2, no. 1 (1950), p. 2.

32. Poem quoted in Henke, "Fraternization," p. 199.

33. Heinz Graupner, "Das normale Geschlechtsleben und seine Gefahren," *Liebe und Ehe* 1, no. 2 (1949), p. 4. This is an excerpt from Graupner, *Geschlechtshygiene und Geschlechtskrankheiten* (Konstanz: Südverlag, 1949).

34. Hans Giese, review of Max Marcuse's essay, "Zur Psychologie der Eifersucht und der Psychopathologie ihres Fehlens," *Psyche* 3 (1950), published in *Zeitschrift für Sexualforschung* 1, nos. 3–4 (1950), p. 307.

35. Letter to the editor, reprinted in Dr. K., "Was halten Sie vom Frauenüberschuss?" p. 10.

36. For example, see "Der Orgasmus," *Sexologie*, no. 1 (1950), pp. 15–25.

37. See Ludwig von Friedeburg, *Die Umfrage in der Intimsphäre*, Beiträge zur Sexualforschung, vol. 4 (Stuttgart: Enke, 1953), pp. 24, 27, 46, 50. There is no reason to think that either of the surveys' findings resulted from inadequately sophisticated sampling techniques. It is unlikely that with more advanced tech-

niques the results would have tended toward greater conservatism. The wealth of other interpretive evidence from the era—from both supporters and detractors of the liberalizing trends—suggests the results' representativeness. It is further notable that those who reported on and analyzed the findings clearly did not feel any need to contradict the results. (In addition to Lund, Undeutsch, and von Friedeburg, see also I. Phönix, "Moderne Intimmoral," in *Mensch, Geschlecht, Gesellschaft: Das Geschlechtsleben unserer Zeit gemeinverständlich dargestellt*, ed. Hans Giese and A. Willy (Paris: G. Aldor, 1954), pp. 201–9.) Moreover, for example, when the sociologist von Friedeburg wrote up the results of the 1949 Institute for Demoscopy survey in his 1953 book, one of the findings he deemed most remarkable was that the Germans interviewed in the study had expressed strong commitment to the institution of marriage. In the early 1950s, when he was formulating his analysis, this commitment was not obvious.

38. See L. R. England, "Little Kinsey: An Outline of Sex Attitudes in Britain," *Public Opinion Quarterly* 13, no. 4 (1949), pp. 587–600; and for a concise summary of Kinsey's findings for the United States, see John D'Emilio and Estelle B. Freedman, *Intimate Matters: A History of Sexuality in America* (New York: Harper and Row, 1988), p. 286.

39. A. Busemann, "Aufgaben sexueller Erziehung in der Gegenwart," *Die Kirche in der Welt* 2, no. 70 (1949), p. 436.

40. Leppich, " 'Thema 1,' " p. 44; and "Gefahren und Ursachen des Sexualismus," *Bonifatiusbote* 63, no. 9 (1952), p. 5.

41. Karl Siegfried Bader, "Die Veränderung der Sexualordnung und die Konstanz der Sittlichkeitsdelikte," *Zeitschrift für Sexualforschung* 1, nos. 3–4 (1950), p. 217.

42. See L. M. Lawrence, "Der Kinsey Report," *Merkur* 3, no. 5 (1949), pp. 495–99. The reviewer in *Die Weltwoche* also thought American women were sexually deprived. Declaring his own belief in "the normalcy of sexual life" and presuming that American attitudes were "for the European perhaps incomprehensible," the reviewer also averred that American women were responsible for their own deprivation. "From earliest childhood on," he announced, the American male was not only taught "to be the wooing one, but also to strive for something that is only granted him with reluctance and repugnance." Ha., "Puritanismus und Wirklichkeit: Kinseys 'Sex Report' und sein Widerhall," *Die Weltwoche* 16, no. 765 (1948), p. 9.

43. For instance, continuities between the sexual liberalities of Weimar and Nazism were taken to be self-evident in such remarks as those of a Catholic activist involved in youth work who urged in 1946 that it should become possible "also to say the word virgin" again "without being met with that disdainful smirk that has in the last decades become the rule." H. Klens quoted in Mark Edward Ruff, "Katholische Jugendarbeit und junge Frauen in Nordrhein-Westfalen 1945–1962," *Archiv für Sozialgeschichte* 38 (1998), p. 272.

44. Conversation with R. S., 1999.

45. Paul Althaus, *Von Liebe und Ehe: Ein evangelisches Wort zu den Fragen der Gegenwart* (Göttingen: Vandenhoeck und Ruprecht, 1949), pp. 3–4.

46. Otto Bernhard Roegele, "Ein heikles Thema . . . Geburtenbeschränkung und Ehenot," *Rheinischer Merkur* 3, no. 3 (1948), p. 3.

47. Hermann Heilweck, "Ein heikles Thema . . . Geburtenbeschränkung und Ehenot," *Rheinischer Merkur* 3, no. 22 (1948), p. 3.

48. For example, one female Bavarian politician declared that "I would like to go so far as to say that if we are again to be a nation among nations [*ein Volk unter Völkern*] then that depends on two matters: on the purity of our marriages and on the fulfillment of our natural right and our highest duty in the education of our children." Elisabeth Meyer-Spreckels, "Ehe und Familie in der Verfassung: Bericht vor dem bayerischen Verfassungsausschuss," *Frankfurter Hefte* (Jan. 1947), p. 93.

49. "Wort der ausserordentlichen Landessynode der Evangelisch-Lutherischen Kirche in Oldenburg an die Gemeinden Oktober 1945," in *Kirchliches Jahrbuch für die evangelische Kirche in Deutschland 1945–1948*, ed. Joachim Beckmann (Gütersloh: Gütersloher Verlagshaus, 1950), pp. 43, 45.

50. "Kundgebung der Landessynode der Evangelisch-Lutherischen Kirche in Bayern in Ansbach, 9.-13. Juli 1946," in Beckmann, *Kirchliches Jahrbuch*, p. 48.

51. Robert Grosche, "Der deutsche Katholizismus 1945–50"; P. Audomar Scheuermann, "Abriss des kirchlichen Eherechts," and Pope Pius XII's remarks to Berlin Catholics (17 June 1949), in "Botschaften und Ansprachen des heiligen Vaters," in *Das katholische Jahrbuch 1951–52* (Heidelberg: Kemper, 1951), pp. 133, 161–75, 210.

52. Bishop quoted in Johannes Kleinschmidt, "Amerikaner und Deutsche in der Besatzungszeit—Beziehungen und Probleme," http://www.lpb.bwue.de/publikat/besatzer/us-pol6.htm.

53. Leppich, "'Thema 1,'" pp. 43–44.

54. See the important anthology, *Kreuz mit dem Frieden: 1982 Jahre Christen und Politik*, ed. Peter Winzeler (Berlin: Elefanten Press, 1982), as well as the main venues in the postwar era for progressive Protestantism (*Junge Kirche*) and progressive Catholicism (*Frankfurter Hefte*). On the ambiguities of postfascist Christianity, see also Dagmar Herzog, "Making Sense of the Past: Antifascist Protestants and the Lessons of the Third Reich, 1945–1965" (paper presented at the Mellon Faculty Forum, Harvard University, 4 Apr. 1994); and Dagmar Herzog, "'Believing in God as an Atheist': Left-Wing Theology and the Confrontation with Secularization" (paper presented at the conference "Formen Religiöser Vergemeinschaftung in der Moderne," University of Chicago, 25 Oct. 2003).

55. "Wort der ausserordentlichen Landessynode der Evangelisch-Lutherischen Kirche in Oldenburg an die Gemeinden Oktober 1945," p. 43.

56. Otto Bernhard Roegele, "Wertloses Leben?" *Rheinischer Merkur*, 30 Aug. 1947, p. 2.

57. For example, see the powerful essay by Eugen Kogon, "Gericht und Gewissen," *Frankfurter Hefte* (Apr. 1946), pp. 25–37.

58. Anton Christian Hofmann, *Die Natürlichkeit der christlichen Ehe* (Munich: J. Pfeiffer, 1951), pp. 5, 9–10, 38–39.

59. For one example among many, contrast the effusively pro-Nazi remarks of Protestant Church activist D. Erich Stange in 1933 with his description of Christians as victims of Nazism in 1951. See Stange quoted in Ernst Klee, *"Die SA Jesu Christi": Die Kirchen im Banne Hitlers* (Frankfurt am Main: Fischer, 1989), pp. 26–27; and D. Erich Stange, "Innere Mission und kirchliche Werke," *Evan-*

gelische Welt 5, no. 22 (16 Nov. 1951), p. 678. But note that also consistently anti-Nazi Christians distorted the relationship between Christianity and Nazism when they emphasized Nazism's anti-Christianity. See, for example, Walter Dirks's remark that "German Catholicism stood on the list of opponents of the German essence that were to be exterminated" (*Der deutsche Katholizismus stand auf der Liste der zur Ausrottung bestimmten Widersacher des deutschen Wesens*). Dirks in *Frankfurter Hefte* (May 1946), p. 45. Postwar Protestants too regularly remarked that Nazism had planned to "liquidate the church," that Nazism wanted to "destroy the church and exterminate the Christian faith," or that "the persecution of Christians was the direct extension of the battle against the Jews. It would have led to a similar extermination program." Link, "Königsberg (1945–1948)," *Junge Kirche. Sonderdruck* (Jan. 1950); "Wort des Bruderrates der EKD zur Reinigung der Kirche vom Nationalsozialismus," *Kirchliches Jahrbuch 1945–1948*, p. 187; Otto Fricke, "Wir Christen und die Juden" (1949), in *Die Juden und wir Christen*, ed. Hans Kallenbach (Frankfurt am Main: Lembeck, 1950), pp. 48–49.

60. Heilweck, "Ein heikles Thema," p. 3.

61. Walter Dirks, "Ein Wort an die Arbeiterschaft in Sachen Paragraph 218," *Frankfurter Hefte* (Dec. 1946), pp. 793–94.

62. Hermann Frühauf, "Paragraph 218," *Frankfurter Hefte* (Oct. 1946), p. 590. Protestants were less active than Catholics in efforts to defeat the campaign to decriminalize abortion, but Protestant opponents of abortion made some related claims—for instance, stressing how difficult it was to "reawaken" awe and respect for "the right to life" in the wake of "an epoch which succumbed to the spirit of killing." Frau Dr. Schwörer speaking before a Protestant Church–organized gathering of midwives in 1951, summarized in "Verantwortung für die Ungeborenen," *Evangelische Welt* 5, no. 22 (16 Nov. 1951), p. 682.

63. See Romano Guardini, "Die soziale Indikation für die Unterbrechung der Schwangerschaft," *Frankfurter Hefte*, Sept. 1947, p. 930.

64. Probst quoted in Angela Delille and Andrea Grohn, "Es ist verboten . . . Empfängnisverhütung und Abtreibung," in *Perlonzeit*, ed. Delille and Grohn (Berlin: Elefanten Press, 1985), p. 124.

65. Gröber quoted in ibid.

66. "Gefahren und Ursachen des Sexualismus," p. 5.

67. Klaus von Bismarck, summarized in "Familienförderung als kirchliche Aufgabe," *Evangelische Welt* 5, no. 22 (16 Nov. 1951), p. 682.

68. Rosine Speicher, "Um das Leben der Ungeborenen," *Die Welt der Frau* 1, nos. 8–9 (Feb.–Mar. 1947), p. 61.

69. Hans March, "Zur Sexual-Ethik," *Stimmen der Zeit* 156 (1955), pp. 290–91, 299, 301. "Pure sexual intercourse, that supposedly is done only for its own sake, that is sought for the sake of the pleasurable release of a bodily urge and knows or wants to know nothing of a deeper soul-spiritual expressive content," March announced, "actually leaves the more differentiated person unsatisfied."

70. Theodor Bovet, "Die Ehe, ihre Krise und Neuwerdung," *Universitas* 2, no. 2 (1947), p. 161.

71. Franz Arnold, "Sinnlichkeit und Sexualität im Lichte von Theologie und Seelsorge," in *Über das Wesen der Sexualität*, Beiträge zur Sexualforschung, vol. 1 (Stuttgart: Enke, 1952), p. 1.

72. Franz Arnold, "Das eheliche Geheimnis in Theologie und Seelsorge," *Universitas* 2, no. 10 (1947): 1155, 1158. Arnold in fact departed from Catholic Church teaching in contending that birth control was acceptable within marriage.

73. Roegele, "Ein heikles Thema," p. 3.

74. Hans Wirtz, *Vom Eros zur Ehe: Die naturgetreue Lebensgemeinschaft* (Heidelberg: F. H. Kerle, 1946), pp. 7, 227, 231, 246, 248, 256–57. Wirtz had used the same language in the earlier edition of the book published during the Third Reich.

75. Hofmann, *Die Natürlichkeit*, pp. 50, 83.

76. Theodor Bovet, *Die werdende Frau* (Bern: Paul Haupt, 1962), pp. 20–21; the book previously appeared in Switzerland in 1944, and was first published in Germany in 1950.

77. Schöllgen in *Die Kirche in der Welt* 1, no. 35 (1947–48), p. 160. Schöllgen's comments about orgasm and fertility were part of a larger phenomenon in Nazi and post-Nazi Germany. A number of specialists speculated that orgasms could trigger ovulation, usually in the context of using this "concern" to dismiss the rhythm method as entirely ineffective (while remaining apparently unconcerned about the crises and conflicts that this "news" would inevitably cause for seriously Catholic couples). See "Die andere Auffassung," *Ärztliche Praxis* 2, no. 42 (21 Oct. 1950), p. 4. Another strand of argumentation, developed under Nazism, claimed to have found that a woman's orgasm permitted sperm to travel more rapidly through the cervix. For example, see B. Belonoshkin, "Weibliche Psyche und Konzeption," *Münchener Medizinische Wochenschrift* 88 (1941), pp. 1007–9.

78. See Meta Holland, *Vor dem Tore der Ehe: Was jede junge Frau wissen muss*, 2nd ed. (Konstanz: Christliche Verlagsanstalt, 1936), pp. 4–5, 91–97, and (Konstanz: Christliche Verlagsanstalt, 1950), pp. 5, 87–89.

79. Ernst Karl Winter, "Das grosse Geheimnis: Ehe und Familie in der christlichen Zivilisation," *Frankfurter Hefte* (Oct. 1951), p. 716.

80. Theodor Bovet, *Von Mann zu Mann: Eine Einführung ins Reifealter für junge Männer* (Tübingen: Katzmann, 1955), p. 47.

81. See Karl P. Rüth, "Ist 'Liebe und Ehe' eine unzüchtige Zeitschrift?" *Liebe und Ehe* 3, no. 5 (1951), p. 212; see also Sven Säger, "Sind wir eigentlich prüde?" *Liebe und Ehe* 2, no. 3 (1950), p. 20. See also Robert Schilling, *Gesamtverzeichnis der jugendgefährdenden Schriften nach dem Stande vom 1. April 1961* (Neuwied: Luchterhand, 1961), p. 59.

82. See *Liebe und Ehe* 1, no. 1 (1949), p. 21.

83. Kurt Fiebich, "Zur Frage der Bordellisierung," *Liebe und Ehe* 2, no. 9 (1950), p. 12.

84. Helmut Meissner, "Dreiecksehe sanktioniert," *Liebe und Ehe* 3, no. 10 (1951), p. 413.

85. Gerhard Ockel, "Tiefenpsychologie und Sinnlichkeit," *Liebe und Ehe* 3, no. 2 (1951), p. 54.

86. Dorothee Löhe, "Menschenpaar," *Liebe und Ehe* 2, no. 1 (1950), p. 1.

87. K. Fischer, "Darf Herr X Frau Y spät abends besuchen?" *Liebe und Ehe* 2, no. 12 (1950), p. 15.

88. Wilhelm Schuh, "Die Eltern, die Tochter, und die Liebe," *Liebe und Ehe* 3, no. 10 (1951), p. 400.

89. Hans Niedermeier, "'Mein Schatz ist ein Matrose . . . ,' " *Liebe und Ehe* 2, no. 11 (1950), p. 19.

90. Kurt Fiebich, "Der Selbstmord der Intelligenz: Die Expansion der Minderbegabten," *Liebe und Ehe* 3, no. 8 (1951), p. 318.

91. Hans von Hohenecken, "Kleine Kulturgeschichte in Heiratsanzeigen," *Liebe und Ehe* 2, no. 8 (1950), p. 40.

92. Martin Brustmann, "Sexuelle Probleme in der SS," *Liebe und Ehe* 3, no. 2 (1951), p. 63; 3, no. 3 (1951), p. 113; 3, no. 4 (1951), p. 148; 3, no. 5 (1951), p. 204.

93. Martin Brustmann, "Sexuelle Probleme in der SS," *Liebe und Ehe* 3, no. 6 (1951), p. 249.

94. Such doubleness of identification and disidentification was also strongly facilitated by the simultaneous hyperventilated fascination with and trivializing banalization of Nazism in the popular postwar press—what one thoughtful critic described as the "smug kitsch of the illustrated magazines," with their "dangerous cult of heroes" and "glorification of the brown celebrities." Karl Gehau, "Der Fluch der guten Tat," *Frankfurter Hefte* (Dec. 1952), p. 963.

95. Gerhard Giehm, "Von der Sexualität in unserer Zeit," *Liebe und Ehe* 1, no. 1 (1949), p. 2. This is an excerpt from Giehm, *Behandlung seelischer und nervöser Sexualleiden* (Hannover: Bruno-Wilkens-Verlag, 1948).

96. Löhe, "Menschenpaar," p. 1.

97. See on this point also the important retrospective reflections of a pastor on the responsibility-diffusing rhetoric used by postwar Germans as they described themselves as having been "victims of the era" (*Opfer der Zeit*, or ODZ). Ingke Brodersen, Klaus Humann, and Susanne von Paczensky, eds., *1933: Wie die Deutschen Hitler zur Macht Verhalfen. Ein Lesebuch für Demokraten* (Reinbek: Rowohlt, 1983), p. 303.

98. Gernot B. quoted in Heinrich Albert, "Über Verhältnisblödsinn," in *Randzonen menschlichen Verhaltens: Beiträge zur Psychiatrie und Neurologie* (Stuttgart: Enke, 1962), p. 195.

99. According to the editors of *Liebe und Ehe*, for example, a battery of hormonal and herbal products to enhance potency were increasingly also being used by quite young men, "so to speak, those in the best years," due not least to the "*emotional* wounds that the last war and the postwar period beat into many millions of men." See "Ihre Sorgen—Unser Rat," *Liebe und Ehe* 2, no. 1 (1950), p. 35.

100. Walter Frederking, "Die Krisis der Ehe: Was der Arzt meint," *Nordwestdeutsche Hefte* 2, no. 10 (1947), pp. 33–34. As Frederking put it, "The German human being has changed more than most of us are aware. One needs only to think of the extent to which feelings and concepts of justice have become blurred and crumbled."

101. Ibid., p. 34.

102. H. H., "Hut ab vor unseren Frauen!" *Constanze* 1, no. 2 (1948), pp. 4–5.

103. Walther von Hollander, "Mann in der Krise: Anklage der Frauen," *Constanze* 1, no. 1 (1948), pp. 3, 22.

104. Ibid., p. 22; and "Aus Walther von Hollanders Privatkorrespondenz," *Constanze* 1, no.1 (1948), p. 19.

105. Walther von Hollander, "Mann in der Krise: Glanz und Elend des Intellekts," *Constanze* 1, no. 2 (1948), p. 15; and Walther von Hollander, "Mann in der Krise: Tristan, Don Juan und der Patriarch," *Constanze* 1, no. 3 (1948), p. 19.

106. Else Feldbinder, "Er und Sie 1948," *Constanze* 1, no. 7 (1948), p. 3.

107. See Hans-Georg Stümke, *Homosexuelle in Deutschland: Eine politische Geschichte* (Munich: Beck, 1989), pp. 73, 81–82.

108. J. Strüder, "Beitrag zur Homosexuellenfrage," *Kriminalistische Monatshefte* 11 (1937), pp. 219–20.

109. Walter Meyer, "Könnte es eine chemisch-physiologische Diagnose und eine erfolgreiche Therapie der echten Homosexualität geben?" *Psychiatrisch-Neurologische Wochenschrift* 39, no. 28 (10 July 1937), p. 309.

110. L. G. Tirala, "Homosexualität und Rassenmischung," *Verhandlungen der Gesellschaft deutscher Naturforscher und Ärzte* 93 (1934), p. 148; J. H. Schultz, "Bemerkungen zu der Arbeit von Theo Lang über die genetische Bedingtheit der Homosexualität," *Zeitschrift für die gesamte Neurologie und Psychiatrie*, no. 157 (1937), pp. 575, 577.

111. For examples of varieties in sentencing, and the general early postwar climate of flux and indeterminacy, see "Rechtliche Beurteilung der Homosexualität," *Geist und Tat* 6, no. 10 (1951), p. 333; Franz Baumeyer, "Zur Beurteilung der Homosexualität," *Die Medizinische* 1 (1952), p. 1603; A. Ohm, "Homosexualität als Neurose," *Der Weg zur Seele* 5 (1953), pp. 51–52; Wilhelm Ellinghaus, "Verfassungmässigkeit des Paragraphen 175 RstGB," *Kriminalistik* 8, no. 3 (1954), pp. 61–63; as well as Mario Kramp and Martin Sölle, "Paragraph 175—Restauration und Reform in der Bundesrepublik," in *"Himmel und Hölle": Das Leben der Kölner Homosexuellen 1945–1969*, ed. Kristof Balser et al. (Cologne: Emons, 1995), p. 126.

112. "Eine Million Delikte," *Der Spiegel*, 29 Nov. 1950, p. 8.

113. Ibid., pp. 8–9. See also Dieter Schiefelbein, "Wiederbeginn der juristischen Verfolgung homosexueller Männer in der Bundesrepublik Deutschland: Die Homosexuellen-Prozesse in Frankfurt am Main 1950/51," *Zeitschrift für Sexualforschung* 5 (1992), pp. 59–73.

114. "Eingabe an die Gesetzgebenden Organe des Bundes in Bonn betr. Paragraphen 175, 175a StGB," *Zeitschrift für Sexualforschung* 1, nos. 3–4 (1950), pp. 311–12.

115. Hans Giese, "Zweck und Sinn der Eingabe," *Zeitschrift für Sexualforschung* 1, nos. 3–4 (1950), pp. 313–15.

116. Horst Pommerening, "Ergebnis der Arbeitstagung vom 11. April 1950," *Zeitschrift für Sexualforschung* 1, nos. 3–4 (1950), pp. 323, 326.

117. Karl Siegfried Bader, "Gutachtliche Äusserung zur Reform der Paragraphen 175, 175a StGB," *Zeitschrift für Sexualforschung* 1, nos. 3–4 (1950), pp. 328, 330, 332.

118. "Rechtliche Beurteilung," p. 334.

119. "Eine Million Delikte," pp. 7–8, 10.

120. Schönke, 1952, quoted in Ellinghaus, "Verfassungsmässigkeit," p. 62.

121. For example, see Maasen, 1954, quoted in ibid.

122. It is revealing that even *opponents* of the paragraph like Bader or Pommerening called attention to the widely felt concern about protection of young men during their, as also Bader put it, potentially "bisexual" phase. Pommerening, despite raising strong doubts about the whole notion of seducibility to homosexuality, nonetheless proposed (perhaps tactically) retaining the age of consent for homosexual acts at twenty-one—because of youth's apparent tendency to "pseudohomoeroticism." Bader, "Gutachtliche Äusserung," p. 330; Pommerening, "Ergebnis," p. 324.

123. "Literatur-Umschau," *Kriminalistik* 6, nos. 13–14 (1952), pp. 167–68. The book under discussion is by a jurist: Gatzweiler, *Das dritte Geschlecht* (Cologne-Klettenberg: Volkswartbund, 1951).

124. "Not um den Paragraphen 175," *Christ und Welt* 4, no. 20 (1951), pp. 4–5.

125. Kramp and Sölle, "Paragraph 175," pp. 132, 139–41.

126. Ellinghaus, "Verfassungsmässigkeit," p. 63.

127. See Robert G. Moeller, " 'The Homosexual Man Is a 'Man,' the Homosexual Woman Is a 'Woman,': Sex, Society and the Law in Postwar West Germany," *Journal of the History of Sexuality* 4, no. 3 (1994).

128. Statistics on registrations and arrests and Schoeps summarized in Kramp and Sölle, "Paragraph 175," pp. 133, 142.

129. Ohm, "Homosexualität als Neurose," p. 56. True to form, Ohm was also convinced that a big reason for homosexuality was many men's inhibitions vis-à-vis real women due to their overidealization of one particular woman, often their mother, or their search for a girl who was so perfect she did not exist. Ohm heaped up anecdotes of homosexuals turned off from the heterosexual "path" by dislike of women's vaginal fluids, or instances in which they felt women had humiliated them. As a result, men "neurotically" built up obstacles so that it became "impossible" for them to "walk" on this "path perceived to be threatening and dangerous" (p. 55).

130. The defendant is quoted in Baumeyer, "Zur Beurteilung," p. 1603.

131. See Ohm, "Homosexualität als Neurose," p. 24.

132. Conversation with G. C., 2002. This man guessed that the four officers were not necessarily homosexually inclined in peacetime but rather that the absence of women was the key factor for "some if not all" of them. See also the findings of Geoffrey Giles, who in his analysis of the few trial records remaining for cases of homosexuality judged before the SS special courts (*Sondergerichte*) found that there was apparently a blurred boundary in many men's minds between a homosexual orientation and acceptable homosexual fondling as a substitute for heterosexual sex in the absence of women. Geoffrey Giles, "The Denial of Homosexuality: Same-Sex Incidents in Himmler's SS and Police," *Journal of the History of Sexuality* 11, nos. 1–2 (Jan.–Apr. 2002), esp. pp. 273–80.

133. Von Friedeburg, *Die Umfrage in der Intimsphäre*, p. 87. When the survey was repeated in 1963, only 10 percent of West German men questioned admitted having "contact with" homosexuality. See Elisabeth Noelle and Erich Peter Neu-

mann, eds., *Jahrbuch der öffentlichen Meinung 1958–1964* (Allensbach and Bonn: Verlag für Demoskopie, 1965), p. 591.

134. For example, see Radu Cernea, *Sexual-Biologische Studien: Betrachtungen eines Arztes über das Wesen und die Bedeutung der Sexualität* (Munich: Akademischer Verlag, 1948), pp. 87, 117–19; Von der Spreu, "Die Wissenschaft meldet," *Liebe und Ehe* 1, no. 1 (1949), p. 34; Von der Spreu, "Störungen der männlichen Potenz III," *Liebe und Ehe* 2, no. 8 (1950), pp. 19–20.

135. See Von der Spreu, "Störung der männlichen Potenz II," *Liebe und Ehe* 2, no. 6 (1950), p. 16; and von der Spreu, "Störung der männlichen Potenz III," pp. 19–20. Von der Spreu took the view that impotence or premature ejaculation could also be the result of a "fundamental homosexual disposition, that rejects the woman as a sexual partner no matter what." Radu Cernea was of the opinion that "Among the cases of war impotence that present themselves to the doctor there are very many latent homosexuals who are not even aware of their homosexuality. They only feel a repulsion toward a woman, or they complain of impotence despite persistent love. Only later they become aware that in the field, under the mask of friendship and comradeship, the homosexual drive announced itself. The more we study the cases of homosexuality, the more we recognize that homosexuality is a neurosis, a flight from the woman." Cernea, *Sexual-Biologische Studien*, pp. 122–23. See in this context also C. Kallwitz, "Das Sexualproblem in der Kriegsgefangenschaft," *Liebe und Ehe* 1, no. 2 (1949), pp. 20, 25.

136. On the thesis that postwar homophobia drew its virulent force not so much from any latent homosexual desires as from quite concrete familiarity with homosexual experiences in wartime, see also Martin Dannecker, "Der unstillbare Wunsch nach Anerkennung: Homosexuellenpolitik in den fünfziger und sechziger Jahren," in *Was heisst hier schwul? Politik und Identitäten im Wandel*, ed. Detlef Grumbach (Hamburg: MännerschwarmSkript, 1997), pp. 35–37.

137. See David K. Johnson, *The Lavender Scare: The Cold War Persecution of Gays and Lesbians in the Federal Government* (Chicago: Univ. of Chicago Press, 2004); John D'Emilio, "The Homosexual Menace: The Politics of Sexuality in Cold War America," in *Passion and Power: Sexuality in History*, ed. Kathy Peiss and Christina Simmons (Philadelphia: Temple Univ. Press, 1989); Barbara Ehrenreich, "Breadwinners and Losers," in *The Hearts of Men: American Dreams and the Flight from Commitment* (New York: Anchor, 1983); Sonya Michel, "Danger on the Home Front: Motherhood, Sexuality, and Disabled Veterans in American Postwar Films," in *American Sexual Politics*, ed. John C. Fout and Maura Shaw Tantillo (Chicago: Univ. of Chicago Press, 1993).

138. See Olav Münzberg, "Wovon berührt? Vom jüdischen Trauma? Von den Traumata der Eltern?" *Ästhetik und Kommunikation* 51 (June 1983), p. 25; and Martin Dannecker, "Die verspätete Empirie," *Zeitschrift für Sexualforschung* 14, no. 2 (June 2001), pp. 173–74. Also see the fascinating reflections on the displacement of moral blame in post-Nazi Austria (from men who had been enmeshed in genocidal warfare onto women who consorted with the occupying Americans) in Ingrid Bauer, " 'Austria's Prestige Dragged into the Dirt'? The 'GI-Brides' and Postwar Austrian Society (1945–1955)," *Contemporary Austrian Studies* (1998).

139. Lauren Berlant and Michael Warner, "Sex in Public," *Critical Inquiry* 24, no. 2 (winter 1998), p. 548; see also pp. 549, 552–53.

140. Dittmann, "Die Krisis der Ehe," p. 34; Leppich, "'Thema 1,'" p. 44.

141. Kolle quoted in Peter Knorr, "Schwierigkeiten bei der Sexualaufklärung," *Pardon* 8, no. 12 (Dec. 1969), p. 65.

142. See Reimut Reiche, "Kritik der gegenwärtigen Sexualwissenschaft," in *Tendenzen der Sexualforschung*, ed. Gunter Schmidt et al. (Stuttgart: Enke, 1970), p. 2.

143. "Tut Scheiden weh?" *Constanze* 21 (1948), p. 3; Luise Heise, "Unverstanden—nicht ernst genommen?" *Constanze* 10 (1948), p. 3.

144. See "Erst die Liebe, dann die Moral? Alles über die Deutschen (15)," *Der Stern*, no. 48 (1963), pp. 43–52; and Noelle and Neumann, *Jahrbuch*, pp. 589–90.

145. See Ulrike Heider, "Freie Liebe und Liebesreligion: Zum Sexualitätsbegriff der sechziger und achtziger Jahre," in *Sadomasochisten, Keusche und Romantiker: Vom Mythos neuer Sinnlichkeit*, ed. Heider (Reinbek: Rowohlt, 1986), p. 93; Michael Schneider, "Fathers and Sons, Retrospectively: The Damaged Relationship between Two Generations," *New German Critique* 31 (winter 1984), p. 9; and Sabine Weissler, "Sexy Sixties," in *CheSchahShit: Die sechziger Jahre zwischen Cocktail und Molotov*, ed. Eckhard Siepmann et al. (Berlin: Elefanten Press, 1984), p. 96.

146. Heipe Weiss, "Freie Liebe war vor allem Reden über Sex," *Frankfurter Neue Presse*, 24 Apr. 1998, p. 9.

147. Along these latter lines, for instance, the self-styled homosexuality expert Theo Lang, one of the most prolific publicists on the subject in the Nazi era, took the occasion of the postwar discussion over whether to abolish Paragraph 175 to try to revive his career. Lang not only reiterated the importance of his Nazi-era research (based on case files supplied by police forces in various German cities) but also asserted that "approximately two-thirds of all cases of homosexuality are genetically determined," and thus that the threat of punishment could not hope to lead to any "change of drive-direction" in these individuals. Nonetheless, he averred, the threat of punishments was still necessary because of these individuals' (also innate) tendency "to propagate their inversion" and to seek to convert others to homosexuality. Theo Lang, "Zum Problem der Homosexualität," *Juristische Rundschau* (1952), pp. 273–75.

148. For example, see the postwar citations of the Nazi-era work of Dr. Hermann Stieve in O. Hajek, "Willkürliche Geburtenregelung," *Ärztliche Praxis* 5, no. 12 (21 March 1953), p. 9; "Die andere Auffassung," p. 4; and F. G. von Stockert, "Kindheit, Pubertät, Reife, Alter," in *Die Sexualität des Menschen: Handbuch der medizinischen Sexualforschung*, ed. Hans Giese (Stuttgart: Enke, 1955), p. 288. On Stieve's "research" under Nazism, see Ulrich Schultz-Venrath and Ludger M. Hermanns, "Gleichschaltung zur Ganzheit: Gab es eine Psychosomatik im Nationalsozialismus?" in *Neues Denken in der Psychosomatik*, ed. Horst-Eberhard Richter and Michael Wirsching (Frankfurt: Fischer, 1991), p. 98.

149. Hans Harmsen, "Das medizinische Übel der Abtreibung," *Die Heilkunst* 66, no. 7 (1953), p. 233. Atina Grossmann has not only documented Harmsen's own embrace of and close collaboration with the Nazis but also explained why, in Cold War West Germany, Harmsen was nonetheless deemed more acceptable by American family-planning organizations than any of the activists who had been

affiliated with the Communist Party's sex reform activities in the Weimar era. See Atina Grossmann, *Reforming Sex: The German Movement for Birth Control and Abortion Reform, 1920–1950* (New York: Oxford Univ. Press, 1995), as well as the concise summary of Harmsen's blatant disdain for the disabled (and his meteoric postwar career) in Ernst Klee, *Was sie taten—Was sie wurden: Ärzte, Juristen und andere Beteiligte am Kranken- oder Judenmord* (Frankfurt am Main: Fischer, 1986), pp. 150–51. The point here is that in 1953 Harmsen felt no need to hide his approval of Nazi policies.

150. March, "Zur Sexual-Ethik," pp. 297–99. On the perception of Muckermann as a "moderate" antisemite, see the review of Muckermann's *Rassenforschung und Volk der Zukunft: Ein Beitrag zur Einführung in die Frage vom biologischen Werden der Menschheit*, 3rd expanded ed. (Berlin and Bonn: Ferdinand Dümmler, 1934), by Peter Schmitz in *Der Seelsorger* 10 (1934), p. 362. Schmitz praised Muckermann for "being in racial matters totally free of all fantastical thinking, putting the significance of races into its proper bounds, but also pointing out forcefully the damages and disadvantages of an unharmonious racial mixing." On Muckermann's openly advanced post-1945 opinions—including his opposition to marriage between European and "Negroid" peoples and his vociferous concern that the disabled cost society more than the healthy ("the thought is unbearable that hopeless progeny from mentally debilitated hereditary lines would be cared for with greater devotion than the progeny of healthy parents")—see Klee, *Was sie taten—Was sie wurden*, pp. 148–49.

151. Y. Michal Bodemann, "Mentalitäten des Verweilens: Der Neubeginn jüdischen Lebens in Deutschland," in *Leben im Land der Täter: Juden im Nachkriegsdeutschland (1945–1952)*, ed. Julius H. Schoeps (Berlin: Jüdische Verlagsanstalt, 2001), p. 15.

CHAPTER THREE
DESPERATELY SEEKING NORMALITY

1. Martin Dannecker, "Die verspätete Empirie: Anmerkungen zu den Anfängen der Deutschen Gesellschaft für Sexualforschung," *Zeitschrift für Sexualforschung* 14, no. 2 (June 2001), p. 173.

2. Ulf Preuss-Lausitz, "Vom gepanzerten zum sinnstiftenden Körper," in *Kriegskinder, Konsumkinder, Krisenkinder: Zur Sozialisationsgeschichte seit dem Zweiten Weltkrieg*, ed. Preuss-Lausitz et al. (Weinheim: Beltz, 1989), pp. 90, 92.

3. See Hans-Peter Schwarz, *Die Ära Adenauer: Gründerjahre der Republik 1949–1957* (Stuttgart: Deutsche Verlags-Anstalt, 1981), p. 382; and Ulrich Herbert, "Legt die Plakate nieder, ihr Streiter für die Gerechtigkeit," *Frankfurter Allgemeine Zeitung*, no. 24 (29 Jan. 2001), p. 48.

4. All quotations in Wolfgang Löhr, "Rechristianisierungsvorstellungen im deutschen Katholizismus 1945–1948," in *Christentum und politische Verantwortung: Kirchen im Nachkriegsdeutschland*, ed. Jochen-Christoph Kaiser and Anselm Döring-Manteuffel (Stuttgart: W. Kohlhammer, 1990), pp. 26–27, 29.

5. See Frank Biess, "Repräsentanten der Not—Christliche Wohlfahrtsorganisationen zwischen Krieg und Nachkrieg" (paper presented at the German Studies Association, San Diego, 5 Oct. 2002).

6. The phrase in quotes is from Hanna Schissler, "'Normalization' as Project: Some Thoughts on Gender Relations in West Germany during the 1950s," in *The Miracle Years: A Cultural History of West Germany, 1949–1968*, ed. Schissler (Princeton: Princeton Univ. Press, 2001), p. 366.

7. See Sophinette Becker, "Zur Funktion der Sexualität im Nationalsozialismus," *Zeitschrift für Sexualforschung* 14, no. 2 (June 2001), pp. 142–43. Becker is here building on the work of historian Ian Kershaw. On the function of withdrawal into privacy as a way of avoiding emotional confrontation with the knowledge of mass murder, see also David Bankier, *The Germans and the Final Solution* (Oxford: Blackwell, 1992).

8. Y. Michal Bodemann, "Eclipse of Memory: German Representations of Auschwitz in the Early Postwar Period," *New German Critique*, no. 75 (fall 1998), pp. 61–72, 88–89.

9. See Frank Stern, *The Whitewashing of the Yellow Badge: Antisemitism and Philosemitism in Postwar Germany* (Oxford: Pergamon, 1992), pp. 302–10; Micha Brumlik, "Post-Holocaust Theology: German Theological Responses since 1945," in *Betrayal: German Churches and the Holocaust*, ed. Robert Ericksen and Susannah Heschel (Minneapolis: Fortress, 1999).

10. See in this context also Maria Hoehn, *GIs and Fräuleins: The German-American Encounter in 1950s West Germany* (Chapel Hill: Univ. of North Carolina Press, 2002), pp. 145–47.

11. Olav Münzberg, "Wovon berührt? Vom jüdischen Trauma? Von den Traumata der Eltern?" *Ästhetik und Kommunikation* 51 (June 1983), p. 25.

12. On the dearth of spiritual renewal and the superficiality of motivations for church attendance in the late 1940s, see also Martin Greschat, *Die evangelische Christenheit und die deutsche Geschichte nach 1945* (Stuttgart: Kohlhammer, 2002), pp. 71–72.

13. Hermann Peter Piwitt, "Autoritär, betulich, neckish und devot," *Konkret*, May 1979, p. 34.

14. Günter Grass, "Geschenkte Freiheit: Versagen, Schuld, vertane Chancen," *Die Zeit*, no. 20 (10 May 1985), p. 21.

15. "Mit Unbehagen," *Die Welt*, 19 Sept. 1952.

16. "Schutz vor Schund und Schmutz," *Frankfurter Allgemeine Zeitung*, 13 Dec. 1949.

17. For an example of early government hesitation about the advisability of an antismut law, see the remarks of the federal minister of justice, Thomas Dehler, summarized in "Gegen Schmutz- und Schundgesetz," *Allgemeine Kölnische Rundschau*, 1 Feb. 1950. See as well the antilegislation stances of politicians in the state of Baden-Württemberg ("Gegen Schund und Schmutz," *Mannheimer Morgen*, 4 Mar. 1950) and in the Free Democratic Party ("FDP-Kulturausschuss lehnt Schundgesetz ab," *Wiesbadener Kurier*, 20 Mar. 1950).

18. "Der 'Skandal der Kioske,' " *HamburgerAllgemeine*, 27 Feb. 1950; Alfred Happ, " 'Feinere Schamlosigkeit,' " *Frankfurter Rundschau*, 3 May 1950.

19. See "Zum Schutz der heranwachsenden Jugend," *Die Welt*, 20 April 1950.

20. Under the 1926 Weimar law 3,660 publications and all the works of an additional 455 authors were put on a blacklist. The Nazis nullified and replaced the Weimar law with their own stricter ruling in April 1935. See Stefan Malin, "Zu diesem Schund und Schmutz: Mit der 'Lex Heintze' begann es," *Die neue Zeitung*, 12 Mar. 1950; "Moral mit Paragraphen," *Die deutsche Zeitung und Wirtschafts Zeitung*, 23 July 1952; and see also the protests of writers and publishers summarized in Gerhard Lüttke, "Verleger und Autoren gegen ein Schund- und Schmutzgesetz," *Frankfurter Rundschau*, 14 Jan. 1950.

21. See "Mit untauglichen Mitteln," *Frankfurter Allgemeine Zeitung*, 26 Aug. 1952. The language about "glorifying war crimes and racial hatred" suddenly appeared as the Bundestag's Committee for Youth Welfare, after almost two years of work, offered a revised version of the law to the Bundestag for final deliberation in July 1952. See "Schmutz- und Schundgesetz fertiggestellt," *Die Neue Zeitung*, 12 July 1952.

22. See the trajectory of the discussion in *Verhandlungen des Deutschen Bundestages. I. Wahlperiode 1949*, vol. 13 (Bonn: Universitäts-Buchdruckerei, 1952), pp. 10532–56. See especially the comments of Maria Niggemeyer of the CDU (p. 10533), Minister of the Interior Robert Lehr, also of the CDU (p. 10536), Anne Marie Heiler of the CDU (p. 10539), Gertrud Strohbach of the Communist Party (KPD) (p. 10542), and Ferdinand Friedensburg of the CDU (p. 10547).

23. See Robert Schilling, *Gesamtverzeichnis der jugendgefährdenden Schriften nach dem Stande vom 1. April 1961* (Neuwied: Luchterhand, 1961), p. 65.

24. See Petra Jäschke, "Produktionsbedingungen und gesellschaftliche Einschätzungen," in *Zwischen Trümmern und Wohlstand: Literatur der Jugend 1945–1960*, ed. Klaus Doderer (Weinheim and Basel: Beltz, 1988), p. 324.

25. See Reimut Reiche, "Über Kinsey," *Zeitschrift für Sexualforschung* 11, no. 2 (1998), p. 167.

26. For example, see Malin, "Zu diesem Schund und Schmutz."

27. Happ, " 'Feinere Schamlosigkeit.' "

28. Erich Kästner, "Schund- und Schandgesetzgebung," reprinted in *Kästner für Erwachsense*, ed. R. W. Leonhardt (Frankfurt am Main and Zurich: S. Fischer/Atrium, 1966).

29. Carlo Schmid, "Schmutz- und Schund-Gesetz—endlose Schraube," *Die Welt*, 13 Jan. 1950.

30. Kästner, "Schund- und Schandgesetzgebung."

31. Communist analyses did not help in offering a more differentiated explanation for the appeals of pornography. KPD politician Renner's remarks in the Bundestag to the effect that the millions of Deutschmark spent on pornographic literature were "indicative of the rotted social order in the Federal Republic" (in contrast to the impressive model provided by the Soviet zone of occupation, "where erotic-decadent literature is not purchasable") only inspired a journalist to sharp sarcasm about the contrast between Stalinist "moralism" on the one hand and the Red Army rapes of German women and concentration and forced labor camps for political opponents of Stalinism on the other. H. H., "Totale Moral," *General-Anzeiger*, 14 Feb. 1952.

32. F. M. Reifferscheidt, "Was steckt hinter 'Schmutz und Schund?'" *Frankfurter Rundschau*, 10 Jan. 1950.

33. See "Schund und Schmutz," *Rhein-Echo*, 2 Mar. 1950.

34. *5 vor 12* (Echter-Verlag, 1950), quoted in Jäschke, "Produktionsbedingungen," p. 321.

35. See Heinz Neudeck, "Pressefreiheit und Jugendschutz," *Die neue Zeitung*, 18 Mar. 1950.

36. Helmut Thielicke, "Schmutz und Schund: Massnahmen von unten her," *Stuttgarter Zeitung*, 4 May 1950.

37. "Was ist 'jugendgefährdend'?" *Frankfurter Neue Presse*, 6 May 1950.

38. Richard Tungel, "Schmutz und Schund," *Die Zeit*, no. 39 (25 Sept. 1952), p. 1.

39. See "Kardinal Frings mahnt Bundesrat," *Kölnische Rundschau*, 29 Aug. 1950.

40. "Das Wichtige und die halbe Wahrheit," *Münchner Allgemeine*, 15 Jan. 1950.

41. See "'Schwarzer Terror,'" *Rheinische Zeitung*, 25 Jan. 1951; "Der erste Scheiterhaufen," *Frankfurter Rundschau*, 8 Apr. 1952.

42. "'Schwarzer Terror.'"

43. Strauss quoted in "Mehr christliche Aktivisten!" *Westfalenpost*, 21 Feb. 1952.

44. "Moral mit Paragraphen," *Deutsche Zeitung und Wirtschafts Zeitung*, 23 July 1952.

45. "Bundestag verabschiedet 'Schmutz- und Schundgesetz,'" *Frankfurter Rundschau*, 18 Sept. 1952.

46. "Mit Unbehagen."

47. *Jugend in Gefahr* (1952), brochure of the Vereinigte Jugendschriftenausschüsse, quoted in Jäschke, "Produktionsbedingungen," p. 394.

48. See the discussion in Jäschke, "Produktionsbedingungen," p. 330.

49. Toska Hesekiel, *Eltern antworten: Eine Hilfe zur Aufklärung unserer Kinder* (Berlin: Burckhardthaus-Verlag, 1955), p. 27.

50. Oesterreich (1954) quoted in Peter Kuhnert and Ute Ackermann, "Jenseits von Lust und Liebe? Jugendsexualität in den 50er Jahren," in *"Die Elvis-Tolle, die hatte ich mir unauffällig wachsen lassen": Lebensgeschichte und jugendliche Alltagskultur in den fünfziger Jahren*, ed. Heinz-Hermann Krüger (Opladen: Leske, 1985), p. 48.

51. Oesterreich (1959) quoted in ibid., p. 49.

52. Hans Wollasch, "Der menschliche Sinn des Geschlechtslebens," in *Familie in Not: Sexualpädagogische Vortragsreihe*, ed. Stadtverwaltung Bad Godesberg (Bad Godesberg, 1954), p. 16.

53. See Erich Schröder, *Reif Werden und Rein Bleiben: Briefe eines Arztes an seinen Patensohn* (Konstanz: Christliche Verlagsanstalt, 1956), p. 29.

54. Gagern quoted in Kuhnert and Ackermann, "Jenseits von Lust und Liebe?" p. 49.

55. Wolfgang Fischer, "Selbstbefriedigung und geschlechtliche Erziehung," *Der evangelische Erzieher* 6, no. 3 (May—June 1954), pp. 74–75.

56. Conversation with F. B., 2001.

57. See Kuhnert and Ackermann, "Jenseits von Lust und Liebe?" esp. pp. 55–72.

58. See ibid., esp. pp. 72–81.

59. Indeed, in the course of the 1960s—as the society was in other ways beginning to liberalize—a number of notorious Federal Court (Bundesgerichtshof) decisions, inspired by church teachings on the indissolubility of marriage, limited individuals' ability to seek divorce even further. Refusal of intercourse with one's spouse (considered one of the "marital duties"), like refusal to conceive, were taken as violations of marriage. The "guilty" party was not permitted to file for divorce, only the guiltless partner could do so. And if the woman was the "guilty" party in these cases, she could lose both her right to alimony and—if the man wanted the children—custody of their children. (These developments, notably, had their roots in the Western occupiers' particular interpretation of the 1938 liberalized Nazi divorce law as a "typically Nazi" law in its concern with dissolving "undesirable" marriages and encouraging reproduction within new marriages. Thus in the wake of the war, the occupiers added a clause that made divorce impossible when it was opposed to the interests of the children.) See Sibylla Flügge, "Der verschlungene Weg zur Gleichberechtigung: Entwicklung der Frauenrechte seit 1945," in *Wir sind so frei: 3 Jahrzehnte Frauenbewegung in Frankfurt*, ed. Frauenreferat der Stadt Frankfurt am Main (brochure, 2001); Ute Gerhard, ed., *Frauen in der Geschichte des Rechts* (Munich: Beck, 1997); Robert Moeller, *Protecting Motherhood: Women and the Family in the Politics of Postwar West Germany* (Berkeley: Univ. of California Press, 1993); Karin Stiehr, "Aspekte der gesellschaftlichen und politischen Situation von Frauen in den 50er Jahren," in *Verdeckte Überlieferungen: Weiblichkeitsbilder zwischen Weimarer Republik, Nationalsozialismus und Fünfziger Jahre*, ed. Barbara Determan et al. (Frankfurt am Main: Haag und Herchen, 1991), pp. 121; Angela Delille and Andrea Grohn, *Blick zurück aufs Glück: Frauenleben und Familienpolitik in den 50er Jahren* (Berlin: Elefanten, 1985), pp. 130, 138–40. For an example of the kinds of sexual responsiveness and cooperation some leading jurists expected wives to show their husbands as a matter of course, see the commentary on the Federal Court decision of 2 Nov. 1966 in *Neue juristische Wochenschrift* 20, no. 23 (8 June 1967), pp. 1078–80. I thank Sibylla Flügge for calling this document to my attention.

60. Schissler, "'Normalization' as Project," p. 368.

61. Excerpt from Franz-Joseph Wuermeling, *Familie—Gabe und Aufgabe*, reprinted in Delille and Grohn, *Blick zurück aufs Glück*, p. 68.

62. Metzger (1957) quoted in Jaeschke, "Produktionsbedingungen," pp. 361, 366.

63. See Delille and Grohn, *Blick zurück aufs Glück*, p. 86.

64. Excerpt from Wuermeling, *Familie—Gabe und Aufgabe*, p. 68.

65. "Hundert Ehefrauen raten einer Braut," reprinted in *Frauenalltag und Frauenbewegung im 20. Jahrhundert*, vol. 4, ed. Annette Kuhn and Doris Schubert (Frankfurt am Main: Dezernat für Kultur und Freizeit, 1980), p. 38.

66. "Sind Sie eine vollkommene Ehefrau?" questionnaire reprinted in Delille and Grohn, *Blick zurück aufs Glück*, p. 122.

67. See Kirsten Plötz, "'Echte' Frauenleben? 'Lesbierinnen' im Spiegel öffentlicher Äusserungen in den Anfängen der Bundesrepublik," *Invertito* 1 (1999), pp. 47–69. For a more disturbing 1950s interpretation of lesbianism—in which lesbianism is intrinsically linked with fascism—see the novel by Wolfgang Koeppen, *Das Treibhaus* (Stuttgart: Scherz and Goverts, 1953).

68. Ruth Seiler, "Vom Kindersegen," in *Mann und Frau*, ed. Liselotte Nold (Nürnberg: Laetare, n.d.), pp. 37–38.

69. Maria Jochum, "Frauenfrage 1946," *Frankfurter Hefte* 1 (June 1946), pp. 24–25.

70. Hanns Lilje, "Zerfall der Familie?" *Sonntagsblatt*, 7 Feb. 1954, p. 24.

71. Wollasch, "Der menschliche Sinn," pp. 7, 17.

72. See in this context, for example, Theodor Bovet, "Sexualethik oder eheliche Partnerschaft," *Radius*, no. 4 (1963), p. 28. For an indication of the durability of religious commentators' worry that noncoital practices could be nothing but "reciprocal masturbation" rather than truly relational, see the rejection of such a view in Siegfried Keil, " 'Zur Jugendliebe gehört die Empfängnisverhütung,' " *Der Spiegel*, 22 Aug. 1966, p. 55; and the reaffirmation of this view in *Denkschrift zu Fragen der Sexualethik: Erarbeitet von einer Kommission der Evangelischen Kirche in Deutschland* (Gütersloh: Gerd Mohn, 1971), p. 28.

73. Numerous doctors and Christian advice writers liked to present the idea that planned pregnancy prevention of *any* kind inhibited female pleasure as an idea advanced by women themselves. For example, see A. Mayer, *Seelische Krisen im Leben der Frau* (Munich: Lehmann, 1954), pp. 80–82, and its approving citation in Anselm Günthör, "Kritische Bemerkungen zu neuen Theorien über Ehe und Eheliche Hingabe," *Theologische Quartalschrift* 144 (1964), p. 343.

74. See the summary remarks about the differences between West Germany and other western nations in Hermann Knaus, "Zur Frage der natürlichen Geburtenregelung und ihrer individuellen Anwendung," *Die Heilkunst* 69 (1956), pp. 272–73; K. Saller, "Zivilisation und Sexualität," *Die Heilkunst* 70 (1957), p. 48; Günter Grund, "Optimale Kontrazeption," *Medizinische Welt*, no. 32 (10 Aug. 1963), p. 1601; and "Die Antikonzeption—in Deutschland noch ein Stiefkind," *Berliner Ärzteblatt* 78, no. 2 (1965), pp. 73–77.

75. Quoted in Hans Harmsen, "Mittel zur Geburtenregelung in der Gesetzgebung des Staates," in *Sexualität und Verbrechen*, ed. Fritz Bauer et al. (Frankfurt am Main: Fischer, 1963), p. 183. See also the 1959 Hamburg case, p. 186.

76. See the discussions in Clemens Bewer, "Verkauf von Gummischutzmitteln durch Aussenautomaten," *Zeitschrift für ärztliche Fortbildung* 50, no. 6 (1961), pp. 460–62; and "Unzucht—schwer gemacht," *Konkret*, Oct. 1963, p. 11.

77. See Harmsen, "Mittel zur Geburtenregelung," p. 185.

78. See Ludwig von Friedeburg, *Die Umfrage in der Intimsphäre*, Beiträge zur Sexualforschung, vol. 4 (Stuttgart: Enke, 1953), p. 50.

79. See "Theologische Stimmen zur ärztlichen Beratung über Empfängnisverhütung," *Wege zum Menschen* 9 (1957), p. 193; "Erst die Liebe, dann die Moral? Alles über die Deutschen (15)," *Stern*, no. 48 (1963), pp. 43–52; and *Jahrbuch der öffentlichen Meinung 1958–1964*, ed. Elisabeth Noelle and Peter Neumann (Allensbach: Verlag für Demoskopie, 1965), p. 589.

80. In this context see also Helmut Schelsky, who—interestingly—gave authority to his own critique of petting by citing anthropologist Margaret Mead's negative assessment of it. Helmut Schelsky, *Soziologie der Sexualität* (Hamburg: Rowohlt, 1955), pp. 121–22. For an example of an ordinary citizen who shared these views that "substitute solutions" like petting would have "the most damaging consequences for a later marriage," see Gerda Ruppricht, letter to the editor, *Twen*, no. 10 (1962), p. 11.

81. L. M. Lawrence, "Der Kinsey Report," *Merkur* 3, no. 5 (1949), pp. 495–99.

82. See "Erst die Liebe, dann die Moral?" p. 50.

83. See "Die gefallene Natur," *Der Spiegel*, 2 May 1966, pp. 64–67.

84. Notably, however, Pope Pius XII in 1951 declared that the rhythm method was only for short-term use; indefinite reliance on the method was unacceptable: "Its use is also a sin against the true nature of marital life if the purpose is continuously to prevent pregnancy without a serious reason." W. F., "Gegen die Geburtenkontrolle: Eine Erklärung des Papstes über die christliche Ehe," *Die Zeit*, 8 Nov. 1951.

85. Hanns Dietel, "Möglichkeiten und Grenzen der natürlichen Geburtenregelung," *Hamburger Ärzteblatt*, Nov. 1953, pp. 234–35.

86. Anne Marie Durand-Wever, "Ärztliche Indikationen zur Empfängnisverhütung," in *Die gesunde Familie*, ed. Hans Harmsen, Beiträge zur Sexualforschung, vol. 13 (Stuttgart: Enke, 1958), p. 129. For a robust defense of the withdrawal method—after more than a decade of very hostile attacks on it by numerous physicians—see Herbert Lax, "Methodik der Antikonzeption," *Deutsches medizinisches Journal* 15, no. 8 (Apr. 1964), pp. 261–67.

87. Conversation with F. T., 2001.

88. See R. Hobbing, "Zur Frage der Haltbarkeit von Minderjährigenehen," *Unsere Jugend* 6, no. 8 (1954), pp. 366–68; "Erst die Liebe, dann die Moral?" p. 46; and "Jung gefreit—Nie gereut," *Twen*, no. 5 (1960), p. 29; and "Darüber spricht man nicht," *Twen*, no. 7 (1960), p. 30. The divorce rate for teen marriages was twice as high as that for marriages between twenty-four- to twenty-six-year-olds.

89. See Delille and Grohn, *Blick zurück aufs Glück*, p. 124; "Ist der Betrieb ein Heiratsmarkt? Alles über die Deutschen (2)," *Stern*, no. 35 (1963), p. 25; Harmsen, "Mittel zur Geburtenregelung," p. 175; Gisela Staupe and Lisa Vieth, "Einführung," in *Die Pille: Von der Lust und von der Liebe*, ed. Staupe and Vieth (Berlin: Rowohlt, 1996), p. 14; and "Heiraten nur weil ein Kind kommt?" *Twen*, no. 6 (1960), p. 26.

90. See Hans Harmsen, "Abtreibung oder Empfängnisverhütung?" *Gesundheitsfürsorge* 3 (1953–54), p. 123; and the informative essay by A. V. Knack and W. Pieper, "Der Stand der Empfängnisverhütung in der ärztlichen Praxis," *Ärztliche Mitteilungen* 41, no. 14 (May 1956), p. 388.

91. Hermann Doerfler, "Was kann die Bayer. Ärzteschaft und was der einzelne Arzt zur Bekämpfung der Abtreibungsseuche beitragen?" *Münchener Medizinische Wochenschrift* 95, no. 17 (24 Apr. 1953), pp. 509–11; and Harmsen, "Mittel zur Geburtenregelung," p. 186.

92. Durand-Wever, "Ärztliche Indikationen," p. 129. Also see Michael Luft, "Abtreibung in Deutschland: Hilfe, ich kriege ein Kind! 1," *Konkret*, May 1964, pp. 7–11. One study done in Kiel in the early 1950s suggested that one out of every twenty abortions was performed by a physician. See Doerfler, "Was kann die Bayer. Ärzteschaft." See also Theodor Bruck, *Geburtenregelung: Empfängnisverhütung—Problem und Praxis* (Flensburg: C. Stephenson, 1964), pp. 129–30.

93. Delille and Grohn, *Blick zurück aufs Glück*, p. 123.

94. Michael Luft discusses this case in "Paragraph 218 oder Baby-Pille für Alle: Hilfe, ich kriege ein Kind! 2," *Konkret*, July—Aug. 1964, p. 8.

95. See Delille and Grohn, *Blick zurück aufs Glück*, p. 123; and the comments about Dr. Hanns Dietel's study in the interview with Dr. Heinz Kirchhoff in "Anti-Baby-Pillen nur für Ehefrauen," *Der Spiegel*, 26 Feb. 1964, p. 87.

96. See Carl Nedelmann, "Abtreibung: Geburtenregelung und Strafrechtsreform," *Konkret*, July 1965, p. 6.

97. See Heike Rieder, letter to the editor, *Konkret*, Sept. 1964, p. 2; and the statistics on West Germany in P. Kühne, "Australiens Frauen und die Pille: Bremswirkung pseudowissenschaftlich erzeugter Karzinophobie," *Berliner Ärzteblatt* 78, no. 7 (1965), pp. 370–73.

98. Kirchhoff quoted in "Anti-Baby Pillen," p. 87.

99. See Bruck, *Geburtenregelung*, pp. 127–28; and Delille and Grohn, *Blick zurück aufs Glück*, p. 123.

100. See "Anhang: Auszüge aus der Bundestagsdrucksache IV/650 vom 4. Oktober 1962 (Regierungsentwurf eines Strafgesetzbuches—E 1962)," in Bauer et al., *Sexualität und Verbrechen*, pp. 406–7, 409–11.

101. Ibid., p. 388.

102. Carl Reiner, "Anmerkungen zum geplanten Sexualstrafrecht," *Diskus* 14, no. 2 (Feb. 1964).

103. Wolfgang Eckhardt, "Unzucht—schwer gemacht: Bedenkliches am Entwurf zum neuen StGB," *Konkret*, Oct. 1963, p. 11.

104. See on this point about Jews and ex-Nazis also Wolf Lepenies, "Exile and Emigration: The Survival of 'German Culture,' " *Occasional Paper*, no. 7, School of Social Science, Institute for Advanced Study, Princeton, NJ (March 2000), pp. 11, 14.

105. Wolfgang Hochheimer, "Das Sexualstrafrecht in psychologisch-anthropologischer Sicht," in Bauer et al., *Sexualität und Verbrechen*, pp. 90, 97–98.

106. Theodor W. Adorno, "Sexualtabus und Recht heute," in Bauer et al., *Sexualität und Verbrechen*, pp. 301–3, 305, 310.

107. Christian Crull and Hans Hagedorn, "Sex und Profit," *Diskus* 12, no. 7 (Aug. 1962), p. 1.

108. As Schoeps put it, "The impression is unavoidable that in present-day public opinion there is apparently a major absence of impartiality, honesty, and courage when it comes to taking a truly independent and objective stand on these questions [of homosexuality]. In fact, anyone who tries to do this can count on being personally suspected, slandered, and vilified. . . . Before 1914 one was in

many ways much further along [since in 1905, five thousand prominent individuals signed a petition against Paragraph 175]. Also the comparison with the 'roaring twenties' makes the present look bad. For back then German intellectuals were less mendacious and cowardly. Undoubtedly the corruption by Hitler is at some considerable fault here, but the greater responsibility lies with the moral decomposition that has in the meantime been self-inflicted." Hans-Joachim Schoeps, "Soll Homosexualität strafbar bleiben?" *Der Monat* 15, no. 171 (Dec. 1962), p. 19. Schoeps did not mention his own homosexuality in this essay.

109. Ibid., pp. 26–27.

110. See "Auf der Rampe," *Der Spiegel*, 18 Dec. 1963, pp. 46–47. For the further impact of this specific assessment of the perpetrators, see the discussion in the section on "legalized criminality" in Arno Plack, *Die Gesellschaft und das Böse: Eine Kritik der herrschenden Moral* (Munich: Paul List, 1967), pp. 304–10. On the enormous importance of the Auschwitz trial for postwar West German culture more generally, see Michael Jeismann, "Glanzstunde der Republik," *Frankfurter Allgemeine Zeitung*, 27 March 2004, p. 33.

111. Heribert Adam, "Spiesser Moral," *Diskus* 15, no. 4 (June 1965), p. 1.

112. Luft, "Paragraph 218 oder Baby-Pille fuer Alle: Hilfe, ich krieg ein Kind! 2," p. 16.

113. Adam, "Spiesser Moral," p. 1.

114. See the discussion of *Konkret* in Ulrike Heider, "Freie Liebe und Liebesreligion: Zum Sexualitätsbegriff der 60er und 80er Jahre," in *Sadomasochisten, Keusche und Romantiker: Vom Mythos neuer Sinnlichkeit*, ed. Heider (Reinbek: Rowohlt, 1986), p. 93.

115. For example, see Ludwig Henze, "Antisemitismus in Deutschland: Der Unsichtbare Stern," and Fritz Bauer quoted in "Lebt Hitler noch?" both in *Konkret*, Apr. 1963, p. 7; Hermann Pieper, letter to the editor and the editors' response, *Konkret*, May 1964, p. 2; Ernest L. Moss, "Jude in Deutschland," *Konkret*, May 1965, pp. 6–10; and Peggy Parnass, "Jüdin in Deutschland," *Konkret*, July 1965, pp. 14–16.

116. For example, see the excerpts from Karlheinz Deschner's *Abermals krähte der Hahn: Eine kritische Kirchengeschichte von den Anfängen bis zu Pius XII* (Stuttgart: H. E. Günther, 1962), a study of the churches' complicity in the Third Reich, serialized in *Konkret* between November 1962 and February 1963.

117. Hermann Kraemer quoted in Heinz Ungureit, "Bernkastels Landrat vergleicht 'Das Schweigen' mit Auschwitz," *Frankfurter Rundschau*, 24 June 1964, p. 22.

118. Wolfgang Fritz Haug, "Vorbemerkung," *Das Argument* 32 (1965), pp. 30–31.

119. "Die gefallene Natur," pp. 57–58.

120. Plack, *Die Gesellschaft und das Böse*, p. 309.

121. See Hannes Schwenger, *Antisexuelle Propaganda: Sexualpolitik in der Kirche* (Reinbek: Rowohlt, 1969), pp. 34–36.

122. Barbara Köster, "Rüsselsheim Juli 1985," interview by Daniel Cohn-Bendit, in *Wir haben sie so geliebt, die Revolution*, ed. Cohn-Bendit (Frankfurt am Main: Athenäum, 1987), p. 244.

CHAPTER FOUR
THE MORALITY OF PLEASURE

1. "Die gefallene Natur," *Der Spiegel*, 2 May 1966, p. 58.

2. To give just one example: while in 1963 one of every five West Germans had insisted women should be virgins at marriage, as of 1970 only one in ten West Germans took this stance. See "Thema eins," *Der Spiegel*, 3 Aug. 1970, p. 46.

3. See "Umfrage in die Intimsphäre: Alles über die Deutschen (13)," *Der Stern*, no. 46 (1963), p. 56; and "Erst die Liebe, dann die Moral? Alles über die Deutschen (15)," *Der Stern*, no. 48 (1963), p. 52.

4. Horst Fischer, *Gruppensex in Deutschland* (Hamburg: Merlin, 1968).

5. For example, see Heinz van Nouhuys's report on Marlies Kolle: "Meine Ehe mit Oswalt Kolle," *Jasmin*, no. 11 (May 1968), pp. 32–40.

6. See the excellent study by Annette Miersch, *Schulmädchen-Report: Der deutsche Sexfilm der 70er Jahre* (Berlin: Bertz, 2003).

7. See "Kosen und Posen," *Der Spiegel*, 13 March 1972, pp. 66–67.

8. "Die gefallene Natur," p. 50.

9. "Amüsiert, ironischer Blick," *Civis*, Nov. 1968, p. 3.

10. See Horst Eglau, "Die Liebesdienerin der Nation," *Die Zeit*, 28 Jan. 1972, pp. 22–23; and "Porno-Markt: Frau Saubermann an der Spitze," *Der Spiegel*, 1 Nov. 1971, pp. 79, 94.

11. See "Porno-Markt," pp. 78–97; Eglau, "Die Liebesdienerin," p. 23; "'Bekennt, dass ihr anders seid,' " *Der Spiegel*, 12 Mar. 1973, p. 58; and Andreas Salmen and Albert Eckert, *20 Jahre bundesdeutsche Schwulenbewegung 1969–1989* (Cologne: Bundesverband Homosexualität e. V., 1989), pp. 8–12.

12. Hartung and Rosenberg quoted in "Porno-Markt," pp. 81, 97.

13. Jean-Francis Held, "Sex über Alles," *Le Nouvel Observateur*, 17 Aug. 1970, p. 51.

14. See Pierre Simon et al., *Rapport sur le comportement sexuel des Français* (Paris: René Julliard/Pierre Charron, 1972); as well as the bemused summary of the findings in "Montags fast nie," *Der Spiegel*, 30 Oct. 1972, pp. 124–26. According to the study, 45 percent of French women between the ages of twenty and twenty-nine were virgins when they married (compared with, depending on the generation, maximally 30 percent, if not only 10 percent of German women); 50 percent of French women had only had one male lover in their lifetime; the average French woman had slept with no more than two men. Most couples did it in the dark; foreplay was brief to nonexistent; positions outside the missionary and woman-on-top, and practices besides coitus, were pursued only by a minority. *Le Nouvel Observateur* noted: "The report paints the picture of a profoundly conservative France."

15. "Jugend forscht," *Der Spiegel*, 22 Mar. 1971, pp. 175, 190.

16. See Wilfried Ruff, "Ist die Sexualethik am Ende?" *Publik*, no. 31 (30 July 1971), p. 12.

17. See Gunter Schmidt, Arne Dekker, and Silje Matthiesen, "Sexualverhalten," in *Kinder der sexuellen Revolution: Kontinuität und Wandel studentischer Sexualität 1966–1996. Eine empirische Untersuchung*, ed. Schmidt (Giessen: Psychosozial-Verlag, 2000), pp. 40, 64.

18. Peter Brügge, "'Ihr könntet uns Liebe erlauben,'" *Der Spiegel*, 8 Apr. 1968, pp. 90–91.

19. "Liebe im Schlafsack," *Der Stern*, no. 49 (1971), pp. 76–77.

20. Conversation with T. D., 1999.

21. Quoted in "Die gefallene Natur," p. 54.

22. Council quoted in "Freude im Haus," *Der Spiegel*, 22 Aug. 1966, p. 54; bishopric quoted in "Thema eins," p. 38.

23. Quoted in Brügge, "'Ihr könntet,'" p. 91.

24. Theologian and biologist Gerd Siegmund quoted in "Thema eins," p. 38.

25. See Siegfried Keil, "Ist Sex des Teufels?" *Die Zeit*, 11 June 1971, p. 48.

26. Thielicke quoted in "'Der Sexus ist kein Sündenpfuhl,'" *Der Spiegel*, 28 Nov. 1966, p. 87.

27. Geno Hartlaub, "Leben für den Sex (II): Ist die Liebesheirat überholt?" *Deutsches Allgemeines Sonntagsblatt*, no. 47 (24 Nov. 1968), p. 17. See the similar sentiments in Wilhelm Quenzer, "Sexuelle Befreiung und Aggressivität," *Information Nr. 47*, ed. Evangelische Zentralstelle für Weltanschauungsfragen (Stuttgart, 1971), p. 3.

28. "Die gefallene Natur," p. 54.

29. See "'Der Sexus,'" p. 75.

30. Lange-Undeutsch quoted in "Diese Dame," *Der Spiegel*, 29 Aug. 1966, p. 51.

31. Cartoon reprinted to accompany "'Der Sexus,'" p. 86.

32. See Koch's remarks from his presentation at a conference sponsored by the YMCA (CVJM) in 1971, quoted in "Liebe im Schlafsack," p. 78; and see Friedrich Koch, *Sexualpädagogik und politische Erziehung* (Munich: Paul List, 1975).

33. Karlheinz Deschner, *Das Kreuz mit der Kirche: Eine Sexualgeschichte des Christentums* (Düsseldorf: Econ, 1974), pp. 385, 390–91, 398–99. The Catholic writer quoted by Deschner is F. Pittet, one of the contributors to the Catholic advice manual *Gesundes Geschlechtsleben: Handbuch für Ehefragen*, ed. Franz Xavier von Hornstein and A. Faller (Olten: Otto Walter, 1950).

34. Siegfried Keil, *Sexualität: Erkenntnisse und Mass-Stäbe* (Stuttgart: Kreuz-Verlag, 1966).

35. Kirchenkanzlei der Evangelischen Kirche in Deutschland, ed., *Denkschrift zu Fragen der Sexualethik: Erarbeitet von einer Kommission der Evangelischen Kirche in Deutschland* (Gütersloh: Gerd Mohn, 1971), pp. 26–29.

36. See Pastor Horst Klingsporn quoted in "Liebe im Schlafsack," p. 78; and Pastor Paul Schulz, ". . . zum Beispiel das sechste Gebot," *Die Zeit*, 8 June 1973, p. 66. Under the caption "The human being must be liberated from the rigid corset of norms—precisely the theologians should be clearing out outdated concepts," Schulz lamented the stultified desires and lack of pleasure evident within many marriages and declared that the sixth commandment, "'thou shalt not commit adultery,' is simply not adequate for the needs of a society in the process of self-emancipation." See also "Schluss mit dem (heimlichen) Seitensprung," *Bild*, 7 Mar. 1969, p. 1.

37. Cartoon accompanying "Liebe im Schlafsack," p. 78.

38. See the photograph accompanying Keil, "Ist Sex des Teufels?" p. 48.

39. See "Jugend forscht," p. 181.

40. See Ruff, "Ist die Sexualethik am Ende?" p. 12.

41. See Hubertus Mynarek, *Eros und Klerus: Vom Elend des Zölibats* (Düsseldorf: Econ, 1978); and Mynarek quoted in "Totale Tröstung," *Der Spiegel*, 20 Feb. 1978, p. 75. More than one-third of all twenty-four thousand priests in West Germany, Mynarek estimated, broke their vows with females, another third with males. Celibacy for him was "an institutionalized untruth," a "systematic sexual oppression."

42. Working-class youth quoted in Gunter Schmidt and Volkmar Sigusch, *Arbeiter-Sexualität: Eine empirische Untersuchung an jungen Industriearbeitern* (Neuwied and Berlin: Luchterhand, 1971), pp. 88–92.

43. Quoted in Rosa Geschichten, ed., *Eine Tunte bist Du auf jeden Fall: 20 Jahre Schwulenbewegung in Münster* (Münster: Schnelldruck Coerdestrasse, 1992), p. 16.

44. Amendt quoted in "Richtige Wohltat," *Der Spiegel*, 31 Aug. 1970, p. 71.

45. See "Liebe im Schlafsack"; and Kentler's study in Hans Grothe, "Ehe 70," *Eltern*, no. 5 (May 1970), pp. 101–8; and Hans Grothe, "Ehe 70 (II)," *Eltern*, no. 6 (June 1970), pp. 124–33.

46. Quoted in "'Wir haben heute eine positive Besessenheit,' " *Der Spiegel*, 3 Aug. 1970, p. 51.

47. Volkmar Sigusch, "Liebe kann doch nichts dafür," *Der Spiegel*, 21 June 1971, p. 136.

48. See Rosa Geschichten, *Eine Tunte*, p. 14; and Schmidt quoted in "Späte Milde," *Der Spiegel*, 12 May 1969, p. 63.

49. Conversation with Volkmar Sigusch, 2002.

50. Martin Dannecker and Reimut Reiche, *Der gewöhnliche Homosexuelle: Eine soziologische Untersuchung über männliche Homosexuelle in der Bundesrepublik* (Frankfurt am Main: Fischer, 1974); "'Bekennt, dass ihr anders seid,' " pp. 46–62; "Ich bin schwul," *Der Stern*, no. 41 (1978), pp. 104–18.

51. See on this point esp. Martin Dannecker, "Die verspätete Empirie," *Zeitschrift für Sexualforschung* 14, no. 2 (June 2001).

52. Klaus Theweleit, . . . *ein Aspirin von der Grösse der Sonne* (Freiburg i.B.: Jos Fritz, 1990), p. 49. Note also Theweleit's observation in 1998: "The interest in the political was manifest among many young people as an interest in the sexual. The bodies of young people in the early sixties were sexually charged in a wholly unusual way." Klaus Theweleit, *Ghosts: Drei leicht inkorrekte Vorträge* (Frankfurt am Main: Stroemfeld Roter Stern, 1998), pp. 106–7.

53. Peter Schneider, "Nicht der Egoismus verfälscht das politische Engagement, sondern der Versuch ihn zu verheimlichen," *Frankfurter Rundschau*, 25 June 1977, p. III.

54. Götz Eisenberg, "Auf der Suche nach Identität," *Frankfurter Hefte* 34, no. 4 (Apr. 1979), p. 88.

55. Claus Offe, "Vier Hypothesen über historische Folgen der Studentenbewegung," *Leviathan*, no. 4 (1998), p. 552.

56. *Berliner Kinderläden: Antiautoritäre Erziehung und sozialistischer Kampf* (Cologne: Kiepenheuer und Witsch, 1970), pp. 108–9.

57. Dannecker and Reiche, *Der gewöhnliche Homosexuelle*, p. 169.

58. Günter Amendt, *SexFront* (Frankfurt am Main: März, 1970), pp. 123, 126.

59. Reimut Reiche, *Sexuality and Class Struggle*, trans. Susan Bennett (New York: Praeger, 1971), pp. 138–39. Like Adorno before him, Reiche called attention to the apoliticism and conformity that appeared to accompany much youth sexual liberalization (p. 171).

60. Quoted in Rosa Geschichten, *Eine Tunte*, p. 16.

61. Theodor W. Adorno, "Sexualtabus und Recht heute," in *Sexualität und Verbrechen*, ed. Fritz Bauer et al. (Frankfurt am Main: Fischer 1963), pp. 300–301.

62. Trial testimony reproduced in Rainer Langhans and Fritz Teufel, eds., *Klau mich* (Frankfurt am Main: Ed. Voltaire, 1968), approximately p. 173 (there are no page numbers).

63. Ulrike Heider, "Freie Liebe und Liebesreligion: Zum Sexualitätsbegriff der 60er und 80er Jahre," in *Sadomasochisten, Keusche, und Romantiker: Vom Mythos neuer Sinnlichkeit*, ed. Heider (Reinbek: Rowohlt, 1986), pp. 92–109, esp. p. 94.

64. Arno Plack, *Die Gesellschaft und das Böse: Eine Kritik der herrschenden Moral* (Munich: Paul List, 1967), pp. 163, 308–9.

65. Erich Fromm, *Autorität und Familie* (1936), quoted in Reiche, *Sexuality*, p. 118.

66. Reinhart Westphal, "Psychologische Theorien über den Faschismus," *Das Argument* 32 (1965), pp. 34, 38.

67. Fromm quoted in Reiche, *Sexuality*, p. 118.

68. For example, see Max Horkheimer, "Theoretische Entwürfe über Autorität und Familie: Allgemeiner Teil," in *Studien über Autorität und Familie*, ed. Horkheimer (Paris: Félix Alcan, 1936); and Max Horkheimer, "Authoritarianism and the Family," in *The Family: Its Function and Destiny*, ed. Ruth Nanda Ashen (New York: Harper and Bros., 1949; rev. ed., 1959).

69. Adorno et al. were concerned to show that while it did appear that racially prejudiced and "potentially fascistic" personalities tended also to manifest a "moralistic rejection of instinctual tendencies," and that "it seems likely that this moral condemnation serves the purpose of externalization of, and defense against, temptation toward immoral and unconventional behavior," "crude promiscuity" was also one of the frequent characteristics of prejudiced individuals. See Theodor Adorno et al., *The Authoritarian Personality* (New York: Harper and Bros., 1950), esp. pp. 1, 393, 395, 420.

70. See *Berliner Kinderläden*, pp. 13–14, 90–91.

71. See Hille Jan Breiteneicher et al., *Kinderläden: Revolution der Erziehung oder Erziehung zur Revolution?* (Reinbek: Rowohlt, 1971), pp. 13, 16–17.

72. Eckhard Siepmann, "Genital versus Prägenital: Die Grossväter der sexuellen Revolution," in *CheSchahShit: Die Sechziger Jahre zwischen Cocktail und Molotow*, ed. Siepmann et al. (Berlin: Elefanten, 1984), p. 101; "Ich will das so alles nicht," *Pflasterstrand*, no. 21 (15 Dec. 1977–11 Jan. 1978), p. 33.

73. Wilhelm Reich, *Die Funktion des Orgasmus: Sexualökonomische Grundprobleme der biologischen Energie* (1927; reprint., Cologne: Kiepenheuer und Witsch, 1969), p. 139.

74. Gunter Schmidt, "Aus der Zauber? Eine kurze Geschichte der Sexualität in der BRD," in Schmidt, *Kinder der sexuellen Revolution*, p. 11.

75. See Peter Mosler, *Was wir wollten, was wir wurden: Studentenrevolte—zehn Jahre danach* (Reinbek: Rowohlt, 1977), p. 159.

76. Heider, "Freie Liebe," p. 94.

77. Dietrich Haensch, *Repressive Familienpolitik: Sexualunterdrückung als Mittel der Politik* (Reinbek: Rowohlt, 1969), pp. 12, 14, 66–67.

78. Dieter Duhm, *Angst im Kapitalismus: Zweiter Versuch der gesellschaftlichen Begründung zwischenmenschlicher Angst in der kapitalistischen Warengesellschaft* (Lampertheim: Kübler, 1972), p. 100.

79. "Kinderschule Frankfurt, Eschersheimer Landstrasse," in *Erziehung zum Ungehorsam: Kinderläden berichten aus der antiautoritären Praxis*, ed. Gerhard Bott (Frankfurt am Main: März, 1970), p. 55.

80. The children were horrified. See Klaus Hartung, "Die Psychoanalyse der Küchenarbeit: Selbstbefreiung, Wohngemeinschaft und Kommune," in Siepmann et al., *CheSchahShit*, p. 106.

81. Sophinette Becker, "Bewusste und unbewusste Identifikationen der 68er Generation," in *Erinnern, Wiederholen, Durcharbeiten: Zur Psycho-Analyse deutscher Wenden*, ed. Brigitte Rauschenbach (Berlin: Aufbau, 1992), p. 273.

82. See Lutz von Werder, "Kinderläden: Versuch der Umwälzung der inneren Natur," in Siepmann et al., *CheSchahShit*, p. 108; Gerhard Bott, "Erziehung zum Ungehorsam: Bericht über antiautoritäre Kindergärten" (film script for the documentary televised by the Norddeutscher Rundfunk in 1969), in Bott, *Erziehung zum Ungehorsam*, p. 106.

83. For details on the battles between the founding women and the usurping men, see the essay by Helke Sander, "Mütter sind politische Personen: Die Kinderfrage seit '68," *Courage* 9 (1978).

84. Ursula Gröttrup, "Im 'Kinderladen' hat Mao das Rotkäppchen verdrängt: Junge Eltern wollen antiautoritäre und aggressive Erziehung," *Berliner Morgenpost*, 19 Jan. 1969, reprinted in *Berliner Kinderläden*, p. 151.

85. Heiko Gebhart, "Kleine Linke mit grossen Rechten: Berliner APO-Mitglieder experimentieren mit ihren Kindern," *Der Stern*, no. 9 (1969).

86. See *Berliner Kinderläden*, pp. 15–17, 205; Breiteneicher et al., *Kinderläden: Revolution*, p. 103; as well as the remarks of the translators for the English-language version of *Berliner Kinderläden: Storefront Day Care Centers: The Radical Berlin Experiment*, trans. Catherine Lord and Renée Neu Watkins (Boston: Beacon, 1973), p. viii; Christian Büttner, "Chancen kollektiver Erziehung," *Neue Praxis* 3 (1974), pp. 228–29; Rüdiger Beier and Christian Büttner, "Kinderläden und Reformtendenzen im Elementarbereich," *Neue Praxis* 5 (1975), pp. 7–14; Lottemi Doormann, "Aufbruch aus dem Mütterghetto: Die Kinderfrage in der Frauenbewegung seit 1968," in *Der grosse Unterschied: Die neue Frauenbewegung und die siebziger Jahre*, ed. Kristine von Soden (Berlin: Elefanten, 1988), esp. pp. 25–27; Lutz von Werder, "Bedeutung und Entwicklung der Kinderladenbewegung in der Bundesrepublik," in *Was kommt nach den Kinderläden? Erlebnis-Protokolle*, ed. von Werder (Berlin: Klaus Wagenbach, 1977), esp. pp. 21–23 and 37–39; Traude Bremer, *Kinderladen Frankfurterstrasse: Versuch einer pragmatischen Hermeneutik* (Frankfurt am Main: Peter Lang, 1986).

87. Conversations with Z. S., L. L., K. T., 1990s.

88. Bott, "Erziehung," pp. 84–86, 89.

89. Ibid., pp. 92, 99.

90. Letters from viewers, reprinted and quoted in *Erziehung zum Ungehorsam*, pp. 111, 114.

91. Excerpt from Annie Reich, *Wenn Dein Kind Dich Fragt . . . Gespräche, Beispiele und Ratschläge zur Sexualerziehung* (Leipzig: Verlag für Sexualpolitik, 1932), reprinted in *Für die Befreiung der kindlichen Sexualität! Kampf den falschen Erziehern!* ed. Zentralrat der sozialistischen Kinderläden West-Berlins (Berlin: Sozialistischer Kinderladen Charlottenburg I, 1969), p. 54.

92. See Zentralrat der sozialistischen Kinderläden, *Für die Befreiung*, pp. 68–70; Kommune 2 (Christel Bookhagen, Eike Hemmer, Jan Raspe, Eberhard Schultz), "Kindererziehung in der Kommune," *Kursbuch* 17 (June 1969), pp. 165 and 168–69.

93. See, for example, Theweleit, *. . . ein Aspirin von der Grösse der Sonne*, pp. 56–57.

94. See Monika Seifert, "Kinderschule Frankfurt, Eschersheimer Landstrasse," *Vorgänge* 5 (1970), p. 162; and "Kinderschule Frankfurt," in Bott, *Erziehung zum Ungehorsam*, pp. 57–58. For an earlier criticism by Frankfurt *Kinderladen* founder Monika Seifert of the Berliners' purported masturbation obsessions, see Sepp Binder, "Erst das Kind und dann die Politik," *Die Zeit*, 24 Jan. 1969, p. 50.

95. "Kinderladen Stuttgart: Bericht über einen Prozess," in Bott, *Erziehung zum Ungehorsam*, pp. 43–44.

96. "Kinderschule Frankfurt," pp. 51, 54, 56–57.

97. Peter Schneider, "Die Sache mit der 'Männlichkeit': Gibt es eine Emanzipation der Männer?" *Kursbuch* 35 (Apr. 1974), p. 121.

98. Zentralrat der sozialistischen Kinderläden, *Für die Befreiung*, p. 88; "Kinderschule Frankfurt," pp. 55–56.

99. Von Werder, "Bedeutung und Entwicklung," p. 7.

100. *Berliner Kinderläden*, p. 126.

101. Zentralrat der sozialistischen Kinderläden, *Für die Befreiung*, p. 35.

102. Zentralrat der sozialistischen Kinderläden West-Berlins, ed., *Kinder im Kollektiv* (Berlin: Sozialistischer Kinderladen Charlottenburg I, 1969), p. 79.

103. Kruse quoted in Gebhart, "Kleine Linke."

104. Breiteneicher et al., *Kinderläden: Revolution*, p. 16.

105. Zentralrat der sozialistischen Kinderläden, *Kinder im Kollektiv*, pp. 83, 87, 93. For an outstanding and detailed critique of this document, see Reimut Reiche, "Sexuelle Revolution—Erinnerung an einen Mythos," in *Die Früchte der Revolte: Über die Veränderung der politischen Kultur durch die Studentenbewegung*, ed. Lothar Baier et al. (Berlin: Wagenbach, 1988), pp. 65–67.

106. Eberhard Knödler-Bunte, "Verlängerung des Schweigens," *Ästhetik und Kommunikation* 51 (1983), pp. 43–45.

107. See Dany Diner, "Fragmente von Unterwegs: Über jüdische und politische Identität in Deutschland," *Ästhetik und Kommunikation* 51 (1983), pp. 11–13; Elizabeth Domansky, "'Kristallnacht,' the Holocaust, and German Unity: The Meaning of November 9 as an Anniversary in Germany," *History and Memory* 4 (spring—summer 1992).

108. Hermann Peter Piwitt, "Kristallnacht und Nebel," *Konkret*, Dec. 1978, p. 33.

109. For two powerful (very different) preliminary analyses, see Inge Deutsch-kron, "Normalisierungen der Beziehungen?" in *Israel und die Deutschen: Das besondere Verhältnis* (Cologne: Verlag Wissenschaft und Politik, 1983), esp. pp. 336–46; and Y. Michal Bodemann, "Das Klappern der Holzschuhmänner: Der Weg zur Erinnerungsexplosion in Deutschland 1960–1975," in *In den Wogen der Erinnerung: Jüdisches Leben in Deutschland* (Munich: DTV, 2002), esp. pp. 70–76. Bodemann quotes the left-wing activist and *Konkret* author Ulrike Meinhof's cutting assessment of the right-wing newspaper *Bild*'s enthusiasm for Israel's victory: "In the Sinai, *Bild* finally, after twenty-five years, won the battle of Stalingrad after all. Anticommunist resentment seamlessly merged into the destruction of Soviet Mig-fighters. . . . If [in the Second World War], one had taken the Jews along to the Ural mountains instead of gassing them, the Second World War would have ended differently. The mistakes of the past were acknowledged as such, anti-semitism was regretted, self-cleansing took place, the new German fascism has learned from the old mistakes. Not against, but with, the Jews anticommunism leads to victory" (p. 72). Deutschkron emphasizes the way young leftists inter-preted the pro-Israeli stance of their elders as a belated admission of the elders' own guilt. "So the young believed, that they now had the obligation to act noncha-lant vis-à-vis Israel and Jews. The past was not their concern. Following their new teachers [Mao, Castro, Ho Chi-minh, etc.] Israel was an imperialist state. . . . Without even bothering to research the problem of the Middle East, they took up the battle against Israel and declared the Arabs to be the revolutionaries that de-served support" (pp. 343–44). Deutschkron also holds the New Left student movement, due to its unpopularity with the German populace, to be co-responsi-ble (along with the beginning economic recession) for the strong rise of the neo-Nazi National Democratic Party of Germany (NPD) in the late 1960s.

110. Cartoon accompanying Diner, "Fragmente."

111. Henryk M. Broder, " 'Ihr bleibt die Kinder eurer Eltern.' 'Euer Jude von heute ist der Staat Israel': Die neue deutsche Linke und der alltägliche Antisemit-ismus," *Die Zeit*, 27 Feb. 1981, pp. 9–11.

112. See Klaus Hartung, "Versuch, die Krise der antiautoritären Bewegung wieder zur Sprache zu bringen," *Kursbuch* 48 (June 1977), pp. 19–20, 28. Aside from this indicative but disturbing discussion of gassing, this essay is a very per-ceptive and thought-provoking analysis of the New Left's problems. Yet contrast Hartung's later far more sensitive autocritique: Klaus Hartung, "Erinnyen in Deutschland: Überlegungen zur 'Historikerdebatte,' zum Faschismusbegriff der '68er,' und zu Peter Schneiders Selbstkritik," *Niemandsland* 2, no. 1 (1987).

113. Peter Schneider, "Im Todeskreis der Schuld," *Die Zeit*, 27 Mar. 1987, p. 66.

114. Claus Leggewie, "Antifaschisten sind wir sowieso," *Die Zeit*, 19 Feb. 1988, p. 62.

115. See Reiche, "Sexuelle Revolution," pp. 50–51, 67.

116. Ibid., pp. 63, 65.

117. Dutschke quoted in " 'Wir fordern die Enteignung Axel Springers,' " *Der Spiegel*, 10 July 1967, pp. 32–33.

118. See Cordt Schnibben, "Vollstrecker des Weltgewissens," *Der Spiegel*, 2 June 1997, p. 109; Breiteneicher et al., *Kinderläden: Revolution*, p. 16; Hartung, "Versuch," p. 42.

119. Theweleit, . . . *ein Aspirin*, pp. 43–44.

120. Among the further avenues that could be explored to make sense of these "circuitous" mechanisms might be the ways New Left demonstrators experienced beatings by police truncheons as repetitions of beatings by parents and teachers (but which, because they experienced them together with others, could be borne better than those earlier beatings). See the moving reflections on this in SDS/KU Autorenkollektiv, "Der Untergang der Bild-Zeitung" (1969), reprinted in *Berliner Kinderläden*, pp. 30–31; see also Klaus Hartung and Max Thomas Mehr, "Der Schuss, der die Studenten in Bewegung setzte," *Die Zeit*, 30 May 1997, p. 11. Another avenue that deserves further study is New Leftists' relationships to their mothers, or as Heipe Weiss put it, this " 'squeaky clean' Lady Macbeth–generation of mothers," these "former BDM-girls" who tormented their children both with an "anal compulsion to clean house" and with a "strict silence . . . about their worship of Hitler." Weiss also quotes 68er bad-boy Bernward Vesper's devastating comment that "Even when I'm lying in my coffin, Mommy, you'll still say I didn't wash my feet!" Heipe Weiss, "Freie Liebe war vor allem Reden über Sex," *Frankfurter Neue Presse*, 24 Apr. 1998, p. 9. See also the remarks about the generation of 1968's mothers sweeping the "wreckage of fascism" "under the carpet, just like the majority of German men," in Ulrike Schmauch, "Alte oder neue Sexualaufklärung?" *Zeitschrift für Sexualforschung* 7, no. 4 (Dec. 1994), p. 354; as well as the extended reflections about the New Leftists' dysfunctional relationships to their mothers in Sibylla Flügge, "1968 und die Frauen—Ein Blick in die Beziehungskiste," in *Gender und soziale Praxis*, ed. Margit Göttert and Karin Walser (Königstein/Taunus: Ulrike Helmer, 2002), esp. pp. 283–84.

CHAPTER FIVE
THE ROMANCE OF SOCIALISM

1. Michel Foucault, *The History of Sexuality*, vol. 1: *An Introduction* (New York: Vintage, 1980), p. 103.

2. See Ina Merkel, *Utopie und Bedürfnis: Die Geschichte der Konsumkultur in der DDR* (Cologne: Böhlau, 1999), pp. 12–13; and Rainer Land, "Unvereinbar: Avantgardismus und Modernismus, Diskussion: Waren die Reformsozialisten verhinderte Sozialdemokraten? Teil 1," *Neues Deutschland*, 23–24, Apr. 1994, p. 10.

3. See Sigrid Meuschel, *Legitimation und Parteiherrschaft: Zum Paradox von Stabilität und Revolution in der DDR 1945–1989* (Frankfurt am Main: Suhrkamp, 1992); and Thomas Schmidt, "Civil Religion in the GDR" (paper presented at the conference "Formen Religiöser Vergemeinschaftung in der Moderne," University of Chicago, 25 Oct. 2003). Schmidt especially emphasizes that the core values of "labor," "equality," and "peace" were shared by regime and populace. The point is that, although citizens did not much like the state, they endorsed the values promoted *by* the state.

4. The aggressive invasiveness is well described in Bürgerkomitee Leipzig, ed., *Stasi intern: Macht und Banalität* (Leipzig: Forum, 1998), esp. pp. 198–212; and Vera Wollenberger, *Virus der Heuchler: Innenansicht aus Stasi-Akten* (Berlin: Elefanten Press, 1992), esp. pp. 7, 18, 37, 40, 106, 121 (Wollenberger was reported on by her own husband). The use by the Stasi of sex as bait is discussed in Belinda Cooper, "Patriarchy within a Patriarchy: Women and the Stasi," *German Politics and Society* 16, no. 2 (summer 1998); and Eduard Stapel, "Schwulenbewegung in der DDR" (interview conducted by Kurt Starke), in *Schwuler Osten: Homosexuelle Männer in der DDR*, ed. Kurt Starke (Berlin: Christoph Links Verlag, 1994), pp. 101–2. On the Stasi's use of prostitutes, see Uta Falck, *VEB Bordell: Geschichte der Prostitution in der DDR* (Berlin: Links, 1998), pp. 108–41. For a thought-provoking critique of the intensity of affect directed against the former collaborators with the Stasi, see Matthias Wagner, *Das Stasi-Syndrom: Über den Umgang mit den Akten des MfS in den 90er Jahren* (Berlin: Edition Ost/Das Neue Berlin, 2001), esp. pp. 7–9, 174–87.

5. See on these points also Detlef Pollack, "Über die 68er und ihr Verhältnis zur DDR," *Leviathan*, no. 4 (1998), p. 545; and Konrad Jarausch, "Jenseits von Verdammung und Verklärung," *Frankfurter Rundschau*, 30 May 2000, p. 22. For a concise and thoughtful summary of the significant differences between the East German dictatorship and the Nazi one (along with some fascinating insights into the complex roles played by the several hundred thousand "informal collaborators" working for the Stasi—not just as functionaries of repression but also "paternalistic caregivers and privilege-distributors" and as mediums for the articulation of the infantilized citizenry's interests)—see Jürgen Habermas, "Bemerkungen zu einer verworrenen Diskussion: Was bedeutet 'Aufarbeitung der Vergangenheit' heute?" *Die Zeit*, 10 Apr. 1992, p. 18.

6. See Ursula Sillge, *Un-Sichtbare Frauen: Lesben und ihre Emanzipation in der DDR* (Berlin: LinksDruck, 1991), pp. 82–87.

7. Conversations with T. T., 2001, and J. T., 2002.

8. H. Ruppert, "Sexuelle Erziehung vom Blickpunkt des Gynäkologen," *Zeitschrift für ärztliche Fortbildung* 50, nos. 1–2 (15 Jan. 1956), p. 63. See also the remarks of Hilde Benjamin a year earlier: "The SS ideology, the Nazi racial madness dissolved the moral relationships within many families, the relationships between man and woman, parents and children. The moral degradation, above all also the fascist war of plunder, allowed primitive sexual lusts to develop unrestrainedly." Hilde Benjamin, "Familie und Familienrecht in der Deutschen Demokratischen Republik," *Einheit* 10, no. 5 (May 1955), p. 450.

9. Friedrich Heilmann, "Die sexuelle Erziehung als pädagogisches Problem," *Zeitschrift für ärztliche Fortbildung* 50, nos. 1–2 (15 Jan. 1956), pp. 65, 67.

10. Ibid., p. 65. This remained a favorite device. Popular advice writer Rolf Borrmann in the 1960s, for example, criticized the "hostility to the body" encouraged by Christianity even as he lamented that "also in the GDR many people still have a false stance toward the sexual." So also in the 1970s, sexologist Siegfried Schnabl continued to bemoan the damage being done by "the formula: the pleasure of the flesh is sin" through "almost two thousand years under the influence of the Christian religion." Rolf Borrmann, *Jugend und Liebe* (Leipzig: Urania,

1966), pp. 42–43; Siegfried Schnabl, *Intimverhalten Sexualstörungen Persönlichkeit* (Berlin: Deutscher Verlag der Wissenschaften, 1972), pp. 14–15.

11. On both the routineness of premarital heterosexual intercourse in the mid-1950s GDR and doctors' acceptance of it, see H.-D. Rösler, "Sexuelle Interessen des Großstadtkindes," and Elfriede Paul, "Die sozialhygienische Bedeutung der sexuellen Aufklärung," both in *Zeitschrift für ärztliche Fortbildung* 50, nos. 1–2 (15 Jan. 1956), pp. 57, 61. On the prevalence of extramarital sex, see Rudolf Neubert, *Das neue Ehebuch: Die Ehe als Aufgabe der Gegenwart und Zukunft* (Rudolstadt: Greifenverlag, 1957), pp. 100, 111.

12. See Wolfgang Bretschneider, *Sexuell Aufklären—Rechtzeitig und Richtig* (Leipzig: Urania, 1956), p. 154.

13. See Atina Grossmann, "A Question of Silence: The Rape of German Women by Occupation Soldiers," *October* 72 (spring 1995); and Atina Grossmann, "Unfortunate Germany: Victims, Victors, and Survivors at War's End, Germany 1945–1950: Notes Toward a Research Project" (paper presented at the Center for the Study of Social Transformations, University of Michigan, Ann Arbor, 16 March 1995).

14. See Gerhard Klumbies, "Zur Jugendsexualität," *Zeitschrift für Psychotherapie und Medizinische Psychologie* 6, no. 6 (Nov. 1956), p. 264.

15. Wolfgang Höfs, "Erfahrungen aus einer Ehe- und Sexual-Beratungsstelle für Männer," *Das deutsche Gesundheitswesen* 7, no. 18 (1952), p. 571.

16. Neubert, *Das neue Ehebuch*, pp. 7, 171.

17. Kühne, "Geburtenkontrolle," *Das deutsche Gesundheitswesen* 2, no. 23 (1947), pp. 746–47. These reflections were in part inspired by Kühne's reading of J. C. Flugel, *Population, Psychology and Peace* (London: Watts, 1947).

18. See Atina Grossmann, *Reforming Sex: The German Movement for Birth Control and Abortion Reform, 1920–1950* (New York: Oxford Univ. Press, 1995), pp. 196–201.

19. "Zweihundertachtzehn: Gestern, Heute und Morgen," *Für Dich* 1, no. 18 (1946), p. 3.

20. Hilde Benjamin, "Juristische Grundlagen für die Diskussion über den Paragraph 218" (25 Feb. 1947), reprinted in Kirsten Thietz, *Ende der Selbstverständlichkeit? Die Abschaffung des Paragraph 218 in der DDR* (Berlin: Basis Druck, 1992), p. 49.

21. See on this point also Annette F. Timm, "Guarding the Health of Worker Families in the GDR: Socialist Health Care, *Bevölkerungspolitik*, and Marriage Counselling, 1945–1970," in *Arbeiter in der SBZ-DDR*, ed. Peter Hübner and Klaus Tenfelde (Essen: Klartext, 1999), p. 470.

22. Maxim Zetkin, "An den Vorstand der SED," in Thietz, *Ende*, p. 29.

23. "Gesetz über den Mutter- und Kinderschutz und die Rechte der Frau vom 27 Sep. 1950," in Amt für Information der Regierung der Deutschen Demokratischen Republik, ed., *Gesunde Familie—Glückliche Zukunft* (Berlin: Deutscher Zentralverlag, 1950), pp. 43–44.

24. Otto Grotewohl, "Zur Begründung des Gesetzes," in Amt für Information, *Gesunde Familie*, pp. 7–8, 19; and "Frauen Fragen, Der DFD Antwortet," in Thietz, *Ende*, p. 77.

25. See Thietz, *Ende*, p. 19.

26. Neubert, *Das neue Ehebuch*, p. 192.

27. A valuable source on ordinary GDR citizens' attitudes about premarital sex in the 1950s are the letters collected in Hanns Schwarz, *Schriftliche Sexualberatung: Erfahrungen und Vorschläge mit 60 Briefen und Antworten* (Rudolstadt: Greifenverlag, 1959). The letters make clear that in the populace premarital heterosexual activity was simply taken as a given; it was *the* common sense behavior in 1950s East Germany. Whenever qualms or anxieties were expressed, they had to do with masturbation, not premarital intercourse. The letters also make clear that girls and women were hardly fearful shrinking violets but rather often the active ones who willingly made overtures to men. Not only do the letter writers remark in passing on their experiences with premarital sex; they also openly asked Schwarz for advice in resolving sexual problems they were having within nonmarital relationships. See also the remarks that while extramarital sex is deemed immoral in the prevailing popular value system, premarital sex is "not seen as indecent" in Karl Dietz and Peter G. Hesse, *Wörterbuch der Sexuologie und ihrer Grenzgebiete* (Rudolstadt: Greifenverlag, 1964), pp. 37, 314.

28. Hanns Schwarz, *Sexualität im Blickfeld des Arztes: Vortrag* (Berlin: Verlag Volk und Gesundheit, 1953), pp. 10–11.

29. Schwarz, *Schriftliche Sexualberatung*, pp. 34, 48.

30. Neubert, *Das neue Ehebuch*, pp. 130, 188.

31. See "Der Jugend Vertrauen und Verantwortung" (1963), in *Dokumente zur Jugendpolitik der DDR* (Berlin: Staatsverlag der DDR, 1965), pp. 93–94; and see the discussion in Heinz Grassel, *Jugend, Sexualität, Erziehung: Zur psychologischen Problematik der Geschlechtserziehung* (Berlin: Staatsverlag der DDR, 1967), pp. 11–12.

32. Wolfhilde Diehrl, *Liebe, Ehe—Scheidung?* (1958, 1961), reprinted in Wolfhilde Diehrl and Wolfgang Bretschneider, *Liebe und Ehe* (Leipzig: Urania, 1962), pp. 198, 201.

33. A classic expression of all three of these assumptions can be found in Bretschneider, *Sexuell Aufklären*, pp. 63–64.

34. Rudolf Neubert, *Die Geschlechterfrage: Ein Buch für junge Menschen* (Rudolstadt: Greifenverlag, 1955, 1966), pp. 80–82.

35. Some scholars surmise that the legal tolerance implemented in 1957 was preceded by a discreet directive from the GDR's Ministry of Justice not to prosecute consensual adult homosexuality already in 1950. See Eike Stedefeldt, *Schwule Macht oder Die Emanzipation von der Emanzipation* (Berlin: Elefanten, 1998), pp. 111, 113; Gudrun von Kowalski, *Homosexualität in der DDR: Ein historischer Abriss* (Marburg: Verlag Arbeiterbewegung und Gesellschaftswissenschaft, 1987), pp. 26–27; James Steakley, "Gays under Socialism: Male Homosexuality in the GDR," *Body Politics* (Toronto), no. 29 (1976–77), pp. 15–18; and Johannes Wasmuth, "Strafrechtliche Verfolgung Homosexueller in BRD und DDR," in *Nationalsozialistischer Terror gegen Homosexuelle: Verdrängt und ungesühnt*, ed. Burkhard Jellonek and Rüdiger Lautmann (Paderborn: Ferdinand Schöningh, 2002), p. 178.

36. The "Committee of Antifascist Resistance Fighters," for example, rejected the East German physician and homosexual rights activist Rudolf Klimmer's efforts to get homosexual victims of Nazism officially acknowledged as victims of

fascism with the following words: "The overwhelming majority of surviving homosexuals are in the FRG. . . . In the rule they belonged to bourgeois or petty bourgeois strata and were hostile to the socioeconomic changes that took place in the GDR after 1945." Quoted in von Kowalski, *Homosexualität*, p. 26. See also Günter Grau, "Return of the Past: The Policy of the SED and the Laws against Homosexuality in Eastern Germany between 1946 and 1968," *Journal of Homosexuality* 37, no. 4 (1999), pp. 1–21; and Marianne Krüger-Potratz, *Anderssein Gab Es Nicht: Ausländer und Minderheiten in der DDR* (Münster: Waxmann, 1991), p. 2.

37. Gerhard Weber and Danuta Weber, *Du und ich* (Berlin: Verlag Volk und Gesundheit, 1965), pp. 102–3. On *Du und ich*'s popularity, see Werner Kirsch, *Zum Problem der sexuellen Belehrung durch den Biologielehrer* (Berlin: Verlag Volk und Wissen, 1967), pp. 78–79.

38. For example, even as medical school professor Helmut Rennert was manifestly pleased to report, based on his empirical studies in Halle in the early 1960s, that young GDR citizens were not only sexually healthy but also sexually active, he also had a hard time disguising his sense of pride that the incidence of homosexual activity was remarkably low. Rather than self-reflexively wondering whether his informants, in view of a homophobic climate, might be evasive on this point as they filled out his questionnaires, perhaps not fully trusting that their answers would remain anonymous (even though on other issues he considered the possibility of false answers), Rennert—while presenting himself as progressive by expressing pleasure that the draft of the new East German criminal code decriminalized homosexuality—nonetheless pandered to the regime's preoccupation with normality by stressing how low rates of homosexual activity apparently were in the GDR in comparison with the findings of researchers like Magnus Hirschfeld in Weimar Germany or Alfred Kinsey in the United States. See Helmut Rennert, "Untersuchungen zur Gefährdung der Jugend und zur Dunkelziffer bei sexuellen Straftaten," *Psychiatrie, Neurologie und Medizinische Psychologie: Zeitschrift für Forschung und Praxis* 17, no. 10 (Oct. 1965), p. 364; Helmut Rennert, "Untersuchungen zur sexuellen Entwicklung der Jugend," *Zeitschrift für ärztliche Fortbildung* 60, no. 3 (Feb. 1966), p. 152; Helmut Rennert, "Untersuchungen über die sexuelle Entwicklung der Jugend in der DDR," *Wissenschaftliche Zeitschrift der Universität Rostock* (Mathematisch-Naturwissenschaftliche Reihe) 17, nos. 6–7 (1968), p. 707; and Helmut Rennert, "Die geschlechtliche Entwicklung der heutigen Jugend am Beispiel unserer Medizinstudenten," in *Jugendprobleme in pädagogischer, medizinischer und juristischer Sicht*, ed. Hanns Schwarz (Jena: Gustav Fischer Verlag, 1967), pp. 93, 95.

39. Conversation with L. S., 2003.

40. Bretschneider, *Sexuell Aufklären*, pp. 40–41, 67–68, 131.

41. This widely held 1950s conviction about the need to sublimate libidinal energies into reconstruction is documented persuasively by Matthias Rothe in "Semantik der Sexualität" (European University Viadrina, Frankfurt an der Oder, unpublished manuscript, 2001). Only in the 1960s, Rothe finds, did the SED—turning to the theory of "cybernetics"—consider the possibility that sex could be a source of energy rather than an energy drain.

42. See André Steiner, "Dissolution of the 'Dictatorship over Needs'? Consumer Behavior and Economic Reform in East Germany in the 1960s," in *Getting*

and Spending: European and American Consumer Societies in the Twentieth Century, ed. Susan Strasser et al. (Cambridge: Cambridge Univ. Press, 1998), pp. 167–85.

43. Hans-Joachim Hoffmann and Peter G. Klemm, *Ein offenes Wort: Ein Buch über die Liebe* (Berlin: Verlag Neues Leben, 1972), pp. 175–76.

44. Conversation with L. U., 2001.

45. Kurt Starke, ". . . ein romantisches Ideal" (interview conducted by Uta Kolano), in Uta Kolano, *Nackter Osten* (Frankfurt an der Oder: Frankfurter Oder Editionen/Sammlung Zeitzeugen, 1995), pp. 83, 86.

46. Conversation with Volkmar Sigusch, 2002.

47. Starke, ". . . ein romantisches Ideal," pp. 82–83; and conversation with Kurt Starke, 2001.

48. Conversation with L. U., 2001; Heiner Carow, ". . . da kommt niemand gegen an," in Kolano, *Nackter Osten*, p. 153. For the transcript of a 1967 SED shaming session, see Felix Mühlberg, "Die Partei ist eifersüchtig," in *Erotik macht die Hässlichen Schön: Sexueller Alltag im Osten*, ed. Katrin Rohnstock (Berlin: Elefanten Press, 1995), pp. 122–43.

49. For example, see Lykke Aresin, *Eheprobleme* (Berlin: Verlag Volk und Gesundheit, 1963), p. 6; Heinz Grassel, "Studentin und Mutterschaft," *Wissenschaftliche Zeitschrift der Universität Rostock (Gesellschaftliche und Sprachwissenschaftliche Reihe),* no. 13 (1964), pp. 541–47; K. Lungwitz, "Die Stabilität frühzeitig geschlossener Ehen im Spiegel der Statistik," *Neue Justiz* 19 (1965); and Karl-Heinz Mehlan, "Die Abortsituation im Weltmassstab," in *Arzt und Familienplanung: Tagungsbericht der 3. Rostocker Fortbildungstage über Probleme der Ehe- und Sexualberatung vom 23. bis 25. Oktober 1967 in Rostock-Warnemünde* (Berlin: Verlag Volk und Gesundheit, 1968), pp. 85–86.

50. See Siegfried Mempel, "Zum Gesetz der DDR über die Unterbrechung der Schwangerschaft," *Recht in Ost und West* 16, no. 5 (Sept. 1972), p. 208. Karl-Heinz Mehlan estimated in 1964 that for the year 1959 there had been at least 60,000 illegal abortions in the GDR and that annually in the GDR in the early 1960s there was approximately 1 abortion for every 3.5 to 4.5 births. Karl-Heinz Mehlan, "Die Familienplanung aus gesellschaftlicher Sicht," *Das Deutsche Gesundheitswesen* 19, no. 16 (1964), p. 743. This was proportionally fewer abortions than in West Germany, where the ratio of abortions to births in these years was estimated at 1 to 1.

51. See H. Rayner and J. Rothe, "Zur Entwicklung von Richtlinien über Arbeitsweise und Organisation des medizinischen Zweiges der Ehe- und Familienberatung (Ehe- und Sexualberatung)," in *Arzt und Familienplanung.*

52. See Siegfried Schnabl, "Die Sexualberatung bei der Anorgasmie der Frau und der Impotenz des Mannes," *Zeitschrift für ärztliche Fortbildung* 60, no. 132 (1966), p. 815; Lykke Aresin and M. Bahder, "25 Jahre Ehe- und Sexualberatung an der Universitäts-Frauenklinik Leipzig" (1973–74), Magnus Hirschfeld Archive, Berlin; the entry on the GDR in "Familienplanung in Europa aus persönlicher Sicht," and "Hindernisse für die Kontrazeption," both in *IPPF Europa: Regionale Informationen* 8 (1979); and Lykke Aresin, "Ehe- und Sexualberatungsstellen und Familienplanung in der DDR," in *Sexuologie in der DDR*, ed. Joachim Hohmann (Berlin: Dietz, 1991), pp. 72–94.

53. See, for example, Grassel, *Jugend*, p. 110; Weber and Weber, *Du und ich*, p. 107.

54. See Heinrich Brückner, *Das Sexualwissen unserer Jugend, dargestellt als Beitrag zur Erziehungsplanung* (Berlin: Deutscher Verlag der Wissenschaften, 1968), pp. 134–37; and "Hüben wie drüben," *Der Spiegel*, 26 May 1969, pp. 72, 75.

55. Klaus Trummer, *Unter vier Augen gesagt . . . : Fragen und Antworten über Freundschaft und Liebe* (Berlin: Verlag Neues Leben, 1966), pp. 7, 11–12.

56. Bernd Bittighöfer in *Deine Gesundheit*, June 1966, pp. 169–71.

57. See the discussion in Grassel, *Jugend*, pp. 141, 155–56. As Erich Honecker put it in 1965, "we are no disciples of hypocrisy and are most certainly in favor of the realistic representation of all sides of human life in literature and art." But "effusions of disinhibition [*Ergüsse der Enthemmung*]" and "pornographic traits" were not acceptable. See Erich Honecker, *Bericht des Politbüros an die 11. Tagung des Zentralkomitees der Sozialistischen Einheitspartei Deutschlands 15.– 18. Dezember 1965* (Berlin: Dietz, 1966), pp. 59, 61. How this played out concretely could be seen for example in the SED's direct censorship, also in 1965, of Irmtraud Morgner's novel *Rumba auf einen Herbst*. The party bureaucrats among other things rejected as overly detailed and/or entirely inappropriate sex scenes in which unfaithful spouses appeared to be having fun and/or to be finding themselves; although the novel had originally been accepted for publication, if Morgner was not willing to change key moments in her text and cut certain scenes, it would simply not be able to appear in the GDR. Morgner soon turned to a more fabulist, magical realist prose style and never published *Rumba*, instead reworking portions of it in a later text. I am grateful to Matthias Rothe for sharing with me copies of the SED memoranda pertaining to *Rumba*.

58. Peter G. Hesse, *Empfängis und Empfängnisverhütung* (Berlin: Verlag Volk und Gesundheit, 1967), p. 39. See also Peter G. Hesse et al., eds., *Sexuologie: Geschlecht, Mensch, Gesellschaft*, 3 vols. (Leipzig: S. Hirzel, 1974–77).

59. See Donna Harsch, "Society, the State, and Abortion in East Germany, 1950–1972," *American Historical Review* 102, no. 1 (Feb. 1997), pp. 62–66.

60. See Lykke Aresin, "Sexologische Probleme in jungen Ehen," *Psychiatrie* 20 (1967), pp. 3–7; Aresin and Bahder, "25 Jahre," p. 87; Schnabl, *Intimverhalten*, p. 265; and Siegfried Schnabl, "Sexuelle Störungen—Verbreitung, Zusammenhänge, Konsequenzen," in Hohmann, *Sexuologie in der DDR*, pp. 116–41, esp. pp. 117, 124, 128. Before she became a strong advocate for the pill, Aresin's clinic in Leipzig dispensed diaphragms and also recommended coitus interruptus, the rhythm method, spermicidal jellies, and condoms. Aresin, *Eheprobleme*, p. 17; and Aresin, "Ehe- und Sexualberatungsstellen," p. 77.

61. See Siegfried Schnabl, *Mann und Frau intim: Fragen des gesunden und des gestörten Geschlechtslebens*, 5th ed. (Berlin: Verlag Volk und Gesundheit, 1972).

62. Starke, ". . . ein romantisches Ideal," pp. 87–88.

63. Staatssekretariat für westdeutsche Fragen, "Das schöne Geschlecht und die Gleichberechtigung in der DDR," *Visite*, no. 3 (1971), pp. 17–21.

64. "Das Kind ist krank—wer bleibt zu Haus?" *Für Dich*, no. 47 (1974), pp. 20, 22.

65. "Zwei Liebeserklärungen," *NBI*, no. 16 (Apr. 1971), pp. 12–14.

66. Ibid., p. 14.

67. Ibid., pp. 14, 16.

68. Marlies Allendorf and Ingeburg Hirsch, "Auf dem Lehrplan steht die Liebe," *Für Dich*, no. 12 (Mar. 1972), p. 6.

69. Prof. Dr. Grandke quoted in Helga Bobach, "Junge Ehe besonders gefährdet?" *Für Dich*, no. 12 (Mar. 1972), p. 38.

70. K. v. Billerbeck, "Rund um Sex," *Für Dich*, no. 12 (Mar. 1972), p. 27.

71. The Schnabl movie was discussed and clips were shown in the made-for-TV movie directed by Tilman Jens, *Liebeslehrer der Nation: Oswalt Kolle zum 70.* (Westdeutscher Rundfunk, 1998).

72. Schnabl, *Intimverhalten*, p. 15–18.

73. Conversation with T. T., 2001.

74. Wolfgang Polte, *Unsere Ehe*, 8th rev. ed. (Leipzig: Verlag für die Frau, 1980), pp. 131, 137–38.

75. See on this point also Starke, ". . . ein romantisches Ideal," p. 94.

76. Kurt Starke and Walter Friedrich, *Liebe und Sexualität bis 30* (Berlin: Deutscher Verlag der Wissenschaften, 1984), pp. 187, 202–3.

77. Ulrich Clement and Kurt Starke, "Sexualverhalten und Einstellungen zur Sexualität bei Studenten in der BRD und in der DDR," *Zeitschrift für Sexualforschung*, no. 1 (1988), pp. 30–44; conversations with Ulrich Clement and Kurt Starke, 2001 and 2002. See also Gunter Schmidt, "Emanzipation zum oder vom Geschlechtsverkehr?" *Pro Familia Magazin*, no. 5 (1993); and Wolfgang Engler, "Nacktheit, Sexualität und Partnerschaft," in *Die Ostdeutschen: Kunde von einem verlorenen Land* (Berlin: Aufbau, 1999), pp. 271–72.

78. See Hans-Joachim Ahrendt, "Neue Aspekte der Familienplanung und Geburtenregelung in Ostdeutschland," in *Sexualität und Partnerschaft im Wandel: Jahrestagung 1991 der Gesellschaft für Sexualwissenschaft*, Leipziger Texte zur Sexualität 1, no. 1 (1992), p.6.

79. Conversation with N. U., 1997.

80. Conversation with H. N., 1998.

81. Conversation with L. U., 2001.

82. See Hans-Joachim Maaz, *Der Gefühlsstau: Ein Psychogramm der DDR* (Berlin: Argon, 1990); and Dietrich Mühlberg, "Sexualität und ostdeutscher Alltag," *Mitteilungen aus der kulturwissenschaftlichen Forschung* 18, no. 36 (1995), p. 10.

83. "DDR-Frauen kriegen *öfter* einen Orgasmus," *Bild*, 30 May 1990, p. 1.

84. Holger Kaukel, *Schweriner Volkszeitung*, 23 Oct. 1993, quoted in Ina Merkel, "Die Nackten und die Roten: Zum Verhältnis von Nacktheit und Öffentlichkeit in der DDR," *Mitteilungen aus der kulturwissenschaftlichen Forschung*, 18, no. 36 (1995), p. 80.

85. Conversation with Kurt Starke, 2001.

86. See Carmen Beilfuss, " 'Über sieben Brücken musst Du geh'n . . .' : Der schwierige Weg der Liebe in der Marktwirtschaft," in *Sexualität und Partnerschaft*, pp. 18–27.

87. Katrin Rohnstock, "Vorwort," in Rohnstock, *Erotik macht die Hässlichen Schön*, pp. 9–10.

88. Conversation with T. T., 2001.

89. D. Mühlberg, "Sexualität und ostdeutscher Alltag," p. 20.

90. Beilfuss, " 'Über sieben Brücken.' "

91. See Bert Thinius, "Vom grauen Versteck ins bunte Ghetto: Ansichten zur Geschichte ostdeutscher Schwuler," in Starke, *Schwuler Osten*, p. 73; Starke, *Schwuler Osten*, pp. 300–301; Kolano, *Nackter Osten*; Konrad Weller, *Das Sexuelle in der deutsch-deutschen Vereinigung: Resümee und Ausblick* (Leipzig: Forum, 1991); Werner Habermehl, *Sexualverhalten der Deutschen: Aktuelle Daten, intime Wahrheiten* (Munich, 1993), pp. 26–31. For a *Wessi* who largely concurs with this assessment, see Karl Scheithauer, "Männerpositionen," in *Stiefbrüder: Was Ostmänner und Westmänner voneinander denken*, ed. Katrin Rohnstock (Berlin: Elefanten Press, 1995), p. 42.

92. See Aleksandar Stulhofer, "Sexual Freedom and Sexual Health in Times of Post-Communist Transition" (paper presented at the International Academy of Sex Research, Hamburg, Germany, 20 June 2002); and Katrin Rohnstock, "Der Bierbauch," in Rohnstock, *Stiefbrüder*, esp. pp. 47–48, 54.

93. Kurt Starke makes these points in "Die Unzüchtige Legende vom prüden Osten," in Rohnstock, *Erotik macht die Hässlichen schön*, p. 157. See also Stapel, "Schwulenbewegung in der DDR," pp. 91–110.

94. Diehrl, *Liebe, Ehe—Scheidung?*, p. 199.

CHAPTER SIX
ANTIFASCIST BODIES

1. Johann August Schülein, "Von der Studentenrevolte zur Tendenzwende oder der Rückzug ins Private: Eine sozialpsychologische Analyse," *Kursbuch* 48 (June 1977), p. 101; and Heinrich Mehrmann, "Erobern Kommunen Deutschlands Betten? Mehr Sex mit Marx und Mao," *Pardon*, Aug. 1967, p. 22. Especially important reflective essays include Peter Schneider, "Die Sache mit der 'Männlichkeit': Gibt es eine Emanzipation der Männer?" *Kursbuch* 35 (Apr. 1974); Lothar Binger, "Kritisches Plädoyer für die Gruppe," *Kursbuch* 37 (Oct. 1974); and Klaus Hartung, "Versuch, die Krise der antiautoritären Bewegung wieder zur Sprache zu bringen," *Kursbuch* 48 (June 1977).

2. Peter Schneider, " 'Nicht der Egoismus verfälscht das politische Engagement, sondern der Versuch ihn zu verheimlichen,' " *Frankfurter Rundschau*, 25 June 1977, p. III.

3. Eckhard Siepmann, "Unergründliches Obdach für Reisende," and "1969—Die grosse Sonnenfinsternis," both in *CheSchahShit: Die sechziger Jahre zwischen Cocktail und Molotow*, ed. Siepmann et al. (Berlin: Elefanten, 1984), pp. 194, 204.

4. The best example—a marvelously funny and thoughtful sex-affirmative curriculum that incorporated feminist and lesbian and gay issues—is Peter A. W. Figge et al., *Betrifft: Sexualität. Materialien zur Sexualerziehung im Medienverbund für Jugendliche, Eltern und Pädagogen* (Braunschweig: Westermann, 1977), sponsored by the Norddeutscher Rundfunk television company and the Federal Office for Health Education (Bundeszentrale für gesundheitliche Aufklärung). In 1982, when the Christian Democrats came back into office under Chancellor Hel-

mut Kohl, all copies of the curriculum remaining in the Federal Office were shredded, and all the educational films for classroom use that had been used in conjunction with the curriculum were officially recalled.

5. On the Alternative Draft, see Herbert Jäger, "Zur Gleichstellung von Homosexualität und Heterosexualität im Strafrecht," *Vorgänge*, no. 4 (1981), p. 19.

6. See CDU/CSU representative Max Güde's remarks in the Bundestag debate of 9 May 1969 (232. Sitzung), in *Verhandlungen des Deutschen Bundestages, 5. Wahlperiode: Stenographische Berichte*, vol. 70 (Bonn, 1969), pp. 12829, 12832; and "Erster Schriftlicher Bericht des Sonderausschusses für die Strafrechtsreform [Drucksache V/4094]," in *Verhandlungen des Deutschen Bundestages, 5. Wahlperiode: Anlagen zu den stenographischen Berichten* (Bonn, 1969), p. 3. The CDU/CSU was adamant about retaining twenty-one as the age of consent, on the grounds that homosexuality among men held "dangers for the sexual development" of young people, even as it (in keeping with the old idea of youth bisexuality) agreed that judicial leniency might be appropriate when homosexual acts engaged in by the under-twenty-one group were the sign of "developmental disturbances or other age-specific difficulties." The SPD, fully aware of the enormity of the change the legal reform represented ("it is the first time that something that was criminalized in our *Volk* is to be decriminalized"), felt the compromise was acceptable. See the remarks of Jungmann (CDU/CSU) and Kübler (SPD) in debate of 7 May 1969, pp. 12787–88.

7. See Karena Niehoff, ". . . der werfe endlich den letzten Stein," *Der Tagesspiegel*, 31 July 1971; "Will Selbstbewusstsein stärken: Rosa von Praunheim," *Münchner Merkur*, 18 Dec. 1971; and Dietrich Kuhlbrodt, "Nicht der Homosexuelle ist pervers, sondern die Situation, in der er lebt," in *Rosa von Praunheim*, ed. Wolfgang Jacobsen (Munich: Carl Hanser, 1984), pp. 113–26.

8. For an important testimonial, see Elmar Drost, "Mit dem Schwanz gedacht: Meine Geschichte fängt da an, wo schwule Geschichte aufgehört hat," in *Schwule Regungen—schwule Bewegungen*, ed. Willi Frieling (Berlin: Rosa Winkel, 1985). See also Andreas Salmen and Albert Eckert, *20 Jahre bundesdeutsche Schwulenbewegung 1969–1989* (Cologne: Bundesverband Homosexualität e.V., 1989), pp. 23–45.

9. Quotes in Kuhlbrodt, "Nicht der Homosexuelle ist pervers," p. 123; and Wolfgang Selitsch in the journal *him* in 1971, quoted in Salmen and Eckert, *20 Jahre*, p. 20. See also " 'Bekennt, dass ihr anders seid,' " *Der Spiegel*, 12 Mar. 1973, pp. 46–62; Michael Föster, "Gegen Spott und Schmach: Homosexuelle formieren sich in Partei- und Gewerkschaftsgruppen," *Vorwärts*, 19 July 1979; and "Hallo, Gerda," *Der Spiegel*, 20 Aug. 1979. See also "Geschichte der Rosa Lüste," http://home.t-online.de/home/rosalueste/histrolu.htm.

10. "Wir sind schwul," *Der Stern*, no. 41 (1978), cover page for the story "Ich bin schwul," pp. 104–18.

11. See graffiti on church wall in Ele Schöfthaler, "Zweierlei Mass: Die evangelische Kirche und der Paragraph 218," in *Das Kreuz mit dem Frieden: 1982 Jahre Christen und Politik*, ed. Peter Winzeler (Berlin: Elefanten Press, 1982), p. 145; banner about gynecologists in "Abtreibung: Massenmord oder Privatsache?" *Der Spiegel*, 21 May 1973, p. 39; cartoon of pregnant Jahn in "Wir müssen uns selber helfen," *Frauen-Zeitung* 1, no. 1 (Oct. 1973), p. 4. See also the

arguments made by feminists in Mainz and Frankfurt in "Warum der Paragraph 218 keine Klassenjustiz ist—oder: Was die Genossin mit der Betschwester zu tun hat!" *Frauen-Zeitung* 1, no. 1 (Oct. 1973), p. 5; and by feminists in the Berlin women's group Bread and Roses in "Brot und Rosen: Paragraph 218," reprinted in *Autonome Frauen: Schlüsseltexte der Neuen Frauenbewegung seit 1968*, ed. Ann Anders (Frankfurt am Main: Athenäum, 1988), pp. 89–93.

12. See "Abtreibung," pp. 38, 44, 50. *Pardon* cartoon also reprinted here.

13. Quotations in "Abtreibung," p. 39.

14. See Ann Anders, "Chronologie der gelaufenen Ereignisse," in Anders, *Autonome Frauen*, pp. 16–21.

15. See Kristina Schulz, *Der lange Atem der Provokation: Die Frauenbewegung in der Bundesrepublik und in Frankreich 1968–1976* (Frankfurt am Main: Campus, 2002), esp. pp. 188–90, 217–25; Kristine von Soden, ed., *Der grosse Unterschied: Die neue Frauenbewegung und die siebziger Jahre* (Berlin: Elefanten Press, 1988); Alice Schwarzer, *So fing es an! 10 Jahre Frauenbewegung* (Cologne: Emma, 1981); and Lottemi Doormann, ed., *Keiner schiebt uns weg: Zwischenbilanz der Frauenbewegung in der Bundesrepublik* (Weinheim: Beltz, 1979).

16. See Eine Frau aus dem Rheinland, "Lesben gemeinsam sind stark" (1972), and Eine Frau aus Heidelberg, "Wie ich gemerkt habe, das ich lesbisch bin," both in *Frauenjahrbuch 1*, ed. Frankfurter Frauen (Frankfurt am Main: Roter Stern, 1975), pp. 200–207; "Lesben: Geschichte der Lesbengruppe im Weiberrat," *Frauen-Zeitung*, no. 1 (Oct. 1973), pp. 13–14; and Ina Kuckuc, *Der Kampf gegen Unterdrückung: Materialien aus der deutschen Lesbierinnenbewegung*, 2nd ed. (Munich: Frauenoffensive, 1977), pp. 73–80. On lesbians' experiences and on the distinctive qualities of lesbophobia in West German culture, see the pathbreaking studies by Siegrid Schäfer, "Sexuelle und soziale probleme von Lesbierinnen in der BRD," in *Ergebnisse zur Sexualforschung*, ed. Eberhard Schorsch and Gunter Schmidt (Cologne: Kiepenheuer & Witsch, 1975); and Susanne von Paczensky, *Verschwiegene Liebe: Lesbische Frauen in unserer Gesellschaft* (Munich: Bertekmann, 1981).

17. "Hexenprozess in Itzehoe, oder: Wie der weiblichen Sexualität der Prozess gemacht wird!" and "Lebenslänglich für Notwehr," both in Frankfurter Frauen, *Frauenjahrbuch 1*, pp. 219–24. See also Annette Dröge, "Jetzt reicht's! Lesbische Frauen werden öffentlich," in von Soden, *Der grosse Unterschied*, pp. 53–56.

18. Photo in Frankfurter Frauen, *Frauenjahrbuch 1*, p. 199.

19. For example, see Ellen Carstens-Graeff, "Mein Fühlen hinterlässt Bremsspuren," and Sibylle Plogstedt, "Ich hatte immer das Gefühl, ich muss näher 'ran," both in *Sexualität* (*Courage Sonderheft* 3, no. 5 [1981]), pp. 56–68.

20. For example, see "Einleitung," *Frauenzeitung*, no. 5 (1974), pp. 1–2.

21. Thus, for instance, in praising the 1969 Bundestag vote to decriminalize male homosexuality, *Der Spiegel* had also compared homophobes with Nazis as it reminded its readers that the same "healthy" "sensibility of the *Volk*" that had been used to justify the persecution, imprisonment, and murder of homosexuals in the Third Reich was still alive and well in 1969 West Germany in the form of popular prejudice against homosexuals. "Späte Milde," *Der Spiegel*, 12 May 1969, p. 55. Along related lines, in 1975, *Der Spiegel* pointedly accompanied its criticism of Pope Paul VI's hostility to the pill with contrasting photographs from

the 1940s and the 1970s: one photograph, captioned "Birthing Propaganda," showed a woman in the Third Reich receiving the Nazi "Mother's Cross" for having done her part to raise the birthrate, while the other, captioned "Birthing Protest," showed an abortion rights demonstration from the early 1970s in West Germany with signs declaring "My belly belongs to me" and calling for "Pleasure without burden" (*Lust ohne Last*). Implicitly here, with respect to sexual politics, the pope was placed on the side of the fascists. "Die Kinder wollen keine Kinder mehr," *Der Spiegel*, 24 March 1975, p. 44.

22. For example, see Ute Döser, "Die Schüler wollen noch mehr wissen," *Hamburger Abendblatt*, 7 Mar. 1970, p. 74; Hartmut Wendscheck, "Reform-Vorschlag geht den Eltern zu weit," *Kölnische Rundschau*, 18 Feb. 1971; "Grenze überschritten," *Der Spiegel*, 20 Mar. 1972, pp. 62–63; "Urteil gegen 'Aufklärung' in der Schule," *Frankfurter Allgemeine Zeitung*, 7 June 1972; "Forsch oder Fromm," *Der Spiegel*, 31 July 1972, pp. 39–40; "Sexual-Unterricht ist gesetzlos und verfassungswidrig!" *Bergedorfer Zeitung*, 16 Nov. 1974; "Zurück zum Gürtel," *Der Spiegel*, 8 Nov. 1976, pp. 98–99; Rainer Klose, "Sexualkunde-Unterricht nicht beanstandet," *Süddeutsche Zeitung*, 15 Feb. 1978; Claus Voland, "Kein Werk des Teufels: Karlsruher Richter zum Sexualkundeunterricht," *Die Zeit*, 24 Feb. 1978; " 'Sexualkunde, na, das macht der Kollege,' " *Der Spiegel*, 27 Feb. 1978, pp. 62–76; " 'Lieber ein Jahr zu früh als eine Stunde zu spät,' " *Der Spiegel*, 27 Mar. 1978, pp. 95–105; and Rupp Doinet, "Macht Sexualkunde impotent?" *Der Stern*, no. 7 (1980), pp. 204–5.

23. Alexander von Hoffmann, "Wie Heil ist der Rechts-Staat?" *Konkret*, Apr. 1976, p. 17. See also Axel Eggebrecht, "Was ist Faschismus? Warnung vor einem Wort," *Konkret*, Feb. 1978, pp. 22–23; and Peter Schneider, "Im Todeskreis der Schuld," *Die Zeit*, 27 Mar. 1987, p. 66.

24. Quoted in Binger, "Kritisches Plädoyer," p. 3.

25. Hartung, "Versuch," p. 36.

26. P. Schneider, " 'Nicht der Egoismus,' " p. III.

27. Uli Puritz, "Schreiben über Sexualität oder wie fische ich das Salz aus der Suppe," *Ästhetik und Kommunikation* 40–41 (Sept. 1980), pp.16–17.

28. *Rote Presse Korrespondenz*, no. 36 (24 Oct. 1969), quoted in *Berliner Kinderläden: Antiautoritäre Erziehung und sozialistischer Kampf* (Cologne: Kiepenheuer und Witsch, 1970), p. 239. See also, for example, Detlev Claussen et al., "Einleitung," in Hans-Jürgen Krahl, *Konstitution und Klassenkampf: Schriften, Reden und Entwürfe aus den Jahren 1966–1970* (Frankfurt am Main: Verlag Neue Kritik, 1971), p. 7; Reimut Reiche's self-criticism of 1971 summarized in Stefan Micheler, "Der Sexualitätsdiskurs in der Studierendenbewegung der 1960er Jahre," *Zeitschrift für Sexualforschung* 13, no. 1 (2000), p. 21; and Dietrich Haensch, "Zerschlagt die Kleinfamilie? Frage an eine sozialistische Alternative zur bürgerlichen Familienpolitik," in *Familiensoziologie: Ein Reader als Einführung*, ed. Dieter Claessens and Petra Milhöfer (Frankfurt am Main: Athenäum, 1973), p. 363.

29. P. Schneider, " 'Nicht der Egoismus,' " p. III.

30. Drei aus der Redaktion, "Von Feen und Faunen," *Pflasterstrand*, no. 23a (9–22 Feb. 1978), p. 5.

31. See on this matter also the reflections of Helke Sander, "Referat," reprinted in *Berliner Kinderläden*, pp. 57–61; and Gabriele Huster, "Die Verdrängung der Femme Fatale und ihrer Schwestern: Nachdenken über das Frauenbild des Nationalsozialismus," in *Inszenierung der Macht: Ästhetische Faszination im Faschismus*, ed. Klaus Behnken and Frank Wagner (Berlin: NGBK, 1987), pp. 145–46.

32. Fischer quoted and discussed in Sibylla Flügge, "1968 und die Frauen—Ein Blick in die Beziehungskiste," in *Gender und soziale Praxis*, ed. Margit Göttert and Karin Walser (Königstein/Taunus: Ulrike Helmer, 2002), p. 281.

33. As Ulf Preuss-Lausitz pointed out in the early 1980s, it might have been hard by that point to imagine anymore that this former "battle cry" of the 1960s had ever been considered progressive, but he assured readers that it most certainly had been. "An incredibly chauvinist, heartless, indeed reactionary sentence, I would say today." However, in the 1960s, "the astonishing thing is that almost no one but the 'old moralists' questioned its progressiveness (which was taken as evidence for its progressiveness)." Ulf Preuss-Lausitz, "Vom gepanzerten zum sinnstiftenden Körper," in *Kriegskinder, Konsumkinder, Krisenkinder: Zur Sozialisationsgeschicht seit dem zweiten Weltkrieg*, ed. Preuss-Lausitz et al. (Weinheim: Beltz, 1989), p. 98.

34. See Mehrmann, "Erobern Kommunen Deutschlands Betten?" pp. 17, 21.

35. Klaus Theweleit, *Ghosts: Drei leicht inkorrekte Vorträge* (Frankfurt am Main: Stroemfeld/Roter Stern, 1998), pp. 106–7.

36. Sabine Weissler, "Sexy Sixties," in Siepmann et al., *CheSchahShit*, p. 99.

37. H. Abholz, H. W. Dräger, and B. Witt, "Lautloses Platzen," *FU Spiegel*, Feb. 1968.

38. Flyer written by the Frankfurt "Broads' Collective" (*Weiberrat*) and distributed at the national SDS convention in Hannover in 1968. Text reprinted in Sibylla Flügge, "Der Weiberrat im SDS," in Siepmann et al., *CheSchahShit*, p. 174.

39. Conversation with R. G., 2002.

40. Verena Stefan, *Häutungen* (Munich: Frauenoffensive, 1975), p. 25.

41. "Psychische Verelendung und Emanzipatorische Selbsttätigkeit" (collective statement produced by a women's group circa 1974), p. 5. Personal archive, Sibylla Flügge, Frankfurt am Main.

42. Elisabeth Skerutsch, "Was soll der Abtreibungsparagraf?" mimeograph flyer (circa 1974). Personal archive, Sibylla Flügge, Frankfurt am Main.

43. "Zum Wandel der Sexualmoral" (seminar paper, University of Frankfurt, early 1970s). Personal archive, Sibylla Flügge, Frankfurt am Main.

44. "Psychische Verelendung," pp. 6–7.

45. For example, see the reflections in Binger, "Kritisches Plädoyer," pp. 11–14.

46. See Karin Rasch, "Geschichte des ersten Weiberrats" (manuscript from early 1971). Personal archive, Sibylla Flügge, Frankfurt am Main.

47. Conversation with T. S., 2002.

48. "Psychische Verelendung," p. 6.

49. Stefan Hinz, "Die Kunscht des Liebens," *Konkret*, Apr. 1981, p. 50.

50. "Sexualität: Wenig Fortsetzung . . . ," *Pflasterstrand* 22 (12–25 Jan. 1978), p. 19.

51. Drei aus der Redaktion, "Von Feen und Faunen," p. 4.

52. "Sexualität: Wenig Fortsetzung . . . ," p. 19.

53. "Intern," *Sexualität Konkret* 1 (1979), p. 4.

54. "Kontroverse zum 'Stammheim-Fick,' " *Pflasterstrand* 22 (12–25 Jan. 1978), p. 23; "Sexualität: Wenig Fortsetzung . . . ," p. 19.

55. Dany, in *Pflasterstrand* 23 (late Jan.–early Feb. 1978), p. 3.

56. Puritz, "Schreiben," p. 13; "Gedanken eines Sauriers," *Pflasterstrand* 21 (15 Dec. 1977–11 Jan. 1978), p. 40; "Vögeln," ibid., p. 28.

57. Harry Oberländer, "Notizen aus der Provinz," *Pflasterstrand* 23 (late Jan.–early Feb. 1978), p. 3.

58. Micky, "Warum ich mich an dieser Diskussion nicht beteilige . . . ," *Pflasterstrand* 23a (9–22 Feb. 1978), p. a.

59. "Gedanken eines Sauriers," p. 42.

60. "Antwort eines Sauriers," *Pflasterstrand* 22 (12–25 Jan. 1978), p. 23.

61. Gernot Gailer, "Eine Traumfrau zieht sich aus," *Ästhetik und Kommunikation* 40–41 (Sept. 1980), pp. 84–85, 91.

62. Cover caption "Zurück zur Weiblichkeit," *Der Spiegel*, 30 June 1975; see also Wilhelm Bittorf, "Der anatomische Imperativ," ibid., p. 42: "Demanding women and men who have become insecure exhaust each other with expectations that they cannot fulfill, get snarled up in ego battles, in which the man often loses not only his feeling of superiority but also his potency and the woman loses all the magic that once upon a time had awakened passion and love."

63. "Bis 25: Täglich Liebe. Ab 30: Ich bin so müde," *Bild*, 24 Jan. 1969.

64. *Der Stern* cartoon reprinted in "Jüngstes Gerücht," *Der Spiegel*, 28 Feb. 1977, p. 190.

65. "Jüngstes Gerücht," p. 191.

66. "Mild bis wild," *Der Spiegel*, 7 Mar. 1977, p. 207.

67. "Stunde der Wahrheit," *Der Spiegel*, 18 Apr. 1977, p. 231.

68. Leona Siebenschön, "Noch genauso frigide," *Die Zeit*, 18 July 1975, p. 37 (a review of the interviews collected in Alice Schwarzer's *Der "kleine" Unterschied* [1975]).

69. SEAT study and quotation in Ingrid Kolb, "Zwischen Lust und Frust," *Der Stern*, no. 21 (1980), p. 132.

70. Quoted in Conrad Zander, "Die Männer werden keusch: Schluss mit dem Sex," *Der Stern*, no. 51 (1982), p. 50.

71. Kolb, "Zwischen Lust und Frust," p. 120.

72. Zander, "Die Männer werden keusch," pp. 48–49. On the striking lack of impact of feminist perspectives on sex in the advice columns of mainstream women's magazines in the early 1980s, see Cheryl Barnard and Edit Schlaffer, "Der Mann im Bett," in *Viel erlebt und nichts begriffen: Die Männer und die Frauenbewegung* (Reinbek: Rowohlt, 1985), pp. 77–81.

73. For example, see "Eine Welle von Nazi-Drohungen gegen Feministinnen," *Emma*, Dec. 1983, p. 5; Margarete Mitscherlich, "Die Unfähigkeit zu kämpfen," *Emma*, Apr. 1991, p. 28; Ingrid Schmidt-Harzbach, "Die Lüge von der Stunde Null," *Courage*, June 1982, p. 34; and Annemarie Troeger, "Die Dolchstosslegende der Linken: 'Frauen haben Hitler an die Macht gebracht.' Thesen zur Geschichte der Frauen am Vorabend des Dritten Reichs," in *Frauen und Wissen-*

schaft: Beiträge zur Berliner Sommeruniversität für Frauen, Juli 1976, ed. Gruppe Berliner Dozentinnen (Berlin: Courage, 1977), p. 324.

74. See FIL, "Sieg Macho," *Emma*, Dec. 1987, p. 6; Ingrid Strobl, "Justine und Justiz," *Emma*, Feb. 1988, p. 33; and the section on "Playboy bis TAZ," in *Schwesternlust und Schwesternfrust: 20 Jahre Frauenbewegung*, ed. Alice Schwarzer (Cologne: Emma, 1991), p. 129.

75. Die Frankfurter Stadthexen et al., in *Pflasterstrand* 23 (late Jan.–early Feb. 1978), p. 1.

76. "Der Aufstand der Frauen: Am 6. Juni 1971 ging es los!" *Emma*, June 1991, pp. 18, 20–21.

77. See the discussion in Karin Windaus-Walser, "Gnade der weiblichen Geburt? Zum Umgang der Frauenforschung mit Nationalsozialismus und Antisemitismus," *Feministische Studien* 1 (1988), p. 111.

78. See the discussions in Annette Kuhn, "Der Antifeminismus als verborgene Theoriebasis des deutschen Faschismus: Feministische Gedanken zur nationalsozialistischen 'Biopolitik,' " in *Frauen und Faschismus in Europa: Der faschistische Körper*, ed. Leonore Siegele-Wenschkewitz and Gerda Stuchlik (Pfaffenweiler: Centaurus, 1990), p. 39; and Frauen gegen Antisemitismus, "Der Nationalsozialismus als Extremform des Patriarchats: Zur Leugnung der Täterschaft von Frauen und zur Tabuisierung des Antisemitismus in der Auseinandersetzung mit dem NS," *Beiträge zur feministischen Theorie und Praxis*, no. 35 (1993), pp. 77–89.

79. Henryk M. Broder, "Ich bin ein Chauvi," *Konkret*, Oct. 1979, pp. 55, 57.

80. Berndt Nitzschke's lecture before sexologists in Salzburg, 5 Nov. 1988, excerpted in *Emma*, Feb. 1989, p. 29.

81. See Troeger, "Die Dolchstosslegende," p. 325.

82. In Fest's work (*Das Gesicht des Dritten Reiches: Profile einer totalitären Herrschaft* (Munich: R. Piper, 1963), and *Hitler: Eine Biographie* (Berlin: Propyläen, 1973), there are repeated descriptions of supposedly "unsatisfied," sexually frustrated "overripe" older women "worshiping" Hitler with "turbid yearning." Fest also wrote that "Hitler increasingly became the object of desire around which neurotic petty bourgeois women gathered for collective wantonness, greedy for the moment of disinhibition, of the great release, which—in the overflowing scream of the mass—decisively revealed the carnal character of these events and their extraordinary similarity to the public sexual acts of primitive tribes." Noting that the immense extent of male enthusiasm for Hitler was quietly sidestepped in Fest's "analysis," and amazed both at the brazenness of Fest's claim and the obvious allusions to "rut, ecstasy, orgasm," feminist sociologist Eva Sternheim-Peters concluded with caustic sarcasm: "Here a 'woman' can only ask pityingly and politely whether at least a few neurotic petty bourgeois *men* were able to enjoy a miserable scrap of pleasure in this 'great release.'" Eva Sternheim-Peters, "Brunst, Ekstase, Orgasmus: Männerphantasien zum Thema 'Hitler und die Frauen,'" *Psychologie heute* 8, no. 7 (1981), pp. 36, 38–39.

83. See Troeger, "Die Dolchstosslegende," p. 325.

84. Sternheim-Peters, "Brunst, Ekstase, Orgasmus," p. 36.

85. Rudolf Augstein, "Frauen fliessen, Männer schiessen," *Der Spiegel*, 19 Dec. 1977, p. 132; and Lothar Baier, "In den Staub mit allen Feinden der Frau," *Frankfurter Allgemeine Zeitung*, 18 Apr. 1978.

86. Bazon Brock, "Frauen, Fluten, Körper, Geschichte: Ein wichtiger Beitrag linker Theorie zur Faschismusdebatte," *Die Zeit*, 25 Nov. 1977, p. 11.

87. "Blut und Widerstand: Der Traum vom Terror," *Pflasterstrand* 21 (15 Dec. 1977–11 Jan. 1978), p. 19.

88. Thomas Kühne, "Männergeschichte als Geschlechtergeschichte," in *Männergeschichte—Geschlechtergeschichte: Männlichkeit im Wandel der Moderne*, ed. Kühne (Frankfurt am Main: Campus, 1996), p. 16.

89. Klaus Theweleit, *Male Fantasies*, vol. 1: *Women, Floods, Bodies, History*, trans. Stephen Conway with Erica Carter and Chris Turner (Minneapolis: Univ. of Minnesota Press, 1987), p. xx.

90. Theweleit is very uneven on homosexuality. At one point—precisely in the context of trying to *refute* the old canard that all Nazis were homosexual—Theweleit claims to find similarities between homosexuals and fascists and suggests that homosexuals, like psychotic children, might be "incompletely born." See Klaus Theweleit, *Male Fantasies*, vol. 2: *Male Bodies: Psychoanalyzing the White Terror*, trans. Erica Carter and Chris Turner with Stephen Conway (Minneapolis: Univ. of Minnesota Press, 1989), pp. 314–18.

91. Ibid., p. 104.

92. Ibid., pp. 189, 195, 201, 432. See also Theweleit, *Male Fantasies*, 1:430–32.

93. Theweleit, *Male Fantasies*, 2:61, 127, 279, 315.

94. Ibid., pp. 301–3.

95. See the brief considerations of the problem in Michael Rogin, "Fascist Fantasies," *Nation*, 18–25 July 1987, p. 65; and Jessica Benjamin and Anson Rabinbach's foreword to Theweleit, *Male Fantasies*, 2:xiv. One way Jews continually reappear is as part of the standard triumvirate of things fascist men were said to hate: women, communists (or proletarians), and Jews (as in a sort of tired rattling-down of the three analytic categories of gender, class, race). But what is interesting here is the way Theweleit often makes this triplet fit better into his argument by linking Jews with sex or, in other words, by subsuming Jews into his sexual argument, as in such phrases as "contagious Jewish lust" (ibid., p. 162) or "lascivious or avaricious Jews" (ibid., p. 348).

96. For example, Theweleit, *Male Fantasies*, 2:118, 213, 348–49.

97. Ibid., pp. 6–7, 9, 237. As an antifascist strategy Theweleit recommended the following type of analytic treatment for a soldierly male: since he is "locked . . . in his totality-armor," "analysis might perhaps involve guiding him toward an acknowledgment of his bodily openings and of the interior of his body, in order to protect him from immediate inundation by the fear of dissolution if his bodily periphery becomes pleasurably invested" (ibid., p. 261; also see pp. 267–68 on "political work with potential fascists").

98. See Richard Herzinger, "Wandlungen eines Mythos: Die Kulturrevolutionäre von 1968—Garanten der liberalen Kultur in Deutschland?" in *Die Nacht hat zwölf Stunden, dann kommt schon der Tag: Antifaschismus—Geschichte und Neubewertung*, ed. Claudia Keller (Berlin: Aufbau, 1996), pp. 252–67; Helmut Dubiel, "Linke Trauerarbeit," *Merkur* 496 (June 1990), pp. 482–94; Detlev Pol-

lack, "Über die 68er und ihr Verhältnis zur DDR," *Leviathan* 26, no. 4 (1998), pp. 540–49; and Jan-Werner Müller, "Melancholy, Utopia and Reconciliation: Left-Wing and Liberal Responses to Unification," in *Another Country: German Intellectuals, Unification and National Identity* (New Haven: Yale Univ. Press, 2000).

99. See Hartmut Schergel, "Reise in eine andere Galaxie," *Kölner Stadt-Anzeiger*, 2–3 Jan. 1999, p. 7 (especially the summary of *Bild*'s study, "Zwischen Cola und Corega Tabs"); and Cordt Schnibben, "Vollstrecker des Weltgewissens," *Der Spiegel*, 2 June 1997, pp. 113, 115. For the prevalence of this argument also in France, see Kristin Ross, *May '68 and Its Afterlives* (Chicago: Univ. of Chicago Press, 2002), pp. 19–21.

100. See the critical discussions in Friedrich Christian Delius, "Die Dialektik des Deutschen Herbstes," *Die Zeit*, 1 Aug. 1997, p. 3; Klaus Theweleit, "Very Important Grown-Ups," *tageszeitung*, 23 Apr. 1999; and Belinda Davis, "New Leftists and West Germany: Violence, Fascism, and the Public Sphere, 1967–1974" (paper presented at the German Studies Association conference, Washington, DC, 7 Oct. 2001). See also Heinrich August Winkler, "Ende aller Sonderwege," *Der Spiegel*, 11 June 2001, p. 176; and Jeremy Varon, *Bringing the War Home: The Weather Underground, the Red Army Faction, and the Revolutionary Violence in the Sixties and Seventies* (Berkeley: Univ. of California Press, 2004).

101. See "Die Verräter sind unter uns," *Die Zeit*, 22 Apr. 1999; and Gerd Holzheimer, *Wider den genitalen Ernst: Sex von den 68ern bis zur Love-Parade* (Leipzig: Reclam, 2002).

102. See Elazar Barkan, *The Guilt of Nations: Restitution and Negotiating Historical Injustices* (New York: Norton, 2000); Hans-Georg Betz, "Towards a Community of Values? Reflections on Europe's Future from North America" (York University, Toronto, unpublished manuscript, 2002); Winkler, "Ende aller Sonderwege," p. 180; and Karl Schlögel, "Der Dämon der Gewalt," in *Experiment Europa* (*Spiegel Spezial*, no. 1 [2002]), pp. 86–95.

103. See Hanno Loewy, "A History of Ambivalence: Post-Reunification German Identity and the Holocaust," *Patterns of Prejudice* 36, no. 2 (2002); and Susanne Klingenstein, "Wer sind diese Deutschen?" *Frankfurter Allgemeine Zeitung*, 6 Oct. 2001.

104. See Jörg Friedrich, *Der Brand: Deutschland im Bombenkrieg 1940–1945* (Berlin: Propyläen, 2002); W. G. Sebald, "Air War and Literature," in *On the Natural History of Destruction* (New York: Random House, 2003); Robert G. Moeller, *War Stories: The Search for a Usable Past in the Federal Republic of Germany* (Berkeley: Univ. of California Press, 2001); Günter Grass, *Im Krebsgang* (Göttingen: Steidl, 2002); Vera Neumann, *Nicht der Rede Wert: Die Privatisierung der Kriegsfolgen in der frühen Bundesrepublik: Lebensgeschichtliche Erinnerung* (Münster: Westfälisches Dampfboot, 1999); Elisabeth Domansky and Harald Welzer, eds., *Eine offene Geschichte: Zur kommunikativen Tradierung der nationalsozialistischen Vergangenheit* (Tübingen: Edition Diskord, 1999); Elisabeth Domansky and Jutta de Jong, eds., *Der lange Schatten des Krieges: Deutsche Lebens-Geschichten nach 1945* (Münster: Aschendorff, 2000); Klaus Naumann, ed., *Nachkrieg in Deutschland* (Hamburg: Hamburger Edition, 2001); Jason

Cowley, "Forgotten Victims," *Guardian Weekly*, 4–10 Apr. 2002, p. 22; and Alice Förster and Birgit Beck, "Post-Traumatic Stress Disorder and World War II: Can a Psychiatric Concept Help Us Understand Postwar Society?" in *Life after Death: Approaches to a Cultural and Social History of Europe during the 1940s and 1950s*, ed. Richard Bessel and Dirk Schumann (Cambridge: Cambridge Univ. Press, 2003).

105. On the self-exculpatory function of narratives of non-Jewish German victimization, see, for example, Moeller, *War Stories*; Frank Stern, *The Whitewashing of the Yellow Badge: Antisemitism and Philosemitism in Postwar Germany* (Oxford: Pergamon, 1992).

106. On Walser, see esp. Jan-Holger Kirsch, "Identität durch Normalität: Der Konflikt um Martin Walsers Friedenspreisrede," *Leviathan* 27, no. 3 (1999).

107. Schäffer quoted in Stern, *Whitewashing*, p. 380; see also p. 383 on Adenauer's mixed motives. For more on Schäffer's and Adenauer's views about restitution, and on how very popular Schäffer was in West Germany, specifically because of his overt antisemitism, see Christian Pross, *Wiedergutmachung: Der Kleinkrieg gegen die Opfer* (Frankfurt am Main: Athenäum, 1988), esp. pp. 31–32, 58–68.

108. On Gruber, see Richard Rubenstein, "The Dean and the Chosen People," in *Holocaust: Religious and Philosophical Perspectives*, ed. Michael Berenbaum and John K. Roth (New York: Paragon, 1989); and Philipp Gassert, " 'Der Nazi-Kanzler': Kurt Georg Kiesinger und die Auseinandersetzungen um die NS-Vergangenheit in den späten 1960er Jahren" (paper presented at the German Studies Association Conference, Washington, DC, 7 Oct. 2001).

109. Von Dohnanyi quoted in the superb essay by Reinhard Mohr, "Total normal?" *Der Spiegel*, 30 Nov. 1998, p. 46.

110. Conversation with F. C., 2003. See also Armin Himmelrath, "Neue, alte Ängste: Jeder dritte Student will Ende der Holocaust-Debatte—jüdische Studenten in Sorge," *Unicum* (July 2002), p. 12; Anton-Andreas Guha, "Ablehnung von Juden, Amerikanern und Arabern hat zugenommen: Studie des Freud-Instituts und der Universität Leipzig/Antisemitismus in Westdeutschland stärker verbreitet als im Osten," *Frankfurter Rundschau*, 15 June 2002, p. 1; and Robin Detje, "Im freien Fall," *Die Zeit*, no. 26 (18 June 2003), p. 34. In November 2002, *Die Zeit* reported that a study found 52 percent of Germans believing that "many Jews try to draw advantage out of the Holocaust." On the special avidity of attention paid by Europeans to Israel, see Andrei S. Markovits, "Der salonfähige Antisemitismus," *tageszeitung*, 11 May 2002. On the earlier history of German reactions to the Middle East conflict, see Dietrich Wetzel, ed., *Die Verlängerung von Geschichte: Deutsche, Juden und der Palästinakonflikt* (Frankfurt am Main: Neue Kritik, 1983).

111. Rex quoted in Mohr, "Total normal?" p. 46.

112. Daniel Jonah Goldhagen, *Hitler's Willing Executioners: Ordinary Germans and the Holocaust* (New York: Knopf, 1996).

113. See Ulrike Jureit, ed., *Verbrechen der Wehrmacht: Dimensionen des Vernichtungskrieges 1941–1944* (Hamburg: Hamburger Edition, 2002); Bernd Ulrich, ed., *Eine Ausstellung und ihre Folgen: Zur Rezeption der Ausstellung "Vernichtungskrieg—Verbrechen der Wehrmacht 1941 bis 1944"* (Hamburg:

Hamburger Edition, 1999); Omer Bartov, Atina Grossmann, and Mary Nolan, eds., *Crimes of War: Guilt and Denial in the Twentieth Century* (New York: New Press, 2002).

114. Hannes Heer, "The Difficulty of Ending a War: Reactions to the Exhibition 'War of Extermination: Crimes of the Wehrmacht 1941 to 1944,' " *History Workshop*, no. 46 (1998), p. 194.

115. See, for example, Michael Burleigh, *Death and Deliverance: "Euthanasia" in Germany 1900–1945* (Cambridge: Cambridge Univ. Press, 1994); Heidrun Kaupen-Haas and Christiane Rothmaler, eds., *Moral, Biomedizin und Bevölkerungskontrolle* (Frankfurt am Main: Mabuse, 1997); Christa Schikorra, *Kontinuitäten der Ausgrenzung: "Asoziale" Häftlinge im Frauenkonzentrationslager Ravensbrück* (Berlin: Metropol, 2001); Michael Zimmermann, *Rassenutopie und Genozid: Die nationalsozialistische "Lösung" der Zigeunerfrage* (Hamburg: Christians, 1996); Guenter Lewy, *The Nazi Persecution of the Gypsies* (Oxford: Oxford Univ. Press, 2000); Frank Sparing, "*. . . wegen Vergehen nach §175 verhaftet": Die Verfolgung der Düsseldorfer Homosexuellen während des Nationalsozialismus* (Düsseldorf: Grupello, 1997); Joachim Müller et al., eds., *Homosexuelle Männer im KZ Sachsenhausen* (Berlin: Rosa Winkel, 2000); Burkhard Jellonek and Rüdiger Lautmann, eds., *Nationalsozialistischer Terror gegen Homosexuelle: Verdrängt und ungesühnt* (Paderborn: Schöningh, 2002); Frank Bajohr, "*Arisierung" in Hamburg: Die Verdrängung der jüdischen Unternehmer 1933–1945* (Hamburg: Christians, 1997); Marion A. Kaplan, *Between Dignity and Despair: Jewish Life in Nazi Germany* (New York: Oxford Univ. Press, 1998); Götz Aly and Susanne Heim, *Vordenker der Vernichtung: Auschwitz und die deutschen Pläne für eine neue europäische Ordnung* (Hamburg: Hoffmann und Campe, 1991); and Christian Gerlach, *Krieg, Ernährung, Völkermord: Forschungen zur deutschen Vernichtungspolitik im Zweiten Weltkrieg* (Hamburg: Hamburger Edition, 1998).

116. See, for example, Jörg Friedrich, *Die kalte Amnestie: NS-Täter in der Bundesrepublik*, 2nd rev. ed. (Munich: Piper, 1994); Norbert Frei, *Vergangenheitspolitik: Die Anfänge der Bundesrepublik und die NS-Vergangenheit* (Munich: Beck, 1996); Ernst Klee, *Deutsche Medizin im Dritten Reich: Karrieren vor und nach 1945* (Frankfurt am Main: Fischer, 2001).

117. Atina Grossmann, "The 'Goldhagen Effect': Memory, Repetition, and Responsibility in the New Germany," in *The "Goldhagen Effect": History, Memory, Nazism—Facing the German Past*, ed. Geoff Eley (Ann Arbor: Univ. of Michigan Press, 2000), pp. 89–90, 93, 107.

118. Klaus Hartung, "Errinyen in Deutschland: Überlegungen zur 'Historikerdebatte,' zum Faschismusbegriff der '68er,' und zu Peter Schneiders Selbstkritik," *Niemandsland* 2, no. 1 (1987), pp. 88–89.

119. On this self-styling of former members of the generation of 1968 as the ones who brought democracy to postwar Germany, see also the critical remarks of Herzinger, "Wandlungen eines Mythos," pp. 252–67; and Ulrich Herbert, "Legt die Plakate nieder, ihr Streiter für die Gerechtigkeit," *Frankfurter Allgemeine Zeitung*, no. 24 (29 Jan. 2001), p. 48.

120. See, for example, Hartmut Häusserman, "Was '1968' bedeutet," Ingrid Gilcher-Holtey, " '1968' in Frankreich und Deutschland," and Claus Offe, "Vier

Hypothesen über historische Folgen der Studentenbewegung," all in *Leviathan* 26, no. 4 (1998); and Heer, "The Difficulty." For the earlier and more critical consensus, see Michael Schneider, *Den Kopf verkehrt aufgesetzt, oder Die melancholische Linke: Aspekte des Kulturzerfalls in den siebziger Jahren* (Darmstadt: Luchterhand, 1981); Jessica Benjamin and Anson Rabinbach, "Germans, Leftists, Jews," and Marion A. Kaplan, "To Tolerate Is to Insult," both in *New German Critique* 31 (winter 1984); Anson Rabinbach and Jack Zipes, eds., *Germans and Jews since the Holocaust: The Changing Situation in West Germany* (New York: Holmes and Meier, 1986); and Andrei S. Markovits, "Coping with the Past: The West German Labor Movement and the Left," in *Reworking the Past: Hitler, the Holocaust, and the Historians' Debate*, ed. Peter Baldwin (Boston: Beacon, 1990).

121. For example, see Claus Leggewie, "Antifaschisten sind wir sowieso," *Die Zeit*, 19 Feb. 1988, p. 62; P. Schneider, "Im Todeskreis"; and Hartung, "Erinnyen."

122. See the thoughtful remarks in "Einleitung," *Inszenierung der Macht*, pp. 7–10; and Peter Reichel, *Der schöne Schein des Dritten Reiches: Faszination und Gewalt des Faschismus* (Munich: Carl Hanser, 1991), pp. 7–10.

123. See Anson Rabinbach, "Reponse to Karen Brecht, 'In the Aftermath of Nazi Germany: Alexander Mitscherlich and Psychoanalysis—Legend and Legacy,' " *American Imago* 52, no. 3 (1995).

124. Volkmar Sigusch, "Editorial," *Operation AIDS* (*Sexualität Konkret*, no. 7 [1986]), pp. 4–5.

125. See *Rosa Flieder*, no. 52 (Apr.–May 1987), p. 11; Dieter Schiefelbein, "Auftakt," in *Der Frankfurter Engel, Mahnmal Homosexuellenverfolgung: Ein Lesebuch*, ed. Initiative Mahnmal Homosexuellenverfolgung (Frankfurt am Main: Eichborn, 1997), p. 12; and the discussion in Erik N. Jensen, "The Pink Triangle and Political Consciousness: Gays, Lesbians, and the Memory of Nazi Persecution," *Journal of the History of Sexuality* 11, nos. 1–2 (Jan.–Apr. 2002), p. 332.

126. See Dirk Ruder, "Es sterben immer die anderen," *Jungle World*, no. 49 (2 Dec. 1998); and "Safer Sex: Worauf es wirklich ankommt," *Du bist nicht allein—Das OnlineMagazin für schwule Jugendliche*, http://www1.dbna.net/junxzone/reports/safersex1.shtml.

127. See Michael Bochow, *Schwule Männer, AIDS und Safer Sex* (Berlin: Deutsche AIDS-Hilfe, 2001); and Michael Bochow, *Die Reaktionen homosexueller Männer auf AIDS in Ost- und Westdeutschland* (Berlin: AIDS-FORUM DAH, 1993).

128. On the conviction that HIV/AIDS did end the sexual revolution, see Ariane Barth, "Eine Infektion der kollektiven Phantasie," *Der Spiegel*, 6 Apr. 1987, pp. 114, 117. On more widespread use of pornography and sex-toys as crucial responses to HIV/AIDS, see, for example, Paul Schulz, "100 Jahre Sex," *Siegessäule* 16 June 2000; and Fabian Kress, Paul Schulz, and Andrea Winter, "Sex: Was Berlins Lesben und Schwule wirklich tun," *Siegessäule*, 30 Nov. 2002.

129. See Ursula Knapp, "Karlsruhe lässt 'Homo-Ehe' zu," *Frankfurter Rundschau*, 19 July 2001, p. 1; Jan Feddersen, "Homoehe? Ein Luftschloss" (interview with Martin Dannecker), *taz-magazin*, 28–29 July 2001, p. vii; Holger Wicht, "100 Jahre Integration," *Siegessäule*, Sept. 1999; Eike Stedefeldt, *Schwule*

Macht oder Emanzipation von der Emanzipation (Berlin: Elefanten, 1998); and Norbert Blech, "Homo-Ehe ohne Grenzen: Signal aus Brüssel," *EuroGay*, 13 Feb. 2003, http://www.eurogay.de/8420.html.

130. Tanja Rest, "Als die Lust am Verbotenen blühte," *Frankfurter Neue Presse*, 24 Apr. 1998, p. 7; and cover caption "Nackt bis auf die Seele: Die exhibitionistische Gesellschaft," *Der Spiegel*, 14 July 1997.

131. " 'Der Tanz ums goldene Selbst,' " *Der Spiegel*, 14 July 1997, p. 92.

132. See, for example, Gunter Schmidt, *Sexuelle Verhältnisse: Über das Verschwinden der Sexualmoral* (Hamburg: Ingrid Klein, 1996), pp. 7–20.

133. See, for example, Volkmar Sigusch, "Die Trümmer der sexuellen Revolution," *Die Zeit*, 11 Oct. 1996, pp. 17–18; Volkmar Sigusch, "The Neosexual Revolution," *Archives of Sexual Behavior* 27, no. 4 (1998), pp. 331–59; and Volkmar Sigusch, "Lean Sexuality: On Cultural Transformations of Sexuality and Gender in Recent Decades," *Zeitschrift für Sexualforschung* 15, no. 2 (June 2002).

134. On Viagra, see Leonore Tiefer, "Doing the Viagra Tango: Die Sex-Pille als Symbol und als Substanz," *Zeitschrift für Sexualforschung* 11, no. 4 (Dec. 1998); and Volkmar Sigusch, "Viagra: Forschungsstand," *Zeitschrift für Sexualforschung* 13, no. 4 (Dec. 2000). On "ego trip" see " 'Der Tanz,' " p. 92; and the interview with fashion designer Wolfgang Joop—who deemed the mirror-gazing, body-fetishizing, tricep-pumping world of fitness studios "profoundly asexual"— in " 'Jeder ist heute ein Diva,' " *Der Spiegel*, 14 July 1997, p. 104. On optimizing time investment, see Bert Thinius, in "Aufbruch aus dem grauen Versteck, Ankunft im bunten Ghetto?" in *Schwuler Osten: Homosexuelle Männer in der DDR*, ed. Kurt Starke (Berlin: Christoph Links Verlag, 1995), p. 11; and the remarks about "modern autistic variants" of sexual behavior and " 'fast food, fast fuck, fast fitness,' " in Konrad Weller, *Das Sexuelle in der deutsch-deutschen Vereinigung: Resümee und Ausblick* (Leipzig: Forum, 1991), p. 57.

135. Schuller cited in Rüdiger Lautman, Jakob Pastoetter, and Kurt Starke, "Germany," *The Continuum Complete International Encyclopedia of Sexuality*, ed. Robert T. Francoeur, Raymond J. Noonan, and Martha Cornog (New York: Continuum, 2003): and Rainer Gruber, "Die Verbindung von Computer und Sexualität—Möglichkeiten," 21 Jan. 1996, http://www.eberl.net/dk/ws95/Gruber/d_index.html.

136. "Jeder Fünfte in Deutschland hat *Erektionsprobleme.*—Sie auch?" (Pfizer ad), in *Der Stern*, no. 12 (2002), p. 39.

137. Leonore Tiefer, "The Medicalization of Women's Sexuality," *American Journal of Nursing* 100, no. 12 (Dec. 2000); Jack Hitt, "The Second Sexual Revolution," *New York Times Magazine*, 20 Feb. 2000. See also Sarah Boseley, "Drug Firms 'Invented' Female Sex Problems," *Guardian Weekly*, 9–15 Jan. 2003, p. 8.

138. Schmidt, *Sexuelle Verhältnisse*, p. 14. Also see Gunter Schmidt, "Weshalb Sex alle (Un)schuld verloren hat," *taz-magazin*, 24 Apr. 1999; Gunter Schmidt, "Motivationale Grundlagen sexuellen Verhaltens," in *Psychologie der Motive*, ed. Hans Thomae (Göttingen: Verlag für Psychologie, 1983); Volkmar Sigusch, "Lob des Triebes," and Gunter Schmidt, "Kurze Entgegnung auf Volkmar Siguschs 'Lob des Triebes,' " both in *Sexualtheorie und Sexualpolitik*, ed. Martin Dannecker and Volkmar Sigusch (Stuttgart: Enke, 1984).

139. Micha Hilgers, "Tote Hose im Bett," *Frankfurter Rundschau*, 6 May 2000, p. 6.

140. *Freundin* study cited in "Sex in den Medien verunsichert die Deutschen," *Frankfurter Allgemeine Zeitung*, 5 Nov. 2002.

141. Rest, "Als die Lust," p. 7.

142. Starke on sex in the late twentieth-century West, quoted and discussed in Dietrich Mühlberg, "Sexualität und ostdeutscher Alltag," *Mitteilungen aus der kulturwissenschaftlichen Forschung* 18, no. 36 (1995), p. 21.

143. For example, see Rest, "Als die Lust," p. 7.

144. Susanne Beyer, Nikolaus von Festenberg, and Reinhard Mohr, "Die jungen Milden," *Der Spiegel*, 12 July 1999, pp. 94, 103.

145. Ralf König, "Veteranen," in *Trau keinem über 30! Die 68er*, ed. Andreas Knigge (Hamburg: Carlsen, 1998), pp. 40–43.

146. For example, see Mariam Lau, "Der neue Mensch als Bote des Eros," *Neue Zürcher Zeitung*, 17–18 Nov. 2001, pp. 53–54; and Schulz, "100 Jahre Sex."

147. See Alexandra Rigos, " 'Eltern sind austauschbar,' " *Der Spiegel*, 16 Nov. 1998, p. 129; and Werner Bohleber, "Schweigen der Generationen: Autorität und Freiheit heute—Sind die 68er schuld am Rechtsextremismus?" *Polis* 6 (1994), pp. 4–5. On the scandal surrounding Bettina Röhl's accusations against Daniel Cohn-Bendit, see Roger-Pol Droit, "Sexual Politics Haunts 60s Rebels," *Guardian Weekly*, 15–21 Mar. 2001, p. 34 (note the headline: "Left's fight against 'fascistic heterosexual ideology' may have been naive, but was far from paedophilia"); as well as Jacqueline Remy, "Le remords de Cohn-Bendit," *L'Express*, 22 Feb. 2001; "Pierre Belfond, éditeur du *Grand Bazar*—'Je l'assume pleinement,' " *L'Express*, 11 June 2001; and Alexander Smoltczyk, "Bettina Röhl: Die letzte Gefangene der RAF," *Spiegelreporter*, no. 3 (2001).

148. Achim Schmillen, "Wir sind besser als die Alten!" *Die Zeit*, 14 Mar. 1997, p. 22.

149. Schnibben, "Vollstrecker des Weltgewissens," p. 149.

150. "Die gefallene Natur," *Der Spiegel*, 2 May 1966, p. 58.

Conclusion

1. For example, see Harry Oosterhuis, *Stepchildren of Nature: Krafft-Ebing, Psychiatry, and the Making of Sexual Identity* (Chicago: Univ. of Chicago Press, 2000); and Volkmar Sigusch, *Karl Heinrich Ulrichs: Der erste Schwule der Weltgeschichte* (Berlin: Rosa Winkel, 2000).

2. This could happen quite unconsciously as well, as for example when observers in the first years of the twenty-first century lamented what they saw as a state of sexual ennui and nonrelationality between partners in the midst of sexual overstimulation. In doing so they were inadvertently echoing comments made first in the aftermath of World War II and then again in the eddying wake of the sex wave of the 1960s and 1970s.

3. See in this context the careful expositions in Stuart Hall, "Signification, Representation, Ideology," *Critical Studies in Mass Communication* 2, no. 2 (June 1985); Mary Poovey, *Uneven Developments: The Ideological Work of Gender in*

Mid-Victorian England (Chicago: Univ. of Chicago Press, 1988); Joan W. Scott, *Gender and the Politics of History* (New York: Columbia Univ. Press, 1988); Joan W. Scott and Judith Butler, eds., *Feminists Theorize the Political* (New York: Routledge, 1992); and Lisa Duggan, *The Twilight of Equality? Neoliberalism, Cultural Politics, and the Attack on Democracy* (Boston: Beacon, 2003).

4. Theodor Adorno and Max Horkheimer, *Dialektik der Aufklärung: Philosophische Fragmente* (Amsterdam: Querido, 1947), p. 244.

5. See on these points also *Das Kreuz mit dem Frieden: 1982 Jahre Christen und Politik*, ed. Peter Winzeler (Berlin: Elefanten Press, 1982); José Casanova, *Public Religions in the Modern World* (Chicago: Univ. of Chicago Press, 1994); Dagmar Herzog, "'Believing in God as an Atheist': Left-Wing Theology and the Confrontation with Secularization" (paper presented at the conference "Religiöse Vergemeinschaftung in der Moderne," University of Chicago, 25 Sept. 2003); and Pascal Eitler, "'Gott ist Rot!': Politische Theologie in der Bundesrepublik Deutschland (1965–1975)" (paper presented at the conference "Politik und Religion (18. bis 20. Jahrhundert)," University of Bielefeld, 6 Feb. 2004).

6. On the intersections between the histories of sexuality and religion in the nineteenth century, see Dagmar Herzog, *Intimacy and Exclusion: Religious Politics in Pre-Revolutionary Baden* (Princeton: Princeton Univ. Press, 1996). Pathbreaking books that begin to tell the histories of sexuality and religion in the twentieth century in conjunction are Callum G. Brown, *The Death of Christian Britain: Understanding Secularisation, 1800–2000* (London: Routledge, 2001); Mark Edward Ruff, *The Wayward Flock* (Chapel Hill: Univ. of North Carolina Press, 2004); and Caroline Ford, *Divided Houses* (Ithaca: Cornell University Press, 2005).

7. See in this context the important article by Gerhard Ringshausen, "Die Kirchen—herausgefordert durch den Wandel in den sechziger Jahren," in *Die Kultur der sechziger Jahre*, ed. Werner Faulstich (Munich: Fink, 2003).

8. For the United States, see especially David K. Johnson, *The Lavender Scare: The Cold War Persecution of Gays and Lesbians in the Federal Government* (Chicago: Univ. of Chicago Press, 2004); and Elaine Tyler May, *Homeward Bound: American Families in the Cold War Era* (New York: Basic Books, 1988). On the role of anticommunism in securing gender conservatism in West Germany, see Robert Moeller, "Reconstructing the Family in Reconstruction Germany: Women and Social Policy in the Federal Republic, 1949–1955," *Feminist Studies* 15, no. 1 (Spring 1989). See also Dagmar Herzog, "Sexuality in the Postwar West," *Journal of Modern History*: forthcoming.

9. For a provocative and useful assertion of the utter noninevitability of political conservatism's coincidence with sexual conservatism, see Rod Liddle, "Back to Basic Instincts," *Spectator*, 28 June 2003, pp. 10–11.

10. See Richard Bessel and Dirk Schumann, eds., *Life after Death: Approaches to a Cultural and Social History of Europe during the 1940s and 1950s* (Cambridge: Cambridge Univ. Press, 2003). This volume grew out of a conference entitled "Violence and Normality." On the need to theorize the post–World War II moment also specifically as a post*war* time (an approach that had been used more frequently to think about the post–World War I era), see also Klaus Naumann, *Nachkrieg in Deutschland* (Hamburg: Hamburger Edition, 2001).

11. On the Vichy law and its persistence into the postwar era, see Michael Sibalis, "Homophobia, Vichy France, and the 'Crime of Homosexuality': The Origins of the Ordinance of 6 August 1942," *GLQ: A Journal of Lesbian and Gay Studies* 8, no. 3 (May 2002); and Mario Kramp, "Homosexuelle im besetzten Frankreich 1940–1944/45: Fragmente einer noch zu schreibenden Geschichte," in *Nationalsozialistischer Terror gegen Homosexuelle: Verdrängt und ungesühnt,* ed. Burkhard Jellonek and Rüdiger Lautmann (Paderborn: Ferdinand Schöningh, 2002).

12. See Dagmar Herzog, "Homosexuality after Fascism," LGBQ Research Initiative Working Paper, Institute for Research on Women and Gender, University of Michigan, 2004.

13. See Julian Bourg, "'Your Sexual Revolution Is Not Ours': French Feminist 'Moralism' and the Limits of Desire," in *Love-in, Love-out: Gender and Sexuality in the Global 1968,* ed. Deborah Cohen and Lessie Jo Frazier (New York: Palgrave, forthcoming); and Todd Shepard, "Not Women, Not Men, Not Arab: Male Same-Sex Radicals and the Revolution in 1970s France" (paper to be presented at the Berkshire Conference on the History of Women, Scripps College, 2–5 June 2005).

14. Siegfried Schnabl, "Sexuelle Störungen," in *Sexuologie in der DDR,* ed. Joachim Hohmann (Berlin: Dietz, 1991).

15. Conversation with Herbert Jäger, 2003.

Acknowledgments

THE INITIAL IDEA FOR THIS BOOK was formulated over a decade ago on a snowy evening in East Lansing, Michigan. It seems entirely fitting that it is now snowing once again. In the meantime, the journey has been winding and long. The first round of research—on antifascist Christianity—was conducted in Harvard University's Divinity School and Widener libraries with the help of an Andrew W. Mellon Faculty Fellowship. Further financial assistance—and with it, above all, time, precious time—was provided by a number of remarkable organizations. The National Endowment for the Humanities took sex out of the title of my proposal for a summer stipend but gave me aid nonetheless; I thank the thoughtful bureaucrat who took matters into his or her own hands. Two other organizations knew exactly what they were funding. Sincerest thanks are due Diane di Mauro, the wonderful director of the Social Science Research Council's Sexuality Research Fellowship Program, whose work is generously underwritten by funds provided by the Ford Foundation, and to the late John D'Arms, who pioneered the American Council of Learned Societies' Frederick Burkhardt Residential Fellowship program. Both individuals offered important personal intellectual support as well. In 1999 Cornell University and the Deutscher Akademischer Austausch Dienst hosted a summer seminar on gender and sexuality in German cultural studies under the excellent direction of (now Provost) Biddy Martin; ties formed there still hold, and I remain grateful for them.

Michigan State University has also contributed to this project with money and time off, and above all with a nurturing environment. I have been especially fortunate to have terrific colleagues. My "bosses" Lewis Siegelbaum and Patrick McConeghy deserve particular thanks for their farsightedness and commitment—and for their friendship. My students contributed greatly as well. Over and over they afforded me the privilege and thrill of being in the room as they—individually and together—worked out their analytic and intuitive thoughts on both the past and the present. I continue to learn from their relentless curiosity and insightful perspectives; they have done much to inform my understanding of Nazism, the Holocaust, sexuality, religion, and many other matters.

Spectacular research assistance was provided by Julia Woesthoff, Constanze Jaiser, and Patricia Szobar. At Princeton University Press, Brigitta van Rheinberg has been the dream editor from start to finish.

This book would not have been possible—and also would have been much less of a pleasure to work on—without the energetic help of a remarkable cohort of German sexologists, psychologists, psychoanalysts, and sex rights and feminist activists who with utmost graciousness shared their homes, lives, personal archives, and opinions with me. I especially thank Günter Amendt, Sophinette Becker, Ulrich Clement, Martin Dannecker, Sibylla Flügge, Reimut Reiche, Gunter Schmidt, Volkmar Sigusch, Kurt Starke, and Uta Starke. The friendship they have shown me has greatly enriched my life; Gunter Schmidt's comradeship—productively disputatious and nurturing at once—has been particularly meaningful. I also want to express my appreciation to the many informants who cannot be named here for their patience with me and their thoughtful and revelatory reflections on life in twentieth-century Germany. In addition, I would like to thank Georg Bussmann for materials on Nazi art and Jakob Pastoetter and Matthias Rothe for providing magnanimous access to crucial sources on East Germany; I thank them as well for sharing their astute and enlightening insights on sexuality and politics. The generosity of Agnes Katzenbach at the Institut für Sexualwissenschaft in Frankfurt am Main was also a great support.

Dozens of professional colleagues in the interlocking worlds of the German Studies Association, the American Historical Association, and the Lessons and Legacies conferences of the Holocaust Educational Foundation have proved by their lived example that solidarity, sharing, and collective intellectual searching are not antiquated values. It is an honor to be part of these worlds. For their mentorship and friendship I am especially grateful to Omer Bartov, Volker Berghahn, Paul Betts, Rebecca Boehling, Michael Geyer, Marion Kaplan, Anson Rabinbach, and Zev Weiss.

Several individuals took the time to read and respond to drafts of chapters or to the whole manuscript. I am very grateful for the careful and thought-provoking readings provided by Volker Berghahn, Frank Biess, Carolyn Dean, Sibylla Flügge, Michael Geyer, Maria Hoehn, Till van Rahden, Gunter Schmidt, Joan Scott, and the anonymous readers for Princeton University Press.

A number of signal conversations that took place en route—sometimes on the spur of the moment and far from home—also deserve acknowledgment. For the challenges they proffered and/or for their engaged brainstorming, I particularly thank Christina von Hodenberg (in San Diego), Jonathan Katz (in Bloomington), Vanessa Schwartz (in Washington), Jonathan Sperber (in Chicago), and Michael Geyer (in Charlottesville). I hope they will see how these discussions inflected my thinking.

More than twenty years ago, Joan Scott took a risk on someone who was at that point working for the Lutheran Volunteer Corps at a shelter for homeless women in Washington, D.C., and who had never heard of Michel Foucault (and had only the faintest of notions about Sigmund Freud). Our first conversation took place (at my end) on a pay phone, with police sirens wailing in the background. My gratitude to her is lasting; throughout, she has been the ideal mentor. In a seminar in women's history in 1985 (which the students—though surely unbeknownst to her—in our emphatic and insouciant insurgent feminism referred to as "the ovular") I and the others took our first serious steps toward making critically informed historical research and writing a lifelong avocation. When she left for the Institute for Advanced Study later that year, I was no longer able to walk into her office but rather was forced to put all thoughts, both stray and systematic, into writing. This turned out to be fortuitous. Joan's unerring instinct for the weak spots in an argument, her record-breaking turnaround time, her brilliance, and above all her unstinting encouragement and kindness have been orienting and sustaining in more ways than I can name. It was a special gift to spend the year in which my research finally turned into this book once again in her vicinity.

In general, the atmosphere in Princeton, New Jersey, was at once stringent and completely magical. Thanks especially to David Holmes, Carol Markowitz, Rachel Tait, and Abby Speck for making everything possible with their extraordinary competence and dedication. And Todd Lewis always had the right touch. The Institute for Advanced Study provided an amazing setting for uninterrupted work. Karen Downing's mindbogglingly efficient Inter-Library Loan skills were beyond outstanding. Adam Ashforth, Clifford Geertz, Albert Hirschman, Eric Maskin, Joan Scott, and Michael Walzer were wonderful hosts, and the community of scholars they gathered in 2002–3 nourished this project in multiple ways. I thank Wolf Lepenies and Martin Mulsow for what turned out to be pivotal conversations, and I especially treasure the hours I was able to spend with Caroline Bynum, Joan Judge, and Debra Keates.

I want to register as well my gratitude for a not-so-secret network of militant and devoted mothers whose clearheaded advice has carried me through many years. To Stephanie Barbatano, Barb Byers, Maria Holter, Lynne Sebille-White, and Cathie Spino (in Michigan) and Eleni Passalaris, Doreen Petrocchi, and Terri Watts (in New Jersey): you're my inspiration. Profuse thanks also go to the friends who have been there from the beginning and have given me such good company through all the stages of this book and so many parts of life: Jennifer Fleischner, Jim Henle, Amy MacKenzie, Dianne Sadoff, and Tracey Wilson.

I am lucky indeed to have family that are friends and friends that have also become family. The enduring love of my mother, Kristin Herzog, and my aunt, Ruth Karwehl, has done so much to maintain my sense of perspective and proportion. The gentle humor and solicitude with which they tolerated my preoccupation with twentieth-century sexuality was as important as the countless clippings they sent my way. Above all, for decades they have modeled for me concern for justice and consistency of commitment; I am deeply grateful for all that they are and stand for.

In 2003 Brendan Hart reconfigured our family by adding himself to it; he has become a dearly beloved and trusted friend. His intelligence and incisive perceptiveness, his constancy and care, are profoundly appreciated.

If the completion of this book more generally demonstrates the at once beautiful and messy reality of human interconnection, in no case is this more true than that of Michael Staub. He envisioned the contours and the texture of this book long before I did. He was always a step ahead of me in figuring out what task came next, and at the same time he did everything to create the atmosphere in which those tasks were possible. His moral acuity and intellectual rigor, his passion and friendship, have been the greatest gifts in my life and I thank him with all my heart.

Finally, to Lucy Milena, my most cherished companion and co-conspirator in those essential activities of reading together, singing, giggling, and hip-hop dancing: thank you forever for being my most important teacher and the bravest and most loving human being I know.

Index